The Continental Dollar

MARKETS AND GOVERNMENTS IN ECONOMIC HISTORY

A series edited by Price Fishback

The Continental Dollar

How the American Revolution Was
Financed with Paper Money

FARLEY GRUBB

THE UNIVERSITY OF CHICAGO PRESS   CHICAGO AND LONDON

The University of Chicago Press, Chicago 60637
The University of Chicago Press, Ltd., London
© 2023 by Farley Grubb
Published 2023
Printed in the United States of America

32 31 30 29 28 27 26 25 24 23   1 2 3 4 5

ISBN-13: 978-0-226-82603-5 (cloth)
ISBN-13: 978-0-226-82604-2 (e-book)
DOI: https://doi.org/10.7208/chicago/9780226826042.001.0001

Library of Congress Cataloging-in-Publication Data

Names: Grubb, Farley Ward, 1954– author.
Title: The continental dollar : how the American revolution was financed
    with paper money / Farley Grubb.
Other titles: Markets and governments in economic history.
Description: Chicago : The University of Chicago Press, 2023. |
    Series: Markets and governments in economic history |
    Includes bibliographical references and index.
Identifiers: LCCN 2022038204 | ISBN 9780226826035 (cloth) | ISBN 9780226826042 (ebook)
Subjects: LCSH: Dollar—History. | Monetary policy—United States. |
    United States—History—Revolution, 1775–1783—Finance.
Classification: LCC E209 .G87 2023 | DDC 332.4/973—dc23/eng/20220823
LC record available at https://lccn.loc.gov/2022038204

♾ This paper meets the requirements of ANSI/NISO Z39.48-1992 (Permanence of Paper).

Contents

Tables

Figures

A Note on Citation Format

Full references are listed at the end of book. In-text and note citations use a version of APA style. Their basic format is Author Year: Page Numbers. If the work does not have an author, then it is cited by title, in the format Title Year: Page Numbers. Only page numbers follow a colon. No comma or period follows the first element of the citation, whether it is the author or the title. When the work cited is a book consisting of several volumes, the style is Author Year, Volume Number: Page Numbers (with no space between the volume number and the page number). A comma always separates the year from the volume number. Some works list only the volume number without a year. Two works without an author that are cited frequently use a shortened title (i.e., *JCC* = *Journals of the Continental Congress* and *PCC* = *Papers of the Continental Congress*).

Preface

In the early 1990s, at the University of Delaware, I created a stand-alone junior-level undergraduate course on the economic history of colonial America. I have taught that course there almost every year since. I created it to teach my research on colonial-era transatlantic indentured immigration and convict transportation. As part of that course, I included a unit on American colonial and revolutionary-era paper monies, because such monies were novel experiments and I wanted some macroeconomic content in the course. I selected several articles from the *Journal of Economic History* and the *Journal of Political Economy* published in the 1980s that addressed these paper-money experiments and taught them to my students. Through the 1990s I slowly stopped using these articles because, as I taught them over and over again, they came to make no sense to me. I had far more questions than I had answers. I started to look deeper into the topic and came to two realizations. First, scholars were forcing inappropriate modern models onto historical institutional structures—a sort of reverse anachronism. The primary goal seemed to be to champion a modern monetary model or in-vogue technique rather than to analyze and understand a historical economy.

Second, I discovered that the data being used were all over the map. Seemingly simple questions such as "How many Continental dollars were emitted during the Revolution?" had a wide range of answers in the secondary literature. Scholars seemed not to notice or care; they just chose what they initially ran across in the prior secondary literature, seemingly oblivious to the wide range of numbers to choose from and seldom justifying why they selected the particular numbers they used.

I found this troubling. One part of my efforts has been to get the numbers right, or as right as I could, and reconcile all the diverse estimates in the secondary literature to get to the same data outcome. The other part started with flushing my head of a lot of those modern models and techniques, seeing them as inappropriate to colonial- and revolutionary-era institutional settings. I wanted to drop back into core economic theory and devise a monetary model de novo that was more appropriate to the institutions of colonial and revolutionary America. This also led to displaying concepts and data differently from the way they have been typically presented in the secondary literature.

Although I started researching the Continental dollar in the late 1990s, numerous ancillary projects intervened, most of which informed my understanding but do not directly appear in this book. I felt I needed to understand the difference between the colonial paper-money economies and the post-Constitution US dollar monetary economy to judge the intervening Continental dollar period. A number of studies not included here were published out of these investigations, namely Grubb (2003, 2005, 2006, 2007a, 2007b, 2010, 2011a). Some of this research does find its way into chapters 16 and 17.

In addition, after some aborted attempts to write this book, I decided that I needed a deeper understanding and demonstration of the value and performance of colonial paper monies to support how I thought the Continental dollar performed. This was because the Continental dollar and colonial paper monies were almost identical in their legal design and institutional structure. A number of studies not included here were published out of these investigations, namely Celia and Grubb (2016); Cutsail and Grubb (2019, 2021); Grubb (2004, 2012b, 2015, 2016a, 2016b, 2016c, 2017, 2018a, 2019a, 2019b, 2020).

Intermittent work on the Continental dollar over these years produced publications on various aspects of the topic that edited, reworked, and augmented show up in the book here. They include Grubb (2008; see appendix A); Grubb (2011b; see chap. 6); Grubb (2012a; see chap. 15 and appendix D); and Grubb (2018b; see chap. 3 and appendix B).

I have always found book-writing to be a mysterious undertaking. I understand how to write journal articles, but book-writing is unfathomable. A book has an infinite variety of ways to be organized and written, with no clear path that is obviously more proper or successful. I am running out of life, however, so I must give it a try before it is too late and entropy overtakes erudition.

I have tried to make sure that each chapter contains some original research, perspective, approach, and evidence, yet also that the chapters

hang together as a unified whole. I think evidence and data are of paramount importance; yet, they can get tediously in the way of the story, so
I moved the most tedious data to the appendices. Although the research
was carried out over a period of two decades, most of the final assemblage was done during the COVID-19 pandemic of 2020–22. While that
pandemic was a misanthrope's paradise that morphed into a solipsist's
nightmare, it did provide the isolation I needed to organize and polish the
project.

I am often asked, "Where do new research ideas come from?" I honestly do not know. The best I can tell the questioner is to know your core
economic theory well (as opposed to particular models or techniques),
then dive deep into original texts and documents; you will see new con-
nections, new perspectives, and new patterns in the data. Maybe it is best
summed up in a bit of doggerel I wrote:

> The urge to create is so great
> Function and form, bend and shape
> Beyond the norm, beyond the ape
> Jove-like it comes from an unknown place
> Not me, not what, not when that I can pace
> But come it does to make the human race

Farley Grubb
Friday Harbor, WA
2021

Introduction

*A*nd so it begins . . .
The British North American colonies from New Hampshire to Georgia assembled in the Second Continental Congress in Philadelphia on May 10, 1775. This assemblage was agreed to at the end of the First Continental Congress, which met from September 5 to October 26, 1774. The Continental Congresses were voluntary associations and lacked coercive governmental powers. The First Continental Congress had met to agree on an all-colony response to the British Parliament's Coercive Acts (the Intolerable Acts). Parliament had passed the Coercive Acts as punishment for the December 16, 1773, Boston Tea Party. The Acts closed Boston Harbor, stripped Massachusetts of some control of its government, and restricted public gatherings in the Massachusetts colony, among other impositions.[1]

The First Continental Congress sent a petition-letter to King George III stating the colonies' grievances and asking for redress. For Parliament to punish everyone in a colony and strip all of them of their sacred English liberties in response to the acts or crimes of a few individuals was seen in all colonies as an existential threat to the English liberties of all colonists. The Coercive Acts were considered an unconstitutional (though there was of course no US Constitution as yet) breach of those liberties. Until Parliament rescinded the Coercive Acts, the First Continental Congress agreed to an all-colonies boycott of British imported goods starting on December 1, 1774, as well as an all-colonies ban on exporting goods to Britain starting on September 10, 1775. Finally, the First Continental Congress agreed to meet in Philadelphia on May 10, 1775, in a Second Continental Congress to assess the response of Parliament and the king to their petition-letter, import boycott, and export-ban threat, and to consider what further actions, if any, were warranted (*JCC* 1:104–24).

Between the adjournment of the First Continental Congress and the assemblage of the Second Continental Congress, events escalated to the point that it was they that drove Congress, rather than Congress driving events. A few weeks before the Second Continental Congress was to assemble, the Battles of Lexington and Concord were fought. British forces, which had retreated to Boston, were under siege by Massachusetts militiamen. Resources and men were, of their own volition, on the move from other colonies to support the Massachusetts revolutionaries. The Second Continental Congress, with no legal authority, made itself the united revolutionary government. This Congress would continue through the Revolution and thereafter until replaced by the Congress created by the US Constitution in 1789. There would be no Third Continental Congress. Congress's immediate problem in May 1775 was marshaling resources for a united military effort against the British occupying Boston.

In the spring of 1775, independence was not yet the dominant sentiment. It would take a full year of open warfare—victory in the battle for Boston, the pending battle for New York, and the campaigns against British Canada—before Congress would declare independence on July 4, 1776 (Randall 1990: 133–317; Tindall 1988: 210–20). While the provision of congressional resources helped sustain the nearly yearlong siege of Boston, it became clear by the end of 1775 that marshaling congressional resources for a united military effort against the British would not be a one-off affair.

As these events unfolded, Congress had to improvise a monetary and fiscal policy, and do so under extreme wartime duress and questionable political legitimacy. Congress was then an improvised extralegal revolutionary body, without any constitutional structure or organization. As such, it exercised power by common consent of the colonies, as represented by their delegates to the Congress. Congress had no enforcement power to tax the public or the states or to enforce its edicts. The Articles of Confederation, the first constituted national government, were not laid before Congress until November 1777, and they were not ratified by the states before March 1781 (*JCC* 9:907–28; 19: 233; Tindall 1988: 247–48).

On the second day of the Second Continental Congress, with the war raging outside of Boston, the state of Massachusetts informed Congress that Massachusetts was issuing interest-bearing bonds (a form of paper money) redeemable in two years at face value in specie to pay for its emergency war expenses. It asked Congress to receive these bonds and help give them a currency throughout the colonies. In early June New Hampshire gave Massachusetts bonds legal-tender status within New Hampshire (*JCC* 2:24–26; Smith 1976–94, 1:470–71).

In response to these developments, the revolutionary government of New York sent instructions to its delegation in Congress, instructions that were not to be made public or disclosed to the other delegates, to dissuade Congress from adopting the paper currencies emitted by individual states or in any way obligating states to accept other states' paper currencies. New York's delegates opposed a union of state currencies (currency union). Instead, New York's delegates were instructed to push Congress to issue its own common paper currency and obligate the "United States" as a group to its redemption. New York saw this as the best way to protect itself against unreasonable monetary obligations imposed on it by neighboring states (Bolles 1969, 1:24–32; Phillips 1866:17–24; Smith 1976–94, 1:419,442; Sparks 1832, 1:38–40).

When Congress acted on June 23, 1775, it adopted what New York had recommended, namely an independent common paper currency issued by Congress and not a union of individual state paper monies. This common paper currency was the Continental dollar (fig. I.1 reproduces a Continental twenty-dollar bill from the first emission). The individual states in Congress obligated themselves as a group to redeem these Continental dollars at face value in specie (gold and silver coin) equivalents after the Revolution and to cover any shortfalls from states that failed to meet their postwar redemption obligations. Congress, however, had no power to enforce these obligations.

Once it became clear that marshaling congressional resources for a united military effort against the British would not be a one-off affair, Congress relied on new emissions of Continental dollars to meet the ongoing costs of paying for troops and supplies. Each new emission had a different authorization date stamped on it, and each looked different, so the public could easily distinguish one emission from another. While the emissions were similar in structural design, each had slightly different components. Four different emissions of Continental dollars are reproduced in figures I.1, I.2, I.3, and I.4. For the most complete set of pictures of the various emissions whose bills have survived, see Newman (2008:37–41,63–72).

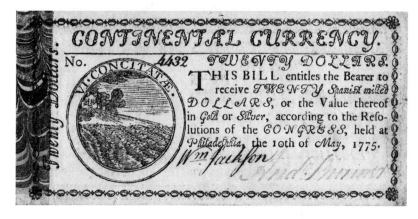

FIGURE I.1. A twenty-dollar bill of credit from the first Continental dollar emission

Source: Newman (2008: 37). Reprinted by permission of the Eric P. Newman Numismatic Education Society.
Note: For emission numbers and dates, see table 1.1.

FIGURE I.2. A two-dollar bill of credit from the second Continental dollar emission

Source: Newman (2008: 38). Reprinted by permission of the Eric P. Newman Numismatic Education Society.
Note: For emission numbers and dates, see table 1.1.

FIGURE I.3. A three-dollar bill of credit from the eighth Continental dollar emission

Source: Newman (2008: 68). Reprinted by permission of the Eric P. Newman Numismatic Education Society.
Note: For emission numbers and dates, see table 1.1.

Congress did not create a true union of state currencies (also known as a currency union). Individual states retained their sovereign power to issue their own separate paper monies, which is what they did throughout the Revolution. Congress overlaid a common paper currency onto a nation where subnational political entities continued to operate independent monetary and fiscal policies and issue their own unique paper monies. No exchange agreements between Continental dollars and the myriad of state paper monies existed in the first years of the war.[2]

How could such a monetary system succeed? Was the Continental dollar doomed at birth, or was there a rational monetary policy that offered some potential for success? I will argue that Congress, at least initially, understood the problems of creating a common currency under such circumstances. Given these conditions and the constraints on taxing power Congress faced, it made reasonable choices to maximize the system's chance of success.

After 1776, however, the Continental dollar's value declined precipitously, and by the end of the Revolution it was close to worthless. In the

FIGURE I.4. A sixty-five-dollar bill of credit from the last Continental dollar emission

Source: Newman (2008: 38). Reprinted by permission of the Eric P. Newman Numismatic Education Society.
Note: For emission numbers and dates, see table 1.1.

end, the demands of a long and expensive war, along with the ascendance of the debt hawks in Congress who failed to grasp the problem of fiscal credibility, overwhelmed and then destroyed the Continental dollar currency system. The adoption of the US Constitution in 1789 ended the sovereign power of the states to issue their own paper currencies, thus paving the way for a true currency union based on the specie US dollar (as a unit of account) for the new nation (Grubb 2006: 43–71).

The Traditional Story

For 230 years traditional historiography has told us that the Continental dollar was a fiat currency—an unbacked paper money. Congress printed and spent an excessive number of these paper dollars from 1775 through 1780. They just turned on the printing presses and flooded the economy with these paper dollars, thus driving their value to near zero by 1781, when they were abandoned as a money. Thereafter, Continental dollars just disappeared; they were no more than trash. We are told that the Continental dollar financing system functioned as an intentional inflation tax on the public and that once it had run its course as an inflation tax (by 1781), it was abandoned.[3] "Not worth a Continental" supposedly became a common derogatory phrase.[4]

This story is simple and appealing. It is a quantity-theoretic story, where the quantity theory of money can be grafted onto the history of the Continental dollar to provide lessons about the follies of legislature-controlled fiat monies.[5] Once a deeper look is taken, however, the story falls apart. First, the unspoken implications of this traditional view is that the founding fathers, who created the Continental dollar system, were either crazy, deceptive, ignorant, evil, or stupid. These are the same founding fathers who are lauded as geniuses for crafting the US Constitution in 1787, especially with regard to governmental monetary powers. Being ignoramuses in the mid-1770s and geniuses in the mid-1780s is incoherent history (Farrand 1966; Grubb 2006).

Second, simple quantity-theoretic patterns are hard to sustain with the evidence. Of course the value of the Continental dollar fell as the quantity of dollars in circulation increased from 1775 through 1779, but its value also fell as the quantity in circulation was reduced after 1781. To argue that a greater quantity reduces value and a lesser quantity also reduces value is unsatisfactory. The quantity theory of money must have symmetry— maybe not perfect symmetry, but not antisymmetry.

Similarly, and often in conjunction with a quantity-theoretic story, it is often asserted that legal-tender laws support a fiat money's value, and thus changes in a fiat money's value are driven by changes in the quantity in circulation. Yet, the Continental dollar had its *highest* relative value when there was no legal-tender law for it (before 1777), and it also had its *lowest* relative value when there was no legal-tender law for it (after 1781). Between 1776 and 1781, when the Continental dollar was a legal tender, its value plummeted. To argue that legal-tender laws were both necessary and unnecessary to supporting a money's value is, again, unsatisfactory. Legal-tender laws, when used to support quantity-theoretic arguments, must have some symmetry in their effect—again, maybe not perfect symmetry, but not antisymmetry.

The quantity-theory-of-money explanation for the value path of Continental dollars also lacks exactitude. While the rate of change in the quantity of Continental dollars in circulation is not expected to be exactly equal to the rate of change in the value of the Continental dollar (in opposite directions), something more exact is required than just saying a positive rate of change in one is associated with a negative rate of change in the other. Yet, nothing more exact can be given. It can always be said that not enough is known about changes in the velocity of circulation and changes in output to calibrate the connection between changes in the quantity of Continental dollars and changes in its value, but again, that is unsatisfactory. In chapters 10–12 I use an asset-pricing model of money that allows me to track the value of the Continental dollar over time more exactly than any quantity-theoretic model can.

Finally, the literary evidence used to support the traditional story is often taken out of context and does not mean what traditional historiography takes it to mean. I will give two examples here, one from Pelatiah Webster in 1776, when the Continental dollar system was just starting, and one from Benjamin Franklin in 1779, the year of the last emission of Continental dollars. These two statements by contemporaries of the Continental dollar are frequently offered by traditional historiography as self-evident proof of what the Continental dollar was. In 1776 a congressman proclaimed, "Do you think, Gentlemen, that I will consent to load my constituents with taxes, when we can send to our printer, and get a wagon-load of money, one quire of which will pay for the whole?" The inference taken from this quote is that no taxes would be laid to support the paper money and so it was a fiat money, and that the whole "wagon-load of [paper] money" would pay for itself via depreciation.

The original source of this statement is an essay by Pelatiah Webster (1969: 7–8) published in the *Pennsylvania Evening Post* on October 5, 1776, wherein Webster remarked in a footnote, "I am told, one member of Congress rose during those debates [over how to fund the Revolution] with this exclamation, 'Do you think, Gentlemen, that I will consent to load my constituents with taxes, when we can send to our printer, and get a wagon-load of money, one quire of which will pay for the whole?'" The congressman's statement is presented by Webster as unattributed and as second-hand hearsay. It is also often misinterpreted. When the congressman says "a wagon-load of money, one quire of which will pay for the whole," he is not talking about the money's paying for its whole self via depreciation, but about the money's being used to pay the whole cost of printing the paper money. The cost of engraving, printing, and endorsing paper money was paid using some of the paper money so printed rather than using real money (gold and silver coins) raised by separate taxes. That is how printing prior colonial paper monies had been paid for. The word in the quote that is unfamiliar to modern ears, "quire," contributes to the passage's misinterpretation. "Quire" simply means several sheets of paper, and several printed sheets of paper money are all that would be needed to pay the engraver, printer, and endorser. In his remark the congressman refers not to taxes to redeem the paper money, but to taxes needed just to pay the paper money's engraver, printer, and endorser.

In 1779 Benjamin Franklin remarked that the depreciation of the Continental dollar from 1775 to 1779 was

> a Kind of imperceptible Tax, every one having paid a Part of it in the Fall of Value that took Place between his Receiving and Paying such Sums as pass'd thro' his Hands. . . . This Currency as we manage it is a wonderful Machine. It performs its Office when we issue it; it pays & clothes Troops, & provides Victuals & Ammunition; and when we are oblig'd to issue a Quantity excessive, it pays itself off by depreciation.[6]

The inference from Franklin's quote seems obvious: the Continental dollar was used as an intentional inflation tax where excessive quantities emitted over time were intended to drive its value down. The Continental dollar paid for itself through depreciation.

The context of Franklin's quote, and thus its real meaning, however, is obscured by focusing just on this part of his letter. Examining Franklin's complete letter and its context reveals a different interpretation. Franklin is really advocating an emergency plan to save the Continental dollar after 1779 by redeeming (and then destroying) some of them with current taxes at the Continental dollar's current value, rather than by redeeming them at their face value at some distant future date. The improper adoption of such a plan by Congress post-1779 contributed to crashing the system. A fuller analysis of Franklin's quote is given in chapter 14.

The traditional story is also used as a lesson. This lesson is summed up best by Alexander Hamilton who, as US Treasury Secretary in 1790, said:

> Paper emissions . . . are of a nature so liable to abuse, . . . so certain of being abused, that the wisdom of the Government will be shewn in never trusting itself with the use of so seducing and dangerous an expedient. . . . [I]n great and trying emergencies, there is almost a moral certainty of its becoming mischievous. The stamping of paper is an operation so much easier than the laying of taxes, that a government, in the practice of paper emissions, would rarely fail in any such emergency to indulge itself too far . . . to avoid as much as possible one

less auspicious to present popularity. If it should not even be carried so far as to be rendered an absolute bubble, it would at least be likely to be extended to a degree, which would occasion an inflated and artificial state of things incompatible with the regular and prosperous course of political economy. (Syrett and Cooke 1962–72, 7:321–22)

In other words, Congress recklessly emitted an excessive quantity of paper Continental dollars. This led to runaway price inflation (runaway currency depreciation) that destroyed the Continental dollar's value and led to its abandonment. The rhetoric presumes that congressmen are by nature irrational, myopic, stupid, and ill-motivated to serve the public interest in monetary matters. If they are given monetary powers, they will mindlessly run off a cliff and crash the system. The history of the Continental dollar proves it.[7]

Or Does It? A New Story (The Real Story)

I did not set out some twenty years ago to overturn 230 years of traditional historiography on the Continental dollar, but only to gain a deeper understanding of that history so I could better teach it to my students. However, at every turn and on every subtopic, I discovered that we have been told an incomplete and often erroneous story about the Continental dollar. That changes here. In every chapter I present some new insight, evidence, perspective, analysis, and thus understanding of the Continental dollar. My research led me into numerous monetary and public finance subtopics dealing with the Continental dollar, many of which have not been addressed in the literature before. The new story I tell is more consistent with rational behavior and the historical record than that embodied in the traditional history. It sharpens our understanding of what was at stake economically and politically in the ubiquitous retelling of the (erroneous) conventional story. It helps us reparse the motives of the founding fathers for transforming governmental monetary powers in the new US Constitution. The end product is nothing short of a revolution in our understanding of the Continental dollar, what it was, how it was used, how it performed, and the calamity that befell it in the end.

The highlights of this new story include the following points:

- fewer Continental dollars were emitted than traditionally thought

- the Continental dollar was a zero-coupon bond and not a fiat currency

- fiscal credibility factored into the Continental dollar's redemption structure and value performance

- through 1779 the emission of new Continental dollars accounted for 77 percent of congressional spending

- one-third of the Continental dollars emitted by Congress were borrowed back by Congress from the public and respent

- the Continental dollar had a unique and bizarre denominational structure

- Continental dollars did not depreciate before 1779 (let me repeat this shocking overthrow of the traditional history: there was no depreciation of the Continental dollar before 1779)

- the Continental dollar system was destroyed by congressional rule changes in 1779 and 1780 that failed to grasp the need for taxation schemes that were fiscally credible

- by 1790 the states had redeemed and removed from circulation 60 percent of the Continental dollars ever emitted

- the final default on the Continental dollar in the 1790 Funding Act was not financially necessary, but may have been necessary to put the United States in a positive net worth position and so help establish its creditworthiness in foreign markets

This new story places a tremendous burden on me to demonstrate its efficacy and veracity. Part I establishes, from many different angles, what the Continental dollar was and how it was used. Its purpose is to convince you that the Continental dollar was a zero-coupon bond and that everyone knew it. It was more like a modern-day US savings bond than a modern-day US dollar bill. In other words, paper money is not just paper money. The structure of money matters, and fiscal credibility matters.[8] Fiscal credibility factored into that structure in a way that made bond redemption messy and the Continental dollar a cumbersome medium of exchange. It also affected the Continental dollar's value and performance.

Part II takes a new approach to measuring the Continental dollar's value and performance. It starts with reevaluating how we (the economics profession) measure what is and is not money. I model money as a value as opposed to a thing and then create a way to measure that value by separating the non-money-value component from the money-value component of the "money thing" in question. As a zero-coupon bond, the

Continental dollar's present value is not its face value, but its face value at its forecast redemption date time-discounted back to the present. This process is explained and applied to the non-money real asset portion of the Continental dollar. Time-discounting per se is not depreciation, as it entails no loss of principal. When a US savings bond is cashed in before its maturity date, it pays less than its face value, but we do not call that value difference depreciation, only time-discounting. I show a similar outcome for the Continental dollar.

Part II then reevaluates the messy and wide-ranging evidence on the actual exchange value of the Continental dollar and establishes the best measure to use. It takes that measure and compares it with the Continental dollar's asset present value. The two are the same from 1777 to 1779, and so the Continental dollar suffered no depreciation before 1779. Lastly, part II reevaluates the causes for the value collapse and onset of true depreciation of the Continental dollar from 1779 through 1781, as well as its abandonment as a medium of exchange thereafter. Congressional rule changes that were not fiscally credible played an important role. Changes in congressional membership and a lack of institutional memory contributed as well.

Part III evaluates what happened to the Continental dollar after its abandonment as a money in 1781. Did the states honor the obligation to redeem the Continental dollar imposed on them by Congress? Was the irrevocable default on Continental dollar embedded in the 1790 Funding Act financially necessary? Finally, I assess how the history of the Continental dollar, and the reshaping of that history into the erroneous story we have been told over the last 230 years, factored into the monetary restructuring that arose at the 1787 Constitutional Convention and was embedded in the new US Constitution as adopted by Congress in 1789.

I hope you enjoy the journey—a journey driven by curiosity rather than ideology.

PART I

What Was the Continental Dollar?
The Intended Structural Design

CHAPTER ONE

Emitting Continental Dollars

The *Journals of the Continental Congress* contain the congressional resolutions for each emission of Continental dollars. Separate emissions are identified by the dates printed on the bills (Newman 2008: 37–41, 63–72). In total, there were eleven emissions, with some having multiple resolutions and emission tranches passed on different dates associated with them. The dates on the bills allowed the public to distinguish between emissions and identify the corresponding congressional resolutions for each emission. The resolutions for each emission determined that emission's quantity, nominal value, denominational spacing, and redemption instructions. Table 1.1 presents this information.

In a series of resolutions from June 22 through December 26, 1775, Congress determined the quantity, nominal value, denominational spacing, and redemption method for the first two emissions of Continental dollars. Congress maintained this structural design in all subsequent emissions, changing only the quantity emitted and denominational spacing. Congressional debates were closed to the public, and the delegates were placed "under the strongest obligation of honor" to keep them secret. Why congressmen structured the Continental dollar the way they did, therefore, must be deduced primarily from their actions and from contemporaneous notes made by one congressman, Richard Smith, in his diary.[1]

The face value of a Continental dollar for redemption purposes was set equal to a Spanish silver dollar, so indicated on the face of each bill

TABLE 1.1 **Continental dollar redemption/maturity dates set by congressional legislation**

Procedural authorization dates	Date printed on the bill (emission no.)	Specie redemption option	Redemption/maturity dates	Current new emission	Redemption order applied to other emissions
July 29, 1775	May 10, 1775 (emission no. 1)	Yes	¼ on or before Nov. 30, 1779 ¼ on or before Nov. 30, 1780 ¼ on or before Nov. 30, 1781 ¼ on or before Nov. 30, 1782	$1,000,000[d]	to $2,000,000 from June 22, 1775
Dec. 26, 1775	Nov. 29, 1775 (emission no. 2)	Yes	¼ on or before Nov. 30, 1783 ¼ on or before Nov. 30, 1784 ¼ on or before Nov. 30, 1785 ¼ on or before Nov. 30, 1786	$3,000,000	
Feb. 21, 1776	Feb. 17, 1776 (emission no. 3)	—	"[O]n the same security as the sums of money heretofore emitted"	$3,937,220	
May 22, 1776	May 9, 1776 (emission no. 4)	Yes[a]	"[I]n such manner . . . as Congress shall hereafter direct"[a]	$5,000,000	
Aug. 13, 1776	July 22, 1776 (emission no. 5)	Yes[a]	"	$5,000,000	
Nov. 2, 1776	Nov. 2, 1776 (emission no. 6)	—	"	$5,000,000	
Feb. 26, 1777	Feb. 26, 1777 (emission no. 7)	—	"[P]eriods . . . that shall be fixed by Congress"[a]	$5,000,000	
May 22, 1777	May 20, 1777 (emission no. 8)	—	Nothing mentioned	$5,000,000	
Aug. 15, 1777	"	—	"	$1,000,000	
Nov. 7, 1777	"	—	"	$1,000,000	
Dec. 3, 1777	"	—	"	$1,000,000	
Jan. 8, 1778	"	—	"	$1,000,000	
Jan. 22, 1778	"	—	"	$2,000,000	
Feb. 16, 1778	"	—	"	$2,000,000	
Mar. 5, 1778	"	—	"	$2,000,000	
Apr. 4, 1778	"	—	"	$1,000,000	
Apr. 11, 1778	Apr. 11, 1778 (emission no. 9)	—	"	$5,000,000	
Apr. 18, 1778	May 20, 1777 (emission no. 8)	—	"	$500,000	
May 22, 1778	Apr. 11, 1778 (emission no. 9)	—	"	$5,000,000	
June 20, 1778	"	—	"	$5,000,000	
July 30, 1778	"	—	"	$5,000,000	
Sept. 5, 1778	"	—	"	$5,000,000	
Sept. 26, 1778	Sept. 26, 1778 (emission no. 10)	—	"	$10,000,100	

					To all prior emissions and to all subsequent emissions to 1780
Nov. 4, 1778	"	—			$10,000,100
Dec. 14, 1778	"	—			$10,000,100
Jan. 2, 1779	Jan. 14, 1779 (Emission no. 11)	Yes[b]	$15,000,000 for 1779 and annually $6,000,000 for 18 years to Jan. 1, 1797, with any additional emissions in 1779 redeemed in the same manner and within the same time period[c]		$8,500,395
Feb. 3, 1779	Sept. 26, 1778 (emission no. 10)	Yes[b]	nothing new added		$5,000,160
Feb. 19, 1779	"	Yes[b]	"		$5,000,160
Apr. 1, 1779	"	Yes[b]	"		$5,000,160
May 5, 1779	"	Yes[b]	"		$10,000,100
June 4, 1779	"	Yes[b]	"		$10,000,100
July 17, 1779	Jan. 14, 1779 (emission no. 11)	Yes[b]	"		$5,000,180
July 17, 1779	Sept. 26, 1778 (Emission no. 10)	Yes[b]	"		$10,000,100
Sept. 17, 1779	Jan. 14, 1779 (emission no. 11)	Yes[b]	"		$15,000,260
Oct. 14, 1779	"	Yes[b]	"		$5,000,180
Nov. 17, 1779	"	Yes[b]	"		$10,050,540
Nov. 29, 1779	"	Yes[b]	"		$10,000,140

Sources: Appendix A; Grubb (2008: 286; 2012a; 2018b); *JCC* (2:103, 105, 207, 221–23; 3:390, 398, 407, 457–59; 4:156–57, 164–65, 339–40, 374, 380–83; 5:599, 651, 724–28; 6:918, 1047; 7:161; 8:377–80, 646–47; 9:873–74, 993; 10:26, 28, 36, 82–83, 86, 174–75, 223–25, 308–12, 337–38, 364–65; 11:521–24, 627, 731–32; 12:884, 962, 967, 1073; 1100–1101, 1133, 1217–18, 1266; 13:20–23, 64–65, 139–41, 209–10, 408–9; 14:548, 557–58, 687–88, 848–49; 15:1076–77, 1171–72, 1285, 1324–25); *PCC* (microfilm 247, reel 33, item 26, "Reports of the Committee on the Treasury and Finance, 1776–1788"; 1–5, 13–14; microfiche 247, reel 145, item 136, "Reports of the Board of Treasury, 1776–1781, vols. 1–2 (1776–1778)": 1:181, 355–57, 462, 507; 2:29, 83, 125, 199, 217, 373, 427, 529, 573, 669, 761; microfiche 247, reel 146, item 136, "Reports of the Board of Treasury, 1776–1781, vol. 3, 1779": 69, 111, 209, 215, 351, 477, 641, 727, 817, 845).

Notes: Dates are for when the most procedural details were given for each emission. An emission is all bills issued with the same date printed on the bill (Newman 1997:58–69, 2008: 62–73). After emission no. 7, each emission had several authorizing resolutions where additional amounts were added to a given emission. Dashes indicate no statement given either way on the presence of a specie redemption option.

[a] Stated in coinage rating resolutions but not in emission resolutions (*JCC* 4:339–40, 382; 5:724; 7:36).

[b] The specie redemption option for citizens at the Continental Treasury was not mentioned in the January 2 and 14, 1779, resolutions, but Congress indicated that it was still operative on June 14, 1779 (*JCC* 14:728).

[c] By the end of 1779 a total of $199,989,995 net new Continental dollars had been emitted. To redeem all the Continental dollars as the January 2, 1779, resolution specified would entail raising the annual payments over the eighteen-year period (1780–97) from $6,000,000 to $10,277,222. See note d. This number is net of some undetermined amount of Continental dollar remittances received from the states after 1779 that the resolution allowed to be respent to pay off loan office certificate principal and interest incurred before 1780. Total state remittances after 1779, therefore, had to be somewhat higher than $10,277,222 per year to account for permanently removing these respent Continental dollars from circulation.

[d] Emission no. 1 had a total of $3,000,000 in it—initially $2,000,000 and then $2,000,000 added to it shortly thereafter. On July 25, 1775, Congress ordered $1,000,000 struck in $30 bills (*JCC* 2:207). This is not possible. Either $999,990 or $1,000,020 can be struck, but not $1,000,000. Which was done and whether other denominations of emission no. 1 were adjusted to accommodate the $1,000,000 target in $30 bills is not known. Because no change in the $1,000,000 total authorized was ever noted by Congress or the Board of Treasury, it is assumed that the discrepancy was made up by adjusting the printing of bills of other denominations from this emission, thus yielding the reported total here of $199,989,995. However, the total cumulative net new emissions could vary between $199,989,985 and $199,990,015 depending on how Congress resolved its order to emit $1,000,000 in $30 bills on July 25, 1775—an outcome that is currently unknown.

(see figs. I.1, I.2, I.3, and I.4; Newman 2008: 37–41, 63–72).[2] For the first
emission, the initial 3 million—those with the date May 10, 1775, printed
on the bills—Congress passed redemption instructions on July 29, 1775.
States were to remit fixed quotas of Continental dollars to the Continental Treasury to be burned. Each state's quota was roughly proportional
to its respective population share in the union. Congress explicitly left
each state free to decide how best to redeem Continental dollars from the
citizens within their respective jurisdictions. State remittances to the Continental Treasury were to be in four equal yearly installments spread out
over a contiguous four-year period, beginning on November 30, 1779, and
ending on November 30, 1782. No contemporaneous taxes or other debts
payable in these Continental dollars were required before the redemption years indicated, no state was required to remit more than its quota,
and Continental dollars paid no interest. States with a quota deficiency of
Continental dollars were to make it up in specie at face value. The Continental treasurer was to retain this specie and advertise its availability.
Citizens with Continental dollars in states that had filled their quotas and
had ceased redeeming Continental dollars could redeem their Continental dollars at face value for specie directly from the Continental Treasury,
in effect claiming the specie remitted by the states with a quota deficiency
of Continental dollars (*JCC* 2:106, 221–23; 3:407).

The adoption of this last provision indicates that Congress anticipated
that by 1779, when state redemption of Continental dollars would com-
mence, a geographic imbalance of Continental dollars relative to state
redemption quotas would exist. The exigency of the war would cause paper money spent on troops and supplies to be concentrated in its theaters,
which were unlikely to be spread evenly among the states. Congress provided an ingenious solution to the anticipated geographic imbalance in
the location of Continental dollars that rebalanced the availability of these
dollars with state quota claims. This was necessary to ensure fairness and
stem jealousies among the states regarding who would shoulder the financial burden of the war. This provision also anchored the value of a Continental dollar to its face value in specie at the specific future dates set for
their redemption.

Before the Revolution, colonies had employed this same method for
rebalancing paper-money redemption requirements within their respective colonies. When a colony emitted paper money, it also set future taxes
to redeem that paper money and remove it from circulation: upon redemption, the paper money would be destroyed. Colonial assemblies real-

ized that future tax burdens to retire the paper money and the possession of that paper money among its citizens would not be perfectly aligned. The transaction costs of trading paper money among a colony's citizens to perfectly realign each citizen's possession of paper money with that citizen's tax obligations by the time taxes were due were burdensome and fraught with potential hold-ups and leveraged rent-seeking of one citizen against another.

Colonial assemblies solved this problem by allowing citizens to pay their taxes either in the colony's paper money or in some other medium, such as grain or specie, at a fixed rate to the colony's paper money. Citizens who did not have, or could not acquire in time, the colony's paper money paid their taxes in these other media. Citizens who had more paper money than they owed in taxes could then directly cash in their excess balances of paper money at the colony's treasury for the grain or specie paid by the citizens who did not have the paper money to pay their taxes. Because the final taxes on paper money redemption were set equal to the quantity of paper money emitted, this method perfectly rebalanced tax obligations and paper-money claims among the colony's citizens.[3] As such, the specie-redemption option in the Continental dollar resolutions would have been familiar to Americans. Its presence, design, and purpose in these Continental dollar resolutions were likely expected and understood by the public.

Congress placed the redemption of the first emission of Continental dollars four to seven years into the future, because that was when the war was expected to be over. For example, Silas Deane, congressman from Connecticut, wrote on July 1, 1775, "The Warr will not last Seven Years if I have any Judgment in Matters."[4] At that point, trade would resume and generate the income necessary to pay the taxes needed to redeem Continental dollars at face value in specie. Most congressmen understood that the colonies were rich in assets—for example, they possessed abundant land, slaves, oxen, and so on—but poor in cash. Specie to pay taxes rested on foreign trade: Americans selling whatever they produced to foreigners for specie. This trade was disrupted by war via import and export embargos imposed by Congress and the British blockade of foreign trade. Congress opened American ports to non-British trade on April 6, 1776.[5] This trade disruption also meant that the ability to acquire specie to pay interest to the holders of Continental dollars in the interim before redemption was in doubt. As such, being unable to make interest payments certain, no interest payments were attached to the Continental dollar in Congress's redemption resolutions.

For the second emission, the next 3 million—those with the date November 29, 1775, printed on the bills—Congress passed redemption instructions on December 26, 1775. These instructions were identical to those for the first emission, except that the four-year redemption window was explicitly voted to be moved forward to begin after the last of the first emission was redeemed, namely November 30, 1783, and to end on November 30, 1786. Richard Smith wrote in his diary on December 23, 1775, that "[James] Duane [congressman from New York] gave in a Sett of Resolves for Sinking the last 3 Millions of Dollars, similar to those of the former 3 Millions & to be sunk in the same Years. They were all agreed to except the Time of Sinking which required further consideration." That further consideration was taken up three days later. Smith wrote in his diary on December 26, 1775, "Duanes Proposition for sinking the last 3 Million of Dollars were gone thro, the Vote was taken Whether that Money shall be sunk in the Years 1779, 1780, 1781 & 1782 as the last 3 Million, or in the Years 1783, 1784, 1785 & 1786 and carried for the latter" (*JCC* 3:457–59; Smith 1976–94, 2:517–18, 524).

This vote is important because it shows that the selection of a redemption window was not an afterthought or just some resolution boilerplate. It was a significant choice based on serious deliberations among alternatives. This vote established that redemption windows would be emission-specific and created a precedent that would govern how expectations could be formed for forecasting the redemption of future emissions. It also provides insight into what motivated the particular structural design of the Continental dollar adopted by Congress.

The redemption of the first emission of Continental dollars amounted to $750,000 per year, which implied an average tax per year per white capita of $0.33. In the thirteen colonies, between 1770 and 1774, the average tax per year per white capita for all taxes was $0.41.[6] Spreading the redemption of the first emission over a contiguous four years to lower per-year per-white-capita taxes to historically acceptable and feasible levels is the only sensible explanation for adopting a multiyear redemption window.

In general, multiyear redemption windows were problematic. They caused uncertainty in the realized values of Continental dollars from the same emission. While the average or expected value of a Continental dollar from the first emission can be estimated given the four-year span of the redemption window, not knowing which specific Continental dollar would be redeemed in 1779 and which in 1782 meant that the realized value of a Continental dollar varied around that average by the waiting cost spanned by the redemption window. If citizens could determine which dollar would be redeemed in which year, they would be willing in 1775 to pay more for a dollar redeemed in 1779 than for one redeemed in 1782. When identical dollar bills are not necessarily of equal present value, this makes for a cumbersome medium of exchange.

The only reason to have a four-year redemption window for the first emission rather than a one-year redemption point was to hold per-year per-white-capita redemption taxes within historically acceptable and feasible limits. If redemption was not fiscally credible—that is, if taxes were so high that the public could not pay them—then the system would collapse, because citizens would doubt that their dollars would be redeemed at face value as promised. In setting the redemption structure of the first emission, Congress made a tradeoff between fiscal credibility and ease of use as a medium of exchange, siding with fiscal credibility. This interpretation plays through the second emission and makes sense of the vote over the redemption window for that emission.

Duane's proposal to redeem the second emission in the same window of time as the first emission would have doubled the redemption quotas for 1779 through 1782. This in turn would have doubled the taxes each state would have to impose on its citizens to an average tax per year per white capita of $0.66, or 61 percent above that for all taxes raised per year per white capita in the years preceding the Revolution. A tax level well above the historically acceptable and feasible range would threaten the fiscal credibility of the system and risk precipitating its collapse. When Congress voted to push the redemption of the second emission into a four-year redemption window that started immediately after the last redemption year of the first emission, they were voting to keep the per-year per-white-capita tax level constant at $0.33 for redeeming both emissions, and thus to maintain the system's fiscal credibility.

Adopting Duane's proposal would have had one good consequence: by having both the first and second emissions redeemed in the same four-year window, Duane's proposal would have caused the expected value of a Continental dollar to be the same regardless of emission, that is, regardless of the date on the bill. Emissions would be fully fungible. Using Continental dollars as a medium of exchange would be easier under Duane's proposal because the expected value of Continental dollars at any point in time would not differ by emission. The realized values of Continental dollars of both emissions would still be subject to the same variance around a common average as discussed above, but that would be a minor inconvenience compared with values varying between emissions.

When Congress rejected Duane's proposal in favor of different redemption windows per emission, they were explicitly accepting that Continental dollars from different emissions at the same point in time would have different expected values. In 1775, having a Continental dollar that would be paid off in specie at face value in 1779 was more valuable than having one that would be paid off in specie at face value in 1786. Not only was there some minor variance in the realized values of Continental dollars per each emission around the average for that emission, but now at any point in time there was a difference in the expected value of a Continental dollar between emissions. The expected value of a Continental dollar was now contingent on the date printed on the bill. This outcome added to the cumbersomeness of using Continental dollars as a medium of exchange. Again, the only sensible explanation for why Congress voted for this redemption structure was that they were making a tradeoff between holding per-year per-white-capita taxes within historically acceptable and feasible limits, thus giving the system fiscal credibility and making Continental dollars an easy-to-use medium of exchange. Again, they sided with fiscal credibility over easy usability.[7]

This choice foreshadows a continuing conflict that by 1779 was won by those congressmen who, like Duane, did not understand the need for fiscal credibility or who believed that current tax levels could be pushed substantially above what had been historically experienced without doing harm. These congressmen either did not see a connection between the fiscal credibility of redemption and the value of the Continental dollar or were willing to sacrifice that connection for other political and economic goals. They gravitated toward reinterpreting the Continental dollar as a pure fiat currency with no value anchor, despite its documented structural design, and viewed the Continental dollar's value as being determined primarily by a naive interpretation of Hume's quantity theory of money (Grubb 2012b, 2018b).

On November 23, 1775, Congress appointed an ad hoc committee on paper money. Richard Smith wrote in his diary on January 11, 1776, "A Report from the Comee. on the Paper Currency was ably argued for 4 Hours, the Report recommended that the present 6 Millions of Dollars be called in and large Notes issued to that Amount bearing Interest."[8] Again, Smith's comments show that Congress debated the structural design of the Continental dollar at length. The choices made were not afterthoughts or resolution boilerplate; they were based on serious deliberations among alternatives. Having the Continental dollar pay yearly interest between emission and redemption was one such alternative design. This proposal was made, debated upon, and not adopted. Most likely the majority of congressmen saw the paying of yearly interest as impractical given the absence of wartime tax revenue. The Continental dollar would remain a zero-coupon bond-type money with defined future payoff dates in specie equivalents.

CHAPTER TWO

Richard Smith and New Jersey's Influence

The influence of Richard Smith, the New Jersey congressman whose diary tells us so much about the Continental dollar, on the dollar's initial structural design may go deeper than just his diary observations noted in chapter 1. Having been present for all congressional paper-money deliberations from May 10, 1775, to March 30, 1776, he was appointed by Congress to a standing committee created on February 17, 1776, for superintending the treasury and overseeing the emission of Continental dollars (*JCC* 4:156–57). He was the only congressman to note the congressional debates on redemption windows and interest payments for the first two emissions. Smith's brother, Samuel Smith, was the New Jersey state treasurer, and Richard left Congress on March 30, 1776, to succeed his brother, who had died, in that post. Richard Smith's public finance expertise and intimate knowledge of colonial New Jersey's paper-money system may have influenced the congressional debates that crafted the initial structural design of the Continental dollar. For an example of colonial New Jersey's paper money, see fig. 2.1.

The Continental dollar and the colonial New Jersey paper pound shared many features. Colonial New Jersey's last emissions of paper money were made during a war, namely the French and Indian War of 1755–64. The redemption of these wartime emissions was designed to take place well after the war had ended. The Continental dollar was emitted under similar wartime circumstances, with the same intention of postwar redemption.

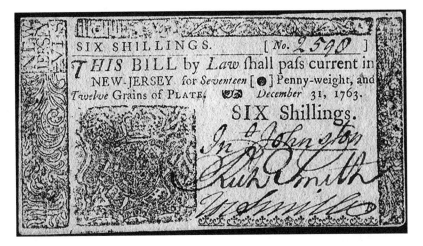

FIGURE 2.1. Example of New Jersey paper money, issued December 31, 1763

Source: Newman (2008: 258). Reprinted by permission of the Eric P. Newman Numismatic Education Society.

Note: "Plate" refers to silver (specie). Twenty pennyweight, of twenty-four grains each, equals one troy ounce of silver plate. Six shillings in New Jersey pounds equals 0.3 New Jersey pound, which is set equal to 0.875 ounces of silver, or 0.3429 New Jersey pound equals one ounce of silver, at face value. One pound sterling equals 3.8715 ounces of silver, or one ounce of silver equals 0.2583 pound sterling. Therefore, by equating both to one ounce of silver, 0.3429 New Jersey pound at face value equals 0.2583 pound sterling, or 1.3275 New Jersey pound at face value equals one pound sterling. See McCusker (1978: 8–10).

Both the Continental dollar and the colonial New Jersey pound had their specie value at redemption printed on the face of each bill (see figs. I.1, I.2, I.3, and I.4 and compare with fig. 2.1). Most colonial paper monies did not have this feature (Grubb 2016a; Newman 1997, 2008). Both the Continental dollar and the colonial New Jersey pound paid no interest. Both had explicit redemption dates set well into the future and spread out to hold per-year per-white-capita taxes within fiscally feasible limits.

Each year the French and Indian War continued, New Jersey emitted more bills of credit to meet unexpected war expenses, until by 1764 a total of 347,500 New Jersey pounds—approximately $1,189,944—in new bills had been emitted (see table 2.1). This was over two and a half times the amount New Jersey had emitted over its entire prior history of issuing paper money, from 1709 to 1754 (Grubb 2015, 2016b). Similarly, new emissions of Continental dollars would be required as long as the War for Independence continued, with the total amount emitted rising to many times what would be considered normal during peacetime. With each new wartime emission (during the French and Indian War), the New Jersey legislature established explicit redemption provisions (maturity dates) by

TABLE 2.1 Colonial New Jersey emissions and redemptions of paper New Jersey pounds, 1755–83

New emissions:	Redemption year and amount (in thousands of New Jersey paper pounds = £NJ)																										
Date and amount	1757	1758	1759	1760	1761	1762	1763	1764	1765	1766	1767	1768	1769	1770	1771	1772	1773	1774	1775	1776	1777	1778	1779	1780	1781	1782	1783
1755																											
Apr. 15,000£NJ	5	5	5																								
Aug. 15,000		5	5	5																							
Dec. 10,000				10																							
1756																											
June 17,500					2.5	15																					
1757																											
Mar. 10,000							10																				
June 5,000							5																				
Oct. 30,000												5	5	5	5	5	5										
1758																											
Apr. 50,000																		10	10	10	10	10					
Aug. 10,000					10																						
1759																											
Mar. 50,000								12.5	12.5	12.5	12.5																
1760																											
Mar. 45,000												7.5	7.5	7.5	7.5	7.5	7.5										
1761																											
Mar. 25,000																		5	5	5	5	5					
1762																											
Mar. 30,000																							15	15			
1763																											
Dec. 10,000																									10		
1764																											
Feb. 25,000																									5	15	5
Total 347,500£NJ	5	10	10	15	12.5	15	15	12.5	12.5	12.5	12.5	12.5	12.5	12.5	12.5	12.5	12.5	15	15	15	15	15	15	15	15	15	5

Sources: Bush (1980: 15–39, 65–74, 81–82, 104, 124–27, 168–72, 195–213, 219–51, 269–88, 303–4, 307–19, 323–24, 327–55, 373–409, 413–36, 451–88, 495–502, 517–31, 539–55, 559–78, 581–97, 621–56, 663–79; 1982: 5–13, 24–28, 73–89, 97–103, 107–11, 125–40, 153–54, 159–66, 191–98, 207–21, 273–76, 289–316, 385–88, 394, 427–31, 453–56, 505–8, 523–64; 1986: 25–29, 53–59, 64–68, 115–21, 171–77, 212–35, 250–51, 301–6, 327–32, 379–93, 419–22, 437–56); Grubb (2015, 2016b); Kemmerer (1940: 279); Sherwood (1851: 147).

fixing future tax obligations to be paid in its bills at the bill's face value. Bills redeemed via taxation were destroyed. The redemption procedure chosen for the Continental dollar was similar to that used by colonial New Jersey.

Finally, as the French and Indian War continued and emissions mounted, the New Jersey legislature deliberately spread the redemption of its wartime emissions evenly over a twenty-seven-year time horizon, from 1757 through 1783 (see table 2.1). For the sequence of new emissions from 1755 through mid-1758 and from 1762 through 1764, the New Jersey legislature deliberately staggered their respective redemptions forward in time. In addition, most individual emissions had a three- to six-year contiguous redemption window with per-year redemption amounts held constant within that window. For emissions from mid-1758 through 1761, the New Jersey legislature deliberately placed the redemption windows for these emissions so as to even out per-year redemptions for the entire amount of wartime emissions over the twenty-seven-year redemption period. In the end, between the last wartime emission in 1764 and 1773, redemption ended up being exactly 12,500, and from 1774 to 1782 it was exactly 15,000 New Jersey pounds per year. This put the average redemption tax per year per white capita for New Jersey residents between $0.37 and $0.45, close to the tax level for redeeming the first two emissions of Continental dollars.[1] This deliberate spreading out of redemptions evenly over a long horizon held per-year per-white-capita taxes within feasible limits, thus giving New Jersey's commitment to its paper-money fiscal credibility.

Like the New Jersey pound, Continental dollars, in the early emissions, were designed to have different contiguous multiyear redemption windows, sequentially pushed further into the future for each new emission. In addition, this redemption structure, like that of the New Jersey pound, was designed to hold taxes within fiscally feasible limits. To sum up: the circumstances of emission, patterns of redemption, and structural design of the Continental dollar closely mimicked those of recent colonial New Jersey paper pounds.

New Jersey successfully redeemed its bills at face value on time as legislatively promised—until the Revolution intervened. The present value of New Jersey's paper money, time-discounted back from its designated redemption dates, closely tracked its current specie exchange rate. These rates fluctuated between 55 and 85 percent of the money's face value (Grubb 2016b: 1223). In other words, the New Jersey paper pound was a zero-coupon, bond-type currency whose current value was explained almost entirely by time-discounting. It traded below face value not because it had depreciated, but because it was a bond that paid no interest and would not be redeemed at face value until sometime in the future.

The initial design of the Continental dollar was virtually identical to, and had all the features of, the colonial New Jersey paper pound. As such, it was not new and would likely be familiar to and well understood by Americans.[2] The history of the colonial New Jersey pound also provided a precedent for what Americans could expect regarding the future performance and redemption structure of the Continental dollar. Specifically, redemption at face value would start only after the war, would be pushed further into the future with each subsequent emission, and would be spread over enough years to keep tax levels within historically acceptable and feasible limits, thus giving the system fiscal credibility.

CHAPTER THREE

Denominational Spacing and Value Size

Among historical and contemporary monies, the Continental dollar used a denominational spacing that was unique, even downright bizarre. The smallest denominations of the Continental dollar were also relatively large in value, making it hard to use as a medium of exchange. These facts are consistent with the notion that with this dollar Congress intentionally created a bond-type money rather than a fiat currency. Chapter 1 showed that Congress debated alternative structural designs for the Continental dollar, namely whether redemption windows should overlap or be staggered per emission, whether bills should pay interest between emission and redemption, and whether bills should be called in and replaced with bills of even larger value. Chapter 2 showed that the Continental dollar had many similarities with the structural designs of colonial paper monies emitted before the Revolution. Congress's explicit discussions regarding the denominational spacing and value size of the Continental dollar have not survived; their decisions have to be inferred from the results. The denominational spacing of the Continental dollar was so unusual that it is difficult to consider Congress's choice regarding that spacing as not being deliberate or not intending some form of monetary control.

Congress may have created the Continental dollar to be a bond-type currency because they expected citizens to hold the Continental dollars they received for future redemption and not use them as a current medium

of exchange. The primary initial recipients of Continental dollars were soldiers, who had no choice but to accept Continental dollars, and at the pay
rates established by Congress. Congress expected soldiers to hold these dollars as bonds for future postwar redemption. For example, on August 6,
1779, General Parsons explained,

> I have not concerned myself with Commerce to increase my Estate Since the
> War . . . I . . . collected my dues [army salary] in Bills [Continental dollars] at
> their nominal Value in full Confidence . . . that at Some future Period my Coun-
> try would do that Justice which they had promis'd me by paying their Debt at
> the nominal Value of the Bills they had emitted . . . to render old age free from
> those miseries arising from Indigence.[1]

The denominational size of Continental dollars was consistent with the
difficulty of their being easily used as a medium of exchange. Continental dollars were large-value bills. The smallest emitted in 1775 was a
$1 bill, equivalent to $31 in 2012 dollars, and in expected present value to
$21 in 2012 dollars when time-discounted from their established redemp-
tion dates at 6 percent. Congress never minted any fractions-of-a-dollar
coins—or any coins whatsoever, for that matter—during the Revolution.
Congress only emitted fraction-of-a-dollar paper notes once, namely
in emission no. 3 on February 17, 1776. These fraction-of-a-dollar notes
amounted only to 0.41 percent of the face value of all Continental dollars ever emitted. The face value of the smallest fraction-of-a-dollar note
emitted was still relatively large, being worth over $5 in 2012 US dollars
(see table B.1).

In 1775 over 60 percent of the bills emitted, in face value and expected
present value, were equivalent to or larger than $124 and $86 in 2012 dollars, respectively. Large denominations were hard to use as transactions
that required change could not be made unless change was given in some
other medium. Congress never made the Continental dollar a legal tender. Thus, while soldiers and other congressional employees had to accept them in payment for their services and goods, private traders in the
marketplace faced no legal penalty if they refused to accept Continental
dollars as a medium of exchange because they could not make change in
Continental dollars.

Soldiers' pay was fixed by Congress in nominal terms in Continental dollars in June and July 1775, at the same time that it established the
structural design of the initial emission of Continental dollars. Soldiers'

pay absorbed nearly half of all Continental dollars emitted through 1777 (Grubb 2011b). American army privates were paid $80 per year. Privates were the primary recipients of military pay, receiving 78 percent of the money paid to each military company. British army privates were paid $55 per year. American privates were paid in paper Continental dollars, whereas British privates were paid in specie. In November 1775 the expected present value of eighty Continental dollars of the first emission when time-discounted at 6 percent from the established redemption dates was between $63 and $53, or comparable with the value of a British private's yearly pay.[2] That Congress initially set an American army private's pay equal to a British army private's pay in expected present value terms rather than in face-value terms is an acknowledgment of the zero-coupon bond nature of the Continental dollar that Congress was creating. The Continental dollar was expected to function as a bond-type money and not a fiat currency.

Before the Revolution, colonial governments had printed reserve sums of their respective paper monies for the sole purpose of swapping such bills one to one for bills in public circulation that had become too ragged and torn to continue being used as a hand-to-hand medium of exchange. Congressmen for the revolutionary government were familiar with such colonial monetary procedures and understood the reasons for their existence. Yet, Congress did not print reserve sums of Continental dollars to serve the same function (Grubb 2018b: 23–24). That Congress did not create a reserve fund of Continental dollars to be swapped one for one with Continental dollars is consistent with Congress expecting Continental dollars to be held primarily as bonds for future redemption and not extensively circulate as a medium of exchange. Again, Congress was treating the Continental dollar as a bond-type money and not a fiat currency.

Lastly, Benjamin Franklin's recommendation during the creation of the Continental dollar shows that he considered the Continental dollar to be a zero-coupon bond rather than a fiat currency. In 1779, while in Paris, Franklin wrote to Samuel Cooper, saying, "I took all the Pains I could in Congress to prevent the Depreciation by proposing first that the Bills [Continental dollars] should bear Interest; this was rejected, and they were struck as you see them" (Oberg 1992–98, 29:354–56). Richard Smith's diary, referred to in chapter 1, provides the first corroboration (that I know of) that Franklin had indeed made such a proposal. Franklin was on the congressional committee that on January 11, 1776, recommended that the current 6 million Continental dollars that had been emitted be called in and swapped for notes of even larger values—notes that would also now pay interest.

In 1764 Franklin explained to the Pennsylvania Assembly that its paper money (bills of credit), which were anchored only by a promise to redeem them at face value at some future date, could not circulate as a currency at their face value owing to time-discounting—the bill's present value was less than its face value. He recommended that the bills be made to pay interest to compensate for this time-discounting cost, thus causing the bills to always circulate at face value (Grubb 2016a: 171–73; Labaree 1966–70, 11:13–17). By 1767, however, Franklin had come to consider interest-bearing bills of credit to be a difficult medium of exchange because of the difficulty of computing the interest portion of the bill when used in day-to-day transactions (Grubb 2016a: 185; Labaree 1966–70, 14:36).

Therefore, Franklin's proposal in January 1776 that the Continental dollar should pay interest is a recognition that the Continental dollar was initially designed to be a zero-coupon bearer-bond money whose present value would always be less than its face value before redemption owing to time-discounting. Interest payments would counterbalance this time-discounting and would cause the bill's present value to always equal its face value. In addition, Franklin's proposal—the proposal of the committee of which he was a member—wanted Continental dollars to be issued as larger-value bills than they were. This only makes sense if they wanted to restrict the medium-of-exchange function of Continental dollars and hoped they would be primarily held as bonds for future redemption.

The Theory of Denominational Structure

Denominational structure is the numerical spacing between denomination values, and the relative real value of the denominational set. I assume that the money creator selects a denominational structure to achieve some purpose. The Continental dollar was a new money, so Congress was free to choose any denominational structure it wanted. Denominational structure is used to infer the monetary policy Congress selected to rationalize their currency system and give it some potential for success.

Denominational theory assumes that the goal of the money creator is to minimize the cost of completing transactions, namely to minimize the cost of making change. This goal is the same as maximizing the medium-of-exchange usage of the money created. Lester Telser (1995: 425–27) mathematically showed that creating a currency with the fewest units needed to execute all transactions entailed choosing a denominational spacing that has a factor of 3 — 1, 3, 9, 27, and so on. The denominational spacing factor is found by taking the value of a given denomination and dividing it by the value of the immediately preceding denomination. Dividing the sum of these factors over all sequential denominational pairings by the number of pairings equals the average denomination factor for a given currency. The denomination factor, both for individual pairings and for the average of all pairings, has a lower boundary of one.

Telser's analysis only considered minimizing the cost of producing the monetary units needed to execute all transactions, and it assumed all monetary units have the same cost of production. By contrast, minimizing the cost of making transactions from the consumer's perspective entails incorporating computational ease and historical familiarity. Ease of computation puts considerable weight on units divisible by 5 and on having a denomination factor of 2. Such cost considerations push denominational structures, conditional on being able to make change in all transactions in said money, toward incomplete binary-decimal triplets—for example, 1, 2, 5; 10, 20, 50; and so on. When such computational cost-minimizing considerations are added to minimizing the cost of currency production, the full cost-minimizing denominational spacing yields average denomination factors between 2 and 3 (Tschoegl 1997: 546–54; Van Hove 2001: 1015–21; Wynne 1997: 221–25).

For example, the modern US dollar has the following spacing between denominations: 0.01, 0.05, 0.10, 0.25, 0.50, 1.00, 2.00, 5.00, 10.00, 20.00, 50.00, and 100.00. The denomination factors are 5, 2, 2.5, 2, 2, 2, 2.5, 2, 2, 2.5, and 2, respectively, with an average of 2.41. The factor of 2 dominates—the mode factor, with an occasional higher factor that is the result of making the next higher nonzero denomination number divisible by 5. The average denomination factor for the euro is 2.18 and for the yen is 3.06—both currencies having a mode factor of 2.

Besides optimal denominational spacing, relative denominational size also matters in achieving the goal of maximizing the use of the currency as a circulating medium of exchange. If the smallest denominations of a currency are large relative to the value of goods being exchanged, then the ability to use that currency as a transacting medium is reduced. Either many transactions cannot take place or change must be made in some other money, barter good, or book credit. If making change entails using alternative monies, then these alternative monies will dominate the medium of exchange. The currency in question will be pushed toward being hoarded as a store of value, exported if it is outside money, or used only in the occasional large transaction.[3] This outcome is the result of an indivisibility of the currency at the lower-value end of its denominational range (Redish and Weber 2008; Sumner 1990; Wallace and Zhou 1997).

In summary, the objective of an optimal denominational structure, namely optimal spacing and value size, is to maximize the use of the currency as a circulating medium of exchange, that is, to make it easy and feasible to execute all transactions in the economy with that money. This result also implies being able easily to make change in that money. The considerations that yield this outcome include minimizing the cost of making computations for consumers, minimizing the cost of monetary-unit production for the money creator, and setting the lower-value denominations in the range of the value of most transactions desired by society.

Why create a currency with a denominational structure that makes it difficult to use that currency as a medium of exchange? One answer would be to mitigate its effect on prices. Under the simple quantity theory of money, increases in the quantity of money (M_x), given the velocity of circulation of that money (V_x), must drive up prices (P) given production constraints on real output (Y) (see equation 3.1; Bordo 1987; Fisher 1912).

Eq. 3.1 $M_x V_x = PY$ (where M_x = money issued by subnational entities, V_x = the velocity of circulation of that money, P = prices expressed in that money, Y = real output)

Suppose that M_x is controlled not by the central authority but by subnational political entities. How can the central authority create its own common currency, M_z, to pay for emergency military expenses, then overlay it on top of these subnational currencies, without affecting P? Under the simple quantity theory of money, if the central authority creates a currency whose circulation (V_z) is reduced to near zero by its denominational structure, P would not be affected.[4] Equation 3.2 adds M_z to equation 3.1. However, as $V_z \rightarrow 0$, equation 3.2 $\rightarrow$ equation 3.1, and there is little inflationary effect from adding M_z to the mix of currencies. The new common currency is held as a store of value for future liquidation. M_x continues to be the primary circulating medium of exchange.

Eq. 3.2 $M_x V_x + M_z V_z = PY$ (where M_z = money issued by the national authority, V_z = the velocity of circulation of that money)

For this strategy to succeed, money entrepreneurs must not be able to undo the denominational constraint placed on M_z's usage as a circulating medium of exchange. A money entrepreneur could undo the above strategy by accepting deposits of M_z bills that were denominationally difficult to circulate and, for a small fee, issue private money claims on those deposits that were denominationally easy to circulate. The M_z bills taken on deposit provide the reserves, redeemable upon demand, for the private money issued. Even without a fractional reserve structure—that is, even with 100 percent reserves backing this private money—this process puts the full value of M_z into circulation, thus undoing the effort to restrict M_z's contribution to wartime inflation.

In the late eighteenth and early nineteenth centuries, this process was essentially what private and publicly chartered banks did: they took in deposits and issued their own private banknotes as claims against those deposits, with the banknotes circulating as a local inside money.[5] Banks and banknotes, however, did not exist in colonial America, owing largely to British restrictions on chartering corporations. The exigencies of war meant that even with the removal of British restrictions, banks were unlikely to form during the Revolution. The Bank of North America, chartered in 1781, was the first successful US bank.[6] Without money entrepreneurs, and the risk of their undoing a denominational control strategy, controlling the wartime circulation of M_z through selection of a restrictive denominational structure, thus mitigating M_z's contribution to wartime inflation, had some chance of success.

The above strategy was chosen by the Continental Congress during the Revolution to maximize the potential success of its common currency system. It was a rational strategy given the circumstances and constraints faced by Congress, and given state resistance to forming a true currency union (see the introduction). Its failure was not preordained.

American Colonial- and Revolutionary-Era Denominational Spacing of Paper Monies

Congress established the denominational structure for each emission of Continental dollars in each emission's authorizing resolution. There were eleven separate emissions, the first in 1775 and the last in 1779. Table B.1 reports the denominational structure separately for each of these eleven emissions in terms of the percentage of units and the percentage of their

TABLE 3.1 **Denominational spacing**

Colony/nation			
Currency	Factor average	Factor mode	Factor range
Modern Nations			
US dollar	2.41	2.00	2.00 to 5.00
Euro	2.18	2.00	2.00 to 2.50
Yen	3.06	2.00	2.00 to 5.00
1775–79 (American Revolution)			
US Continental dollar	1.36	1.50	1.08 to 2.50
1775–77 (American Revolution)			
Virginia currency	1.39	1.25	1.20 to 2.00
Pennsylvania currency	1.30	1.25/1.33	1.07 to 1.60
New Jersey currency	1.84	2.00	1.25 to 2.00
New York currency	1.60	1.50	1.33 to 2.00
1755–64 (Seven Years' War)			
Virginia currency	1.82	2.00	1.25 to 2.00
Pennsylvania currency	1.62	1.33/1.50	1.25 to 2.50
New Jersey currency	1.84	2.00	1.25 to 2.00
New York currency	1.73	2.00	1.25 to 2.00

Sources: Derived from tables B.1, B.2, and B.3.
Notes: The factor spacing is calculated by taking the value (X_t) of a denomination (d_t) at location (t) and dividing it into the value of the next higher denomination, i.e., $(X_{t+1}d_{t+1} / X_t d_t)$. The average factor spacing is the summation of factor spacing across the full range of denominations emitted into circulation, i.e.,

$$[\sum_{t=1}^{N} (X_{t+1}d_{t+1} / X_t d_t)] / (N-1),$$ where N = the complete sequential list of denominations.

face value issued per each denomination for that emission, as well as for the cumulative total for all Continental dollars ever emitted.

Table 3.1 uses the data in tables B.1, B.2, and B.3 to construct the average, mode, and range of denomination factors for all Continental dollars ever emitted, and for the currencies issued by Virginia, Pennsylvania, New Jersey, and New York during the Seven Years' War and during the first years of the Revolution. For comparative purposes, table 3.1 also reports similar information for the modern currencies of the euro, yen, and US dollar. The comparison to state currencies during the Revolution is restricted to pre-1778 because on November 22, 1777, Congress asked the states to restrict their emission of large-value bills, thus altering the desired denomination factor for their post-1777 emissions (*JCC* 7:125; 9:955–56). The comparison to colonial currencies is restricted to the Seven Years' War, 1755–64, to draw out similar circumstances to the Continental dollar, namely large emergency wartime paper-money emissions that had occurred within the lifetimes of most congressmen in 1775.

Compared with modern and contemporary North American currencies, the Continental dollar had a relatively low average, mode, and minimum denomination factor. Its denominations were more tightly spaced
than those of other currencies. This pattern was not unique, however. The
average, mode, and range of the Continental dollar's denomination factor were comparable to those of the Virginia and Pennsylvania state currencies issued at the same time. It was, however, unprecedented in prior
experience. Colonial paper-money emissions under similar circumstances
yielded denomination factors with substantially higher average and mode
values.

While possessing lower average denomination factors than modern
currencies, colonial currencies had the same mode factor as modern currencies. Comparing denomination factors, the Continental dollar had an
88 and 29 percent lower average, and a 33 and 25 percent lower mode,
than that of modern and recent colonial currencies, respectively. The denominational spacing of the Continental dollar was unusual.

A closer examination of the denominational spacing within individual
emissions of Continental dollars in table B.1 reveals that the denominational spacing was odder than that revealed in table 3.1. Each emission
has a concentration of units in the denomination sequence of two-, three-,
four-, five-, six-, seven-, and eight-dollar bills. I have not found such a core
denominational sequence for any other money. For eight of the first nine
emissions, 78 to 88 percent of the units issued were in this sequence. For
the total emission of Continental dollars, 53 percent of the units issued
were in this sequence. This denominational spacing is not only unconven-
tional and unprecedented, but downright bizarre and inexplicable. No one
has noted this before or commented on its oddity. What was Congress
thinking? What were they up to?

The explanation of this denominational spacing cannot be simple igno-
rance. Most congressmen had either been closely involved with or lived
under the paper-money regimes of the colonies they represented. Congress
selected congressmen with prior experience with colonial paper monies to
craft the Continental dollar, such as Benjamin Franklin and Richard Smith.
In 1775 and 1776 Congress debated at length on how to structure the Continental dollar system it created (see chaps. 1 and 2).

While the sequence two-, three-, four-, five-, six-, seven-, and eight-
dollar bills is generally an inexplicable denominational spacing, a reasonable explanation may be related to the fact that Continental dollar
bills were relative large in value (see the next section). Most of these bills

were used to pay soldiers' salaries. Soldiers' pay was fixed by Congress in June and July 1775 at the same time it was deciding on the denominational structure of the initial emissions of Continental dollars. Soldiers' pay absorbed nearly half of all Continental dollars emitted through 1776. American army privates were paid 80 Continental dollars per year. Privates were the primary recipients of military pay, receiving 78 percent of the money paid to each military company (Grubb 2011b: 275; *JCC* 2:89–90, 93–94, 209–10, 220–23).

The unusual denominational spacing of the Continental dollar makes sense if Congress intended to pay soldiers in the fewest bills necessary, and thus in large-value bills that would be difficult to use as a circulating currency. Three months' pay for a private, twenty Continental dollars, could be accommodated with one or various combinations of three, four, or five large-value bills. One month's pay for a private after clothing deductions, five Continental dollars, could be accommodated with one or various combinations of two large-value bills. For higher-ranked military personal, paying them with a few large-value bills was even easier. Thus, the strange denominational spacing of the Continental dollar and its unusual denominational size were linked.

Congress's behavior is consistent with their hope that soldiers would simply hold their pay, being in large-value bills, as assets for future liquidation after the war. Furthermore, it is consistent with their thinking that it would be too difficult for soldiers to spend their pay as money, given the bills' large value. Thus, the emission of Continental dollars would not function as a circulating medium of exchange for everyday transactions. As such, it would not contribute to wartime inflation.

American Colonial- and Revolutionary-Era Denominational Value Sizes

Tables B.1, B.2, and B.3 convert the denominational units of the Continental dollar and of various colonial and state currencies into comparable values, namely Spanish silver dollars, pounds sterling, and 2012 US dollars. Table 3.2 and figure 3.1 use the conversion into 2012 US dollars to compare the value of these denominations, as well as to provide a sense of the relative magnitude of these values. Table 3.2 and figure 3.1 show that the Continental dollar consisted of relatively large-value bills, with 82 percent being over $50 and 69 percent being over $100 in 2012 US dollars. Only

TABLE 3.2 **Distribution of denominational sizes by number of units emitted**

| | Measured in 2012 US dollar equivalents | | | | | |
| | Percentage below | | | | Percentage above | |
Currency	$5	$10	$15	$20	$50	$100
1775–79 (American Revolution)						
US Continental Dollar	0.00	3.69	7.38	11.07	81.91	69.27
1775–77 (American Revolution)						
Virginia currency	0.00	23.72	47.43	47.43	42.36	34.51
Pennsylvania currency	56.00	65.40	72.90	74.80	18.70	11.40
New Jersey currency	0.00	41.40	41.40	55.80	31.80	11.90
New York currency	31.90	53.80	57.80	76.40	14.40	7.20
1755–64 (Seven Years' War)						
Virginia currency	0.00	31.20	48.00	48.00	35.30	22.40
Pennsylvania currency	26.80	38.80	50.20	50.20	36.10	14.20
New Jersey currency	0.00	41.00	41.00	50.30	53.00	27.20
New York currency	0.00	0.00	0.00	0.00	95.70	91.60

Sources: Derived from tables B.1, B.2, and B.3.

4 percent were under $10, and none were under $5 in value. Large-value bills were difficult to use as a medium of exchange without making change in some other currency, barter good, or book credit. Some sense of the large value of a Continental one-dollar bill can be taken from Congress's payment of one Continental dollar per week in 1775 to cover an enlisted man's entire weekly subsistence expense while waiting in quarters after recruitment to join the Continental Army (*JCC* 3:289, 309, 322, 415, 419).

By contrast, state currencies issued during the first years of the Revolution had a substantial proportion that were small-value bills; for example, 56 and 32 percent of Pennsylvania and New York bills, respectively, were under $5 in 2012 US dollar value, and 24 and 41 percent of Virginia and New Jersey bills, respectively, were under $10 in value. State currencies during the Revolution were similar in value size to colonial currencies issued during the Seven Years' War, with the exception of New York. New York only issued large-value bills during the Seven Years' War. New York's behavior during the Seven Years' War was the one exception to the general colony/state pattern of issuing a preponderance of small-value bills. As such, it provides the one precedent for Congress issuing only large-value bills during the Revolution. Why New York issued only large-value bills during the Seven Years' War has not been previously noted, nor have the reasons been explained. Whether this example influenced Congress's denominational choice for the Continental dollar is unknown. The coincidence is

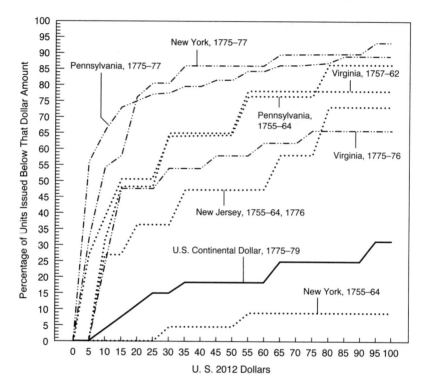

FIGURE 3.1. Percentage of units issued below the listed value

Source: Derived from tables B.1, B.2, and B.3.

Note: The lines are accumulated percentages to that point. The 2012 US dollar equivalents are used to provide a common metric for comparison. Separate lines for New Jersey in 1755–64 and in 1776 were not drawn because they were approximately the same.

suggestive, given the fact that New York shifted to small-value bills for its emissions in 1775–77, as though there were an intentional policy to separate state and congressional monies by denominational sizes.

John Hanson II (1979: 281–86; 1980a: 165–75; 1980b: 411–20) noted the high proportion of small-value bills issued by colonial governments and argued that this behavior was an intentional effort by each colony to make their paper money easy to use as a medium of exchange in local transactions. The corollary implication is that only issuing large-value bills was an intentional effort to restrict the bills' use as a circulating medium of exchange. Several pieces of evidence are consistent with Congress intentionally making Continental dollars large-value bills in the hope that the bills would not circulate as money, but instead be held like bonds for postwar liquidation.

First, as large a value as the smallest Continental dollar bill had in 1775, a congressional committee that included Benjamin Franklin recommended on January 11, 1776, that the first two emissions, totaling 6 million Continental dollars, be called in and replaced with even larger denominations (*JCC* 3:367–68; Smith 1976–94, 3:83). Second, Congress through the first seven emissions did not make, or request that the states make, the Continental dollar a legal tender. Without legal-tender status, purveyors in the marketplace could refuse to accept payment in Continental dollars. In particular, they could refuse to make change in other currencies when offered large-value Continental dollar bills. Third, when, on November 22, 1777, Congress asked the states to curtail their emission of state paper monies, Congress explicitly exempted the emission of small-value state currencies, noting the necessity of making change in some currency other than Continental dollars (*JCC* 9:955–56).

Finally, colonial paper-money acts often included a reserve sum of bills to be printed for the sole purpose of replacing worn, torn, and ragged bills that were no longer fit to remain in circulation. Citizens would bring these unfit bills to the issuing treasury and receive replacements, with the unfit bills being destroyed by the treasury. The size of these reserve funds provides a gauge of how extensively these bills were expected to circulate hand to hand, and thus experience wear and tear, as a local medium of exchange.

For example, the New Jersey emissions of 1733, 1737, and 1769 (the 1769 emission having, however, been disallowed by the Crown) each set aside enough extra bills to replace 25 percent of the amount authorized. These emissions had a circulation life of sixteen to twenty years. The New Jersey emission of June 1756 set aside enough extra bills to replace 20 percent of the amount authorized; this emission had a circulation life of seven years. Finally, the New Jersey emission of 1746 set aside enough extra bills to replace 60 percent of the amount authorized (Bush 1977: 427–28, 474–87; 1980: 21–28, 413–25; 1982: 523–47).

Maryland provides a similar example. The Maryland emission of 1733 set aside enough extra bills to replace 12 percent of the amount authorized, and that of 1770 set aside enough extra bills to replace 6 percent of the amount authorized. The latter emission had a circulation life of twelve years. The Maryland treasury reported that 3.4 percent of this emission had been replaced within the first three years of being placed in circulation.

This rate of replacement, if it continued, would exhaust the quantity of extra bills set aside for that purpose well before the end of that emission's circulation life. As a result, Maryland increased the number of replacement bills in its next paper-money act. The Maryland emission of 1774 set aside enough extra bills to replace 28 percent of the amount authorized. This emission also had a circulation life of twelve years (*Archives of Maryland* 40:28–31, 266–69; Celia and Grubb 2016). Such evidence makes it hard to deny that colonial paper money experienced extensive hand-to-hand usage as a medium of exchange.

By contrast, Congress only once authorized a reserve of Continental dollar bills to be printed for the sole purpose of replacing worn bills that could no longer continue in circulation. On January 5, 1776, Congress authorized "the sum of ten thousand dollars, be struck, for the purpose of exchanging ragged and torn bills of the continental currency; that the bills, making this sum . . . be lodged in the treasury, to be applied to the sole purpose aforesaid." A total reserve of ten thousand Continental dollars represented only 0.005 percent of the total emission of Continental dollars and only 0.17 percent of the February 17, 1776, emission (Grubb 2008: 283–84; *JCC* 4:32). Only a small number of replacement bills would be required if they were primarily needed to replace bills damaged in storage, say, because of water seepage, as opposed to being damaged by hand-to-hand circulation. This behavior is consistent with Congress expecting Continental dollar bills not to experience significant hand-to-hand circulation as a medium of exchange and so not experience wear and tear.

The Inferred Monetary Strategy

The Second Continental Congress chose to create a common inside paper currency rather than a currency union for the colonies/states in rebellion (see the introduction). They overlaid this common currency on top of states issuing their own inside paper monies and running their own fiscal and monetary policies. Congress's choice regarding the denominational structure of its currency is consistent with a rational strategy to maximize the prospects of success for the common currency system adopted. State monies were in low-value denominations and so functioned as the local medium of exchange. Congress's Continental dollars were in high-value denominations and so were difficult to use as a medium of exchange. They were to be held as if they were bonds for liquidation after the war. Thus, the common currency would not contribute to wartime inflation. No linkages between state monies and the common currency were instituted before 1777. With a short war, this strategy had reasonable prospects of success. It, however, unraveled by mid-Revolution.

When the primary use of Continental dollars was to pay soldiers, no legal-tender law was required. Soldier had to accept them as pay. If soldiers could not effectively spend them, but had to hold them as if they were bonds for postwar redemption, no congressional funding issues were threatened. After 1776, however, the majority of congressional spending was on military supplies purchased in the marketplace rather than on soldiers' pay. In the marketplace, purveyors could refuse Continental dollars because the bills had no legal-tender status. Thus, Congress on January 14, 1777, asked the states to make Continental dollars legal tender within their respective states (see chap. 6; Grubb 2011b: 36).

The states moved quickly to accommodate this request. For example, Pennsylvania made Continental dollars legal tender after February 6, 1777, Delaware after February 22, 1777, and Virginia after May 5, 1777. By the eighth new emission of Continental dollars, authorized on May 22, 1777 (see table 1.1), Continental dollars were a legal tender. When a state made the Continental dollar a legal tender within its jurisdiction, this established a legal equivalence between Continental dollars and that state's paper money. The two monies were now linked, and the exchange of one for the other could be enforced (Cushing 1981: 599–602; Hening 1969, 9:297–98; *Statutes at Large of Pennsylvania* 1903–4, 9:34–40). Thus, once Continental dollars were made legal tender, they could be more easily used as a medium of exchange. Legally, purveyors could not refuse them nor refuse making change in other currencies when offered Continental dollars. The establishment of legal-tender status helped make $V_z > 0$ which in turn allowed increases in Continental dollars to contribute to wartime inflation.

Finally, the massive volume of Continental dollar emissions, given a long and costly war, overwhelmed Congress's denominational control strategy. By early 1779 some 200 million Continental dollars in face value had been emitted. If held and treated like bonds, the expected redemption of such a volume of bills was now so far in the future that it reduced the value of Continental dollars by 1778 to being small-value bills in present-value terms (see chap. 10 and table 10.1). At these low present values, they could be more easily used as a medium of exchange, especially in terms of making change. A quantity-theoretic assessment yields the same outcome,

namely an excessive amount of Continental dollars emitted would depreciate their value until they were now small-value bills easily used as a medium of exchange.

The last emissions of Continental dollars were denominationally restructured to be even larger-value bills (in face value). Congress was apparently trying to offset the loss of value discussed above and so make
the bills large-value again (see table B.1). This effort did not succeed. The
Continental dollar collapsed to 2.5 percent of face value by 1780. It ceased
to circulate shortly thereafter (see chap. 10, table 10.1, and chap. 14).

The common currency versus currency union problem for the United
States was finally resolved by the adoption of the US Constitution in 1789.
States lost the constitutional power to issue their own paper currencies.
This paved the way toward forming a true currency union among the
states based on the specie US dollar, in unit-of-account terms, for the new
nation (Grubb 2006).

CHAPTER FOUR

Informing the Public

The structural design for the first and second emission of Continental dollars, including instructions for their redemption, was widely disseminated. Congress circulated a handbill that contained its Continental dollar resolutions passed before July 30, 1775, including all the relevant redemption provisions for the first emission (see fig. 4.1). This handbill was reprinted in its entirety in numerous newspapers, beginning with the *Connecticut Journal, & New-Haven Post-Boy*.

During the fall of 1775 this handbill was reprinted in its entirety in the *Connecticut Journal, & New Haven Post-Boy*, New Haven, Connecticut, on October 25; the *Pennsylvania Evening Post*, Philadelphia, Pennsylvania, on November 2; the *Pennsylvania Ledger or the Virginia, Maryland, Pennsylvania, & New Jersey Weekly Advertiser*, Philadelphia, Pennsylvania, on November 4; the *Connecticut Courant and Weekly Intelligencer*, Hartford, Connecticut, on November 6; the *Norwich Packet and the Connecticut, Massachusetts, New-Hampshire, and Rhode Island Weekly Advertiser*, Norwich, Connecticut, on November 6; the *New-York Journal; or, The General Advertiser*, New York, New York, on November 9; *Thomas's Massachusetts Spy or, American Oracle of Liberty*, Worcester, Massachusetts, on November 10; the *Providence Gazette and Country Journal*, Providence, Rhode Island, on November 11; the *New-England Chronicle or The Essex Gazette*, Cambridge, Massachusetts, on November 16; and the *Boston Gazette and Country Journal*, Watertown, Massachusetts, on December 4.

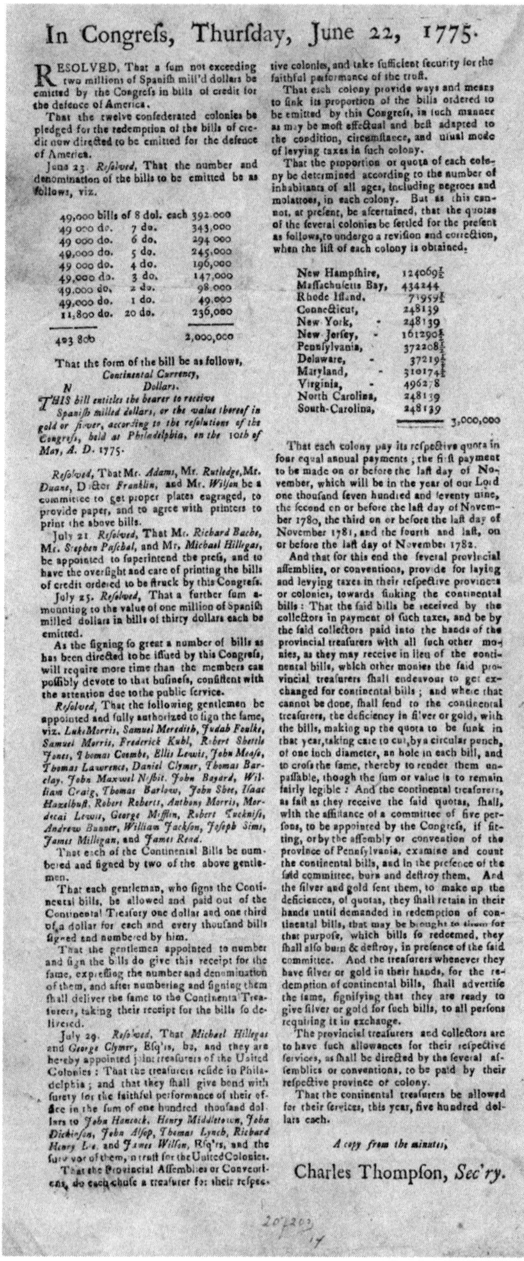

In Congreſs, Thurſday, June 22, 1775.

RESOLVED, That a ſum not exceeding two millions of Spaniſh mill'd dollars be emitted by the Congreſs in bills of credit for the defence of America.

That the twelve confederated colonies be pledged for the redemption of the bills of credit now directed to be emitted for the defence of America.

June 23. *Reſolved*, That the number and denomination of the bills to be emitted be as follows, viz.

49,000 bills of	8 dol.	each	392.000
49 000 do.	7 do.		343,000
49 000 do.	6 do.		294 000
49,000 do.	5 do.		245,000
49 000 do.	4 do.		196,000
49,000 do.	3 do.		147,000
49.000 do.	2 do.		98.000
49,000 do.	1 do.		49.000
11,800 do.	20 do.		236,000
403 800			2,000,000

That the form of the bill be as follows,

Continental Currency,

N *Dollars.*

THIS bill entitles the bearer to receive Spaniſh milled dollars, or the value thereof in gold or ſilver, according to the reſolutions of the Congreſs, held at Philadelphia, on the 10th *of May, A. D.* 1775.

Reſolved, That Mr. *Adams*, Mr. *Rutledge*, Mr. *Duane*, Doctor *Franklin*, and Mr. *Wilſon* be a committee to get proper plates engraged, to provide paper, and to agree with printers to print the above bills.

July 21. *Reſolved*, That Mr. *Richard Bache*, Mr. *Stephen Paſchal*, and Mr. *Michael Hillegas*, be appointed to ſuperintend the preſs, and to have the overſight and care of printing the bills of credit ordered to be ſtruck by this Congreſs.

July 25. *Reſolved*, That a further ſum amounting to the value of one million of Spaniſh milled dollars in bills of thirty dollars each be emitted.

As the ſigning ſo great a number of bills as has been directed to be iſſued by this Congreſs, will require more time than the members can poſſibly devote to that buſineſs, conſiſtent with the attention due to the public ſervice.

Reſolved, That the following gentlemen be appointed and fully authorized to ſign the ſame, viz. *Luke Morris, Samuel Meredith, Judah Foulke, Samuel Morris, Frederick Kuhl, Robert Shettle Jones, Thomas Coombe, Ellis Lewis, John Meaſe, Thomas Lawrence, Daniel Clymer, Thomas Barclay, John Maxwel Neſbit, John Bayard, William Craig, Thomas Barlow, John Shee, Iſaac Hazelhurſt, Robert Roberts, Anthony Morris, Mordecai Lewis, George Mifflin, Robert Tuckniſs, Andrew Bunner, William Jackſon, Joſeph Sims, James Milligan*, and *James Read*.

That each of the Continental Bills be numbered and ſigned by two of the above gentlemen.

That each gentleman, who ſigns the Continental bills, be allowed and paid out of the Continental Treaſury one dollar and one third of a dollar for each and every thouſand bills ſigned and numbered by him.

That the gentlemen appointed to number and ſign the bills do give this receipt for the ſame, expreſſing the number and denomination of them, and after numbering and ſigning them ſhall deliver the ſame to the Continental Treaſurers, taking their receipt for the bills ſo delivered.

July 29. *Reſolved*, That *Michael Hillegas* and *George Clymer*, Eſq'rs, be, and they are hereby appointed joint treaſurers of the United Colonies: That the treaſurers reſide in Philadelphia; and that they ſhall give bond with ſurety for the faithful performance of their office in the ſum of one hundred thouſand dollars to *John Hancock, Henry Middletown, John Dickinſon, John Alſop, Thomas Lynch, Richard Henry Lee*, and *James Wilſon*, Eſq'rs, and the ſurvivor of them, in truſt for the United Colonies.

That the Provincial Aſſemblies or Conventions, do each chuſe a treaſurer for their reſpective colonies, and take ſufficient ſecurity for the faithful performance of the truſt.

That each colony provide ways and means to ſink its proportion of the bills ordered to be emitted by this Congreſs, in ſuch manner as may be moſt effectual and beſt adapted to the condition, circumſtance, and uſual mode of levying taxes in ſuch colony.

That the proportion or quota of each colony be determined according to the number of inhabitants of all ages, including negroes and molattoes, in each colony. But as this cannot, at preſent, be aſcertained, that the quotas of the ſeveral colonies be ſettled for the preſent as follows, to undergo a reviſion and correction, when the liſt of each colony is obtained.

New Hampſhire,	124069½
Maſſachuſetts Bay,	434244
Rhode Iſland,	71959½
Connecticut,	248139
New York,	248139
New Jerſey,	161290½
Pennſylvania,	372208½
Delaware,	37219½
Maryland,	310174½
Virginia,	496278
North Carolina,	248139
South-Carolina,	248139
	3,000,000

That each colony pay its reſpective quota in four equal annual payments; the firſt payment to be made on or before the laſt day of November, which will be in the year of our Lord one thouſand ſeven hundred and ſeventy nine, the ſecond on or before the laſt day of November 1780, the third on or before the laſt day of November 1781, and the fourth and laſt, on or before the laſt day of November 1782.

And that for this end the ſeveral provincial aſſemblies, or conventions, provide for laying and levying taxes in their reſpective provinces or colonies, towards ſinking the continental bills: That the ſaid bills be received by the collectors in payment of ſuch taxes, and be by the ſaid collectors paid into the hands of the provincial treaſurers with all ſuch other monies, as they may receive in lieu of the continental bills, which other monies the ſaid provincial treaſurers ſhall endeavour to get exchanged for continental bills; and where that cannot be done, ſhall ſend to the continental treaſurers, the deficiency in ſilver or gold, with the bills, making up the quota to be ſunk in that year, taking care to cut, by a circular punch, of one inch diameter, an hole in each bill, and to croſs the ſame, thereby to render them unpaſſable, though the ſum or value is to remain fairly legible: And the continental treaſurers, as faſt as they receive the ſaid quotas, ſhall, with the aſſiſtance of a committee of five perſons, to be appointed by the Congreſs, if ſitting, or by the aſſembly or convention of the province of Pennſylvania, examine and count the continental bills, and in the preſence of the ſaid committee, burn and deſtroy them. And the ſilver and gold ſent them, to make up the deficiences, of quotas, they ſhall retain in their hands until demanded in redemption of continental bills, that may be brought to them for that purpoſe, which bills ſo redeemed, they ſhall alſo burn & deſtroy, in preſence of the ſaid committee. And the treaſurers whenever they have ſilver or gold in their hands, for the redemption of continental bills, ſhall advertiſe the ſame, ſignifying that they are ready to give ſilver or gold for ſuch bills, to all perſons requiring it in exchange.

The provincial treaſurers and collectors are to have ſuch allowances for their reſpective ſervices, as ſhall be directed by the ſeveral aſſemblies or conventions, to be paid by their reſpective province or colony.

That the continental treaſurers be allowed for their ſervices, this year, five hundred dollars each.

A copy from the minutes,

Charles Thompſon, *Sec'ry.*

FIGURE 4.1. Handbill issued by Congress informing the public of the design and redemption structure of the first emission of Continental dollars, circa August–October 1775

Source: http://memory.loc.gov/service/rbc/bdsdcc/00301/0001.jpg, accessed January 30, 2013.

The newspapers consulted where no evidence could be found that this handbill was reprinted either in its entirety or in parts include the *New-Hampshire Gazette and Historical Chronicle* (Portsmouth, New Hampshire); *Freeman's Journal* (Portsmouth, New Hampshire); the *Essex Journal and Merrimack Packet: The Massachusetts and New-Hampshire General Advertiser* (Newburyport, Massachusetts); the *Newport Mercury* (Newport, Rhode Island); the *Constitutional Gazette* (New York, New York); *New-York Gazette and the Weekly Mercury* (New York, New York); *Rivington's New-York Gazette; Or, The Connecticut, Hudson's River, New Jersey, and Quebec Weekly Advertiser* (New York, New York); the *Pennsylvania Gazette* (Philadelphia, Pennsylvania); *Dunlap's Pennsylvania Packet or the General Advertiser* (Lancaster, Pennsylvania); the *Pennsylvania Journal; and The Weekly Advertiser* (Philadelphia, Pennsylvania); *Maryland Gazette* (Annapolis, Maryland); *Virginia Gazette* (Williamsburg, Virginia); *South-Carolina Gazette; and Country Journal* (Charleston, South Carolina); and the *South-Carolina Gazette* (Charleston, South Carolina).

In total, between October 25 and December 4, 1775, all three newspapers in Connecticut, three of the four in Massachusetts, one of the two in Rhode Island, one of the four in New York, and two of the five in Pennsylvania reprinted this handbill. Out of the surviving newspapers consulted, ten out of twenty-four reprinted the handbill. Because the newspapers consulted did not have a complete run of surviving copies or had terminated early in this period, the ratio of those reprinting the handbill out of the total newspapers consulted is biased low.

The redemption procedures covering the second emission were reprinted in the *Pennsylvania Evening Post*, March 12, 1776. This information was also disseminated when Congress published its journals at the end of 1775 and later in 1776.[1] The *Constitutional Gazette*, December 20, 1775; the *New-York Gazette and the Weekly Mercury*, December 25, 1775; the *New-York Journal; or, The General Advertiser*, December 21, 1775; the *Pennsylvania Journal; and the Weekly Advertiser*, December 13, 1775; and the *Pennsylvania Gazette*, October 23, 1776, advertised the proceedings of the Continental Congress for sale.

Between the direct circulation of the handbill, the reproduction of it in the nation's newspapers, the publication of Congress's journal, and the publication of congressional resolutions in the *Pennsylvania Evening Post*, the public was well informed, with the possible exception of citizens in the southern colonies, about the structural design of the Continental dollar, including its redemption procedures.

Once the public was informed of the Continental dollar's structural design, they acted as if they understood that the Continental dollar was a zero-coupon bond requiring time-discounting to ascertain its present value. The first reports of Continental dollars trading below face value appeared before Congress in Philadelphia on November 23, 1775. It had occurred immediately after the structural design of the Continental dollar was first reported in Pennsylvania newspapers.[2] After the public was told that Continental dollars were a zero-coupon bond-type money with defined maturity dates, they started to accept them below their face value.

The first congressional committee to investigate reports of depreciation was formed in November 1775. It was comprised of John Jay, Benjamin Franklin, Samuel Adams, Thomas Johnson, George Wythe, Edward Rutledge, and Thomas Jefferson. This committee recognized that Continental dollars were being accepted below their face value, but the resolution and published announcements that were adopted did not explicitly condemn this practice. They condemned only the nonacceptance of Continental dollars. Not explicitly condemning this "depreciation," but only nonacceptance, was consistent with Congress's recognizing that time-discounting was not really depreciation per se, and that the public was right to accept Continental dollars below their face value given that they were zero-coupon bonds, just as they had done with the bills of credit emitted by colonial governments.[3]

CHAPTER FIVE

Descriptions by Contemporary Leaders

A number of important citizens and national leaders, all members at some point of the revolutionary government, knew about time-discounting and the present-value calculation that reduced a future value to a current value. They explained the Continental dollar as a zero-coupon bond needing such discounting to understand its current value. In their descriptions, the Continental dollar was not a fiat currency, and time-discounting was not depreciation per se. These ideas were not totally new; many colonial writers had articulated the time-discounting embedded in colonial paper monies.[1]

Congressional Committees

On April 19, 1776, Congress created a committee to ascertain the comparative value of different silver and gold foreign coins. The committee consisted of James Duane, George Wythe, John Adams, Roger Sherman, Joseph Hewes, Thomas Johnson, and William Whipple. Thomas Jefferson joined the committee on July 24, 1776. The structural design of the Continental dollar required that Congress rate the relative value of foreign coins. By congressional resolution, the Continental dollar was redeemable at maturity in Spanish silver dollars or the value thereof in gold and silver (see figs. I.1, I.2, I.3, and I.4). Thus, for future redemption purposes the equivalence of

other foreign specie coins to Spanish silver dollars had to be established by
Congress. That this task was the sole initial purpose of this April 19, 1776,
committee is seldom noted. However, the committee's report, both on
May 22, 1776, and on September 2, 1776, clearly stated that that was its
purpose.[2] The second paragraph of the committee's report reads:

> Whereas, the holders of bills of credit [Continental dollars] emitted by author-
> ity of Congress will be entitled, at certain periods appointed for redemption
> thereof to receive out of the treasury of the united colonies the amount of the
> said bills in spanish milled dollars, or value thereof in gold or silver; and the
> value of such dollars, compared with other silver and with gold coins, is esti-
> mated by different standards in different colonies, whereby injustice may hap-
> pen in some instances to the public, as well as to individuals which ought to be
> remedied. . . . Therefore,
>
> *Resolved*, that the several gold and silver coins passing in the said colonies
> shall be received into the public treasury of the continent, and paid out in ex-
> change for bills emitted by authority of Congress, when the same shall become
> due, at the rates set down in the following table: . . .

This committee clearly operated with the understanding that Continental
dollars would not be redeemed until some future date, and at that date
their redemption would be, or could be, in specie coins paid out of the
Continental Treasury at face value. In other words, the Continental dollar
was a type of bearer bond anchored to face-value specie payments at some
future date.

Commissioners of the New England States Report

In January 1778 the commissioners of the New England states, along with
commissioners from New York, Pennsylvania, and New Jersey, met in
New Haven, Connecticut to discuss economic issues related to the Revolution. Their letter to Congress of January 30, 1778, ended with the following observation:

> Before we Conclude we beg leave to mention that the public have never yet
> been notified, when the Continental Bills are to be redeemed, except the two
> first Emissions. Their being at an uncertainty about this matter has been com-
> plained of as having a tendency to lessen the Credit of the bills, Whereas if they

were to be Ascertained when they were to be redeemed, Especially if it was at
a short period, it would give them a confidence in the money, and greatly tend
to Establish its Currency.[3]

The commissioners' observations were consistent with understanding the
Continental dollar to be a zero-coupon bond rather than a fiat currency.
They noted that the time to redemption influenced the value of the bills,
with a more distant redemption being associated with a lower current (present) value. They also noted that Congress had not yet fixed the redemption
of emissions that came after emission no. 2, and so people had to guess or
forecast what those redemption windows would be. If they guessed a more
distant redemption date, that would lessen the current (present) value of
the bills. Therefore, if Congress set a redemption window that was closer to
the present, that would raise the current value of the bills.

Roger Sherman

Roger Sherman was a delegate from Connecticut to the Continental Congress from 1774 through 1781. He was often a member of Congress's finance committees, took an active part in congressional debates on money,
and was regarded as knowledgeable about monetary matters. In a letter to
the governor of Connecticut, Jonathan Trumbull, Sr., on October 27, 1778,
Sherman gave a clear explanation of the nature of the Continental dollar:

> A note for £100 on compound interest, payable at the expiration of 20 years
> would be equal to one for £321 for the same term without interest. If the Bills of
> public credit [Continental dollars], so far as they exceed a sufficient quantity for
> a medium of trade, are to be considered only as securities for money without in-
> terest, rebating the compound interest for the time before they are redeemable
> will determine their present value, and they will gradually appreciate as time of
> their redemption approaches. Enclosed is a computation of the annual increase
> of £100 for 21 years on compound interest. (Smith 1976–94, 11:136–39, 306–7)

Sherman's description of the Continental dollar is that of a zero-
coupon bond. He views a Continental dollar as a security for money to
be delivered in the future without interest paid in the interim, as opposed
to money itself. He also describes the time-discounting that must be done
to determine a Continental dollar's current value. He even uses the term

"present value" to describe that current value. He describes the rise, or appreciation, in that value as the time to redemption approaches. In his example, the implied interest rate that discounts £321 from twenty years in the future to £100 in the present is 5.83 percent, that is, $100 = 321 * e^{(-0.583*20)}$. Sherman even provided his correspondent with a table for performing time-discounting calculations. Sherman's table of present-value calculations, enclosed in his letter to Trumbull, spans twenty-one years. This suggests that in mid-1778 Sherman did not expect all the Continental dollars outstanding at that point to be redeemed before 1800.

Gouverneur Morris

Gouverneur Morris was a delegate to Congress from New York, attending between January 20, 1778, and late November 1779. He was a member of Congress's 1778 committee attempting to reorganize the treasury and sort out the government's finance system. He would go on to become a central actor on monetary issues for the US government under Robert Morris when Morris was superintendent of finance, and then a key shaper of the monetary provisions in the US Constitution at the 1787 Constitutional Convention.[4] In the course of working on the 1778 congressional committee's report on currency finance, of which he was the author, he wrote a treatise on money. That committee's report was delivered on September 19, 1778, but Congress shelved it, deeming it too controversial. In Morris's preparatory treatise on money, alluding to paper money like the Continental dollar, he reasoned:

> If a Legislature . . . should utter a Paper Medium payable at a distant Day it would or would not be received according to the Want of such Medium among the People. And when received it's [sic] Value would depend on the Consideration 1st. of the Want 2ly. of the Distance of the Day of Payment & 3ly. of the Certainty or Uncertainty of such Payment.[5]

Gouverneur Morris viewed the value of paper money, such as the Continental dollar, as being determined by (1) the transaction premium attached to that money compared with its next best alternative, that is, the "Want"; (2) the time to redemption, that is, time-discounting; and (3) the fiscal credibility of the future promised redemption payment. Therefore, if no excess transaction premium existed and future redemption was certain, then the present value of a Continental dollar would depend only on time-discounting—that is, the Continental dollar was a zero-coupon bond. Morris saw the credibility of the government's promise of a future money payoff, namely the government's willingness and ability to meet that payoff at the time of redemption, along with the time to redemption, as key determinants of the present value of the Continental dollar. It is hard to interpret this passage without saying that Morris understood the Continental dollar to be a zero-coupon bond and not a fiat currency.

On February 17, 1780, Gouverneur Morris, who was by then out of Congress and working as a lawyer in Philadelphia, published an analysis of America's finances in the Philadelphia newspaper *Pennsylvania Packet, or General Advertiser*. He ended with the following observation:

> I have spoken of paper [money] hitherto without marking particularly the effects which follow from the idea of redemption. But now let us advert for this purpose to our paper [the Continental dollar]. Suppose a full confidence prevailed that in twenty years it would be appreciated to its nominal [face] value; then every man possessed of forty dollars would believe that if he kept it twenty years it would be worth forty dollars in specie.[6] Now if we reckon a compound interest of six per cent. forty dollars payable twenty years hence will be worth at present about twelve and a half, which deducting two and a half leaves ten. Wherefore it would follow, that he who purchases paper [Continental dollars] at the rate of four for one, would have the best possible security to receive a compound six per cent. interest on his money, with an ultimate additional profit of twenty-five per cent. at the end of twenty years. (Barlow 2012: 103, 109–10)

As in the Morris passage quoted earlier, here Morris treats the Continental dollar as a zero-coupon bond and not a fiat currency. Its present value, under the ideal condition of being paid off in the future with certainty, is determined only by time-discounting. He goes on to give an example using 6 percent as the discount factor and twenty years as the time to redemption. He calculates that $40 at face value in twenty years is only worth $12.50 today. He does not call this lower present value today "depreciation." It is just time-discounting.

James Madison

James Madison was elected to Congress on December 14, 1779. To prepare for his role, he studied the finances of the United States and, sometime between December 14, 1779, and March 18, 1780, wrote down his thoughts. While these observations—his treatise on money—would not be published until 1791, it seems unlikely that he wrote in a vacuum. Fellow Virginians familiar with the history of congressional paper-money emissions were likely consulted by Madison before he made his way to Philadelphia. If so, his observations may reflect some consensus beyond the reasoning of just one man. Madison's treatise on money is the most clear, consistent, and cogent analysis of the nature and structural design of the Continental dollar written by any American during or in the decade after the Revolution, including anything written by the financial luminaries of the American Revolution, namely Benjamin Franklin, Alexander Hamilton, Gouverneur Morris, Robert Morris, and Pelatiah Webster. Madison's entire treatise is recommended reading. A brief portion highlighting the zero-coupon bond nature of the Continental dollar states:

> If the circulating medium be a municipal one, as paper currency. . . .
>
> It consists of bills or notes of obligation payable in specie to the bearer, either on demand or at a future day. [Madison indicates that for the illustrative exercise to follow, the credibility of redemption whether on demand or at a fixed future day will always be assumed.] Of the first kind is the paper currency of Britain [banknotes], and hence its equivalence to specie. Of the latter kind is the paper currency of the United States [the Continental dollar], and hence its inferiority to specie.
>
> Let us suppose that the circulating notes . . . instead of being payable on demand, were to be redeemed at a future day, at the end of one year for example, and that no interest was due them. . . . They would in that case represent not the nominal sum expressed on the face of them, but the sum remaining after a deduction of one year's interest. . . . We may extend the time from one, to five, or to twenty years; but we shall find no other rule of depreciation than the loss of the intermediate interest.
>
> [The United States] Being engaged in a necessary war without specie to defray the expense, or to support paper emissions for that purpose redeemable on demand, and being at the same time unable to borrow, no resource was left, but to emit bills of credit [Continental dollars] to be redeemed in the future. The inferiority of these bills to specie was therefore incident to the very nature of them. If they had been exchangeable on demand for specie, they would have been equivalent to it; as they were not exchangeable on demand, they were inferior to it. The degree of their inferiority must consequently be estimated by the time of their becoming exchangeable for specie, that is the time of their redemption.

> Suppose the period necessary for its [the Continental dollar's] redemption to be 18 years, as seems to be understood by Congress;[7] 100 dollars of paper 18 years hence will be equal in value to 100 dollars of specie; for at the end of that term, 100 dollars of specie may be demanded for them. They must consequently at this time be equal to as much specie as, with compound interest, will amount, in that number of years, to 100 dollars. . . . Admit, however the use of money to be worth 6 per cent. about 35 dollars will then amount in 18 years to 100. 35 dollars of specie therefore is at this time equal to 100 of paper; that is, the man who would exchange his specie for paper at this discount, and lock it in his desk for 18 years, would get 6 per cent. for his money.[8]

Madison explained the difference between a paper currency convertible to specie at face value on demand versus one convertible to specie at face value but only at some future date. Assuming certainty of convertibility, the one convertible on demand will circulate at its face value because it is equal at any point in time to its face value in specie. But even assuming certainty of redemption, the present value of the one convertible at some future date, by its very nature, will not equal its face value, but only its face value reduced by time-discounting from the future date of redemption. Madison even gives an example of what the value of 100 Continental dollars redeemed in eighteen years for 100 silver dollars would be today at a 6 percent discount rate, namely 35 silver dollars. Madison terms this reduced value "depreciation," but the term means only the loss of interest, not depreciation per se or a loss of principal at redemption. He also concludes that its present value is governed by the time-span to redemption. The further into future the promised redemption is, the lower the present value must be. As such, Madison does not mean "depreciation" as everyone else used the term, for there was no loss in value separate from time-discounting. Madison also notes the importance of, and even uses the phrase, "credibility of redemption" for determining a Continental dollar's present value. Future redemption based on levied taxes had to be fiscally possible, a burden able to be sustained by the public, to prevent depreciation beyond time-discounting. Madison understood Continental dollars, by the "incident to the very nature of them," to be zero-coupon bonds and not a fiat currency.

Pelatiah Webster

Pelatiah Webster was an influential contemporary writer on political and economic matters and a sharp commentator on congressional actions. In an essay published on October 5, 1775, in the *Pennsylvania Evening Post*, he asked, in reference to the Continental dollar, "Why should the soldier ... be paid in promises, which are not so good as money, if fulfilment is at a distance?" Webster saw the Continental dollar as a zero-coupon bond, namely as being only a promise to pay at a distance, and not a fiat currency or even as money per se.

Thomas Jefferson

In addition to his work on Congress's coin rating committee discussed above, Thomas Jefferson explained in 1786 that paying taxes during the war, given the disruption to commerce, was impossible, and so Congress could only promise that taxes would be laid at some future postwar date for the purpose of redeeming Continental dollars (see Boyd 1953–55, 10:25, and chap. 10).

Thomas Jefferson, James Madison, Gouverneur Morris, Roger Sherman, the commissioners attending the January 1778 New Haven conference, and the 1776 congressional committee that rated foreign coins — James Duane, George Wythe, John Adams, Roger Sherman, Joseph Hewes, Thomas Johnson, William Whipple, and Thomas Jefferson — all explicitly articulated an understanding of the Continental dollar consistent with its being a zero-coupon bond and not a fiat currency.

CHAPTER SIX

Congressional Spending

The Continental Currency is the great Pillar, which Supports our Cause, and if that Suffers in its Credit, the Cause must Suffer: if that fails the Cause must fail. — John Adams to Samuel Cooper, July 10, 1776 (Smith 1976–94, 4:423)

Much of the spending by Congress during the first five years of the war was in the form of a paper money that Congress had created — the Continental dollar. This chapter establishes what share of congressional spending took this form and tallies Congress's yearly budgets with respect to deficits and surpluses during the era spanned by the Continental dollar. Estimating the breakdown of congressional spending by source, type, and location for each year as well as establishing the distribution of resource demands requested from each state by Congress can be used to reevaluate the fiscal/monetary course of the war. This method of congressional resource creating and spending collapsed in 1780–81.

Public-Goods Theory

A theoretical discussion of congressional organization can help identify the fiscal constraints Congress faced and evaluate state incentives to accommodate congressional resource requests. Congress can be viewed as producing a public good — for instance, independence. Each state gets to consume the same independence regardless of how much each state contributes to Congress's production of that independence. The public-goods nature of independence creates the incentive to free-ride. Individual states have no incentive to voluntarily contribute to Congress's production of independence. Each state comes out ahead by letting the other states contribute the resources to produce the independence from which it cannot be excluded. Given that Congress was not given the power to compel states to contribute resources, the economic prediction is that no state will contribute resources to Congress, and thus the Revolution will fail. This is the classic underproduction-of-public-goods outcome in economic theory (Baack 2008; Dougherty 2001; Olson 1965).

States, however, transferred substantial resources, both men and matériel, voluntarily to Congress to support the war effort. This does not mean that the public-goods-induced incentive to free-ride was not operative. In Congress individual states kept an eye out for and often voiced concern about any fellow state that lagged behind their own contribution. Often retribution via reducing their contribution was the unspoken, and occasionally spoken, threatened reaction to perceived laggards among their fellow states. Thus, one possible explanation for why states did not perfectly free-ride is that shared norms within a self-regulating ethical realm, and the knowledge that if no one contributed resources then independence would be lost, created voluntary contributions. An equilibrium amount of voluntary contributions was created and enforced through a game-theoretic outcome where monitoring of individuals and the threat of retaliatory action (if you don't contribute then I will stop) kept states in the game of providing resources to Congress. In other words, Adam Smith's *The Theory of Moral Sentiments* and patriotism triumphed over a perfect free ride (Neem 2009: 475–77; Smith 1976). This was possible because individual state contributions to Congress via contributions of men and matériel to the Continental Army were observable.

Ben Baack (2008: 109, 112) asserts that Congress's emission of a Continental dollar paper currency was a circumvention of the free-rider problem regarding state contributions to Congress. He asserts that Congress simply printed and spent fiat paper money at will. This claim, however, ignores the fact that states, through their delegates in Congress, voted for each emission and voted to be held accountable for redeeming said money after the war based on their share of the union's population. Substantial compliance occurred after the war such that over half of the Continental dollars Congress emitted before 1780 were redeemed by the states by 1790 (see chap. 15). In addition, the states, at their own expense, contributed considerable manpower to the common cause of Revolution (Grubb 2011b).

State assemblies pushed Congress into using the Continental dollar system precisely to prevent an individual state from issuing its own paper money in excessive quantities and then free-riding on the required redemption imposed on other states (see the introduction). The fact that states redeemed substantial amounts of Congress's Continental dollars that were issued during the war well after independence—well after gaining the public good—raises questions about whether either a pure public-goods theory, a public-goods theory with localized private benefits, or a theory of patriotic sentiment can account fully for positive state contributions and the variation in state contributions to Congress during the Revolution.

Resource Request Apportioned among the States

How did Congress apportion its resource demands among the states? In June 1775, one month after convening, Congress committed itself to a united military effort against the British in Boston. It had to raise substantial sums of money to finance this effort, namely to pay monthly wages to soldiers, provision them, and provide military arms for the Continental Army as well as to meet sundry expenses that accompany a functioning central government. It could not directly tax the public or the states, and it had no resources or assets of its own. The states were not in a position to immediately deliver money to Congress. Thus, Congress had to borrow. As a government with questionable legitimacy, it could not easily borrow from foreigners or even directly from its own people. Thus, it resolved to borrow from itself, namely from its constituent states, as a united entity, rather than merely to sanction separate state borrowings with some sort of national endorsement.

Congress accomplished this borrowing by issuing zero-coupon bonds, that is, Continental dollars, which the states assembled in Congress pledged to redeem and return to the congressional treasury to be burned at distant future dates. Congress left it up to the individual states to decide on their own how to redeem their share of Continental dollars—for example, which state taxes could and could not be paid with Continental dollars. Congress also asked the states, after 1776, to make Continental dollars legal tender within their respective states to force acceptance of them, as congressional agents spent them to acquire resources — a request with which states complied (see chap. 7; Grubb 2008; *JCC* 2:221–23, 3:458, 13:20–21, 64–65; Newman 1997: 33–35, 59–68).

In this initial action Congress also established how the states would contribute resources to Congress, in this case what share of the total Continental dollars issued by Congress each state would be required to redeem. The resolution stated:

> That each colony provide ways and means to sink its proportion of the bills [Continental dollars] ordered to be emitted by this Congress, in such manner as may be most effectual and best adapted to the conditions, circumstances, and usual mode of levying taxes in such colony.
>
> That the proportion or quota of each colony be determined according to the number of Inhabitants of all ages, including negroes and mulattoes in each colony; But as this cannot, at present, be ascertained, that the quotes of the several colonies be settled for the present, as follows, to undergo a revision and correction, when the list of each colony is obtained. (*JCC* 2:221)

The contribution percentages are listed in table 6.1, column 2. Georgia was not yet in Congress and so received no quota. The basic idea was that the total resources needed for the united war effort as executed by Congress would be supplied by the states in proportion to each state's relative economic strength and ability. How to assess that relative economic strength was not obvious or easy to estimate with any accuracy. The initial choice was by relative population shares in the union, in part because it was highly correlated with economic strength and ability to deliver resources, but mostly because it was an easy-to-measure expedient. Even relative population shares, as indicated in the resolution quoted above, were not known with exact certainty.

Article 8 of Congress's Articles of Confederation, dated November 15, 1777, stated:

> All charges of war and all other expenses, that shall be incurred for the common defence or general welfare, and allowed by the United States, in Congress assembled, shall be defrayed out of a common treasury, which shall be supplied by the several states, in proportion to the value of all land within each State, granted to or surveyed for any person, as such land and the buildings and improvements thereon shall be estimated according to such mode as the United States, in Congress assembled, shall, from time to time, direct and appoint.

TABLE 6.1 **Percentage distribution across the states of fiscal, monetary, and military quotas, 1775–83: Congressional resource and revenue demands**

| State | 1780 % of population: total [white only] | Initial Continental dollar (1775) redemption quota % | Recommended Nov. 22, 1777, funding % | Troop quota % | | | Remaining Continental dollar (1781) redemption quota % | Funding % set Apr. 1783 |
				1777	1778	1779 & 1780		
New Hampshire	3.16 [3.96]	4.14	4.00	3.41	3.49	3.75	2.67	3.51
Massachusetts	11.43 [14.17]	14.47	16.40	17.07	17.44	18.75	15.33	14.96
Rhode Island	1.90 [2.28]	2.40	2.00	2.27	1.16	2.50	1.33	2.15
Connecticut	7.43 [9.11]	8.27	12.00	9.09	9.30	10.00	11.33	8.81
New York	9.29 [10.75]	8.27	4.00	4.55	5.81	6.25	5.00	8.55
New Jersey	5.02 [5.86]	5.38	5.40	4.55	4.65	3.75	6.00	5.56
Pennsylvania	11.77 [14.49]	12.41	12.40	13.64	11.62	13.75	15.33	13.68
Delaware	1.63 [1.92]	1.24	1.20	1.14	1.16	1.25	1.13	1.50
Maryland	8.83 [7.48]	10.34	10.40	9.09	9.30	10.00	10.53	9.43
Virginia	20.97 [16.11]	16.54	16.00	17.05	17.44	13.75	16.67	17.10
North Carolina	10.08 [8.51]	8.27	5.00	10.23	10.47	7.50	6.67	7.27
South Carolina	6.47 [3.76]	8.27	10.00	6.82	6.98	7.50	8.00	6.41
Georgia	2.02 [1.60]	–	1.20	1.14	1.16	1.25	–	1.07
Respective totals	2,708,369 [2,204,949]	$3,000,000	$5,000,000	59,840	44,892	83,520	$195,000,000	$1,500,000 (annually)

Sources: Derived from *Historical statistics* (1975: 1168).—Maine was included in Massachusetts; Vermont in New York; Kentucky in Virginia; and Tennessee in North Carolina for population counts; Knox (1790); Ferguson et al. (1973–99, 1:193–94); *JCC* (9:955, 15:1150, 24:259).
Notes: The total amount of Continental dollars that Congress thought it had emitted was $200 million (Grubb 2008). The amount to be assigned to Georgia was left unstated and presumably reflects the difference between the $195 million sum and the total Congress thought it had emitted. Georgia, having been invaded, may have also been excused from its quota, and the $195 million total by June 1781 may have reflected $5 million already paid in by the states.

> The taxes for paying that proportion shall be laid and levied by the author-
> ity and direction of the legislatures of the several states, within the time agreed
> upon by the United States, in Congress assembled. (*JCC* 9:913–14)

Thus, by mid-November 1777 relative land value, including improvements made to the land across the states, was to be the criterion for determining what share of total resources demanded by Congress each state would be required to provide. While the articles would not be ratified by the states until March 1781, its ratification basically legitimized the status quo in that from November 15, 1777, Congress operated under its auspices (Jensen 1981: 376; Tindall 1988: 248). However, it is unclear whether the relative-land-value criterion for apportioning resources to be supplied to Congress was ever implemented. The lack of accurate information on relative land values, including improvements made to the land, as well as the difficulty of obtaining such information under wartime circumstances, may have made the criterion unusable.

On April 18, 1783, Congress formally switched back to using relative population shares among the states as the apportionment criterion, albeit with slaves now counted as only three-fifths of a person. This change was also made retroactive in application. The revision revoked the language in paragraph 1 of Article 8 of the Articles of Confederation and replaced it with:

> All charges of war and all other expenses, that have been or shall be incurred
> for the common defence or general welfare, and allowed by the United States,
> in Congress assembled, shall be defrayed out of a common treasury, which shall
> be supplied by the several states in proportion to the whole number of white
> and other free citizens and inhabitants, of every age, sex and condition, includ-
> ing those bound to servitude for a term of years, and three-fifths of all other
> persons not comprehended in the foregoing description, except Indians, not
> paying taxes, in each State; which number shall be triennially taken and trans-
> mitted to the United States in Congress assembled, in such mode as they shall
> direct and appoint. (*JCC* 24:260–61)

The criteria used to apportion congressional resource demands among the states are assessed in table 6.1, which presents the percentage dis-
tribution across the states of several specific congressional requests and compares them with the modern estimate of the population distribution across the states in 1780 (column 1). Columns 2 and 7 present the distribu-

tions of Continental dollars to be redeemed—the first and last distribution of Continental dollars mentioned by Congress. Columns 3 and 8 present distributions of non-Continental dollar revenue requests—one from 1777 and one from 1783. Lastly, columns 4, 5, and 6 present distributions of troop requests from the states to fill the ranks of the Continental Army.

The comparisons show that while each distribution is slightly different—and, it seems, randomly so—they are all basically consistent with the distributions' being based on each state's population share in the union. Columns 2 and 8 were supposed to be based on the population distribution, the only difference being that column 8 but not column 2 was to be based on counting slaves as three-fifths of a person. Columns 3–7 were set under the auspices of the Articles of Confederation, which were supposed to use improved land value as the criterion for apportionment. Yet, it is difficult to see systematic differences between the distributions in these columns. Finally, it is hard to see any systematic difference across any of these resource distributions established by Congress and the modern estimate of the distribution of population across the states in 1780.

While the evidence in table 6.1 indicates that throughout the war Congress demanded that resources and revenues be provided by each state in proportion to that state's population share in the union, Congress did not know with great exactitude what those shares were, certainly not at the level of the modern estimate of population shares (column 1). This lack of exact knowledge may explain some of the seemingly random variation across the distributions. States may have sought adjustments from year to year in their congressional apportionments.

That said, it is still interesting to note what Congress thought the shares should be relative to the modern estimates of those shares; compare column 1 of table 6.1 with the other columns in the table. Requests were set consistently higher for Massachusetts, Maryland, and South Carolina, and lower for New York, Delaware, and Georgia, than they should have been. On average, requests were set slightly higher for New Hampshire and Connecticut, and slightly lower for Virginia and North Carolina, than they should have been. For several states both in the north and in the south, the distributions track their white-population-only share, while for other states they track their total population share, in the union. The cases of New York and Georgia may also reflect the fact that large portions of these two states, that is, their most important economic areas, were occupied by the British during a substantial portion of the war, and so they may have been excused from their full share. The other cases probably represent simple misestimates of population totals by Congress. In conclusion, congressional resource demands from the states throughout the war can be taken as apportioned by state population shares in the union. In other words, national revenue and resources were to be extracted by population and thus geographically by population location.

Where Were Resources Spent?

While congressional resource obligation and extraction demands were prorated by population and thus geographically based on population location within the union, congressional spending was driven by military necessity and thus was targeted geographically at the theaters of war. The theaters were not spread evenly across the states or across the population of the union; rather, they were regionally if not locally focused, moving geographically over time as military strategy changed. Table 6.2 tracks the location of the major theaters of war. Roughly, the war moved from north to south. The first year of the war, April 1775 through April 1776, was waged largely in New England, with Boston being the major focus but with smaller campaigns waged in northern New England and into Canada. The next four years of war, May 1776 through May 1780, were waged almost exclusively in the middle states—between the environs of New York City and Philadelphia, with one major engagement in upstate New York. Thereafter, the war turned to the southern states, but on a smaller scale than what had gone before. The main Continental Army would not travel into the southern states to fight until after August of 1781.

Congressional spending in this period was primarily in the paper money it created—the Continental dollar. If congressional spending followed the theater of war exclusively, then approximately 10 million Continental dollars (face value) were injected into the New England economy, principally in the Boston area, during the first year of the war, with little thereafter. The remaining 190 million Continental dollars (face value), emitted between May 1776 and November 1779, were injected into the economies of the middle states, excluding New York City, which was occupied by the British for most of the period.

This crude approximation of spending flows highlights the issue of geographic fiscal/monetary imbalance. Throughout this period, the southern states received far less congressional spending compared with the resource and revenue obligations, or future responsibility for revenue obli-

TABLE 6.2 **Major theaters of war by region, 1775–81**

Dates	Major campaigns theater/region	Major battles (date)	Approximate American forces engaged	American commander
Apr. 1775– Apr. 1776	**New England** [Massachusetts, New Hampshire, Rhode Island, Connecticut]	Siege of Boston	1775: 16,000 1776: 10,000	George Washington George Washington
May 1776–80	**Middle states** [New York, New Jersey, Pennsylvania, Delaware]	New York City (May–Nov. 1776)	19,000	George Washington
		Trenton/Princeton, NJ (Dec. 1776–Jan. 1777)	6,800	George Washington
		Brandywine, PA (Sept. 1777)	11,000	George Washington
		Germantown, PA (Oct. 1777)	11,000	George Washington
		Saratoga, NY (Sept.–Oct. 1777)	11,000	Horatio Gates
		Monmouth, NJ (June 1778)	13,400	George Washington
		[Main army remained in New Jersey, New York, and Pennsylvania until Aug. 1781]		
1780–81	**Southern states** [Maryland, Virginia, North Carolina, South Carolina, Georgia]	Charleston, SC (May 1780)	5,000	Benjamin Lincoln
		Camden, SC (Aug. 1780)	3,052	Horatio Gates
		Cowpens, SC (Jan. 1780)	1,040	Daniel Morgan
		Guilford Court House, NC (Mar. 1781)	4,400	Nathaniel Greene
		Hobkirk's Hill, SC (Apr. 1781)	1,551	Nathaniel Greene
		Eutaw Springs, SC (Sept. 1781)	2,200	Nathaniel Greene
		Yorktown, VA (Sept.– Oct. 1781)	8,845	George Washington

Sources: Esposito (1995, maps 4–9); Puls (2008); Tindall (1988: 210–42).

gations, demanded of them by Congress. This imbalance was also true for New England after the first year of the war. By contrast, the middle states, after the first year of the war, received more congressional spending than they owed Congress in return.

Continental dollars were the dominant form of congressional spending, especially early in the war. Table 6.3 estimates the source of congressional monies spent from 1775 through 1779. While the exact amount

TABLE 6.3 **Percentage distribution of congressional monies spent, 1775–79, estimated by source and measured in Continental dollars (face value)**

Source	1775	1776	1777	1778	1779	Total
Continental dollars emitted	100.00%	99.03%	58.79%	74.69%	76.66%	76.68%
Domestic loans	0.00%	0.00%	33.20%	5.50%	16.62%	12.80%
Foreign loans and gift aid	0.00%	0.97%	8.01%	19.81%	6.72%	10.52%
Total	$6,000,000	$19,122,420	$22,113,250	$85,017,038	$128,564,501	$260,817,209
Converted to Spanish dollars (specie value)	$6,000,000	$19,122,420	$7,371,083	$17,003,408	$6,428,225	$55,925,136

Sources: Derived from tables 1.1 and 6.5.

Notes: These yearly percentages are estimates in that the information on domestic loans was not kept by calendar year, so some cross-year overlaps were unavoidable; see table 6.5. In addition, the monetary portion of the foreign aid that Congress could use to spend domestically is unknown; see table 6.5. It is assumed here that all foreign loans and gift aid were in cash that Congress could spend, thus giving a biased-low estimate to the Continental dollar percentage of the budget. These numbers also exclude goods and services confiscated or otherwise acquired for IOUs in the form of Quartermaster Notes, Warrants, and Certificates; see table 6.5. Finally, the conversion factor for going from Continental dollar face value to Spanish dollar (specie value) are crude yearly averages; see table 6.5.

TABLE 6.4 **Congressional troop costs in just soldier salaries: Expressed in Continental dollars (face value) per year, 1775-79**

	1775*	1776	1777	1778	1779
Number of men in Continental pay	27,443	46,901	34,820	32,899	27,699
Biased-low annualized expected troop pay	$1,380,874	$8,106,346	$6,018,272	$5,686,247	$4,787,481
As a percentage of Continental dollars emitted that year	23.01%	42.81%	46.29%	8.95%	4.86%

Sources: Table 1.1; Knox (1790); *JCC* (2:89–90).

Notes: * = 1775 covers only from June on. Congress set the monthly pay for troops in Continental pay on June 14, 1775. The pay for privates through captains for a company of eighty-one men sums to $582.25 per month. Annualized, this is $14,000 per company of eighty-one men per year in expected cost. This information is used to generate the annualized expected troop pay in the table. These numbers are biased low in that they do not include the pay for military personal above the rank of captain, nor do they include recruitment bonuses or any equipage cost. Not all troops were necessarily enlisted for the entire year; thus, these numbers represent the expected cost if those enlisted that year in fact stayed enlisted for that year.

and yearly placement of domestic loans as well as foreign loans and gifts cannot be determined with perfect certainty, the general pattern can be taken with some confidence. From 1775 through 1779 Continental dollars represented approximately 77 percent of the monies spent by Congress. It was 100 percent in the first two years. In other words, the first five years of the war were fought on the back of the Continental dollar. These massive monetary injections, if regionally targeted, could have produced regional differences, at least in the short run, in who suffered the declining present value of the national currency.

Having established the dominance of spending in Continental dollar currency, the above approximation on the geographic imbalance of this spending can be further refined by showing that in fact the majority of congressional spending actually flowed to where the theater of war was located. While harder to establish conclusively, a strong case can be made for such a flow. A first stab can be taken by looking at the monthly pay of soldiers in the Continental Army, annualized to get an expected yearly cost. Because the vast majority of Continental troops—those at and below the rank of captain—were likely to be located where the theater of war was, their total expense can give an impression of where Continental dollars were flowing. Table 6.4 provides these estimates and shows that around 43 to 46 percent of all the Continental dollars authorized by Congress in 1776 and 1777 can be accounted for as just monthly salary flowing to soldiers in the field. The numbers are lower in 1775, 1778, and 1779, at

23, 10, and 5 percent, respectively. These figures are indicative of a substantial flow of Continental dollars going narrowly into where the theaters of war were located.

The Knox Report

A full accounting of congressional spending by type of expense for each year of the war is hard to find. As far as I know, only one exists. It was prepared by Henry Knox, Secretary of War in the first Washington administration, in 1790 and was included in a document compiled by Joseph Nourse, Registrar of the Treasury, for Congress explaining the "receipts and expenditures of public monies during the administration of the finances by Robert Morris." This report has often been overlooked, perhaps because it was made by a man little known to most Americans today.[1]

Knox, however, may be the most underappreciated revolutionary hero and founding father of the current scholarly literature. He was there at the beginning of hostilities, quickly rose to command Washington's artillery corps, and was a key advisor to Washington on strategy, logistics, and supplies. In some ways he was Washington's right-hand man, and Washington viewed him as critical to his military success. In addition, Knox became a principal in organizing ordnance supplies, including the foundation and running of armories during the war at Springfield, Massachusetts and Carlisle, Pennsylvania (Puls 2008).

After the Revolution, Knox was put in charge of the War Department under the Confederation government and then became the only department head held over into the first Washington administration under the new US Constitution as Washington's Secretary of War (Puls 2008). He and Nourse were the two longest-continuously-serving administration appointees from the end of the war into the 1790s. Finally, from the beginning of the Revolution into the early 1790s, the war office was extensively involved in the disbursement of congressional spending authorizations, whereas the congressional treasury was more in charge of managing the revenue and finance side of the ledger (Jensen 1981: 55). Henry Knox was in the right place to observe congressional spending and had been continuously and directly involved in these spending issues longer than any other administrator, civilian or military.

As such, Knox's 1790 report should carry considerable weight in any assessment of congressional wartime spending. But it is doubly important in that the war office and all its records were destroyed by fire in November 1800. Knox's report, being embedded in Nourse's report to Congress in 1790, is, as far as I can tell, the only surviving account of the record of congressional spending from 1775 through 1781 kept by the war office (Knox 1790). It forms the basis for what follows.

Knox's report lists between eleven and fourteen categories or types of spending for each year of the war — 1775 being included in 1776, since congressional spending on the war did not begin until late June 1775. From 1775 to 1780 amounts were kept in Continental dollar units of account. Table 6.5 presents Knox's data for 1775–80 by year in percentages spent by category out of the total spending listed that year. Knox's data have been slightly rearranged by consolidating some categories, so that only twelve are listed, and by grouping the categories according to whether the spending was more or less targeted into the current theater of war — thus trying to get at the issue of geographic spending imbalances by region.

While table 6.4 estimated the expected yearly cost of monthly pay just to the Continental Army at the rank of captain and below and found it to be a substantial component of congressional spending through 1777, Knox's first category in table 6.5 reports the actual spending on all pay plus recruiting costs and "other contingencies" of the Continental Army. It shows that direct army personnel and contingency expenses dominated congressional spending through 1777 and remained sizable thereafter — coming in second behind military supplies (the Commissary and Quartermaster categories) after 1777. Through 1777 congressional spending was dominated by direct army pay; after that it was dominated by the cost of supplying the army with provisions and equipment — well over half the budget in the years after 1777 (Carp 1984: 17–135).

Direct military pay was not the only budget item that was likely to be war theater–specific spending. Because of logistics and transport costs, supplying the army with food, clothing, equipment, and other necessary support materials was largely a local or at least regional affair (Carp 1984: 53–135). Thus, when the Commissary, Quartermaster, Special Expeditions, and Clothing, Hospital, and Prisoner Departments are included with the army pay category (the first five categories in table 6.5), the share of total congressional spending that was likely targeted narrowly at the region where the theater of war was located amounted to two-thirds in 1775–76, rose to three-quarters by 1777, and peaked at 90 percent of the budget in 1779. These numbers are likely biased low because the largest spending category not included among the war theater–specific categories was

TABLE 6.5 **Yearly distribution of congressional spending by type of expense, 1775–80**

	Percentage of total spent per year				
Type of expense	June 1775–1776	1777	1778	1779	1780[a]
1. Spending that was relatively "current" war-theater specific					
Army recruiting, pay, and other contingencies	46.71%	36.45%	22.00%	10.55%	23.30%
Commissary Department	12.66	21.78	31.36	35.52	40.32
Quartermaster Department	3.82	11.86	26.59	37.94	16.88
Clothing, Hospital, and Prisoner Departments	3.37	5.81	7.30	6.21	4.04
Special Expedition against Detroit	0	0	1.39	0	0
Subtotal	66.56%	75.90%	88.64%	90.22%	84.54%
2. Spending that was less "current" war-theater specific					
Military Stores and Barrackmaster Departments	0	0.09	0.87	2.55	6.39
Indian Affairs and Post Office	0.21	0.13	0.03	0.06	0.37
Contingent expenses and civil list	1.53	1.57	1.82	0.39	2.38
Marine Committee	7.21	3.61	1.79	1.10	1.31
Secret Committee	6.43	2.51	0	0	0
Commercial Committee	0	0	0.54	0.56	0.61
Advances to the states	18.07	15.22	6.30	5.11	4.38
Subtotal	33.45%	23.13%	11.35%	9.77%	15.44%
Total spending in Continental dollars (face value)	$20,064,667	$26,426,333	$66,965,269	$149,703,857	$82,908,320[a]
Authorized emissions of Continental dollars by Congress (face value)	$19,937,220 [June 1775–July 1776]	$18,000,000 [Nov. 1776–Dec. 1777]	$63,500,300 [Jan. 1778–Dec. 1778]	$98,552,480 [Jan. 1779–Nov. 1779]	0
Deficit of Continental dollars (face value)	$127,447	$8,426,333	$3,464,969	$51,151,377	$82,908,320[a]

TABLE 6.5 *(continued)*

Type of expense	June 1775–1776	1777	1778	1779	1780[a]
			Percentage of total spent per year		
Made up for by: domestic interest-bearing loans (bonds) in Continental dollars (face value)	0	$7,342,275 [Before Mar. 1778]	$4,675,113 [Mar. 1778 to Sept. 1778]	$21,372,021 [Sept. 1778 to Sept. 1779]	$13,169,826 [Sept. 1779 to Mar. 1780]
Domestic deficit in Continental dollars (face value)	$127,447	$1,084,058	+$1,210,144 [surplus]	$29,779,356	$69,738,494[a]
Made up for by (?): Foreign loans and gift aid (in Spanish dollars)[b]	$185,200	$590,325	$3,368,325	$432,000	$555,600
Converted to Continental dollars (face value)[c]	$185,200	$1,770,975	$16,841,625	$8,640,000	$22,224,000
Residual deficit—made up for by (?): [Quartermaster notes, indents, warrants (IOUs), and direct state loans in Continental dollars at face value, plus confiscations]	+$57,753 [surplus applied to 1777]	+$744,760 [surplus applied to 1778]	+$18,796,529 [surplus applied to 1779]	$2,342,827	$47,514,494[a]

Sources: Table 1.1; appendix A; Boyd (1953–55, 10:42–43); Ferguson (1961: 38–42); Jensen (1981: 38–39); *JCC* (8:650, 731; 9:953–8; 14:626; 15:1147–50; 16:263; 24:285–6); *PCC* (microfilm 247, reel 146, item 136:647); all other numbers derived from Knox (1790).

Notes:

[a] Represents spending denominated in Continental dollars of the old emission only and not spending rated in the new Continental-state dollar (see chap. 14). Thus, 1780 is only a partial accounting.

[b] Equals the conversion of loan, subsidy, and gift amounts from *livres* into Spanish dollars (specie) at the rate stated in the sources cited. Apportionment across the years, while somewhat unclear, follows Ferguson (1961: 40–42) and Jensen (1981: 38–39) as closely as possible, with the Dutch loan and the Spanish gift aid placed in 1779, and the three million *livres* floating debt to individuals in Europe placed in 1780 somewhat arbitrarily. How much of the foreign loans were in cash versus in credit subsidies for foreign purchases is still to be determined. Thus, how much to count toward deficit balancing of domestic spending is unclear. The full amount is used here, thus yielding a biased-low estimate of the residual deficit.

[c] Foreign loans and gifts are converted from Spanish dollars (specie) to Continental dollars following the depreciation table reported by Jefferson on January 24, 1786, using either the average or the mid-year rate for each year, respectively (Boyd 1953–55, 10:42–43). The conversion factors used are 0, 3, 5, 20, and 40 Continental dollars to one Spanish dollar for 1775–76, 1777, 1778, 1779, and 1780, respectively.

"advances to the states." This category included some states that were within the current theater of war. Thus, separating that category into war-theater versus non-war-theater spending would increase the percentage of war-theater spending.

Spending versus Resources Flows

Knox's report tallies total congressional spending per year in Continental dollar units of account (see table 6.5). Assuming Knox's totals are the true totals, comparing them with the authorized emissions of Continental dollars by Congress within the same approximate time frame indicates that Continental dollars once authorized and printed were probably spent rapidly. The congressional treasury was constantly empty of Continental dollars; congressional authorization of new emissions of paper money could not keep up with spending. This has never been shown before, though many have suspected it. In part, this explains the explosion in the Continental dollar money supply and its resulting rapid decline in value. Remember, no Continental dollars were required to be redeemed by the states and returned to the congressional treasury, where they were to be burned, before 1780.

While the deficit in Continental dollar currency needed to meet current spending was small through 1776: only $127,447 that year, it ballooned to over $8.4 million in 1777 and just under $3.5 million in 1778. After that it exploded to crisis levels—over $51 million in 1779 and over $82 million in 1780. Much of this change was driven by the expanding share of the Commissary and Quartermaster Departments in the congressional spending budget. Military supplies, not men, were breaking the budget. How were these deficits made up?

The remaining part of table 6.5 attempts to account for how these deficits in Continental dollars were covered—something that has not been charted well before. The evidence is fragile and sketchy, yet of some interest and generally coherent. First, domestic borrowing via loan office certificates, while relatively small, helped reduce the deficit dramatically in the early years, yielding a deficit of only about $1 million in 1777 and then even putting the budget into surplus by $1.2 million in 1778. Thereafter, domestic borrowing was not enough to keep the deficit from ballooning, yielding deficits of about $30 million in 1779 and $70 million in 1780 (see chap. 8).

Foreign loans and gifts may have helped reduce these remaining deficits. This is more difficult to determine, because it is not known how much of these foreign loans and gifts were in cash given to the congressional treasury that found their way into Knox's accounting of congressional spending. Foreign loans and gifts in the form of direct goods or credits in Europe seem unlikely to have been included in Knox's spending tally. A biased-low estimate of the residual deficit can be made by assuming that all foreign loans and gifts were cash that the treasury could spend. Under this assumption, the congressional budget, using Knox's spending data, was in good shape through 1778, basically being in a small surplus from 1776 to 1778. Thereafter, the residual deficits mounted to $2.3 million in 1779 and $47.5 million in 1780.

While the exactitude of the accounting cannot be relied on, the general pattern over time and approximate magnitudes appear sound. What they indicate is that a budgetary fiscal/monetary crisis was held in check well into 1778 but then rapidly escalated into crisis. The residual deficit in these latter years, especially after 1778, was largely made up by direct state loans to Congress and/or by confiscation of supplies and services, as well as nonpayment of soldiers' salaries. While Congress's requested amounts of direct state loans in this period could have balanced the budget, the actual amount lent by the states to Congress is unclear and may have been deficient (see chap. 8). Paper IOUs—for example, quartermaster notes, indents, and warrants—were handed out to the lucky ones whose goods and services were requisitioned (legally impressed), while others just had their goods taken (confiscated) (Carp 1984: 71, 90, 97; Jensen 1981: 34).

These sums appear large. A conservative estimate using the data in table 6.5 is that about $50 million in current Continental dollar unit-of-account value of these IOUs, state loans, and accumulated payment arrears were used to balance the budget in 1779–80. This is consistent with the Commissary and Quartermaster Departments' having risen to dominate the lion's share of congressional spending after 1778. Again, this spending was largely focused on where the theater of war was located (Carp 1984: 53–135).

The imbalance of spending locations across the states versus resource obligations based on population by state led to lengthy negotiations and accounting efforts after the war to rebalance claims among the states (see Elliot 1843). It also helps explain the differences among the states in the extent and timing of remitting their quotas of redeemed Continental dollars to the US Treasury through the 1780s (see fig. 15.2).

CHAPTER SEVEN

Legal Tender

When we sit here in Legislation, we have great Power, but we are not almighty. We cannot alter the Nature of Things. Values will be as they are valued or valuable, and not as we call them. We may stamp on a Piece of Paper, This is Ten Shillings, but if we do not make some other Provision that it always be worth Ten Shillings, the Say-so of our Law [a legal-tender law] will signify little. Experience in other Colonies as well as in ours, have demonstrated this. Benjamin Franklin, from his speech to the Pennsylvania Assembly, January 14, 1764 (Labaree 1966–70, 11:13–14)

Legal-tender laws typically entailed two requirements. First, they made refusal to accept the designated legal tender as a medium of exchange illegal. Second, they fixed the legal tender's exchange value in specie. If the legal tender was paper money, it fixed the bill's face value to its specie equivalent, making it illegal to accept it at less than that specie equivalent. Many contemporaries, and numerous scholars since, have assumed that legal-tender laws, especially the second requirement, supported the value of paper money, making bills trade at face value or closer to face value than they would have without the legal-tender law.

This assumption is erroneous. Legal-tender laws per se, even when rigorously enforced, do not support the value of the legal tender.[1] Legal-tender laws accomplished two things. First, they prevented traders in the marketplace from refusing, under legal penalty, to accept the designated legal-tender paper money as a medium of exchange (the first requirement). Second, as an unintended consequence of the second requirement, they cause pricing in the marketplace to be dominated by the designated legal tender. While legal-tender laws may have increased the designated legal-tender paper money's usage as a medium of exchange, they did not affect its market value relative to its face value in specie. This chapter will show why and, in the process, eliminate the claim that legal-tender laws directly controlled the market value of the Continental dollar—with the exception of how legal-tender laws altered the fungibility of emissions in redemption (see chaps. 10 and 12).

Recap

Congress never made the Continental dollar a legal tender. It is unknown why, as it never stated its reasoning. Either members thought it was un-necessary, or they thought they did not have the power to do so. Congress eventually asked the individual states to make the Continental dollar a legal tender within each state's respective jurisdiction and then later en-couraged the individual states to revoke that legal-tender status. These re-quests suggest that Congress thought either that it did not have the power to make the Continental dollar a legal tender or that such a power was unenforceable without state concurrence.

During the first year and a half of the Revolution, when the primary use of Continental dollars was to pay soldiers, no legal-tender law was required. Soldier had to accept them as pay at the pay-grade-rates set by Congress. If soldiers could not effectively spend them, but had to hold them as if they were bonds for postwar redemption, no congressional funding issues were threatened. After 1776, however, the majority of con-gressional spending was on military supplies purchased in the market-place rather than on soldiers' pay. In the marketplace, purveyors could refuse Continental dollars because the bills had no legal-tender status. Thus, Congress on January 14, 1777, asked the states to make Continen-tal dollars legal tender within their respective states (see chap. 6; Grubb 2011b: 36).

The states moved quickly to accommodate this request. For example, Pennsylvania made Continental dollars legal tender after February 6, 1777, Delaware after February 22, 1777, and Virginia after May 5, 1777. By the eighth new emission of Continental dollars, authorized on May 22, 1777 (see table 1.1), Continental dollars were a legal tender. When a state made the Continental dollar a legal tender within its jurisdiction, it established a legal equivalence between Continental dollars, that state's paper money, and the specie face value of the Continental dollar. The two monies, the state's paper money and the Continental dollar, were now linked through that specie equivalence, and the exchange of one for the other could be enforced (Cushing 1981: 599–602; Hening 1969, 9:297–98; *Statutes at Large of Pennsylvania* 1903–4, 9:34–40). Thus, once Continental dollars were made legal tender, Continental dollars could be more easily used as a medium of exchange. Purveyors could not refuse them nor refuse making change in other currencies, like the state's paper money, when offered Continental dollars.

Unintended Consequences

The unintended consequence of imposing legal-tender laws was that they pushed the pricing of current transactions to being denominated by the designated legal tender. Sellers had to price only in the legal tender to avoid being forced to accept bills at above their present value, namely at the legal tender's face-value equivalent in specie monies. By pricing only in the legal tender, sellers could adjust their prices upward to compensate for the fact that the bill's present value was below its face value.

Figure 7.1 shows this effect in the Philadelphia market. The weekly *Pennsylvania Gazette*, Benjamin Franklin's old newspaper, was the most prominent newspaper in the Philadelphia region. A typical issue had a couple of pages of news and then several pages of commercial advertisements. I read through every issue between 1770 and 1790, with the exception of the period when the British occupied Philadelphia and the paper was not issued, and recorded the monetary unit used in every advertisement and transaction. A total of 15,170 separate monetary statements were taken from this source over these twenty-one years. By far, the two most prominent monetary units mentioned were "dollars" and "pounds," often with no other qualifier. "Dollars" could refer either to Spanish silver dollars or, after mid-1775, to paper Continental dollars. "Pounds" could refer either to Pennsylvania paper pounds or to pounds sterling. From the tenor of the texts, the paper versions—the Pennsylvania pounds and the Continental dollars—were what advertiser meant unless they qualified the statement with the word "silver" or "sterling."

Out of all these commercial transactions, pricing in dollars did not gain a clear majority of transactions until after January 1777, that is, until af-

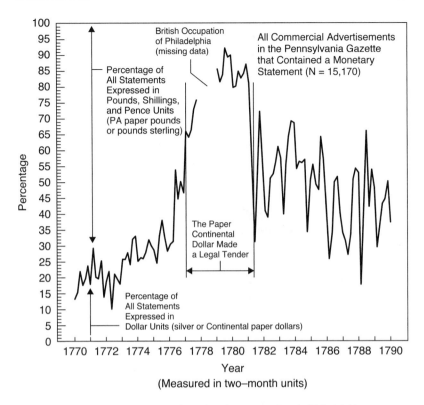

FIGURE 7.1. Prevalent unit of account in marketplace transactions in Philadelphia, 1770–90

Source: Pennsylvania Gazette.

Note: All commercial advertisements placed in the *Pennsylvania Gazette* were examined. Data are organized in two-month units. Line breaks indicate missing data (newspapers). Dollar units include Spanish silver dollars and Continental paper dollars. Pounds, shillings, and pence units include Pennsylvania paper pounds and pounds sterling monies.

ter the Continental dollar had been made a legal tender in Pennsylvania. Shortly thereafter pricing in dollars rose to capture 80–90 percent of all transactions listed. This proportion held into early 1781, when, at Congress's recommendation, states removed the Continental dollar's legal-tender status in their respective jurisdictions.[2] After 1781 the reference to "dollars" almost universally meant Spanish silver dollars. Newspaper price currents, merchant account books, and George Washington's account book all stopped quoting prices in Continental dollars in May 1781 (Bezanson 1951: 12, 344; Breck 1843: 16; Ferguson 1961: 66; Webster 1969: 502).

Figure 7.1 shows that pricing in Continental dollars rose significantly in 1776 and then dominated pricing through 1780. This finding supports Anne Bezanson's (1951) proposition that the price index created for the Philadelphia region based on local newspaper price currents, the only price index currently known to exist for the Revolution, is indeed capturing pricing in Continental dollars, and thus the market value of the Continental dollar, from mid-1776 through 1780 (see chap. 11). The data in figure 7.1 are also consistent with the proposition that legal-tender laws drive pricing in the marketplace to be in the designated legal tender.

Legal-Tender Laws and Colonial Paper Money: What Congressmen Knew in 1775

Each colony, when legally allowed by the British, made their paper monies a legal tender, though not for every emission (Grubb 2016a: 209–24). Legal-tender laws were a point of contention with the British government, who moved to discourage, disallow, and then outright ban legal-tender laws. Parliament's Currency Act of 1751 (24 Geo. II c. 53) banned legal-tender laws in the New England colonies, and Parliament's Currency Act of 1764 (4 Geo. III c. 34) extended that ban to all the colonies. The colonies resisted these restrictions, often arguing that legal-tender laws were necessary to give their paper monies a currency and to support their value.

With these acts banning legal-tender laws in the colonies, colonial assemblies were initially unsure whether their tax-redemption method of anchoring the value of their paper monies would work. Several colonies— New York, New Jersey, and Delaware, and perhaps North and South Carolina (Grubb 2016a)—either stopped or substantially curtailed their emission of bills of credit after 1764, at least through 1775. Other colonies discovered that the method of emitting bills of credit backed by future tax redemptions would still work even without a de jure legal-tender law if the issuing government acted as if it were still bound by a legal-tender law, that is, if it operated a de facto legal-tender law for public debts (taxes and government-issued mortgage payments); examples include Pennsylvania, Maryland, Virginia, and Georgia (Celia and Grubb 2016; Grubb 2016a). Parliament's 1773 Currency Act revised the 1764 Currency Act to formally allow legal-tender laws, but only for the payment of public debts, that is, provincial taxes (Ernst 1973: 308–11). Evidence on exchange rates and prices shows little difference in the performance of bills of credit between before and after the 1764 ban on legal-tender paper monies (Celia and Grubb 2016; Grubb 2016a, 2016b, 2018a, 2020).

That legal-tender laws did not support or fix the value of bills of credit was well-known. In 1764 Benjamin Franklin, in the longest speech of his career (among his surviving texts), explained to the Pennsylvania Assembly the fallacy of thinking that legal-tender laws per se could support, determine, or fix the specie value of their bills of credit:

And indeed of what Force can it [a legal-tender law] be to fix an arbitrary Value on the Bills [of Credit], unless the Value of all Things to be purchased by the Bills could be fix'd by the same Law. I want to buy a Suit of Cloth, and am told by the Seller, that his Price is 20s. [20 Shillings or 1 Pound] a Yard. Very well, say I, cut me off 5 Yards, and here are five 20s. Bills for you. I beg your Pardon, says he, the 20s. that I mean is 20s. lawful Money, according to such an Act of Parliament: Your Paper Money is greatly depreciated of late; it is of no more than half its nominal Value, your 20s. is really worth but ten; so that if you pay me in those 20s. Bills you must give ten of them for five Pounds. Don't talk so to me, says I, you are oblig'd by Act of Assembly to take these Bills at 20s. each. Very well, says he, if I *must* take them so I must; but as the Law sets no Price on my Goods, if you pay me with those Bills at 20s. each, my Cloth is 40s. a Yard, and so you must still give me ten of them; and pray then what becomes of your [legal-tender] Law? (Labaree 1966–70, 11:14)

In 1767 Franklin also pointed out that in colonies where bills of credit had been made a legal tender, they still traded below face value (Labaree 1966–70, 14:35).[3] In 1788 Franklin delivered a clearer, more succinct statement of this principle: "The making of paper [money] with such a sanction [a legal-tender law] is . . . a folly, since, although you may by law oblige a citizen to take it for his goods, you cannot fix his prices; and his liberty of rating them as he pleases, which is the same as setting what value he pleases on your money, defeats your sanction" (Smyth 1907: 638).

In 1776 Adam Smith, in *The Wealth of Nations*, echoed Franklin's point: "A positive law may render a shilling a legal tender for a guinea; because it may direct the courts of justice to discharge the debtor who has made that tender. But no positive law can oblige a person who sells goods, and who is at liberty to sell or not to sell, as he pleases, to accept of a shilling as equivalent to a guinea in the price of them" (Smith 1937: 311).

In other words, suppose I have a good for sale that is worth 1 £$_{Sterling}$ and I post its price as 1 £$_{Sterling}$ which at par or face value would be the same as 1.33 $£_{MD}$ (Celia and Grubb 2016; Grubb 2019b; with $£_{MD}$ = Maryland's paper pounds). However, suppose that the present value of a $£_{MD}$ is currently 90 percent of its face or par value. As such, I would set my posted prices for the good in question to be 1 $£_{Sterling}$ or 1.48 $£_{MD}$. I would have a two-tier price system that reflected the present value of the bills of credit in the current marketplace relative to their face or par value. A legal-tender law that requires that I accept the bills of credit but does not control prices or exchange rates cannot by itself support the value of the bills of credit and push their present value toward trading at their face value in sterling or specie.

Now suppose that legal-tender law also includes a statement fixing the face value of the bills of credit in specie, for example, saying that not only are $£_{MD}$ a legal tender and cannot be refused in payment, but that the valuation in exchange must be at its par or face value of 1.33 $£_{MD}$ equals 1 $£_{Sterling}$. Under such a restriction the good I had for sale, for which I posted a price of 1 $£_{Sterling}$, would now sell for 1.33 $£_{MD}$ if someone offered 1.33 $£_{MD}$ for it (I could not refuse this offer under the legal-tender law that also fixed the par of exchange), even if the present value of a $£_{MD}$ was currently 90 percent of its face or par value in the marketplace. I want to be paid 1.48 $£_{MD}$ for the good, but I cannot post that price or refuse the offer of 1.33 $£_{MD}$ if I post the good's price as 1 $£_{Sterling}$. I cannot post a two-tier price of 1 $£_{Sterling}$ or 1.48 $£_{MD}$ because, having posted a price of 1 $£_{Sterling}$, I could not refuse 1.33 $£_{MD}$ in payment under the legal-tender law, which also fixes the par of exchange.

The solution, however, is easy. I simply stop posting or contracting prices in sterling or specie units. I only contract or post prices in bills of credit. I post my price for the good in question to be 1.48 $£_{MD}$ only. Under the legal-tender law, 1.48 $£_{MD}$ is equal to 1.11 $£_{Sterling}$. But I cannot sell the good for 1.11 $£_{Sterling}$ because that price is above its worth and no one will pay it. The good is actually worth, and I would accept, 1 $£_{Sterling}$ in lieu of 1.48 $£_{MD}$, but I do not publicly say that. I would take the offer of 1 $£_{Sterling}$ in lieu of 1.48 $£_{MD}$ but only under the table or off the record, as a favor, or discount off the 1.11 $£_{Sterling}$ par equivalence to the 1.48 $£_{MD}$ posted price fixed by the legal-tender law. Thus, I have completely nullified the legal-tender law's effort to support the par value of the bills of credit by fixing a par exchange rate.

The testable hypothesis that results from this discussion is that when legal-tender laws with fixed par exchange rates to sterling or silver dollars are passed and enforced, then pricing in the marketplace and in contracts should gravitate to being dominated by pricing in the designated legal-tender paper-bills-of-credit monetary unit. This hypothesis has yet to be systematically tested for colonial America, though casual observation is consistent with it. Figure 7.1 provides a successful test of it for the Continental dollar in the Philadelphia region.

Why Did the British Object to Legal-Tender Laws?

Legal-tender laws with fixed exchange rates cause havoc in noncontemporaneous trades that end up in court when contracts are breached. Noncontemporaneous trades are when the payments by one party are at some future date from the initial contract, or the initial delivery of the goods that corresponds to those payments. Breach of contract is when the party who pays last, the debtor or purchaser, reneges on the promised payment to the party who paid first, the creditor or seller. The creditor or plaintiff would sue the debtor in court, seeking to recover the promised payment. When finding in favor of the plaintiff or creditor, courts would make the plaintiff whole by enforcing the payment promised. In cases where the defendant or debtor either could not deliver the specific payment promised—for instance, he did not have the specific horse he promised to deliver, or the specific specie coins he promised to pay—or where the contractual payment was vague regarding the monetary instrument, such as "16 pounds," the courts had to assign a monetary substitute that would make the plaintiff whole.

The presence of a legal-tender law essentially tied the hands of the courts in these breach-of-contract cases. The monetary substitute assigned to make the plaintiff whole had to be the designated legal tender. The issue for the courts was whether the legal-tender monetary substitute would be priced at its present value or at its face value. If the courts priced it at its present value, then the plaintiff was indeed made whole, and no injustice would be done. Benjamin Franklin claimed that in Pennsylvania this was indeed the case. In 1767 Franklin observed that "it [has] ever been a constant rule there [in Pennsylvania] to consider British debts [those in sterling] as payable in Britain, and not to be discharged but by as much paper [money] as would purchase a bill for the full sterling sum." Franklin goes on to write in a draft petition: "In the Courts of Justice [in Pennsylvania], full satisfaction has ever been given in discharge of debts due to the British merchant [in sterling valuation . . .]." In 1760 the British Board of Trade made the same observation. They concluded that Pennsylvania had been exempted from Parliament's 1751 Currency Act, which forbade making paper money a legal tender, because "the province had, without a Law, come of itself very near the regulation which the Law would have prescribed" (Labaree 1966–70, 9:149; 14:34–36, 80, 185).

But what if the courts used the legal-tender par rate to make the plaintiff whole in breach-of-contract cases? This may have been the case in colonies such as Virginia in the early 1760s and New England in the 1740s (though this needs to be researched and established more thoroughly). In such cases, the plaintiff would not be made whole but would be paid less than the sum originally contracted, the size of the underpayment being the gap between the current present value of the bills of credit and their face value. Knowing that judges and courts would use the par value rather than the present value when using the legal tender to make plaintiffs whole in breach-of-contract cases could lead to strategic behavior by debtors and unjust outcomes for creditors, especially among non-repeat traders. During periods when bills of credit had a present value well below their respective face values, debtors would be increasingly tempted to breach their contracts, knowing that courts would count bills at their par rates. Such suspected behavior in New England in the 1740s, and in Virginia in the early 1760s, appears to have been behind Parliament's passage of the 1751 and 1764 Currency Acts, respectively.

In 1776 Adam Smith, in *The Wealth of Nations*, made a similar observation:

> The paper currencies of North America consisted . . . in a government paper, of which the payment was not eligible till several years after it was issued: And though the colony governments paid no interest to the holders of this paper, they declared it to be, and in fact rendered it, a legal tender of payment for full value for which it was issued. But allowing the colony security to be perfectly good, a hundred pounds payable fifteen years hence . . . in a country where interest is at six per cent. is worth little more than forty pounds ready money. To oblige a creditor . . . to accept of this as full payment for a debt of a hundred pounds actually paid down in ready money, was an act of such violent injustice, as has scarce . . . been attempted by the government of any other country which pretended to be free. It bears the evident mark of having originally been . . . a scheme of fraudulent debtors to cheat their creditors. . . .
>
> No law, therefore could be more equitable than the act of parliament, so unjustly complained of in the colonies, which declared that no paper currency to be emitted there in time coming, should be a legal tender in payment. (Smith 1937: 310–11)

Smith's analysis of the initial conditions of colonial paper money regarding discounted valuation is not that different from what Franklin stated in his 1767 essay "The Legal Tender of Paper Money in America" (Labaree 1966–70, 14:32–39). Their conclusions regarding the effect of legal-tender laws on these initial conditions were, however, diametrically opposed. Smith assumes that courts would assign the legal-tender substitute at its par exchange value to specie, whereas Franklin points out that, at least in the middle colonies, the courts used the present value of the legal tender when assigning it as a payment substitute in breach-of-contract cases. Smith relied heavily on William Douglass, a strident anti–paper money polemicist from New England, for his information about paper money in America (Davis 1964: 3–4; Smith 1937: 310). Smith's views of colonial paper money may have been colored by this reliance.

What Positive Role Did Legal-Tender Laws Serve?

If legal-tender laws did not support the value of paper money, and they potentially caused havoc when misapplied by judges and courts in breach-of-contract cases, what good were they? Franklin gives a hint in 1767 when he wrote that the purpose of legal-tender laws was "the convenience to the possessor where *every one* is oblig'd to take them" (Labaree 1966–70, 14:34), namely the first requirement identified in legal-tender laws. While not fully articulated by Franklin, or by any other writer that I know of from this period, from the totality of Franklin's writings on the subject this appears to mean solving the short-run or temporary hold-up problem in trade. Franklin saw outside monies (specie or sterling values) as being prone to substantial and unexpected short-run fluctuations in availability, say, owing to unexpected foreign trade shocks. Inside monies (the paper bills of credit of the colonies) were not susceptible to these effects, as they had no exportable value. If a creditor who was owed a payment in outside money could refuse being paid in an equivalent amount of inside money at its present value exchange rate, then the creditor could exert undue short-term leverage over the debtor when outside money was unexpectedly and temporarily scarce. Under such circumstances, the creditor could extract (extort) more payment than the expected present value equivalent of the outside money owed by the debtor by threatening the debtor with debtor's prison for nonpayment of the specific outside money contracted. Given enough time, the debtor could solve this problem, exchanging inside for outside money at the present value rate of exchange. It is the presence of short-run trade disruption that creates these temporary hold-up extortion opportunities for creditors, such as occurred during the Revolution. Legal-tender laws removed this creditor-extortion possibility by requiring the creditor to accept the market equivalent of bills of credit in payment.

But then why have legal-tender laws that state the par equivalence of the bills in sterling, or in Spanish silver dollars, or in some other outside money unit (the second requirement identified in legal-tender laws)? In most cases, this appears to be how colonial assemblies anchored in law the tax-redemption payment equivalence of bills of credit for tax-receipt purposes. When a bill was to be redeemed through paying a future tax or mortgage payment designed to pull the bill out of circulation, the taxpayer or a mortgage holder could always pay in specie or sterling instead. In fact, if a taxpayer or mortgage holder did not have the bills of credit needed to pay their tax or mortgage, they had to be allowed to pay in some other lawful way. The government had to specify the equivalence of value between bills and this other lawful payment. It was this alternative payment in sterling or specie that anchored the value of the bills of credit to a par exchange rate in sterling at final redemption. Legal-tender laws with a set par exchange rate of bills for sterling or silver dollars were simply fixing the par value at the final redemption year designated in law. Legal-tender laws with fixed par exchange rates were simple ways for the colonial government to state and allow this outcome.

Legal-tender laws may have served one other positive function within the colonial monetary system. While not fully articulated as argued here, in 1767 Franklin offered the following reason for the presence of legal-tender laws in America (Labaree 1966–70, 14:35–36). For bills of credit anchored by a tax-redemption and mortgage-redemption structure, a time discount was built into their current value. Staggered overlapping emissions could stabilize the average present value of these bills of credit (Grubb 2016a). However, having bills of credit from different emissions with different redemption dates and hence different current present values circulating concurrently created a cumbersome medium of exchange. If each emission was priced correctly at its present value, valuation differences among concurrent emissions in circulation would raise the transaction cost of using the paper money as a medium of exchange. A legal-tender law that did not make a distinction between which bills were paid to satisfy which taxes among concurrently circulating bills from overlapping emissions, as long as total taxes were equal to or greater than the total bills to be redeemed, would reduce such present value difference among overlapping emissions currently outstanding. As such, legal-tender laws may have served to remove confusion over the relative valuation of a colony's paper-money emissions that overlapped and were circulating concurrently. This effect for the Continental dollar is shown in chapter 10.

The implementation of legal-tender laws under the redemption design of colonial paper monies as well as the Continental dollar, while improving the ease of using the money as a medium of exchange, had costs. While all bills regardless of emission would now have a comparable expected present value, the variance in the realized present value of an individual bill at a point in time around that average value was dramatically increased. This was because merging redemption intervals across emissions currently outstanding created a much longer redemption interval for each current bill. In other words, under a legal-tender law, and given the structural design of sequential overlapping emissions, whether a particular bill is redeemed today at face value or not for, say, twenty years at face value is indeterminate. See the discussion in chapters 1 and 10 (Grubb 2016a: 169).

CHAPTER EIGHT

Loan Office Certificates

The Delegate of North Carolina [to Congress Thomas Burke] could not be satisfied that Loan-Office certificates, & bills of credit [Continental dollars], ... were not in effect the same thing: he therefore thought Loan certificates another emission in bills of another denomination, with this unjust inequality, that one part of the community would thereby be taxed to the other. —Thomas Burke, February 8, 1777 (Smith 1976–94, 6:238)

A loan-office certificate differs in nothing from a common bill of credit [a Continental dollar], except in its higher denomination, and in the interest allowed on it; and the interest is allowed, merely as a compensation to the lender, for exchanging a number of small bills, which being easily transferable, are most convenient, for a single one so large as not to be transferable in ordinary transactions. As the certificates, however, do circulate in many of the more considerable transactions, it may justly be questioned, ... whether the advantage to the public from the exchange, would justify the terms of it. —James Madison, September 1779–March 1780 (Hutchinson and Rachal 1962–65, 1:308–9)

I will finish part I by considering the emission of loan office certificates and their role in the Continental dollar story. I will explain what loan office certificates were and why they were created. Furthermore, I will consider whether they count as new emissions of Continental dollars, and thus as augmentations to the Continental dollar money supply, or not. I will also relate the data on loan office certificates to the evidence on congressional spending in chapter 6. Lastly, I will point out that there is a lot I and the profession do not yet know about how the system of loan office certificates worked, in terms of process, amounts, and timing. I will present as much data as I could gather in the hope that it will prove useful to future scholars.

What Were Loan Office Certificates?

Instead of emitting more new Continental dollars, Congress borrowed back from the public Continental dollars that it had already spent into public circulation. Congress would then spend those borrowed Continental dollars. The vehicle for this borrowing was the loan office certificate. Figure 8.1 shows an example of a loan office certificate. It reveals that loan office certificates differed from Continental dollars in numerous ways (compare figs. I.1, I.2, I.3, and I.4 with fig. 8.1). Unlike Continental dollars, loan office certificates had blank spaces where the lender's name was written in by hand, as well as blank spaces where the date that the specific certificate was put into operation and when it was witnessed as being put into operation were written in. And unlike Continental dollars, loan office certificates also had an annual interest rate printed on them. No one would confuse a Continental dollar with a loan office certificate.

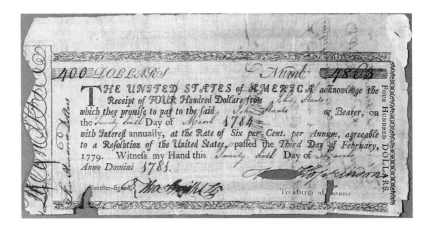

FIGURE 8.1. Loan office certificate from the sixth loan office authorization, February 3, 1779

Source: Photo © Christie's Images / Bridgeman Images. Single use rights purchased by Farley Grubb, April 7, 2022.

Note: See table 8.1. The resolution date typeset on the certificate is February 3, 1779, and so it is from authorization no. 6. Certificates were not printed and made available until after the resolution date. March 26, 1781, is the date the certificate was issued to John Staats. The maturity date on the certificate is March 26, 1784, which makes it a three-year bond. The note paid 6 percent per annum. Notice that unlike Continental dollars, loan office certificates had the bearer's name written on the note. See also an example in Anderson (1983: 84).

TABLE 8.1 **Loan office certificates: Amounts, conditions, and dates authorized**

Authorization no. Date	Amount authorized in Continental dollars	Purpose	Years to maturity	Annual interest rate	Medium in which interest will be paid	Borrowing media	Unrestricted bearer bond?
No. 1 Oct. 3, 1776	$5,000,000	Borrow and spend	3	6%[a]	In specie via bills of exchange on France[b]	Continental dollars only	Yes
No. 2 Jan. 1, 1777	2,000,000	"	Unstated (3)	6%[a]	"	Also local state bills of credit	"
No. 3 Feb. 22, 1777	13,000,000	"	"[j]	6%[a]	"	Unstated (same as no. 1 and no. 2)	"
No. 4 Jan. 7, 1778	10,000,000	"	"	6%	"	"	"
No. 5 May 2, 1778	250,000	Lottery payoff	"	4%[c,g]	Unstated (in Continental dollars)	"	"
No. 6 Feb. 3, 1779	20,000,000	Borrow and spend	"	6%+[g]	"	Continental dollars only[d]	No
No. 7 Apr. 27, 1779	4,000,000	Denomination swap[e]	"	6%+[g]	"	"	"
No. 8 June 29, 1779	20,000,000[h]	Borrow and spend	3+[f]	6%+[f]	"	"	?
No. 9 Oct. 30, 1779	600,000	Lottery payoff	5	6%+[g]	"	"	?
No. 10 Jan. 2, 1781	850,000	"	Unstated	6%	"	"	?
Borrow-and-spend total	71,283,600 to 74,000,000[h]						
Lottery payoff total	1,700,000[i]						
Grand total	72,983,600 to 75,700,000[h]						

Sources: JCC (5:845–46, 849–50; 6:955–56; 7:36–37, 40, 143, 158; 8:724–26, 730–31;9:777–78; 10:59; 11:415–16; 12:1147; 13:112, 141–42; 14:523, 717–20, 783–85, 772, 798–99; 15:1052, 1148, 1225–26; 16:392).

a The initial authorization (no. 1) stated the annual interest rate to be 4 percent. Authorizations no. 2 and no. 3, did not explicitly state the annual interest rate. On February 26, 1777, Congress changed the annual interest rate to 6 percent on all future borrowings and applied that rate retrospectively to all past borrowings, i.e., to all loan office certificates issued regardless of the interest rate printed on them (*JCC* 7:158). This resolution came soon enough for the certificates of authorization no. 3 to have the new 6 percent annual interest rate preprinted on them.

b The initial authorizations (no. 1, no. 2, and no. 3) did not indicate in what medium interest would be paid, though it was presumed that it would be Continental dollars. On September 9 and 10, 1777, Congress made interest payments on all prior and future loan office certificates issued before March 1, 1778, to be paid in bills of exchange drawn on the United States commissioners in Paris at a rate of five French *livres* for every Spanish milled silver dollar due in interest, or in Continental dollars, at the borrower's option. The resolution presumes that the nominal dollar interest arising from loan office certificates, whose principal was expressed in Continental dollars, would be paid in Spanish silver dollars.

c The resolution explicitly states a 4 percent annual interest rate on these loan office certificates. Whether the 6 percent annual interest rate mandated in the resolutions of September 9 and 10, 1777, and May 2, 1778, that said "any resolution to the contrary" overrode this stated 4 percent annual interest is unclear.

d On November 19, 1778, Congress directed that only bills of credit that have been emitted by Congress (Continental dollars) be received for loan office certificates, thus effectively removing the acceptability of state bills of credit for loan office certificates (*JCC* 12:1147).

e Issued in $1,000 denominations and to be of the same tenor and date as the immediately prior authorization (no. 6). To be swapped for certificates of lower denominations still on hand and unlent. These lower-denomination certificates were to "be retained in the hands of the treasurer of loans until the further orders of Congress" (*JCC* 14:523). Further orders came on July 2, 1779 (*JCC* 14:798–99). See note h.

f The borrower could continue the principal at interest indefinitely as long as the whole amount of Continental dollars currently circulating exceeded the amount circulating at the time the loan was made. The annual interest rate was set at 6 percent but would be raised in proportion to the proportional increase in the quantity of Continental dollars outstanding between the time the loan was made and when the interest payment was due (*JCC* 14:784–85).

g The indexed interest rate adjustment adopted in authorization no. 8 on June 29, 1779 (see note f), was retrospectively applied to all loans made on or after March 1, 1778, i.e., to all loans where interest was paid in Continental dollars. On October 6, 1779, Congress extended this interest-rate adjustment to all loans taken out on or before March 1, 1780. See *JCC* (14:784–85; 15:1148); Smith (1976–94, 14:51–52); appendix C, table C.1 from *Early American imprints* (1983, microfiche S 269, nos. 16634, 16635; "U.S. Board of Treasury, 1779, A Table of First Year's Interest. Philadelphia, 1779" and "U.S. Board of Treasury, 1779. Table of the Sums Actually in Circulation. Philadelphia, 3 December 1779," respectively).

h On July 2, 1779, Congress ordered all unused (unlent) loan office certificates from prior authorizations to be used to meet the $20 million required to be borrowed by authorization no. 8. On April 4, 1780, Congress authorized the printing of $4,800,000 new loan office certificates to meet what was required by authorization no. 8. How much of the rest of this authorization entailed printing new loan office certificates and how much entailed using leftover (unlent) certificates from prior authorizations is unknown. See *JCC* (14:798–99; 16:392). The accounting of lent and unlent certificates by March 3, 1783, in table 8.2 indicates that a total of $71,220,600 certificates had been printed in the borrow-and-spend category, and an extra $63,000 certificates had been printed and added to the lottery-payoff category, which in turn was placed here in the borrow-and-spend category total. This accounting implies that $2,716,400 certificates authorized were not in fact printed. Part of this amount was likely the certificates unused from prior authorizations that were then applied to fulfilling authorization no. 8, thus obviating the need to print the full authorized amount of $20,000,000.

i The total lottery pay out in loan office certificates was reported to be $1,763,000 by March 3, 1783, see table 8.2. The extra $63,000 was assumed taken from the left over and unlent loan office certificates on hand. That number is used to calculate (added to) the lower number in the totals reported.

j Figure 8.1 indicates a maturity date of December 1, 1781.

As with Continental dollars, a loan office certificate also had the date of its authorizing legislation preprinted on it. Thus, the public could always determine the unique features of the given loan office certificate, and how it differed from Continental dollars and other loan office certificates, by consulting the authorizing legislation.

Table 8.1 lists the separate congressional authorizations of loan office certificates along with the legislated features of their structural design. Ten separate authorizations were made, the first in October 1776 and the last in January 1781. The primary purpose of these authorizations was to borrow and spend Continental dollars—authorizations nos. 1–4 and 6–7. The last borrow-and-spend authorization was in June 1779. Authorizations no. 5, in May 1778, and nos. 9 and 10, in October 1779 and January 1781, respectively, were used to pay off lottery winners.[1] Annual interest rates were initially set at 4 percent but were raised to 6 percent in 1777 and made retrospective for all past borrowings; that was the rate for all future borrowings using loan office certificates. The maturity date was set at three years in authorization no. 1 in October 1776. It was left unstated in future authorizations until it was restated as three years in authorization no. 8 in June 1779. Holders were allowed to continue holding and accruing annual interest on their certificates past the maturity date.

The medium in which annual interest was to be paid went unstated in the first three authorizations, as well as in the last six authorizations. It is presumed the intention was that interest would be paid in Continental dollars. Congress attempted to have authorization no. 4, and then, retrospectively, authorizations nos. 1–3, pay annual interest in specie via bills of exchange drawn on the United States commissioners in Paris. To what extent annual interest payments were actually made, if any, and in what medium is unclear. The accumulation of interest arrears appears to have been common.

What could be borrowed in authorizations nos. 2–5 was not exclusively Continental dollars. Authorization no. 2 explicitly allowed state bills of credit (state paper monies) to be borrowed as well, and while authorizations nos. 3–5 did not explicitly list what could be borrowed, it may have been understood as continuing what was allowed in authorization no. 2. Not until authorization no. 6 in February 1779, and continuing for all authorizations thereafter, was borrowing restricted to Continental dollars only, as was the case for authorization no. 1. Authorizations nos. 2–5 totaled $25,250,000. It is currently unknown what share of this amount was borrowed in Continental dollars as opposed to state paper monies. This observation makes the summed total borrowings in table 8.1 biased high in terms of just Continental dollars.

Why Congress instituted a system to borrow already-spent Continental dollars rather than just printing more new Continental dollars as a revenue source was never clearly articulated. Based on the comments of some congressmen, there was a faction that felt that borrowing already-spent Continental dollars rather than issuing more new ones would have a salutary effect on the value of the currency, arresting or at least retarding its decline in value. In crude quantity-theoretic terms, in which some congressmen thought (see chap. 3 and Grubb 2012b), borrowing already-spent Continental dollars and then spending them did not augment the Continental dollar money supply (that is, when not counting loan office certificates as Continental dollars per se) and so would not affect prices or cause the Continental dollar to depreciate further. That borrowing and spending Continental dollars likely increased their velocity of circulation and so affected prices in the quantity-theoretic formula (driving prices up) was something apparently not addressed by congressmen.

A similar logic comes from thinking of the Continental dollar as a zero-coupon bond with fiscally credible redemption maturity dates with operative legal-tender laws (see chaps. 1, 2, 5, 10, and 12). Each new emission of Continental dollars before any redemptions started meant that the expected redemption of the average Continental dollar in circulation was necessarily pushed further into the future, thus lowering the present value of all Continental dollars in circulation. Borrowing and spending Continental dollars via loan office certificates did not alter or elongate the redemption structure. As long as loan office certificates did not negatively affect the government's ability to redeem Continental dollars or the public's ability to pay the taxes necessary to pay off the loan office certificates at their maturity, the value of Continental dollars would be maintained at current present-value levels.

Whether the added taxes needed to pay the annual interest and then repay the principal on loan office certificates were within the fiscally credible feasible set was not addressed by congressmen. Table 8.2 lists the issuances of loan office certificates by state through March 3, 1783, as well as the approximate per-white-capita amount of these certificates. It indicates that the taxes needed to pay off these certificates at their three-year maturity dates, let alone covering the annual interest payments, when added to the taxes needed to redeem Continental dollars as expected, went well beyond what was historically feasible and so was not fiscally credible (see chap. 1 and table 10.1). Thus, the move by Congress to borrow via loan office certificates helped crash the Continental dollar system by destroying its fiscal credibility regarding expected future redemptions at face value in the years after 1779. The addition of the loan office certificate

TABLE 8.2 Loan office certificates issued for Continental dollars by state to March 3, 1783

State	Face value: beginning–Feb. 28, 1778	Face value: Mar. 1, 1778–Sept. 10, 1779	Face value: Sept. 10, 1779–Dec. 31, 1779[a]	Face value: Dec. 31, 1779–Sept. 30, 1780[b]	Face value: cumulative total as of Nov. 10, 1780[b]	Face value: Nov. 10, 1780–Mar. 3, 1783[m]	Face value: cumulative total as of Mar. 3, 1783[n]	Residual on hand and unlent[o]
New Hampshire	$350,000	$445,717	$34,283	$142,700	$972,700	$0	$972,700	$602,300
Per white capita	$4.01	$5.11	$.039	$1.64	$10.63	$0.00	$10.63	$6.90
Massachusetts	2,068,200	3,075,000	1,115,200	987,700 [1,287,700]	7,246,100 [7,546,100]	846,807 [546,807]	8,092,907	50,893
Per white capita	6.71	0.98	3.57	3.16–4.12	23.19–24.15	1.75–2.71	25.90	0.16
Rhode Island	608,846	857,841	236,013	164,000[c]	1,866,700[c]	100	1,866,800	1,109,500
Per white capita	12.11	17.06	4.69	3.26	37.13	0.00	37.13	22.07
Connecticut	947,375	2,286,600	551,025	508,200	4,293,200	0	4,293,200	250,300
Per white capita	4.72	11.39	2.74	2.53	21.38	0.00	21.38	1.25
New York	850,000	1,660,723	369,277[d]	625,800[e]	3,505,800[c]	4,000	3,509,800	851,200
Per white capita	3.59	7.01	1.56	2.64	14.79	1.69	14.81	3.59
New Jersey	370,900	1,298,724	2,708,276[f]	—	4,377,900[f]	172,000	4,549,900	193,600
Per white capita	2.87	10.05	20.97	—	33.89	1.33	35.22	1.50
Pennsylvania	2,074,400	10,316,300	4,739,300	9,281,600[g]	26,411,600[g]	2,110,900	28,522,500	311,800
Per white capita	6.49	32.29	14.84	29.05	82.68	6.61	89.29	0.98
Delaware	39,176	221,731	142,793	92,200[f] [107,700]	495,900[f] [511,400]	41,100 [25,600]	537,000	273,500
Per white capita	0.92	5.23	3.37	2.18–2.54	11.70–12.06	0.60–0.97	12.67	6.45
Maryland	93,600	2,691,400	273,400	807,900	3,866,300	127,000	3,993,300	448,900
Per white capita	0.57	16.32	1.66	4.90	23.44	0.77	24.21	2.72
Virginia	57,000	3,068,200	-275,100[h]	57,200[i]	2,907,300[h] [3,182,400]	52,500 [-222,600][h]	2,959,800	477,200

Per white capita	0.18	9.67	?	0.18	9.16–10.03	0.00–0.17	9.32	1.50
North Carolina	33,700	33,000	—	—	66,700[j] [740,000] [756,000]	1,143,100 [469,800] [453,800]	1,209,800	474,700
Per white capita	0.19	0.18			0.37–4.22	2.53–6.38	6.75	2.65
South Carolina	52,000	31,250	3,181,208[k]		3,264,458	581,947	3,846,405	720,595
Per white capita	0.63	0.38	38.33		39.33	7.01	46.34	8.68
Georgia	—	—	—	—	—	951,000	951,000	151,000
Per white capita		—	—			26.99	26.99	4.28
Total sum	$7,545,197	$25,986,486	$13,075,675	$12,667,300	$59,229,658[l]	$6,075,454[m]	$65,305,112	$5,915,488
Per white capita	$3.50	$12.04	$6.06	$5.87	$27.44	$2.81	$30.25	$2.74
Maximum Alternative totals		[$26,188,909]	$13,350,775	$12,982,800	$60,509,558[l]	$4,795,554		
Per white capita		$12.13	$6.18	$6.01	$28.03	$2.22		
Lottery loan office certificates issued							$1,763,000	
Per white capita							$0.82	
Grand total for all loan office certificates issued or paid out							$67,068,112	
per white capita							$31.07	
Grand total of all loan office certificates printed[p]							$72,983,600	
Per white capita							$33.81	

continues

TABLE 8.2 (continued)

Source: Carter, Gartner, Haines, Olmstead, Sutch, and Wright (2006, 5:652); Ferguson et al. (1973–99, 7:546–47); PCC (microfilm 247, reel 146, item 136, "Reports of the Board of Treasury, 1776–1781, vol. 3, 1779"; microfiche 247, reel 41, item 34, "Reports of a Committee Appointed to State the Public Debt and Estimates of Expenses, with Related Papers 1779–1781", no. 143 and no. 145); table 8.1.

Notes: Expressed in nominal Continental dollar values (face value). The numbers in brackets are the totals reported in the PCC sources when they differed from the summation of the component parts reported in that source. Since certificates were issued in hundred-dollar units, the below-one-hundred numbers reported do not make sense. They are either recording errors or represent the total after deductions were made for things such as commissioner fees. Population numbers are for 1780. The Vermont population is included in that for New York, and the Maine population is included in that for Massachusetts.

a The total in this column is derived by taking the total reported in the PCC sources for the opening of the loan office to the date listed and then subtracting the amount reported in the prior two columns.

b While the PCC source states November 10, 1780, as its reporting date, the individual state returns listed in the source actually end between July 31, 1780, and October 31, 1780. See notes c–k.

c Runs through July 31, 1780.

d Through October 31, 1779.

e From November 2, 1779, through July 31, 1780.

f Runs through August 31, 1780.

g Runs through October 31, 1780.

h Runs through June 30, 1780. The total reported for this period is less that that reported in the prior two columns, which are subcomponents of this estimate. Thus the value is entered here as a negative number to indicate the accounting discrepancy; see note a. The sum of the positive row values, $3,182,400, is more than that reported in the PCC source for the Total as of Nov. 10, 1780 column by $275,100, thus explaining the negative entry of that amount in the Sept. 10–Dec. 31, 1779 column for Virginia. This accounting discrepancy carries through and explains the negative entry in brackets in the Nov. 10, 1780–Mar. 3, 1783 column for Virginia.

i Ran from June 30, 1780, through September 30, 1780.

j The PCC source reports no returns after September 10, 1779, but the total reported [740,000] is more than the reported sums from the first two columns through September 10, 1779, which in turn is less than the subcomponent parts reported for that total [756,000].

k Runs through May 6, 1780.

l The PCC source reported a grand total as of November 10, 1780, of $60,263,458. The row values do not sum to the last column total owing to the accounting adjustments explained in notes a–k. The total loan office debt was reported to be $60,558,444 as of February 16, 1781 (JCC 19:161–62).

m Derived by subtracting the cumulative total reported on March 3, 1783, from the cumulative total reported as of November 10, 1780. The column does not sum to the total reported due to accounting adjustments; see note l.

n From a report delivered to Congress by Robert Morris, Superintendent of Finances, on March 10, 1783, based on data gathered by Joseph Nourse, Registrar of the Treasury through March 3, 1783 (Ferguson et al. 1973–99, 7:543–48).

o Derived by subtracting the amount in the column Nov. 10, 1780–Mar. 3, 1783 from the amount listed in table 8.1. The sum in brackets in the column Nov. 10, 1780–Mar. 3, 1783 is used for Massachusetts, Delaware, and North Carolina, but not for Virginia. The bracketed numbers are the more accurate and internally consistent numbers, except for Virginia. See note h.

p Sums the immediately prior row with the last entry in the last column.

system may have been pushed by congressmen like James Duane (see chap. 1), who thought only in crude quantity-theoretic terms and so did not see the need for a fiscally credible redemption tax structure based on historically feasible taxing levels.

Finally, while Congress was borrowing Continental dollars that had already been put into circulation, it continued to emit new Continental dollars through 1779, thus adding to the stock in circulation (compare table 1.1 with table 8.1). Under legal-tender laws, new emissions that added to the stock already in circulation reduced the present value of all Continental dollars outstanding, whether evaluated in quantity-theoretic terms or as zero-coupon bonds under rational bond pricing (see chaps. 10 and 11). This created a problem for paying back the principal of loan office certificates at their maturity dates. While paying annual interest on loan office certificates meant that they did not suffer a loss of value owing to time-discounting, as Continental dollars did, the repayment of principal at maturity would likely be in Continental dollars that had a lower present value than did the Continental dollars initially borrowed.

By June 1779 Congress appears to have recognized that given the continuing decline in the value of the Continental dollar (see chap. 11), citizens were reluctant to loan Continental dollars to Congress via loan office certificates. If the value of the principal expressed in Continental dollars when lent was much higher than the expected value of that principal expressed in Continental dollars when repaid at a later date, citizens would suffer a substantial loss of principal when buying and holding loan office certificates. Therefore, they would be reluctant to loan Continental dollars to Congress via this mechanism unless something was done to counter the expected loss.

Congress's last authorization for borrowing Continental dollars via loan office certificates for the purpose of "borrow and spend" was for 20 million on June 29, 1779 (see table 8.1). With this authorization, Congress also attempted to counter the loss lenders expected by (1) allowing holders of loan office certificates to continue to hold them and collect annual interest past the three-year maturity date as long as the amount of Continental dollars in circulation was greater than at the time the loan office certificate was purchased and (2) increasing the annual interest earned on all loan office certificates issued after February 1778 "in proportion to the increase of the sum of continental paper money which may be in circulation after the date of such loans respectively" (*JCC* 14:783–85). This process amounted to an indexing of loaned values to changes in the amount of Continental dollars outstanding.

Whether interpreted in quantity-theoretic terms or as zero-coupon bonds under rational bond pricing, increases in the quantity of Continental dollars outstanding caused a reduction in the Continental dollar's current real value. Being allowed to not require repayment of the loan office certificate's principal before the quantity of Continental dollars outstanding returned to the amount when the loan was originally made implies repayment of principal at a comparable real value. Requiring the annual interest earned to increase in proportion to the increase in the amount of Continental dollars outstanding is a Fisher-type equation compensation where the nominal interest rate is set equal to the real rate (6 percent) plus the inflation rate when paid in the money affected.

As far as can be determined, these conditions in the June 29, 1779, authorization of loan office certificates were never implemented or made operational. No record of payments that used this indexing or linking of loan office certificate interest rates to inflation rates could be found. Citizens could hold their certificates past the stated maturity date and continue to collect annual interest (or accumulated interest arrears), but that condition was more a default outcome of the government's inability to meet scheduled payments of either interest or principal through the mid-1780s. Interest arrears seem to have just accumulated (Grubb 2007a).

The June 29, 1779, authorization also had a caveat attached to the interest-rate indexing scheme stating, "until some more accurate standard of value can be devised" (*JCC* 14:784). This more accurate standard of value was devised on June 28, 1780, and expressed in the form of a depreciation table (*JCC* 17:567–69). Depreciation tables replaced the June 29, 1779, indexing scheme for calculating compensation due loan office certificate holders. That is why no record of the indexing scheme being implemented as laid out on June 29, 1779, can be found—depreciation tables supplanted it. Depreciation tables were now used to adjust the payoff value between the borrowing date and repayment date for both principal and interest combined, so that what was repaid was comparable in present value to the principal borrowed and interest owed. Depreciation tables as constructed still relied on some proportional link to changes in the amount of Continental dollars outstanding in their construction, just like what the June 29, 1779, indexing scheme had.

Scholars over the last 230 years have used these depreciation tables as a measure of the market value of Continental dollars. These tables, however, do not measure the current value of the Continental dollar per se in a continuous way; they were intended only to establish what a compensated repayment of loan office certificate principal would be. Congress explicitly stated as much when creating its depreciation table on June 28, 1780: it listed six exchange-rate points between 1777 and 1780 and ordered that the depreciation table run its calculations in "geometric proportion to time, from period to period" (chap. 11; *JCC* 17:567–69).

None of the depreciation tables—those from Congress, from the various states, and reported by Thomas Jefferson—start before 1777 (Boyd 1953–55, 10:42–43; Bullock 1895: 135; *JCC* 17:567–69; *Pennsylvania Gazette* July 19, 1780; United States Congress 1834, 2:2243–51). That fact is consistent with loan office certificates not being sold before 1777. These depreciation tables also vary considerably from source to source. Why they do is unclear, but it would be consistent with political motivations affecting the values chosen to be in the depreciation tables rather than the tables reflecting true market values. Whether accrued-interest payments are factored into these depreciation tables is also unclear. Overall, these depreciation tables show a slower and less extreme decline in the value of the Continental dollar than that gleaned from price indices in Continental dollars (see fig. 11.1).

In total, Congress borrowed and respent approximately $67,068,112 Continental dollars (see table 8.2). This is a biased-high estimate, as some unknown portion of the borrowings in authorizations nos. 2–5 may be in state paper monies. This means that Congress borrowed and respent roughly one-third of all the net new Continental dollars it had initially emitted through direct spending out of the Continental Treasury.

Should Loan Office Certificates Be Counted as Continental Dollars?

The case for counting loan office certificates as just more new Continental dollars is best made in the two initial quotes, one by Congressman Thomas Burke and the other by James Madison, at the start of this chapter. If we so count them as new Continental dollars, then the total emissions and amounts outstanding over time of Continental dollars, as shown in table 1.1 and appendix A, have to be augmented. It is difficult to do so precisely, given the current data. There are inconsistencies in the loan office certificate data reported. The timing when certificates were actually put into circulation and then redeemed and pulled out of circulation cannot be easily pinned down. Some of this is revealed in the notes to tables 8.1

and 8.2, where alternative estimates and inconsistencies are highlighted. Some of this is due to the fact that loan office certificates were not emitted like Continental dollars out of Congress's Continental Treasury, but were provided to the states that ran the loan programs. Loan office certificates were a passive emission vehicle in that they depended on the public's willingness, solely at the public's volition, to buy loan office certificates. As such, the public determined both the amount and the timing of such lending. Why the amounts of loan office certificates sent to each state to be loaned out by that state varied across states is unclear (see table 8.2).

Not all loan office certificates authorized, printed, and provided to the states were used. Between $9.5 and $11 million worth of certificates remained unlent by November 1780, and approximately $6 million remained unlent by March 1783 (see tables 8.2 and 8.3). Thus, if loan office certificates are considered to be just more Continental dollars, the cumulative total of net new Continental dollars ever placed in public hands would be $267,058,107. This total is composed of $199,989,995 in Continental dollars and $67,068,112 in loan office certificates (see tables 1.1, 8.2, and A.1).

Charting the amount of combined Continental dollars and loan office certificates in public circulation over time is hard to pin down because information on exactly when loan office certificates were lent and when loan office certificates were redeemed is currently lacking. The best that can be done is three spot estimates before the start of 1780 using the first three columns in table 8.2. These three dates are before either Continental dollars or loan office certificates were redeemed and removed from circulation. Combining the cumulative total of Continental dollars by a given date from table A.1 with the cumulative total of loan office certificates lent by that same given date from table 8.2 yields the following amounts: $50,482,417 at the end of February 1778; $185,925,361 by September 10, 1779; and $246,597,353 by the end of 1779. The last number assumes no loan office certificates from authorization no. 1 (see table 8.1) were yet redeemed.

On the other hand, this may all be irrelevant: the case for not counting loan office certificates as just more Continental dollars is strong and argues against augmenting the Continental dollar money supply with loan office certificate totals. First, no scholar over the last 230 years has counted loan office certificates as part of the Continental dollar total, with the possible exception of Gouge (1833, pt. 2:25) and Elliot (1843: 8, 11), who seem to count everything as Continental dollars. Second, loan office certificates were never made a legal tender by Congress nor, as far as I can determine, by any state.

TABLE 8.3 **Loan office certificates still on hand and unlent by state as of November 10, 1780**

State	As of	Total nominal (face) value	Per white capita	As a percentage of total certificates lent and remaining on hand[b]
New Hampshire	Sept. 30, 1780	$602,300	6.90	39.37%
Massachusetts	Sept. 30, 1780	597,700	1.91	7.34
Rhode Island	July 31, 1780	1,109,600	22.07	37.28
Connecticut	Aug. 31, 1780	250,300	1.25	5.51
New York	July 31, 1780	855,200	3.61	19.61
New Jersey	Aug. 31, 1780	368,600	2.85	7.77
Pennsylvania	Oct. 31, 1780	2,422,700	7.58	8.40
Delaware	Aug. 31, 1780	299,100	7.06	36.90
Maryland	Sept. 30, 1780	575,900	3.49	12.96
Virginia	Sept. 30, 1780	529,700	1.67	14.27
North Carolina	Sept. 10, 1779	628,000	3.51	45.38
	Nov. 10, 1780	(306,500)[a]	(5.22)[a]	(55.28)
South Carolina	May 6, 1780	1,302,542	15.69	28.52
Georgia	No returns reported	(1,102,000)[a]	(31.27)[a]	(100.00)
Total		$9,541,642)	4.42	13.62
		($10,950,142)[a]	(5.07)[a]	(15.32)

Source: Carter, Gartner, Haines, Olmstead, Sutch, and Wright (2006, 5:652); *PCC* (microfilm 247, reel 41, item 34, "Reports of a Committee Appointed to State the Public Debt and Estimates of Expenses, with Related Papers 1779–1781," no. 143 and no. 145), table 8.2.

Notes: Expressed in Continental dollars at face value. The numbers in brackets are the totals reported in the source when they differed from the summation of the component parts reported in the source. Since certificates were issued in hundred-dollar units, the below-one-hundred numbers reported do not make sense. They are either recording errors or represent the total after deductions were made for things such as commissioner fees. Population numbers are for 1780. Vermont population is included in that for New York and Maine population is included in that for Massachusetts.

[a] These are the values of the certificates sent to these respective states, but because no returns had been submitted by November 10, 1780, what portion had been loaned and what portion remained on hand was unknown. These values are added into the totals and the per white capita and percentage estimates reported in parentheses. For North Carolina that entails summing the two entries reported in the "Total nominal (face) value" column.

[b] Uses the largest total for each state from table 8.2, last column.

Third, despite Madison's comment at the start of this chapter, loan office certificates were issued only in extraordinarily large denominations. Given that loan office certificates paid the going interest rate, they would not suffer diminished present value due to time-discounting. Using depreciation tables to repay principal held that value in check from declining, so the denomination of a loan office certificate is approximately its current present value. As such, loan office certificates are like modern-day Treasury bonds, which are not counted as part of the US dollar money supply.

Tables B.4 and B.5 provide the denominational structure of loan office certificates. The smallest was $200, which would be equivalent to walking around today with a $6,200 bill in your pocket (in 2012 US dollars). Such a bill would not be easy to use as a medium of exchange even if change was given in other state or Continental monies. The typical loan office certificate (the mode) was $500 in units and $1,000 in value. These are equivalent to a $15,500 and $31,000 bill, respectively, in 2012 US dollars. If they traded at all it could only be among wealthy individuals as speculative investment vehicles. They could not function as a medium of exchange in the economy.

Finally, table 8.1 shows that most loan office certificates issued after 1778 were not unrestricted bearer bonds. Their transferability was legally unclear. Add to that the fact that, unlike a Continental dollar, a loan office certificate had the name of the initial lender or payee placed on it (see fig. 8.1). This fact raises the specter that if the certificate was transferred or used as a means of payment in the economy, the initial lender might be legally on the hook to honor the repayment of the principal on the certificate at that certificate's maturity date if the government defaulted on its redemption. More research is needed to better sort this out.

All these factors mitigate against considering loan office certificates as just more Continental dollars. I will follow the prior literature in not so counting them in the rest of the book. But I wanted future scholars to see the effect of counting them as just more Continental dollars and to provide as much information as I could for future scholars to explore the issue further if desired.

Loan Office Certificates and Congressional Spending

Whether or not loan office certificates are counted as just more Continental dollars, they were part of the revenue-generation process that fed congressional spending. The amounts in table 8.2 confirm that the domestic interest-bearing loans listed in table 6.5 (using the Knox report) were in fact loan office certificates. While the numbers in the two reports, table 8.2 and table 6.5, for domestic loans do not match up exactly in terms of dates, they are close. For the period prior to March 1778, table 8.2 reports only 2.7 percent more loans than does table 6.5. For the period March 1778–September 1779, the total from table 6.5 is within the range estimate in table 8.2 for those dates. The total for September 1779–March 1780 in table 6.5 is only four percentage points different from the amount in table 8.3 for January–October 1780.

In terms of accounting for the residual deficit in table 6.5, the extra loan office certificates reported in table 8.3 versus table 6.5 would only reduce that deficit in 1779, as reported in table 6.5, by about 6 percent. Thus, almost all the residual deficit reported in table 6.5 had to be made up by some method than through loan office certificates. While the numbers in chapters 6 and 8 cannot be made to exactly match, they are close enough to give confidence to the analysis and approximate numbers reported in both chapters. The lack of detailed evidence on loan office certificates, especially on the exact timing of their issue and redemption, makes a more exacting comparison impossible and likely accounts for the discrepancies.

Finally, how many loan office certificates were redeemed at their maturity date or shortly thereafter can be approximated through 1782. Edwin Perkins (1994: 213) and Donald Swanson (1963: 48) report that the domestic interest-bearing debt in 1782 was approximately $27 million. Taking the total amount of loan office certificates issued—$67,068,112—from table 8.2, and subtracting that $27 million yields about $40 million that are implied to have been redeemed and retired from circulation. The total amount that would have come to maturity by the end of 1782, assuming all matured in three years (see table 8.1), would have been all those issued and outstanding by the end of 1779. That total from table 8.2 is $46,607,358. This implies that roughly 86 percent of the loan office certificates that had matured by the end of 1782 had been redeemed (paid off). That percentage represents a surprising success for this part of the public finance exercise, especially given that it is thought that no principal or interest was paid on the remaining outstanding domestic loans thereafter until they were absorbed by the 1790 Funding Act (Grubb 2007a).[2] It also explains the need for the depreciation tables that were generated by the states and Congress in the pre-1783 period but were not then extended into the post-1782 period. If governments were not redeeming loan office certificates, no depreciation tables to adjust the present value of the principal payoffs would be needed. This estimate is tentative, and future research is needed to establish this outcome with more certainly.

Direct Loans Congress Requested from the States

In an effort to balance the congressional budget late in the war in ways other than issuing more Continental dollars and loan office certificates, Congress asked the states to loan Continental dollars directly to Congress so it could respend them. The states were asked to impose taxes on their citizens to raise this money and then directly loan that tax revenue to Congress, and were given individual loan quotas to fill.[3] The total amount of loans requested were a 5 million Continental dollar loan requested on November 22, 1777, a 45 million Continental dollar loan requested on May 21, 1779, and a 15 million Continental dollar loan requested on October 6–7, 1779 (*JCC* 8:650, 731; 9:953–58; 14:626; 15:1147–50; 16:263).

If these amounts were actually loaned by the states to Congress, they would cover the residual deficit estimated in table 6.5 for the years 1779 and 1780. The amounts the states remitted as loans, however, and when they were remitted, is not exactly clear. Little evidence of compliance with these loan requests can be found. The states may have ignored them because the per capita per year taxes needed to comply with these loan requests in Continental dollars at their face value, around $33, were over eighty times higher than what had been historically feasible, especially when added to the other taxes that would be required to remit state quotas of Continental dollars to the Continental Treasury to be burned, to pay off loan office certificates, and to cover other state-specific spending obligations (see table 10.1). The lack of state compliance with these loan requests is implied by the language used in the remittance request made on March 18, 1780 (see chap. 14).

Overall, the topic of loan office certificates and direct state loans to Congress calls out for deeper research to better account for the timing in the issuance and redemption of the certificates, as well as the type and timing of interest payments, and in the amount and timing of direct state loans made to Congress. We also need a better understanding of how loan office certificates were used by the public—as money or as just investments. Finally, we need to understand the public finance role of the certificates and direct state loans to Congress better. Because each state ran its own loan office for lending the certificates sent it by Congress and levied its own taxes to raise money to loan to Congress, it may take a state-by-state research effort to sort it out better. I hope future scholars will take up the task.

PART II

Value and Performance

CHAPTER NINE

Modeling Value

Part II addresses the value and performance of the Continental dollar over time. To measure its value and performance, we must first understand how to conceptualize its role as a money in revolutionary America. This conceptualization will then allow the construction of a proper way to capture its value and performance as a money. This exercise is particularly important for understanding the Continental dollar because the Continental dollar was emitted into a multimoney environment, namely an environment where many alternative transacting media existed.[1] Choice regarding money usage existed. Individual states issued their own separate paper monies that mediated local exchange, which, along with some foreign specie coins, commodities, such as tobacco, and book credits, were also used to mediate exchange. Measuring the money value of the Continental dollar must be done in a way that takes into account these money alternatives.[2]

What Is Money and What Is Not Money?

To measure the value of money and evaluate its performance, we first need to determine what is and is not money. This is a deeply perplexing problem and one that economists answer poorly. Surprisingly, economists do not use the tools of economics to independently determine what is and is not money. They just assume X is money and Z is not money in their models and then assume for empirical applications that trades in the economy are sufficiently transacted in X so that X captures the relational patterns of behavior in the theory corresponding to money.[3]

Other than just assuming money, economists often define money as anything and everything, such as defining money as anything that changes hands but is not then directly consumed but instead is eventually passed on in trade for something else. Such a concept is too broad to be useful. Or they fall back on the pre-nineteenth-century methodology of using categorization by unweighted characteristics to evaluate what is money—characteristics such as portability, divisibility, storability, countability, identifiability, and so on. Or they focus on functionality characteristics to evaluate what is money, such as store of value, medium of exchange, and unit of account. None of these approaches consistently and coherently determines what is and is not money.

The problem lies in how the general public, as well as economists, talks about money. It is a problem of ontology and epistemology. As humans, we have come to casually talk about a money as a particular "thing," namely, a physical object identified by our senses. Money, in various economies, is a coin, a tobacco leaf, a length of blue cloth, a conch shell, a beaver pelt, a paper bill of credit, a banknote, and so on. But it is always identified as a particular thing—a physical object. Yet that thing or physical object, whatever it is, is just the carrier of the money value and not identical with money itself. If any of the money things listed above were not a money, they would still have real value. The coin can be used as an ornament, the tobacco leaf can be smoked, the length of blue cloth can be used for clothing, the beaver pelt can be made into a hat, the bill of credit and the banknote can be used as a legal claim to a future amount of real assets or outside money such as Spanish silver dollars, and so on. The general conflation of money value with the money "thing," namely with the physical object carrying the money value, creates incoherence in our ability to measure the value of money and evaluate the performance of the money-carrying object.

I decompose the money thing into its non-money real goods or real asset value, namely what its real value is when not a money, and its money value. I refer to this money-value portion of the money thing as the object's "moneyness" to distinguish it from the casual usage of the term "money" by the general public. A heuristic conception of this decomposition exercise is displayed in figure 9.1. This decomposition exercise uses

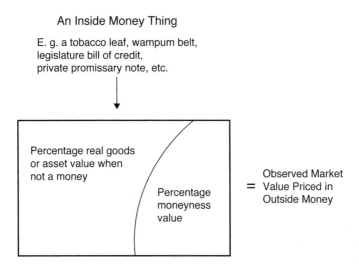

FIGURE 9.1. Counterfactual decomposition approach to measuring moneyness value

Note: In the evaluation of legislature-emitted bills of credit in eqs. 9.1 and 9.2, MEV = observed market value priced in outside money like Spanish silver dollars, $(APV - RD)$ = percentage of real goods or asset value when the bill of credit is not a money, and TP = percentage moneyness value.

the core tools of economics to define what money (moneyness) is. These tools are opportunity cost and counterfactual analysis. Counterfactual analysis asks, if the money thing in question were not a money, what would its real goods or real asset value be? A counterfactual exercise involves estimating values from a hypothetical world, but not just any hypothetical world. The hypothetical world to be measured is determined by opportunity cost, namely identifying the next best non-money use of the money thing in question and estimating that next best non-money value.

Opportunity cost also plays a role in conceptualizing what the moneyness portion of the money thing is. The choice to use the particular money thing as a transacting medium, compared with the next best alternative thing that can also be a carrier of value, means that there must be some convenience value in using that particular money thing over its next best alternative. It is that gap in value that is what money value is, and what I would claim is all that money actually is. I call that gap the transaction premium (TP) or moneyness value attached to the money thing.

While defining money as a value rather than as a thing may seem strange at first, economists should embrace such a definition, as economics defines many important concepts in value terms rather than in physical-object terms.

For example, an accountant defines profits as a thing, such as a physical pile of cash. Economists, however, define profits as that accountant's pile of cash minus the hypothetical pile of cash that could have been made in the next best pursuit. Opportunity cost and counterfactual estimation are used by economists to define profits. As such, profits are no longer a thing per se, but instead must be an estimated value. There is no reason money should not be defined the same way using the same economic tools. Just as it seems impossible to get the general public to conceptualize profits as an economist does, rather than as an accountant does, the public will likely never change how they talk about money as being this thing or that thing, as opposed to a value measure. But to succeed analytically it is useful to embrace measuring money as a value separate from the thing carrying that value.

Economists define profits as a value using opportunity cost and counterfactual analysis in order to determine what activity will be chosen. It only takes an unperceptively small positive economic profit to induce an actor to shift to that activity. The same outcome occurs when defining money as the transaction-premium portion of the money thing. It takes only an imperceptibly small positive transaction premium to lead traders to select that money thing as the primary or dominant medium of exchange. What is currently being used as the primary or dominant medium of exchange does not necessarily imply that it must have a large moneyness or transaction-premium value. The transaction premium just has to be positive, and it also has to be positive for it to be money as defined here. As such, we cannot infer the value of money or moneyness from the fact that a particular money thing serves as the dominant medium of exchange. We need a separate decomposition estimation exercise.

Conceptualizing money as a value allows us a clearer and more coherent way to discuss what a pure fiat money is, what a pure barter exchange is, what a ubiquitous barter good is, and what a commodity money is. If the money thing has no value when it is not a money, then it is a pure fiat money. All of its value, 100 percent, is moneyness value or transaction premium. By contrast, if the money thing has the same value as when it is not a money, then it is a pure barter good. All its value, 100 percent, is real goods or real asset value. A ubiquitous barter good would then be a good that is often used to mediate exchange but that has no transaction premium. It is no better to use to transact and consummate exchanges than the next best alternative barter good.[4] A commodity money or asset money is one where only some portion of its value, less than 100 percent, remains when it is not a money. Estimating that amount determines how much of the commodity money thing is moneyness value and how much is real barter goods value.

Embedded in this definition of money as a transaction-premium value is a trader's faith that subsequent traders will continue to see the object as a more convenient transacting medium than the next best alternative. It is that expected ongoing convenience in transacting compared with using the next best alternative that generates a willingness to pay for the money object over and above its non-money value—its transaction premium amount. Legal-tender laws, and the designation by the government in what media taxes can be paid, contribute to that faith. Who is the guarantor, and their reputation for following through on their guarantee, of the real goods or real asset portion of the money object also affect that faith. Relatively risky real goods and relatively risky real assets are unlikely to possess moneyness value. Guarantors who are private individuals, such as for promissory notes or bills of exchange, may have occasioned less faith in the subsequent moneyness value of the money object than guarantors who had governmental power and law backing them.

This decomposition approach to defining money is based on relative measurement. As such, a baseline value is needed against which any prospective inside money can be measured. I assume, but do not systematically estimate, that specie coins had moneyness value when used in international transactions. The act of minting coins imbued gold and silver with a value beyond their non-money real goods value. Coins had a convenience in executing transactions above the next best alternative medium of exchange across polity borders. As such, the international outside money, gold and silver specie coins, is used here as that baseline for comparative evaluation of the Continental dollar. The face value, or par redemption value, of the Continental dollar was also stated in Spanish silver dollars or their specie coin equivalent.

A Decomposition Model for Inside Monies

The Continental dollar was a "bill of credit" issued by Congress that served as an "inside" money, namely inside the United States only. It had no exchange or market value outside the United States. "Outside" monies were monies that crossed polity borders and so transacted international trade. These monies were primarily specie coins and specie credits.

The observed market exchange value (*MEV*) of the Continental dollar is decomposed into its component parts (see eq. 9.1). The *MEV* equals its expected real asset present value (*APV*) minus its default risk discount (*RD*), that is, its value as just another non-money barter asset, plus its *TP*, which measures its pure "moneyness" value, that is, its extra value as a transacting medium of exchange. The (*APV* – *RD*) value is just rational bond pricing. Positive values for *TP* measure the willingness of the public to pay a premium above the bills' expected real asset present value, because the bills served as a more convenient transacting medium than the next best alternative. The expected real asset present value is further separated into its pure time-discounted component (i.e., *APV*), and its *RD*. All components are calculated as a percentage of face value, where that face value is set equal to an outside money to be in a comparable metric. For Continental dollars, that outside money is Spanish silver dollars (see fig. 9.1). Equation 9.1, being a decomposition exercise, is an identity.

Eq. 9.1 $$MEV_t \equiv (APV - RD)_t + TP_t$$

Congress controlled *APV* and *RD*. They controlled *APV* by choosing the redemption structure, and they influenced *RD* by the fiscal credibility of, and on how they follow through on, that redemption structure. *TP* was determined by the public through the structure of the economy in terms of how the public evaluated and used alternative media of exchange to execute domestic transactions. Empirical measurement is the difficult part of applying this approach. While *MEV* can be measured using price indices or exchange rates to an outside money (Spanish silver dollars), *RD* and *TP* cannot be independently measured. In addition, measuring *APV* entails constructing a counterfactual value of the bills, namely their value when not used as money and when no risk of default is expected.

Continental dollars were bills of credit. The term "bills of credit" should be understood literally: they were credits that the holder had against the issuer (Congress). Structured as zero-coupon bonds, the bills had defined or expected maturity dates when they were paid off, or paid in, at face value in specie (outside money) equivalents by, or to, the government. As such, and given expected redemption time paths and an appropriate risk-free time-discount rate, the *APV* of these bills as risk-free non-money tradable bonds can be calculated independently of their *MEV*. Moving the variables that can be independently measured to the left-hand side and the ones that cannot be independently measured to the right-hand side yields equation 9.2. In terms of proportions, the ratio APV_t/MEV_t shows how much of MEV_t is accounted for by APV_t, with the residual share accounted for by $(TP - RD)_t$. The gap between MEV_t and APV_t measures the magnitude of $(TP - RD)_t$.

Eq. 9.2 $$(MEV_t - APV_t) \equiv (TP - RD)_t$$

Behaviorally, TP is likely a negative function of RD. Thus, as RD takes on positive values, TP is driven to zero. An asset with a high default risk is unlikely to possess a transaction premium—that is, to be the preferred medium of exchange—relative to an asset with a low default risk. Thus, I assume that when $(TP - RD)_t > 0$, it is primarily due to $TP_t > 0$; and when $(TP - RD)_t < 0$, it is primarily due to $RD_t > 0$.[5]

Scholars who see this as a radical departure from their monetary orthodoxy do not have to believe in this approach for it to be a useful tool. If Americans are assumed to have acted *as if* their Continental dollars were zero-coupon bonds and to have acted *as if* they correctly forecast the redemption path of these bonds, then the observed market value of Continental dollars from 1775 through 1779 is more accurately predicted and tracked by this technique than by any other method or theory. This approach was applied to the bills of credit issued by colonial New Jersey, colonial Maryland, colonial Virginia, and colonial North Carolina, with surprising success. The model tracks the market value of these paper monies better than any other method or theory.[6]

To apply equation 9.2, two data sets are required: the counterfactual expected APV of Continental dollars as non-money low-risk bonds must be constructed, and data on the MEV of the Continental dollar have to be gathered. These data sets are constructed in chapters 10 and 11, respectively. Then, in chapter 12, these two data sets are then compared using equation 9.2. The comparison in chapter 12 establishes the moneyness value of the Continental dollar over time.

Some Caveats on *APV* Construction

Congress did not fix exact redemption dates for each emission of Continental dollars for the period 1776–78 (see table 1.1). Redemption dates were set for the first two emissions only and then again for all emissions together in 1779 and thereafter. Starting in 1777, legal-tender laws resulted in all Continental dollars being fungible in redemption. For this reason, I assume that the public responded only to the *expected* or *forecast* redemption of the *average* bill currently outstanding (based on congressional precedent related to fiscal credibility). The *MEV* data measure only the current market value of the average bill in circulation; they do not distinguish between the bills of different emissions. Thus, *APV* is calculated to be a comparable measure to *MEV*.

Equation 9.3 shows how I calculate the expected *APV* of the average bill in circulation. It is adapted from the basic continuous discounting present value formula ($PV = FVe^{-rt}$), where PV is present value, FV is face value, r is the discount rate, and t is the time to maturity. In equation 9.3, the amount of Continental dollars outstanding in a given year is assumed to be redeemed by all bills forecast to be redeemed in the years immediately following until the year when that original amount is fully redeemed. These yearly redemption amounts are divided by the initial amount outstanding from the chosen year to assign a yearly weight to its contribution in the redemption process. The time discounts between the initial year and the redemption year are multiplied by the contribution weights for their respective years. The time-discount weight values for each year are summed to get the expected present value of a representative bill outstanding for that chosen year.

Eq. 9.3 $$APV_j = \sum_{t=j}^{N} (RED_t / M_j) e^{-rt}$$

In equation 9.3, r = the risk-free time-discount rate or opportunity cost of capital, M_j = the face value amount of Continental dollars outstanding in year j, RED_t = the face value amount forecast to be redeemed and retired from circulation each year, and RED_N is the amount in the last year N that satisfies:

$$\sum_{t=j}^{N} (RED_t / M_j) = 1$$

No time series of market-generated interest rates for any class of assets currently exists for revolutionary America. Therefore, I use the r considered normal by contemporaries for assets with relatively low default expectations. This rate is a proxy for what in modern analysis is the risk-free rate. In 1764 Benjamin Franklin stated that the rate for discounting well-funded, legislature-issued zero-coupon bonds was 5 or 6 percent (Labaree 1966–70, 11:13–15). The rate on loan office certificates from 1776 through

1781 was 6 percent (see table 8.1). At the end of 1776 Congress had to offer 6 percent to secure loans in pounds sterling (*JCC* 6:1036–37). On January 17, 1777, Robert Morris said that 6 percent was the opportunity cost of capital placed in private securities (Smith 1976–94, 6:117). The interest rate mentioned most often in the second half of the eighteenth century, including through the Revolution, was 6 percent. In the 1790s the US government borrowed predominantly at 6 percent.[7] Thus, I will use 6 percent as my surrogate for the risk-free discount rate.

CHAPTER TEN

Rational Bond Pricing

On the commencement of the late revolution, Congress had no money. The external commerce of the states being suppressed, the farmer could not sell his produce, and of course could not pay a tax. Congress had no resource then but in paper money. Not being able to lay a tax for its redemption they could only promise that taxes should be laid for that purpose so as to redeem the bills by a certain day. — Thomas Jefferson, January–February 1786 (Boyd 1953–55, 10:25)

Continental dollars were zero-coupon bonds and not a fiat currency (see part I). They resembled today's US savings bonds more than today's US dollar bills, with the exception that Continental dollars were transferable and redeemable in specie equivalents, and they did not list the bearer's name on the bill. As such, the current non-money real value of a Continental dollar was not its face value, but its present value, namely its face value reduced by time-discounting from its expected future redemption (maturity) date. This present value provides the benchmark against which empirical measures of the Continental dollar's current market value should be evaluated. The difference between the Continental dollar's present value and its observed market value measures the Continental dollar's true depreciation or appreciation (inflation or deflation) over time.

This chapter constructs a measure of that present value under the assumption that the Continental dollar was just a zero-coupon bond and not a money. As such, this measure is a counterfactual exercise. It answers the question: what was the expected real value of a Continental dollar if it was not a money and there was no risk of default? The estimated outcome corresponds to the risk-free *APV* in the value model presented in chapter 9 (see equations 9.1 and 9.2).

The First Two Emissions (Nos. 1 and 2) of Continental Dollars

Table 1.1 shows the redemption structure legislated for the first two emissions of Continental dollars, and chapter 1 discusses why Congress chose that design. Figure 10.1 illustrates that discussion and shows the ideal present-value performance of the first two emissions of Continental dollars; it also shows the medium-of-exchange problems arising from its redemption design. Values are discounted back continuously from the final redemption window at 6 percent (see chap. 9) and expressed as a percentage of face value at each respective point in time. The "ideal" present-value path assumes that redemption is viewed as credible or certain and that 6 percent represents the opportunity cost or time preference for such a certain payoff.

The ideal expected present value of a Continental dollar started well below its face value due to time-discounting—72 and 57 percent of face value in November of 1775 for dollars from emissions nos. 1 and 2, respectively. Starting in November 1775 these values rose continuously, reaching face value by the last year of their respective redemption windows, 1782 and 1786 for emissions nos. 1 and 2, respectively.

Figure 10.1 illustrates the two tradeoffs, discussed in chapter 1, that Congress made between the fiscal credibility of redemption and the cumbersomeness of using Continental dollars as a medium of exchange. For a given emission, a four-year rather than a one-year redemption window increased the fiscal credibility of redemption, but at the cost of making a Continental dollar from a given emission at any point in time have a range of realized values. For example, in 1777, not knowing whether a particular Continental dollar from emission no. 1 would be redeemed in 1779 or in 1782 meant that the realized value of that Continental dollar, discounted back from its possible redemption dates, ranged between 87 and 74 percent of face value. For a Continental dollar from emission no. 2, this range was between 70 and 58 percent of face value.

These ranges made using Continental dollars as a medium of exchange cumbersome. When a dollar is not necessarily equal in realized value

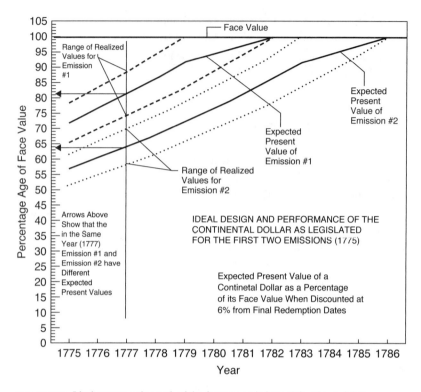

FIGURE 10.1. Ideal present-value path of the first two emissions of Continental dollars

Sources: Chap. 1 and table 1.1.

to an identical-looking dollar at the same point in time, trade becomes problematic.

If a citizen could not determine when any particular Continental dollar from a given emission would be redeemed within its redemption window, the best guess of its ideal present value at any point in time would be the expected discounted value for that emission (see the solid lines in figure 10.1). Given that citizens likely could not determine which dollar would be redeemed when within its respective redemption window, the variance in realized values noted above may have been considered only a minor inconvenience. As long as the redemption window for a given emission was relatively short, trade could function relatively well using the expected present value of Continental dollars from the same emission.

More problematic was Congress's choice of staggered sequential redemption windows for subsequent emissions. Congress spread the redemption of subsequent emissions successively forward in time to maintain the fiscal credibility of redemption. By contrast, had Congress chosen the proposed alternative of having all new emissions redeemed in the same redemption window, the required redemption taxes would have been beyond historically feasible and acceptable limits, making redemption doubtful (see chap. 1). The tradeoff of not choosing this proposed alternative was to make the Continental dollar an even more cumbersome medium of exchange than it already was for each separate emission.

Figure 10.1 illustrates this problem. Emissions nos. 1 and 2 have different expected present values at each point in time. For example, in 1777 the expected present value of a Continental dollar from emission no. 1 was 81 percent of its face value, whereas for emission no. 2 it was 64 percent. In other words, Continental dollars from different emissions were, in effect, different monies. Citizens would have to use the dates printed on the bills to determine what expected present value to assign to each particular bill of the same denomination. Each new emission multiplied this problem, making for an increasingly cumbersome medium of exchange. The Continental dollar could still function as a medium of exchange, but it would necessitate citizens' pricing goods and services separately by Continental dollar emissions, and trading Continental dollars from different emissions at values other than one to one.

The Continental dollar's emission-specific redemption structure created future problems for its initial use as soldiers' pay. Soldiers' pay absorbed nearly half of all Continental dollars emitted through 1777 (see table 6.4). Congress fixed soldiers' pay in nominal terms in June and July 1775 at the same time as it designed the first emission of Continental dollars. American army privates were paid $80 per year. Privates were the primary recipients of military pay, receiving 78 percent of the money paid to each military company. British army privates were paid $55 per year. American privates were paid in Continental dollars, whereas British privates were paid in specie. In November 1775 the expected present value of eighty Continental dollars of the first emission was between $63 and $53, or comparable to the present value of a British private's yearly pay.[1] That Congress initially set an American army private's pay to be equal to a British army private's pay in expected present-value terms rather than in face-value terms is an acknowledgment by Congress of the zero-coupon bond nature of the Continental dollar that it created. As the war continued, however, the present value of soldiers' pay when made in subsequent emissions fell, yet Congress failed to change the nominal pay grades set in mid-1775 for American soldiers.

By November 1775 the expected present value of a full year's pay for an American private, when paid with dollars from the second emission, would be between $50 and $41 —well below the present value of a British private's yearly pay. For subsequent emissions, it was even lower. In effect, Congress was financing the war by systematically reducing the real pay of its citizen soldiers, and it continued to drop as the war progressed. The necessity of adjusting nominal military pay to realign it with the new present value of each successive emission of Continental dollars may have been overlooked, or Congress may just have deemed it too complicated to address constantly. Keeping the pay structure of the military fixed in the nominal values set before August 1775 made it easier for them to estimate and budget military expenses, as well as to finance the war via military-pay price controls.

This action, however, created problems for the financing system regarding military pay over the course of a long war. At some point soldiers would no longer reenlist and fight for a fraction of the present value of their original pay. Late in the war Congress moved to solve this problem by promising military personnel that Congress would make up "the deficiency of their original pay" when feasible.[2] This promise is consistent with Congress's acknowledging the zero-coupon bond design of the Continental dollar monetary system it had created, along with its declining present value as new emissions pushed redemptions further into the future.

Forecasting the Redemption of Emissions Nos. 3–10

For the first two emissions Congress issued redemption instructions. For the next eight emissions (emission no. 3 through part of emission no. 10, totaling $95,500,300 in face value), however, no explicit redemption instructions were issued. At best, statements were made indicating that redemption would be "on the same security as the sums of money heretofore emitted by Congress have been," "in such manner . . . as Congress shall hereafter direct," and for "periods . . . that shall be fixed by Congress." But most often nothing was stated. After 1775 Congress shifted monetary matters from Congress, sitting as a whole, to standing subcommittees. Redemption instructions for subsequent emissions fell between these administrative cracks, each group apparently thinking the other was responsible for establishing the redemption instructions for each new emission. Not

until emission no. 11 did Congress sitting as a whole resolve this administrative oversight (see table 1.1; *JCC* 4:156–57; Smith 1976–94, 3:270–71).

This failure by Congress to explicitly give redemption instructions for
emissions no. 3 through part of no. 10 was noticed, and the fact that everyone was "left to his own conjectures" as to when redemption would occur
was a concern. James Madison, in his treatise on money, explicitly stated
this concern and described the likely forecast:

> Every one must have taken notice that, in the emissions of Congress, no pre-
> cise time has been stipulated for their redemption, nor any specific provision
> made for that purpose. A general promise entitling the bearer to so many dol-
> lars of metal as the paper bills express, has been the only basis of their credit.
> Every one therefore has been left to his own conjectures as to the time the
> redemption would be fulfilled; and as every addition made to the quantity in
> circulation, would naturally be supposed to remove to a proportionally greater
> distance the redemption of the whole mass, it could not happen otherwise than
> that every additional emission would be followed by a further depreciation
> [meaning a lower present value owing to time-discounting]. (Hutchinson and
> Rachal 1962–65: 305–6)

The January 1778 meeting of state commissioners in New Haven also
noted the lack of redemption instructions for these emissions. In their letter to Congress, they concluded that

> the public have never yet been notified, when the Continental Bills are to be
> redeemed, except the two first Emissions. . . . If they were to be Ascertained
> when they were to be redeemed, Especially if it was at a short period, it would
> give them a confidence in the money, and greatly tend to Establish its Currency.
> (Hammond 1889a: 293)

They noted that the distance to redemption was critical, and so what the
public conjectured about redemption distance was important to determining the present value of Continental dollars.

By necessity, therefore, the pattern of redemption for these eight emissions was being forecast by the public. What a rational forecast would be
is constructed using the redemption pattern set by Congress for the first
two emissions of Continental dollars—those issued in 1775—and expectations based on how the colonies had financed the French and Indian
War. This was information the public had (see chaps. 2 and 4), so it would

likely form the basis of any forecast the public made of the unspecified redemption structure for the next eight emissions of Continental dollars—
those issued from 1776 through 1778. In general, redemption would only
start postwar and would be pushed successively into the future with each
subsequent emission. It would also be spread over enough years to keep
tax levels within historically acceptable and feasible limits, thus giving the
system fiscal credibility.

Three forecasts are consistent with the redemption pattern set by
Congress in 1775 (see table 1.1). First, a four-year contiguous redemption interval would be maintained for each subsequent emission starting
the year after the redemption interval for the immediately prior emission ended (forecast 1). Second, redemption intervals would be adjusted
to maintain a constant per-year, per-white-capita tax level until all emissions were redeemed at face value, with $0.33 being that level (forecast 2).
Third, redemption intervals would be adjusted to maintain a constant
$750,000 per-year redemption amount until all emissions were redeemed
at face value (forecast 3).

Forecast 1 is identical to forecast 3 when emission sizes are identical,
which is approximately true for emissions nos. 1–7. After emission no. 7,
emission sizes get so large that by 1779 forecast 3 would entail a redemption period of 267 years. As such, forecast 3 is redundant before and
unrealistic after 1777, and so it is not used. Forecast 2 requires making
projections about population growth. That such projections were made
regarding the redemption of Continental dollars can be seen in John Jay's
published address to the public as president of Congress on September 13,
1779 (*JCC* 15:1056). The construction of forecast 2 uses estimates of the
actual growth in population. Both forecasts 1 and 2 are used to represent
the public's expectations about future redemptions of Continental dollars.

Table 10.1 presents the ideal expected present value of a Continental
dollar at each emission's inception as a percentage of its face value based
on face-value redemption dates, both legislated and forecast, using a
6 percent discount rate. The third column calculates that expected present
value at inception. Figure 10.2 draws the full ideal expected present value
time paths from inception to redemption, for emissions nos. 1–7, using legislated redemption instructions for emissions nos. 1 and 2 and forecast 1
for emissions nos. 3–7. Each emission starts at an expected present value
well below its face value due to time-discounting and then rises to its face
value by its last redemption date. Because each new emission is forecast
to have a four-year redemption window staggered successively forward in

TABLE 10.1 Legislated/forecast redemption dates and valuations for Continental dollar emissions

(1)	(2)	(3)	(4)			(5)					(6)
			Average expected present value to date[b]			Under legal-tender laws: expected present value[c]					
		Expected present value at inception[a]	[Legislated] forecasts	&		Perfect-foresight-expectations forecasts	&		No-foresight-expectations forecasts	&	Implied average tax per year per white capita[d]
Emission no. Date printed on the bills (Amount)	Maturity/redemption interval (L) = legislated (F) = forecast 1	100 = par	1	& 2		1 & 2			1 & 2		
			100 = par			100 = par			100 = par		
No. 1 May 10, 1775 ($3,000,000)	Nov. 30, 1779–Nov. 30, 1782 (L)	69.73	[69.73]	[69.73]							$0.33 0.35–0.31
No. 2 Nov. 29, 1775 (3,000,000)	Nov. 30, 1783–Nov. 30, 1786 (L)	56.68	[64.37]	[64.37]							0.28 0.30–0.27
No. 3 Feb. 17, 1776 ($3,937,220)	Nov. 30, 1787–Nov. 30, 1790 (F)	45.18	57.21	57.16							0.33 0.35–0.32
No. 4 May 9, 1776 ($5,000,000)	Nov. 30, 1791–Nov. 30, 1794 (F)	36.03	50.48	50.38							0.36 0.38–0.34
No. 5 July 22, 1776 ($5,000,000)	Nov. 30, 1795–Nov. 30, 1798 (F)	28.70	45.65	45.35							0.32 0.33–0.31
No. 6 Nov. 2, 1776 ($5,000,000)	Nov. 30, 1799–Nov. 30, 1802 (F)	22.94	41.70	41.46							0.28 0.30–0.27

continues

TABLE 10.1 (*continued*)

(1)	(2)	(3)	(4)		(5)				(6)
			Average expected present value to date[b]		Under legal-tender laws: expected present value[c]				
			[Legislated] forecasts		Perfect-foresight-expectations forecasts		No-foresight-expectations forecasts		
		Expected present value at inception[a]	1	& 2	1	& 2	1	& 2	Implied average tax per year per white capita[d]
Emission no. Date printed on the bills (Amount)	Maturity/ redemption interval (L) = legislated (F) = forecast 1	100 = par	100 = par		100 = par		100 = par		
No. 7 Feb. 26, 1777 ($5,000,000)	Nov. 30, 1803–Nov. 30, 1806 (F)	18.45	38.52	38.43					0.31 0.38–0.24
Legal-tender laws enacted in 1777 made all emissions fungible and so all expected present values cumulative									
No. 8 May 20, 1777 ($16,500,000)	Nov. 30, 1807–Nov. 30 1810 (F)	14.70[i]			13.41	9.61	30.40	30.02	0.36 0.76–0.24
No. 9 Apr. 11, 1778 ($25,000,000)	Nov. 30, 1811–Nov. 30, 1814 (F)	12.18[i]			14.17	10.15	25.11	23.52	0.43 1.03–0.24
No. 10 Sept. 26, 1778 ($75,001,080[e])	Nov. 30, 1815–Nov. 30, 1818 (F)	9.84[i]			14.53	10.41	21.09	18.54	0.49[e] 1.09–0.24
No. 11 Jan. 14, 1779[f] ($53,551,695)	Nov. 30, 1779–Jan. 1, 1797 (L)	62.38	[62.38]	[62.38]	14.80[g]	10.59[g]			3.66[f] 6.95–2.59

All emissions[h] ($199,989,995)	Apr. 1780–Apr. 1781 (L)	2.50[h]	[2.50]	[2.50]	15.70[g]	11.27[g]	86.72 2.17[i]

Average tax per year per white capita in the 13 colonies for all taxes, 1770–74 0.41

Average tax per year per white capita for all US federal government taxes, 1792–95 1.39

Sources: Table 1.1; appendix A; Carter, Gartner, Haines, Olmstead, Sutch, and Wright (2006, 1:36; 5:82, 652); Grubb (2008, 2012a); *JCC* (2:221–23; 3:457–59; 13:20–21; 16:262–67; 17:567–68); Rabushka (2008: 796, 825, 862–63).

Notes: See table 1.1; appendix A; and the text.

[a] Continuously discounted at 6 percent off the face value on the bill from the redemption interval dates to the date printed on the bill expressed as the value of $100 in Continental paper money. See this chap., n. 2.

[b] This is the expected average present values for the cumulative emissions outstanding to that date weighted by their dollar size. In other words, if one had a random draw of Continental dollars currently outstanding at this date, then this is what their average expected present value would be. After emission no. 7, legal-tender laws made all expected values per specific emission average cumulative values for all currently outstanding emissions.

[c] See chap. 7 for details about how legal tender laws work. Perfect-foresight expectations mean that the public knew exactly how many Continental dollars would eventually be emitted. No-foresight expectations mean that the public did not take future emissions of Continental dollars into account when calculating the expected present value of a Continental dollar for the emissions issued so far and currently outstanding.

[d] This is the tax needed to redeem the promised or forecast amount of Continental dollars at face value. It applies to legislated and forecast 1 values only. Forecast 2 by construction is set at $0.33. The range across the redemption interval for each emission is below the average number for that interval. Population is extrapolated linearly between decadal benchmarks and is for the white population only (Carter, Gartner, Haines, Olmstead, Sutch, and Wright 2006, 1:36; 5:652). Only the tax needed to redeem Continental dollars at face value is reported. Taxes are expressed in Spanish silver dollars. Taxes expressed in pounds sterling are converted to Spanish silver dollars following McCusker (1978: 10). Legal-tender laws merged emission redemptions after emission no. 7. Thus, for emissions after emission no. 7, the average tax covers redemption across all prior emissions and redemption years. The high number in the tax range for each emission after emission no. 7 represents the per-year per-white-capita tax for the fourth to the last year of redemption.

[e] Only the $30,000,300 portion of emission no. 10 authorized before January 14, 1779, is used to estimate the average per-year per-white-capita tax. After January 14, 1779, all emissions, including new authorizations of emission no. 10, were merged into one redemption window.

[f] Applies to all past and future net new emissions ($199,989,995) regardless of the date on the bill.

[g] These are counterfactual expected present values using forecasts 1 and 2 under the assumption that the new legislated redemption dates in 1779 and 1780 were not operative.

[h] Enacted March 18, 1780, this covered all past emissions. How to calculate the expected present value at inception is unclear. The resolution's 40-to-1 conversion rate of paper Continental dollars to Spanish silver dollars is used. See *JCC* (16:262–67).

[i] Evaluated at 40 Continental dollars = $1 in specie, as established in the March 18, 1780, resolution.

[j] These are counterfactual expected present values at inception for these individual emissions using forecast 1 under the assumption that legal-tender laws were not adopted.

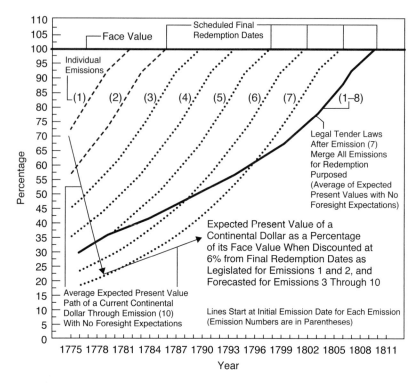

FIGURE 10.2. Ideal expected present value of a current Continental dollar: face value discounted from final redemption at 6 percent for various emissions and cumulative totals using forecast 1

Sources: Derived from the sources in tables 1.1 and 10.1.

Note: See table 10.1 and the text for discussion.

time, each emission's ideal expected present value time path is positioned successively farther to the south and east in figure 10.2. This is not depreciation per se, but merely time-discounting.

While each emission's ideal expected present-value time path rises over time, the frequent addition of new emissions that start at successively lower present values pulls down the average present value of all Continental dollars currently outstanding over the years of active emissions. This was because the frequency and size of new emissions, which add Continental dollars that start at lower present values, outweigh the rising present value of the Continental dollars from prior emissions. Suppose at a given date one took a random drawing of Continental dollars that were currently outstanding. The expected present value of that drawing would be the average of the expected present values of the individual emissions at the date they were drawn. That average would depend on the chance of randomly drawing bills from various outstanding emissions, which in turn would depend on the relative size of each emission.

Column 4 of table 10.1 shows these average expected present values at inception for each new emission through emission no. 7, weighted by the nominal dollar size of all emissions currently outstanding. It uses the legislated redemption dates for emissions nos. 1 and 2, and forecasts 1 and 2 for emissions nos. 3–7. This average of the expected present values at an emission's inception, column four, is above that for that emission's bills, column 3, because bills from earlier emissions with higher present values are being averaged in with this emission. Column 5 of table 10.1 shows these average expected present values at inception for each new emission from emissions nos. 8–11 given the passage of legal-tender laws.

Figure 10.3 illustrates the complete time path for the ideal average expected present values presented in columns 4 and 5 of table 10.1 for emissions nos. 1–11 (1775 to 1779). Forecasts 1 and 2 are so close to each other that they appear as a single dotted line prior to 1777. Comparing figures 10.2 and 10.3 illustrates how the average expected present value is pulled down over time. The frequency and size of new emissions with their lower expected present values at inception outweigh the rise in the expected present value of earlier emissions. Given that the public's estimates of a Continental dollar's current value at any point in time would likely be made on a blind or random chance acquisition of Continental dollars among various outstanding emissions, that is, not knowing in advance which emission a given dollar presented to them would be from, the time paths in figure 10.3 and columns 4 and 5 in table 10.1 represent the overall ideal present value at any point in time of a Continental dollar through early 1779. This value shows that, even under ideal conditions, with no uncertainty or depreciation per se, the average expected present value of a Continental dollar fell from 70 percent of its face value in May 1775 to 38 percent of its face value by March 1777 and then further to between 15 and 11 percent of its face value by early 1779. This was not depreciation, but simply the effect of time-discounting, that is, the result of taking the value of time into account.

While the public could operate on the basis of forecasting an overall average expected present value of a Continental dollar as shown in figure 10.3 through early 1777, it still faced the problem that Continental

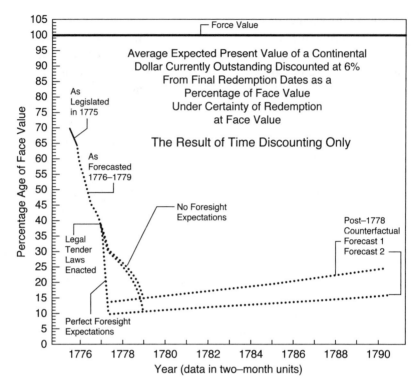

FIGURE 10.3. Ideal average expected present value of a Continental dollar currently outstanding discounted at 6 percent from final redemption dates as legislated and forecast expressed as a percentage of face value

Sources: Derived from tables 1.1 and 10.1.

Note: See table 10.1 and the text for discussion. Ideal means with certainty of redemption as promised.

dollars known to be from different emissions should trade at different expected present values (see fig. 10.2). Once the emission date of a Continental dollar received in trade was revealed, the expected present value of that dollar could depart substantially from the overall average expected present value at that date, as shown in figure 10.3. Congress had created these differences in their initial structural design of the Continental dollar. Such differences across emissions made for a cumbersome medium of exchange.

Before the Revolution, individual colonies had solved this problem by making their respective bills of credit a legal tender at face value within their respective jurisdictions. Legal-tender laws made bills from different emissions that were currently outstanding fungible, in effect merging emission-specific redemption windows for currently outstanding bills into one big window. Under legal-tender laws, which bills were redeemed in which emission redemption window no longer mattered as long as cumulative redemptions over the entire redemption window for all emissions matched cumulative emissions.

Legal-tender laws allowed the public to respond to what the expected present value of a Continental dollar was at each point in time independent of emission dates for all bills currently outstanding. In other words, assessing the expected present value of a Continental dollar no longer depended on a blind random drawing of bills currently outstanding. That assessment remained valid even if a non-random composition of emissions in a sample of Continental dollars was known ahead of time. In figure 10.2, legal-tender laws rendered the expected present value time paths for each emission irrelevant by merging them into the one solid line (1–8). Thus, only the overall expected present-value time path in figure 10.3 mattered for knowing the current value of any Continental dollar.

Because legal-tender laws made emission-specific redemption windows irrelevant, it freed Congress from linking each emission to a unique authorization by breaking the relationship between a specific emission and its accompanying emission-specific redemption instructions (or its forecast instructions). Congress could now authorize additional amounts at several subsequent dates under the umbrella of the same emission. Table 1.1 shows this behavior. Before legal-tender laws—that is, before emission no. 8—each emission had one authorized amount. After legal-tender laws—that is, after emission no. 7—each emission now had multiple authorization dates when additional sums were added to that emission. Under legal-tender laws, individual emissions could and did become much larger in size.

As expectations of a brief conflict waned, the need for more emissions became clear, and the public's use of Continental dollars as a medium of exchange became more likely. Congress moved to solve the structural problem they had created whereby different emissions should trade contemporaneously at different expected present values. They did this by asking the states to make the Continental dollar a legal tender within their respective jurisdictions. On May 22, 1776, the very day that emission no. 4 was authorized, a congressional committee consisting of James Duane, George Wythe, John Adams, Roger Sherman, Joseph Hewes, Thomas Johnson, and William Whipple recommended that Congress ask the states

to make the Continental dollar a legal tender. The committee, now including Thomas Jefferson, made the same recommendation on September 2,
1776. Finally, on January 14, 1777, after emission no. 6 had been authorized, Congress acted on the committee's recommendation and asked the
states to make the Continental dollar a legal tender at face value within
their respective jurisdictions.[3] The states quickly accommodated this request. For example, Pennsylvania made the Continental dollar a legal tender on February 6, 1777, Delaware on February 22, 1777, and Virginia on
May 5, 1777. By emission no. 8, authorized on May 22, 1777, Continental
dollars were legal tender at face value.[4]

With emission no. 8, after May 1777, legal-tender laws made Continental dollars from different emissions have the same expected present
value in contemporaneous trades. Before May 1777, however, Continental
dollars from emissions nos. 1–7 should have traded contemporaneously
at different values. Little direct evidence of differential treatment across
emissions before 1777 has been previously noted, in part because no one
has looked for it, which in turn may be due to data difficulties. Market participants typically recorded monetary transactions in units of account and
not media of exchange (Bezanson 1951: 3–4, 10–11). That said, on February 20, 1777, Congress's Committee on Way and Means for supplying the
Treasury made a recommendation that entailed distinguishing between
the first two emissions and subsequent emissions in terms of current value
credits. Such a distinction only made sense if Continental dollars from different emissions were perceived to have different present values.[5]

After 1777 congressional payments for war supplies absorbed more
Continental dollars than soldiers' pay (see chap. 6). While soldiers' pay
had been fixed in nominal terms by Congress on July 29, 1775, when Congress spent Continental dollars in the marketplace for supplies and services, prices could be raised by suppliers and service providers to reflect
the expected present value of the Continental dollars offered in payment.
Suppliers and service providers were more likely to respend the money
paid them because they had subcontractors and employees to pay. Figure 7.1 shows that market participants in Philadelphia did not start de-
nominating transactions in dollar units, above that used prior to the first
emission of Continental dollars, until sometime after mid-1776. By mid-
1777 the public was pricing goods primarily in Continental dollars.

That Congress waited until 1777 to ask the states to make the Continental dollar a legal tender is consistent with this transition in usage.
As war supplies came to dominate congressional spending, Continental

dollars had to become a less cumbersome transacting medium of exchange. This was difficult to achieve if Continental dollars with different emission dates had different contemporaneous expected present values. Legal-tender laws eliminated this problem. The public could now think in terms of one overall expected present value for any Continental dollar outstanding independent of the emission date on the bill.

When Congress altered the redemption rules on January 2, 1779 (see table 1.1), they explicitly made the expected present value of all Continental dollars identical regardless of emission date. They did this by establishing one overall redemption window for all Continental dollars ever emitted. Theoretically, this action had the same effect as states making the Continental dollar a legal tender within their respective jurisdictions. That Congress explicitly took this action for the first time in 1779 may have added to the certainty that all Continental dollars now had the same expected present value, regardless of emission date. A few market participants took notice. Edward Bonsall and Abraham Shoemaker advertised in the January 27, 1779, *Pennsylvania Gazette* that they would sell a tract of land "*For Continental Currency of any date*" (italics in the original). The implication of this previously unused phraseology is that prior to January 2, 1779, Continental dollars from different emissions may occasionally have been treated differently when settling accounts. Not all citizens may have understood that legal-tender laws had already implicitly accomplished what the January 2, 1779, congressional resolution explicitly accomplished.[6]

Legal-tender laws altered the public's present value forecasts. A simple average of the expected present values of outstanding emissions weighted by emission size—used before legal-tender laws were enacted (col. 4, table 10.1)—was no longer valid. Prior to legal-tender laws, adding a new emission lowered the average expected present value of a random drawing of Continental dollars, but not by lowering the expected present value of any prior emission. It did so merely by adding in the weight of the new emission's lower expected present value. Under a legal-tender law, this was changed. By continuously merging and remerging all prior emissions' redemption windows with each new emission's redemption window into one big constantly growing redemption window, legal-tender laws caused each new emission to lower the expected present value of all prior emissions. In other words, under legal-tender laws, each new emission exerted a negative externality on all prior emissions' expected present values. Because future emissions now impacted prior emissions' expected present values, under legal-tender laws the public now had to also forecast future emissions to calculate a current expected present value of a Continental dollar. Expected present value now depended on forecasting redemption (forecasts 1 and 2) and forecasting future emissions (perfect foresight versus no foresight). These four forecasts are incorporated in the present values illustrated in figure 10.3.

Column 5 of table 10.1 presents two alternative expectations of future emissions used for recalculating the expected present value at inception for emissions nos. 8–11 using forecasts 1 and 2 under legal-tender laws. The first alternative assumes the public had *perfect* foresight regarding the number and size of future emissions of Continental dollars; the second assumes the public had *no* foresight regarding future emissions. In other words, it assumes the public thought each current emission would be the last emission.

The perfect-foresight alternative is likely the most reasonable. As early as mid-1777, and certainly by 1779, there was strong sentiment among Americans that the war had been won and would soon be over. The public could gauge the yearly cost of the war and, with some idea of when the war would end, could then gauge future Continental dollar emissions. Congress had started debating an end to emissions and in 1779 set a $200 million limit for total cumulative emissions.[7] That the last emission occurred when the first redemptions were to be received by the Continental Treasury was likely no coincidence and thus expected by the public.

The forecasts of war costs requiring Continental dollars after mid-1777, based on average monthly war costs from 1775 into 1777, turned out to be fairly accurate. For example, the present value of congressional spending of Continental dollars from emissions nos. 1–7 was approximately $11 million, or $529,101 per month on average from September 1775 through April 1777. This is almost exactly what Thomas Jefferson estimated in July 1775, namely that each six months of war would cost $3 million (Smith 1976–94, 1:689–91). Using this number to forecast the present value of Continental dollars needed per month to continue the war from May 1777 through March 1780 yields approximately $18.5 million. The total present value of Continental dollars emitted after emission no. 7 equaled between $17.6 and $24.6 million using forecasts 1 and 2 with perfect-foresight expectations, respectively.[8] As such, the projected $18.5 million in present value needed to finish the war based on past behavior is close to the perfect-foresight expectation of the number and size of future emissions needed after emission no. 7, in present-value terms using forecasts 1 and 2, to finish the war. Therefore, the perfect-foresight expectation approximates closely the forecast of future emissions based on past behavior.

The difference between the perfect-foresight and the no-foresight forecast (see table 10.1, col. 5, and fig. 10.3) illustrates the size of the negative externality caused by legal-tender laws on the expected present value of currently outstanding Continental dollars. Under perfect foresight, the adoption of legal-tender laws after emission no. 7 caused the expected present value to fall from 38.5 percent of face value at the inception of emission no. 7 to between 9.5 and 13.5 percent of face value at the inception of emission no. 8. This was the lowest forecast expected present value. From that point forecast expected present values would rise continuously between the inception of emission no. 8 and the year when the last Continental dollar ever emitted would be redeemed. This result occurred because the public knew how many future Continental dollar emissions would occur and what the size of those emissions would be. Thus, they knew when the last redemption year would be, and because the inception of emission no. 8 is the furthest in time from the last redemption year, its expected present value is the lowest.

By comparison, if the public has a no-foresight forecast, then, with the adoption of legal-tender laws after emission no. 7, the expected present value falls from 38.5 percent of face value at the inception of emission no. 7 to only 30 percent of face value at the inception of emission no. 8. This is 18.5 percentage points less than the fall under the perfect-foresight assumption. From that point, the forecast expected present value falls with each successive emission under the no-foresight calculation, while it continues to rise under the perfect-foresight calculation, until the two rejoin at the inception of the last emission in January 1779 (emission no. 11) at between 10.6 and 14.8 percent of face value (see table 10.1, col. 5, and fig. 10.3). Thereafter the two foresight expectations yield identical expected present value forecasts for both forecasts 1 and 2. This last result is because, after the last emission, the assumptions that the public pretends no more emissions will occur and that the public perfectly foresees no more emissions will occur are identical.

The adoption of legal-tender laws after mid-1777, assuming perfect-foresight expectations, produced a substantial collapse in the expected present value of Continental dollars outstanding during the critical year of 1777. In effect, by requesting that the states adopt legal-tender laws, Congress was trading a substantial reduction in the expected present value of Continental dollars already outstanding for making Continental dollars a less cumbersome medium of exchange. Even this improved medium-of-exchange function may not have been realized owing to the extreme length of the redemption window needed to create it.

Legal-tender laws gave all Continental dollars, regardless of emission number or date on the bill, the same expected present value, making them a less cumbersome medium of exchange. It accomplished this by merging the redemption windows for all emissions into a single large one. This method, however, increased the variance in the realized value of Continental dollars at any point in time. At the inception of emission no. 8, the redemption windows for forecasts 1 and 2 under perfect foresight were forty-three and seventy-two and a half years, respectively. Under the no-foresight assumption, they were thirty-one and thirty-four and a half years, respectively. These are much longer redemption windows than the typical four-year window forecast for each of emissions nos. 3–7 before legal-tender laws were enacted. This long redemption window increased the range of realized values around the now-common average value.

With emission no. 8 and the adoption of legal-tender laws, under perfect foresight using forecasts 1 and 2, a given Continental dollar could now end up being redeemed at face value as early as 1779 or as late as 1822 or 1852, respectively. If a citizen knew in advance which Continental dollar would be redeemed in 1779 versus which in 1822 or 1852, they would be willing to pay more than the expected average for the one redeemed in 1779, and less for the one redeemed in 1822 or 1852. For example, under perfect foresight using forecasts 1 and 2, at the inception of emission no. 8, while the expected present value of any Continental dollar was 13.4 and 9.6 percent of face value, respectively, the range around these averages was 86.1 to 6.5 percent of face value for forecast 1, and 86.1 to 1.11 percent of face value for forecast 2. Under the no-foresight assumption using forecasts 1 and 2, at the inception of emission no. 8, while the expected present value of any Continental dollar was 30.4 and 30.0 percent of face value, respectively, the range around these averages was 86.1 to 13.4 percent of face value for forecast 1 and 86.1 to 10.9 percent of face value for forecast 2.

While most citizens did not know in advance which Continental dollar would be redeemed in which year within the redemption window and thus would use the common expected present value when transacting in Continental dollars, the sheer range of possible realized values around that common average imparted additional risk to using Continental dollars as a medium of exchange. Congress had created no mechanism to determine which specific Continental dollar would be redeemed in which year. If everyone rushed to the Continental Treasury in 1779 with their Continental dollars, how the Treasury would decide which to accept to fill that year's quota and which to turn away was undetermined. Insider knowledge and political favors intruding into the actual redeeming process must have been a concern and something that would affect the value stability of the system. The variance in realized values produced by a four-year redemption window may have been a minor inconvenience, but that produced by a thirty-one- or seventy-three-year redemption window had to be a major concern, carrying a substantial risk cost, when trading in Continental dollars after emission no. 7.

An additional rationale for Congress's requesting that the states adopt legal-tender laws was to gain purchasing power in Congress's newest emissions. Column 3 in table 10.1 and figure 10.2 show that the expected present value of emissions nos. 6 and 7 at their inceptions were low, 23 and 18 percent of face value, respectively. If nothing was done, the expected present value of the next emission (no. 8) at its inception would be even lower. The purchasing power Congress expected from a new emission, even with zero depreciation, was vanishing rapidly owing to forecast time-discounting.

If the public operated under a no-foresight expectation regarding future emissions, then adopting legal-tender laws would twist and flatten the expected present value time path of the merged emissions nos. 1–8, so that the expected present value of new emission no. 8 at its inception would now be well above what it was for emissions nos. 5–7 at their respective inceptions (see table 10.1, cols. 3 and 5, and fig. 10.2). This action made the expected present value of emission no. 8 at inception 30 percent of face value rather than 15 percent of face value if no legal-tender laws were adopted, or almost twice as high in terms of percentage points. Thus, the purchasing power Congress would enjoy with its new emission no. 8 was enhanced. The differential in Congress's purchasing power for emissions nos. 9 and 10 by adopting legal-tender laws was about 10 percentage points above what it would have been if no legal-tender laws had been adopted. If the public had perfect-foresight expectations regarding the number and size of future emissions, then less was gained by Congress in the purchasing power of its new emissions, at best about an expected present value of 4 percentage points higher by emission no. 10 under legal-tender laws compared with no legal-tender laws.

If this alteration in the time path of redemption, solid line (1–8) in figure 10.2, was Congress's intention, it came at a cost. The adoption of legal-tender laws sacrificed the present value expected by holders of prior emissions to prop up the present value of the new emission Congress was now spending. This was a breach of faith that damaged the credibility of Congress and the Continental dollar financing system. It amounted to a retrospective change in the present value of outstanding zero-coupon bonds through unilaterally imposing a legal postponement in their likely day of redemption. This cost along with the sharp and large collapse in expected present value in 1777 caused by the adoption of legal-tender laws under perfect-foresight expectations put destructive pressure on the Continental dollar financing system.[9] Appendix C illustrates this outcome from a different angle by measuring the cumulative spending of Continental dollars by Congress in both face and present value.

Ideal Redemption Performance after Emission No. 10

The last emissions of Continental dollars were in 1779 (see table 1.1). The dotted lines in figure 10.3 show the ideal expected present value of Continental dollars from 1779 through 1790 under the assumption that Congress adopted forecasts 1 or 2—that it formally adopted the projected pattern of redemptions derived from the 1775 legislated redemption structure for emissions nos. 1 and 2. Under this redemption assumption, the Continental dollar would have reached its low in 1779 at 14 and 11 percent of face value for forecasts 1 and 2, respectively, and then risen continuously thereafter to 25 and 16 percent of face value for forecasts 1 and 2, respectively, by 1790.

In 1779 and then again in 1780 Congress formally altered the redemption rules from the pattern set in 1775 with emissions nos. 1 and 2 by a considerable margin. Figure 10.4 shows how these new post-1778 redemption rules changed the ideal expected present-value time path of the Continental dollar from that forecast in figure 10.3. These rule changes are addressed in detail in chapters 13 and 14, where it will be argued that they were not fiscally credible and so cannot be considered a viable "ideal" present-value time-path expectation that the public would act on. The rule changes Congress implemented from 1779 into 1781 effectively crashed the Continental dollar financing system. The effect of these monetary rule changes is what Edmund Randolph was likely referring to in his opening statement at the 1787 Constitutional Convention when he asserted that "the havoc of paper money had not been foreseen" by the creators of the Articles of Confederation (Farrand 1966, 1:18). Chapters 13 and 14 address how changing personnel in Congress after 1775 led to these

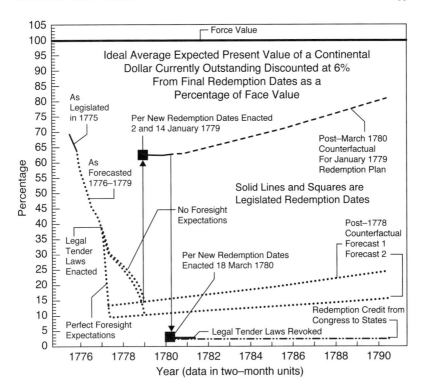

FIGURE 10.4. New post-1778 ideal average expected present value of a Continental dollar currently outstanding discounted at 6 percent from final redemption dates as legislated and forecast expressed as a percentage of face value and as legislated after 1778

Sources: Derived from tables 1.1 and 10.1.

Note: See table 10.1 and the text for discussion. Ideal means with certainty of redemption as promised.

dramatic and wildly out-of-forecast rule changes, why Congress made the changes, and what Congress was attempting to accomplish. It also addresses how the advice from Benjamin Franklin was poorly applied, and why these attempted rule changes failed and so crashed the Continental dollar system.

First, however, chapter 11 charts the market value of the Continental dollar over time, and then chapter 12 compares that market value with the ideal expected present value (non-money real value) of the Continental dollar over time. This comparison focuses on the period from 1775 to 1779 to establish how the Continental dollar performed before the 1779–81 rule changes destroyed the system.

CHAPTER ELEVEN

The Current Market Exchange Value

Chapter 10 calculated the expected present value of Continental dollars as riskless, zero-coupon bonds based on legislated and then, derived from that legislation, forecast redemption time frames (the dotted lines in fig. 10.3). Those values are counterfactual or hypothetical values, the *APV*s from the model of money detailed in chapter 9. Chapter 11 presents evidence that measures the observed current market value of Continental dollars, namely what Continental dollars were actually worth when traded in the marketplace by the public. This evidence corresponds to *MEV* in the model of money in chapter 9. Comparing the *MEV* with the hypothetical value (*APV*) determines the "moneyness" value (the *TP* in the model of money in chap. 9) and, therefore, how the Continental dollar performed. That comparison will be taken up in chapter 12. First, the actual observed *MEV* of the Continental dollar has to be determined.

I will report these values as a percentage of the Continental dollar's face value to make all measures be in the same metric and thus easily comparable, as well as comparable to the *APV* measures in chapter 10. The face value of the Continental dollar was set such that one paper Continental dollar was equal to one Spanish silver dollar coin or its specie equivalent (see figs. I.1–I.4). Thus, if a source reports that it took two Continental dollars to buy what one Spanish silver dollar would buy, that means that Continental dollars were trading at 50 percent of their face value (1/2 = 0.5). Similarly, if a source reports that it took four or ten or forty Continental dollars to buy what one Spanish silver dollar would buy, that means that Continental dollars were trading at 25 or 10 or 2.5 percent of their face value ($1/4 = 0.25$, $1/10 = 0.1$, $1/40 = 0.025$), respectively. If the source is a price index, then dividing the current price index into the based year set at 100 for June 1770–May 1775 — just before the first Continental dollars were emitted — generates a current percentage-of-face-value measure. Thus, if the current price index, say at the start of 1777, stands at 200, that means that the Continental dollar is trading at 50 percent of its face value ($100/200 = 0.5$). If the current price index, say at the end of 1777, stands at 500, that means that the Continental dollar is trading at 20 percent of its face value ($100/500 = 0.2$), and so on.

What the market exchange value of the Continental dollar actually was is not as obvious or as easily measured as the prior secondary literature indicates. Earlier scholars have reported a measure of the value of the Continental dollar, but typically only one such measure.[1] All measures show that the value of the Continental dollar was declining over time. Seldom do these authors indicate that there are many evidential source measures from which to choose, measures that exhibit considerable variance in the timing and extent of the Continental dollar's declining value. Nor do they discuss the intent or potential biases in these measures. In many cases, I suspect authors just grabbed the first measure in an original document or as reported in the secondary literature that they happened to run across without realizing that there are many alternatives from which to choose. Most authors used one or another of the "depreciation tables" (discussed below) as their measure of the market value of the Continental dollar. Depreciation tables are not actual observed market values and thus may erroneously measure the speed and extent of the decline in the value of the Continental dollar.

Four different types of evidence are used to measure the market value of the Continental dollar: depreciation tables, merchant account books, isolated statements by government officials, and price indices. I will evaluate each in turn. First I will show that there are wildly different outcomes across the various existing measures. Numerous depreciation tables exist, all different. Individual states issued their own depreciation tables for the Continental dollar. Congress issued a different depreciation table in 1780, and Jefferson reported a different one in 1786. While only one price index exists for the revolutionary period, value outcomes depend on the mix of goods included in the index, in particular whether import or export prices dominate the index. Finally, merchant accounts and isolated statements by officials are idiosyncratic and therefore hard to evaluate.

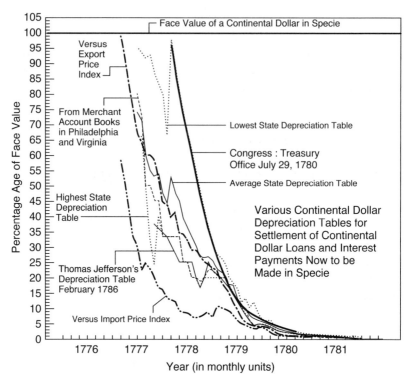

FIGURE 11.1. Various measures of the market value of a Continental dollar, 1776–81

Sources: American state papers (1832: 772–77); Bezanson (1951: 332–44); Boyd (1953–55, 10:42–43); Bullock (1895: 135); *JCC* (1904–37, 17:567–68); *Pennsylvania Gazette*, July 19, 1780; United States Congress (1834–56, 2:2243–51); Webster (1969: 501–2).

Note: For the price indices, only goods with prices reported for each month from 1770 through 1790 in the Bezanson (1951: 332–44) price data are used. The import price index lists eight goods: chocolate, coffee, molasses, pepper, rum, muscovado sugar, tea, and loaf sugar. The export price index lists seven goods: beef, iron bar, pork, wheat, corn, superfine flour, and common flour. See the text for construction.

Figure 11.1 shows these various measures and illustrates their wide range of values. For example, at the start of 1778 these measures range between 70 and 8 percent of a Continental dollar's face value. At the start of 1778, Congress's and the lowest states' depreciation tables rated the Continental dollar at 70 percent of its face value. The average state depreciation table rated the Continental dollar at just under 40 percent of its face value. The export price index rated it at 34 percent of its face value. Merchant account books, and Jefferson's and the highest states' depreciation tables, rated it at 25 percent of its face value. Finally, the import price index rated it at 8 percent of its face value. Clearly, which measure to use matters, and for some applications it matters a lot. All these measures have their problems and drawbacks, which are discussed next.

Depreciation Tables

Depreciation tables are not observed market values per se. They were created by legislatures for determining how the states and the congressional treasury would settle repayment of the loan principal and interest due on loan office certificates (see chap. 8). They were intended to calculate what was needed to compensate lenders for the loss in value between the value of the principal measured in Continental dollars when lent and the lower value of that sum measured in Continental dollars, or its specie equivalent, when repaid by the government. This purpose explains why there are many different depreciation tables, and why none starts before 1777. Individual states ran their own loan offices for selling loan office certificates and were partly responsible for repayment at maturity, and loan office certificates were not issued before 1777 (see chap. 8). Figure 11.2 reproduces the cover page of Congress's depreciation table. It explicitly says it is for calculating the repayment of principal and interest on loans of Continental dollars.

While depreciation tables were obviously related to and reflected what was happening to the Continental dollar in the marketplace, how closely the tables matched that market behavior is unknown. They were created after the fact by legislatures, mostly in the early 1780s; they are not contemporaneous observations. Exactly how each table was constructed by its legislature is unknown. The first depreciation table was recorded in Congress on June 28, 1780. It computed "a progressive rate of depreciation . . . in geometrical proportion to time," starting at face value and running to March 18, 1780 (*JCC* 17:567–68). The starting point was when Congress first borrowed Continental dollars—from late 1776 into early 1777 (see chap. 8).[2]

As can be seen, depreciation tables were not directly constructed from observations, so political bias may have influenced the values chosen. The most obvious bias would come from the incentive legislatures had to reduce the amount of compensation they owed to lenders, thus leaving more funds free for the legislature to spend as it desired. Given that most state and congressional coffers were empty and tax revenue inflows were meager, legislatures had the incentive to make the compensation as small as they could get away with.

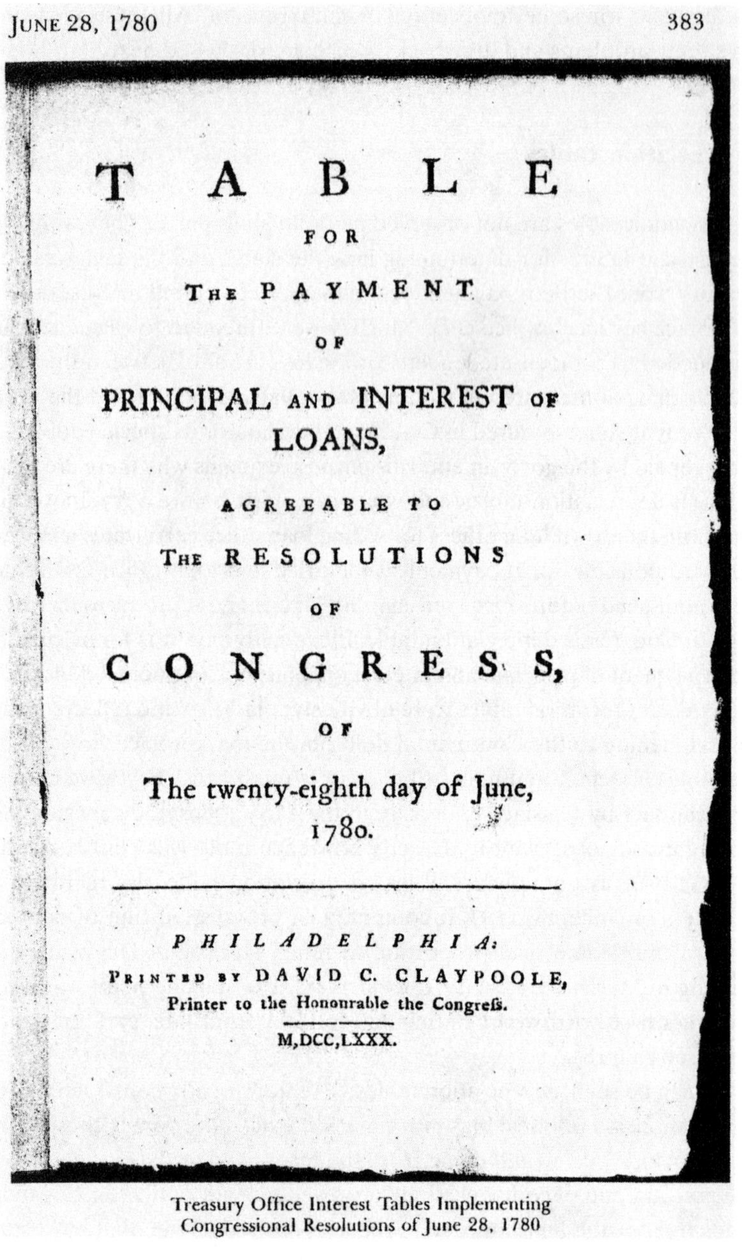

T A B L E

FOR

THE PAYMENT

OF

PRINCIPAL AND INTEREST OF LOANS,

AGREEABLE TO

THE RESOLUTIONS

OF

C O N G R E S S,

OF

The twenty-eighth day of June,
1780.

P H I L A D E L P H I A:
PRINTED BY DAVID C. CLAYPOOLE,
Printer to the Honourable the Congress.

M,DCC,LXXX.

Treasury Office Interest Tables Implementing
Congressional Resolutions of June 28, 1780

FIGURE 11.2. Cover page of Congress's 1780 depreciation table

The incentive to understate required compensation is consistent with the relative position of depreciation table values in figure 11.1 compared with price index and merchant account book values. Congress's and the lowest states' depreciation tables are considerably above the price index and merchant account book measures. The average of all the states' depreciation tables is slightly above the highest price index values (for export prices only) and well above the merchant account book values. Only the highest states' depreciation tables, as well as the depreciation table report by Jefferson in 1786, are comparable to the merchant account book values and fall between the export and import price index values, and this is only for before mid-1778. After mid-1778 all depreciation table values are above those for the price indices.

In conclusion, depreciation tables appear to overstate the market value of Continental dollars and so understate its fall in value. The overstatement is substantial early on, in 1777–78, becoming less dramatic after mid-1779. As such, depreciation tables are a poor measure of the market value of Continental dollars, especially before 1779.

Merchant Account Books

In April 1781 Pelatiah Webster (1969: 485–502) reported the evidence used in figure 11.1 on the market value of Continental dollars found in merchant account books. All he says is that the account books are for merchants in Virginia and Philadelphia. Who the merchants were, how many observations existed, and what commerce was involved are not recounted. The data Webster provides run from January 1777 through May 1781. It is possible that the Philadelphia merchant account book data used by Webster was incorporated into the larger data set used by Bezanson (1951: 332–42) to construct the Philadelphia price index. Bezanson's sources include records from Philadelphia merchants along with newspaper price currents.

Isolated Statements by Government Officials

On December 20, 1776, Robert Morris (delegate to Congress from Pennsylvania) valued a Continental dollar at 50 percent of face value. On September 30, 1777, William Williams (delegate to Congress from Connecticut) valued a Continental dollar at 25 percent of face value. On March 9, 1778, Congress's Committee at Camp valued a Continental dollar at 25 percent of face value. On July 19, 1779, Congress's Commerce Committee valued a Continental dollar at 16.7 percent of face value (Smith 1976–94, 5:623; 8:35; 9:245; 13:257). Upon what foundations these statements were made—whether they were based on direct market observations or just hearsay—is unknown.

Morris's statement is closest to the import price index value for his date. Williams's statement is closest to Jefferson's depreciation table value for his date. The Committee at Camp statement is closest to the export price index value at their date. The Commerce Committee statement is above all the other measures reported in figure 11.1. Such isolated statements are difficult to use as coherent and continuous value series.

The Philadelphia Price Index

Only one price index currently exists that spans the revolutionary years, and that is the Bezanson (1951) price index for the Philadelphia region. The obvious drawback to this evidence is that it covers only Philadelphia and its hinterlands. That said, Philadelphia was the largest city and the largest port of the thirteen colonies in rebellion. New York was occupied by the British after September 15, 1776, and Charleston after May 12, 1780. Boston and Charleston were on the fringe of where the major battles and warfare spending occurred (after 1775 for Boston and before 1780 for Charleston). For most of the Revolution covering the period when Continental dollars were spent by Congress, the middle colonies were where the war was fought and where most Continental dollars were spent (see chap. 6).

Philadelphia was occupied by the British from September 26, 1777, to June 18, 1778, making the Bezanson index based more on the Philadelphia hinterlands than on the port of Philadelphia during that occupation period. How the occupation affected the index is unclear. A price index measures absolute price movements (currency inflation and deflation) only to the extent that relative real-price shocks are netted out. One reason to separate the Bezanson index into imported versus exported goods is to help control for the effect of the British occupation and gauge the size of the relative real-price shocks involved. But for all that, the Bezanson price index is the only direct, purchase-revealed market evidence we have for the actual trade value of Continental dollars. It is a "real-time" monthly time series using contemporaneous observations, as opposed to being an after-the-fact creation, as the depreciation tables were.

The Bezanson index uses evidence from merchant account books and newspaper price currents in the Philadelphia region and thus contains a broad sampling mix of market-derived evidence. The index also measures prices monthly. Only fifteen goods, however, are continuously priced each month throughout the revolutionary period, and these goods are either predominantly imported goods or exported goods (see notes to figure 11.1). No purely domestically traded goods exist as a continuously priced series in the index. Thus, another drawback of this evidence is the mix of imported versus exported goods in the sample and how real shocks to imports and exports might alter the index. Again, for this reason, the export-only and import-only portions of the index are reported separately in figure 11.1.[3]

Figure 11.3 models the relative real-price movements in the Philadelphia price index caused by revolutionary war shocks that could be masking absolute price movements. The top panel in figure 11.3 shows what happened to relative import prices. The model assumes that American demand had its normal downward slope, that there was no American supply of the imported good in question, such as tea, and that Americans were a small part of a large global market for that good and thus were price-takers in that market. As such, Americans faced a perfectly elastic (flat) supply curve for that imported good. The prewar equilibrium is at $P*Q*$.

The First Continental Congress agreed to a boycott of all imports from Great Britain, the main source of colonial imports, starting on December 1, 1774. The top panel in figure 11.3 shows this as a reduction in American demand to the Q# boycott amount at $P*$. The boycott itself would not necessary lead to a long-run rise in import prices, since the British could sell their goods elsewhere in the world. In the short run, either a rise or a fall in relative import prices is possible depending how the pre-boycott stocks on hand in the colonies were demanded and priced (not shown in fig. 11.3). If initial stocks on hand were not considered part of the boycott, prices would rise. If initial stocks on hand were considered something to boycott, prices would fall.

The long-run effect on the relative price of imported goods during the Revolution comes from the British imposing a foreign-trade blockade on the colonies in rebellion, shown as a rise in the relative supply price of imports to $P**$. Congress opened American ports to non-British trade on

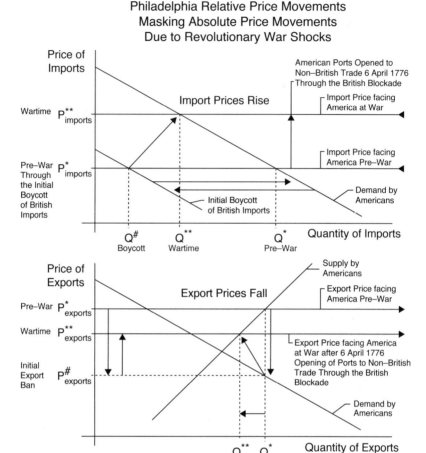

FIGURE 11.3. Philadelphia relative price movements masking absolute price movements owing to Revolutionary War shocks

April 6, 1776, shown as a return to the initial American demand for imports. In addition to the higher supply price cause by running the British blockade, part of the relative higher price of imports could also include having to import from less efficient and thus higher cost non-British suppliers. Regardless of how you adjust the model, the end result is that the relative price of imports rose during the Revolution independent of any depreciation or appreciation of the currency.

The bottom panel in figure 11.3 shows what happened to relative export prices. The model assumes that American demand had its normal downward slope and that American supply had its normal upward slope. It also assumes that Americans both consumed and exported this product—for example, tobacco—and that Americans were a small part of a large global market for that good and so are price-takers in that market. As such, Americans face a perfectly elastic (flat) demand curve for that exported good. The initial prewar equilibrium is at P*Q*.

The First Continental Congress agreed to an all-colony ban on exports to Great Britain starting on September 1, 1775. Most colonial exports to Europe were shipped to and through Britain. Given the export ban's starting date, initial export prices would fall, as the quantities produced in the prior period could not all be exported in a timely fashion to their traditional and primary overseas market. For Americans to consume the total amount produced would drive the price down to P#. Congress opened American ports to non-British trade on April 6, 1776. This trade, however, faced a British blockade of American foreign trade. The cost of running the blockade, plus the fact that non-British foreign buyers might be less willing to pay what British buyers would pay, reduced the wartime relative price of exports to P** from P* over the Revolution (but P** is higher than the initial short-run wartime fall in export prices, P#). Regardless of how you adjust the model, the end result is that the relative price of exports fell during the Revolution independent of any depreciation or appreciation of the currency.

The rise in real import and fall in real export prices caused by the Revolution and its trade boycotts and blockades altered the terms of trade. The percentage change in the terms of trade, the import price index divided by the export price index, is shown in figure 11.4. Initially, in 1776, the terms of trade deteriorated by a sizable 20 to 30 percent over prewar levels. It then deteriorated continuously, reaching four times above prewar levels by early 1778. Thereafter the terms of trade continuously improved, returning to prewar levels briefly by mid-1779 and then again in mid-1780 through mid-1781. Between 1782 and 1783 the terms of trade again deteriorated, reaching twice above prewar levels, only to rise again to prewar levels or better after mid-1783. Figure 11.4 also shows that the British occupation of Philadelphia was not a particularly reshaping event regarding the Philadelphia price index.

In conclusion, figures 11.3 and 11.4 show that export prices understate the decline in the value of the Continental dollar that is due to currency

FIGURE 11.4. Changes in the terms of trade, 1776–85

Source: Derived from Bezanson (1951: 332–42).

Note: See the notes to fig. 11.1 for the list of import and export goods in each index.

effects, and import prices overstate the decline in the value of the Continental dollar that is due to currency effects. The import index is a biased-high measure of that decline, and the export price index is a biased-low measure of that decline. As such, the export and import price indices in figure 11.1 bracket what the true fall in the value of the Continental dollar was due to currency effects. Whether an average price index, whether a weighted or unweighted average of import and export prices, gets you closer to the true fall in value of the Continental dollar cannot be discerned a priori without knowing more about the composition of the index and the dynamics illustrated in figure 11.3 model. For that reason, I will confine my assessment of the fall in value of the Continental dollar to that area bracketed by the export and import price indices in figure 11.1.

One last problem in using the Philadelphia price index as a measure of the declining value of the Continental dollar is determining when the index is tracking prices in Continental dollars versus some other currency. Figure 7.1 showed what unit of account was in dominant use in the Philadelphia region. It indicates that pricing in dollars, meaning Continental dollars, did not reach 50 percent of the prices observed before mid-1776. Thereafter, it was the dominant currency used in pricing until 1781.

Exactly how Bezanson (1951: 10–11) merged data that were largely in Pennsylvania pound currency units with the relatively few observations that were in Continental dollar units pre-mid-1776 is unclear. Market participants typically recorded monetary transactions in units of account, not media of exchange. In figure 7.1, out of 3,127 commercial advertisements placed in the *Pennsylvania Gazette* between March 1775 and April 1780 that listed a monetary statement, only 3 percent referred to a particular money or medium of exchange as opposed to just listing the unit of account used.

Merchant account books and price currents typically converted market transactions from whatever media of exchange were used into a common unit of account. For transactions in dollars, merchants initially used a fixed conversion rate of $1 = 7 shillings 6 pence (Bezanson 1951: 1–11, 26). How long this initial conversion rate stayed in use is unclear. Thus, only when marketplace transactions were typically in dollars can we be sure that the price index reflects changes in the value of dollars. The price indices pre-mid-1776 may not be capturing the decline in the value of the Continental dollar per se. For that reason I start the price index data in figure 11.1 in mid-1776, as it is only after that date that the price data are predominantly in Continental dollar units.[4]

Figure 11.5 shows that the price indices behave differently depending on which currency is the dominant pricing currency. The shift from pricing in Continental dollars to pricing in Pennsylvania pounds can clearly be seen in early 1781, when Continental dollars were abandoned as a medium-of-exchange currency. Thus, price index measures of Continental dollar values cannot be extended past early 1781.

Exactly when we can assume that price indices start measuring the value of Continental dollars is less clear. The price indices in figure 11.5, all versions except the export index, show values below 100 percent of base value starting between the end of 1775 and the beginning of 1776, and then only around 94 percent of face value. The first reports of Continental dollars' trading below face value in the marketplace were brought to Congress in Philadelphia on November 23, 1775, and then again on January 11, 1776. This first report was made immediately after the structural design of the Continental dollar was first reported in Pennsylvania newspapers (see chap. 4). The first congressional committee formed to investigate depreciation

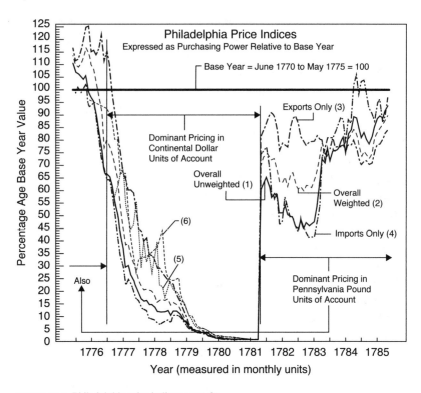

FIGURE 11.5. Philadelphia price indices, 1775–85

Source: Derived from Bezanson (1951: 60–67, 332–44); fig. 7.1.

Note: See text for construction and the notes to fig. 11.1. Indices 5 and 6 are not price indices per se but are derived from Bezanson's (1951: 60–67) data on exchanges of Continental dollars for foreign specie coins and on the prices for the same commodity expressed both in Continental dollars and in foreign coins, respectively, from 1776 to 1781, with interpolated values used for missing months of data. See this chapter, n. 3.

was also in November 1775.[5] Although this timing matches when the price indices dipped below 100 percent of face value (with the exception of the export index), the accuracy of the magnitude of this fall in value by mid-1776 is difficult to determine when currency composition in the index is likely dominated by monies other than Continental dollars.

Choosing the Best *MEV*

I will use the Philadelphia price indices from mid-1776 to early 1781 as my measure of the market exchange value of the Continental dollar. In particular, I will use the area bracketed by the export and import price indices in figure 11.1 as my best guess of where the market value of the Continental dollar resides. The price indices are the only market-revealed evidence we have. In addition, they show a lower value and greater decline in value of the Continental dollar than other measures. Given the surprising and radically important result presented in chapter 12, I want to bias that chapter 12 outcome against myself. In other words, by using the price indices as my measure of market value, I am using the worst-case scenario for making my case in chapter 12 that no depreciation of the Continental dollar in terms of expected loss of principal occurred before 1779. Using any other measure of value would yield a stronger outcome in my favor, so the key result I report next in chapter 12 can be accepted with confidence.

CHAPTER TWELVE

Time-Discounting versus Depreciation

Assessing the performance of the Continental dollar requires distinguishing between time-discounting and depreciation. In the prior literature, scholars have typically confused time-discounting with depreciation, conflating the two concepts and their outcomes. This confusion comes from two sources. One source is from the sloppy use of language where any value that becomes lower is said to have depreciated. The other source is from erroneously assuming that the Continental dollar is a fiat currency, similar to the US dollar today.

Depreciation is defined as the fall in a real asset's value over time. A fiat currency commands only current real values. Thus, if a US dollar bought two apples yesterday, but only one apple today, we would say the US dollar has depreciated by 50 percent between yesterday and today (in real apple value) because it commands only half as many apples today as it did yesterday. Each successive day tells us whether the US dollar has appreciated or depreciated from the prior day (in real apple value) depending on how many apples a US dollar commands that day compared with the prior day. A US dollar, as a fiat currency per se, has no legal claim to any fixed real future value. It is worth only what the market will bear today, and then what the market will bear tomorrow when tomorrow comes.

Time-discounting is different. Time-discounting measures the present value of a future real asset given the certainty of receiving that future real asset and taking into account the cost of time, namely the cost of waiting.

The basic continuous present-value formula is $PV = FVe^{-rt}$, where PV is the present value, FV is the future promised, contracted, or initially expected real value, t is the time interval between the present and the future, and r is the discount rate. The market interest rate for assets with little risk of default is typically used for r.

Given the definition of depreciation, the only relevant real asset in the present-value formula is FV. The fact that $PV < FV$ is not depreciation. It is just time-discounting. If FV remains unchanged, it does not matter what the current PV is, there has been no depreciation. If FV is a bond or loan, the principal remains intact and unaltered if FV remains unchanged. If the current MEV of the FV is its PV and FV is expected to stay at FV, then there is no depreciation, just time-discounting. $MEV = PV < FV$, rising to $MEV = FV$ as $t \rightarrow 0$. This case corresponds to $MEV = APV$ with $(TP - RD) = 0$ in the model of money in chapter 9 (see eq. 9.1).

Depreciation occurs only when the expected FV^* falls below the promised, contracted, or initially expected FV ($FV^* < FV$), such as an expected loss of principal repayment for a loan or for a bond at maturity. The current MEV would fall to reflect this expectation that the real future payoff would be less than promised, contracted, or initially expected. In this case, $MEV = PV - (FV - FV^*)e^{-rt}$. This formula corresponds to $MEV = APV - RD$ in the model of money in chapter 9, where PV equals APV and RD equals the present value of the expected depreciation in the real asset FV, namely $(FV - FV^*)e^{-rt}$. RD represents the expected loss in principal repayment at maturity, in present-value terms, if FV is a loan or bond.

If PV falls but FV remains unchanged, then again there is no depreciation (no loss of principal), just a change in the time-discounting calculation of PV. This can be the outcome when two different claims (claim 1 and claim 2) to two different future values (FV_1 and FV_2) are merged into a current average present value for the two claims in combination. Suppose $MEV_1 = PV_1$, $MEV_2 = PV_2$, $PV_1 > PV_2$, FV_1 remains unchanged, FV_2 remains unchanged and, crucially, the claims to FV_1 and FV_2 are made fungible such that you do not know in advance which claim will be paid off with which FV real assets, FV_1 or FV_2. Under these conditions, the best you can do is take an expectation or average PV of the two claims. Thus, $MEV = [(MEV_1 + MEV_2)/2] = [(PV_1 + PV_2)/2] < MEV_1 = PV_1$. If claim 1 is issued first and claim 2 is issued second and added to the mix, then over this sequence of time MEV will fall as PV falls, MEV to $(MEV_1 + MEV_2)/2$ and PV_1 to $(PV_1 + PV_2)/2$, yet there is no depreciation as FV_1

and FV_2 remain unchanged. This pattern is exactly what happened with the Continental dollar's PV from 1775 through 1779 (see chap. 10).

As part I makes clear, the Continental dollar was not a fiat currency, but a zero-coupon bond. As such, changes in its current MEV, as shown by the measures reported in chapter 11, cannot be used per se as a sign or measure of depreciation. This is because the Continental dollar was not a fiat currency but represented a claim to a real asset (Spanish silver dollars) to be paid at a future date. To measure true depreciation, the Continental dollar's asset present value (PV or APV in chap. 9) must be netted out, such that $MEV = APV - RD$, with RD being the measure of depreciation capturing the expected default or loss of principal of the future value promised or expected by the Continental dollar claim.

I will translate this analysis into a simpler story for the general reader. Suppose you are given a claim check by Farmer Jones to a basket of one hundred crisp new apples from his orchard that you can redeem only from him ten years from now (the claim check playing the role of the Continental dollar). The claim check's face value says one hundred crisp new apples (but only ten years from now, per legally contracted agreement). At a 6 percent discount rate (r = 0.06) you would be indifferent between holding the claim check and redeeming the one hundred apples ten years from now or taking fifty-five crisp new apples from Farmer Jones today. The difference between fifty-five apples today and one hundred apples ten years from now is not depreciation of the claim check. The one hundred future apples remain as one hundred future apples. There is no loss there. The difference between fifty-five apples today and one hundred apples ten years from now is just measuring the value of time, that is, the opportunity cost of waiting. They are equivalent values, as you are indifferent to whether you get one hundred apples in ten years or fifty-five apples now $[(100e^{-0.06*10}) \approx 55]$. The present or current value is below the face value of the claim check, but that does not represent depreciation—just as the current cash-in value of a US savings bond, being less than its face value, does not represent depreciation, just time-discounting.

Now suppose that, shortly after being given the claim check, you expect Farmer Jones will not be able to provide the one hundred crisp new apples due you in ten years. All of a sudden Farmer Jones looks frailer and more sickly than you first thought, and you suspect therefore that his orchard will be neglected in the future. You expect that in ten years you will only get eighty crisp new apples for your claim check. You expect Farmer Jones to default on twenty crisp new apples owed you (maybe you expect him to stick you with twenty worthless wormy apples out of the one hundred owed). At a 6 percent discount rate, you now will be indifferent as to whether you receive forty-four crisp new apples today or hold your claim check for ten years and get only eighty of the one hundred apples listed on its face [$(80e^{-0.06*10}) \approx 44$]. The present value of the expected default (the RD) is eleven crisp new apples [$(20e^{-0.06*10}) \approx 11$]. The current value of your claim check is $PV - RD$, or $55 - 11 = 44$ apples. The loss of twenty apples at maturity, or the present value of those twenty apples today (eleven apples), is the depreciation of your claim check.

Now suppose Farmer Jones gives you two claim checks. First, he gives you a claim check for one hundred crisp new apples in ten years, and then shortly thereafter he give you another claim check for one hundred crisp new apples in thirteen years. You expect him to deliver on both claim checks as promised, but then, frustratingly, he does not tell you which claim check will be honored in which year. He will honor whichever claim check happens to be presented first in ten years, and then, second, in thirteen years. The claim honored in ten years is worth fifty-five apples today, and the one honored in thirteen years is worth forty-six apples today: $(100e^{-0.06*10}) \approx 55$ and $(100e^{-0.06*13}) \approx 46$. When you just had the first claim check, its present value today was fifty-five apples. Then, when you are handed the second claim check, with the uncertainty regarding which claim check corresponds to which redemption date, the present value of either claim check is the expectation or average of the two claim checks, or fifty and a half apples today [$(55 + 46)/2$]. The current value of the average claim check has fallen from fifty-five apples, when you received the first one, to fifty and a half apples on average. The average present value has fallen, but there is no depreciation, as the two tranches of one hundred crisp new apples attached to the two claim checks remain intact. The fall in present value is merely a compositional adjustment to an average claim-check value versus an individual claim-check value. Again, this is what happens to the Continental dollar from 1775 through 1779 (see chap. 10).

In conclusion, to measure the true depreciation of the Continental dollar, the APV of the Continental dollar from chapter 10 has to be subtracted from the MEV of the Continental dollar from chapter 11: ($MEV - APV$) $\equiv$ ($TP - RD$). If $MEV < APV$, then $TP = 0$ and $RD > 0$ (see chap. 9). Depreciation is afoot, with the size of RD measuring the present value of the expected default on the Continental dollar's initially expected payoff at maturity. If $MEV > APV$, then $TP > 0$ and $RD = 0$ (see chap. 9). There is no depreciation, and in fact the Continental dollar is trading at an appreciated value, capturing the willingness of people to pay a transaction premium above its expected APV because it serves as a more convenient transacting medium than the next best alternative. If $MEV \approx APV$, then $(TP - RD) = 0$, and the Continental dollar is just a tradable financial instrument, no better or worse to use as a transacting medium of exchange than the next best barter asset or good. It has no "moneyness" value, but also it suffers no depreciations.

Evaluating the Continental Dollar's *MEV* versus *APV*: Measuring True Depreciation

Figures 12.1, 12.2, and 12.3 merge figure 11.1 (*MEV* measures) and figure 10.3 (*APV* measures) onto the same graph so that *MEV* can be compared with *APV* over time. For clarity, figure 12.1 uses only the Philadelphia export and import price indices as the measure of *MEV*, my preferred measures (see chap. 11), and reports only data from 1775–79. Figure 12.2 reports the same evidence but extends the data out to 1781 and includes the overall weighted price index for Philadelphia. For comparative purposes, figure 12.3 reports the same *APV* evidence but compares it with only two of the lower depreciation-table measures of *MEV*, namely Jefferson's 1786 table (Boyd 1953–55, 10:42–43) and the average of the state depreciation tables reported by Bullock (1895: 135). The other depreciation tables from figure 11.1 lead only to a more dramatic conclusion in the same direction as reported here.

The existence of three distinct periods can be gleaned from the evidence in figures 12.1, 12.2, and 12.3: from the Continental dollar's beginning in late 1775 to late 1776; from 1777 to the end of 1778; and from 1779 on. From the Continental dollar's beginning in late 1775 to late 1776, *MEV* > *APV* and so *TP* > 0, meaning that the Continental dollar not only was not depreciating, but in fact had a positive "moneyness" value, meaning it traded at an appreciated rate compared with its expected *APV*. From 1777 to the end of 1778, the proposition that *MEV* ≈ *APV* cannot be rejected on balance, and so the Continental dollar suffered no depreciation, nor was it valued above its expected *APV* when used as a medium of exchange. From 1779 on, *MEV* < *APV* and so *RD* > 0, meaning that the Continental dollar suffered depreciation. Expectations of default on its forecast future expected face-value payoff became manifest only after 1778.

Before late 1776 all measures of *MEV* were above *APV*. Because all *MEV* measures were above *APV* before late 1776, the claim that *TP* > 0

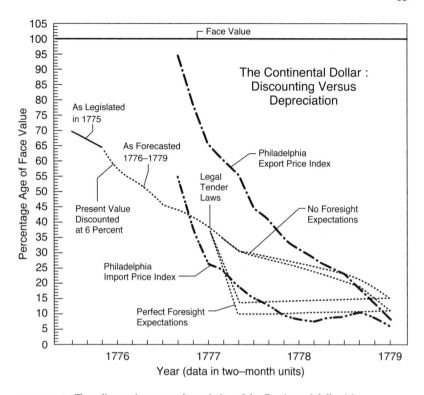

FIGURE 12.1. Time-discounting versus depreciation of the Continental dollar (1)

Sources: Figs. 10.3 and 11.1.

Note: Dotted lines are the asset present value calculations (*APVs*) from chap. 10. All other lines are the market exchange values (*MEVs*) from chap. 11.

in this period can be accepted with confidence. Because *MEV* measures before mid-1776 may not be reliable (see chap. 11), I will use mid-1776 as my starting point. This point is also where *MEV* exceeds *APV* by the most among the post-mid-1776 evidence. At mid-1776, using the overall Philadelphia price index (see fig. 12.2), *MEV* exceeds *APV* by roughly 20 percentage points, that is, $MEV = APV + TP$, namely $65 = 45 + 20$. In other words, while the Continental dollar was trading at roughly 65 percent of face value, it should have traded at only about 45 percent of face value if it was valued only as a non-money zero-coupon bond with no expectations of default. The extra 20 percentage points of face value added to that real *APV* means that traders in the marketplace placed a sizable *TP* on using Continental dollars as the preferred medium of exchange.

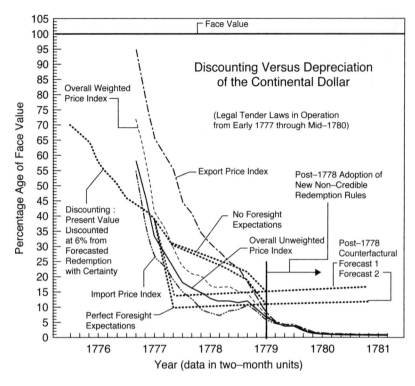

FIGURE 12.2. Time-discounting versus depreciation of the Continental dollar (2)

Sources: Figs. 10.3 and 11.1.

Note: Dotted lines are the asset present value calculations (*APVs*) from chap. 10. All other lines are the market exchange values (*MEVs*) from chap. 11.

Despite trading at roughly 65 percent of face value by mid-1776, the Continental dollar not only suffered no depreciation, but was actually trading at a substantially appreciated value. Exactly why is unclear, though several explanations are possible. First, the Continental dollar was the only paper currency that could cross all state borders without exchange-rate adjustments. That fact could make it a preferred medium of exchange, especially for cross-state-border transactions, compared with state-specific paper monies. A premium would be paid to use Continental dollars rather than a state-specific paper money when trading. Second, patriotic fervor and a desire to be seen as connected to the Revolution may have boosted the Continental dollar's transaction premium early in the Revolution.

For whatever reason, the evidence indicates that there was no depreciation of the Continental dollar before the end of 1776. From mid-1776 to the start of 1777, however, the transaction premium shrank, disappearing by 1777. The decline in the market value of the Continental dollar in this period is due mostly to the decline of its *APV*. In other words, it is just rational bond pricing, given continual new emissions and their forecast redemption. Part of the steep decline in the market value of the Continental dollar from mid-1776 to the start of 1777, however, must be ascribed to the loss of this *TP*. Depreciation made no contribution here.

From the start of 1777 to the end of 1778, the proposition that on balance $MEV \approx APV$, and so $TP = 0$ and $RD = 0$, cannot be rejected. Despite falling from roughly 40 to roughly 10 percent of face value in the marketplace between 1777 and 1779, the Continental dollar on balance

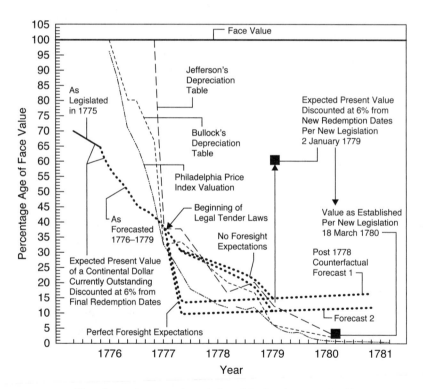

FIGURE 12.3. Time-discounting versus depreciation of the Continental dollar (3)

Sources: Figs. 10.3 and 11.1.

Note: Dotted lines are the asset present value calculations (*APV*s) from chap. 10. All other lines are the market exchange values (*MEV*s) from chap. 11.

experienced no depreciation. Its fall in market value simply tracked its declining (average) APV. It functioned as a tradable financial instrument, no
better and no worse than the next best medium of exchange. This finding
is revolutionary compared with the prior literature, so let me repeat it.
Before late 1778, the Continental dollar did not depreciate. Its fall in value
was all due to the fall in the present value of the average Continental dollar caused by the forecast time to redemption of continued emissions of
new Continental dollars. In other words, rational bond pricing explains
the market value of the Continental dollar from 1777 to 1779 under the
expectation that default on principal repayment at expected maturity
would not occur, namely that RD (depreciation) = 0.

The data on MEV and APV between 1777 and 1779 are messy in terms
of alternative MEVs and APVs that can be used. Legal-tender laws in
early 1777 created a negative externality of future emissions on past emissions' APVs. Future emissions lowered the APVs of past emissions creating a partial present-value loss on pre-1777 emissions from their pre-1777
forecast expectations of redemption. The public's adaptation to how legal-
tender laws would alter their APV calculation depends on how well the
public forecast future emissions (see chap. 10). Because this forecast is unknown, I show both the perfect-foresight and the no-foresight outcomes on
APVs in figures 12.1, 12.2, and 12.3. Most of the MEV measures are bracketed by the perfect-foresight versus no-foresight APV measures, and it can
be concluded that in this period, on balance, $MEV \approx APV$ and so $TP = 0$
and $RD = 0$. However, depending on whether the public was closer to
the perfect-foresight or the no-foresight APV can lead to small $TP > 0$ or
small $RD > 0$ outcomes in the period 1777–79.

If the public thought each new emission of Continental dollars was
the last emission (the no-foresight expectation), then on balance $APV >$
MEV. All the measures of MEV, except the biased-high export price index, are below this APV from mid-1777 to 1779. This implies that $TP = 0$
and $RD > 0$—in other words, that some depreciation was present. At the
start of 1778, APV for the no-foresight case was roughly 25 percent of face
value. The MEV using the overall Philadelphia price index (see fig. 12.2)
was roughly 15 percent of face value. The difference implies the presence
of an RD, that is, depreciation, of about 10 percent of face value, namely
$MEV = APV - RD$ or $15 = 25 - 10$.

Alternatively, if the public had perfect foresight regarding future emissions, which was a good possibility (see chap. 10), then on balance $APV <$
MEV. Most of the measures of MEV, except the biased-low import price

index after mid-1777, were at or above this *APV* from early 1777 to late 1778. This implies that $RD = 0$ and $TP > 0$—in other words, that no depreciation was present and the Continental dollar traded at a small appreciated rate above its expected asset present value. In mid-1777, *APV* for the perfect-foresight case was roughly 12 percent of face value. The *MEV* using the overall Philadelphia price index (see fig. 12.2) was roughly 17 percent of face value. The difference implies the presence of a *TP* of about 5 percent of face value (and no depreciation), that is, $MEV = APV + TP$ or $17 = 12 + 5$.

From 1779 forward the *APV*s based on the forecast expected redemption derived from the 1775 legislated structures (forecasts 1 and 2) exceeded all measures of *MEV*. This pattern began in late 1778, by November of that year, and was clearly the case for all measures of *MEV* by the start of 1779 (January and February of that year). From 1779 the Continental dollar suffered depreciation, and increasing depreciation over time. In mid-1779 the *APV* stood at roughly 14 percent of face value, whereas all the measures of *MEV* were at roughly 4 percent of face value. Thus, $RD = 10$ percent of face value, such that $MEV = APV - RD$ or $4 = 14 - 10$. The Continental dollar did not depreciate before late 1778; it began to do so clearly only at the start of 1779, and then increasingly so onward.

The source of that depreciation and the calamity that befell the Continental dollar comes from actions taken by Congress at the end of 1778 through mid-1780. The Continental dollar experienced a continuous decline in its market value from 1776 onward. But this decline to 1779 was not due to depreciation. It was primarily the outcome of rational bond pricing, namely time-discounting. The congressional actions that precipitated the rise in depreciation, the destruction of the Continental dollar financing system, and finally its abandonment as money lay in the 1779–80 period. That period and those actions are addressed in the next two chapters.

CHAPTER THIRTEEN

1779

The Turning Point

If they [Continental dollars] were to be Ascertained when they were to be redeemed, Especially if it was at a short period, it would give them a confidence in the money, and greatly tend to Establish its Currency.—Commissioners of the New England States' letter to Congress, January 30, 1778 (*JCC* 4:382)

Between a Rock and a Hard Place

Congressional finances were in reasonable shape up to mid-1778 (see table 6.5). Financial disaster, however, was looming. Congressional spending, driven mostly by the expansive spending by the Quartermaster and Commissary Departments, was about to run substantially ahead of Congress's revenues. Congress's traditional and primary revenue source was the printing of new Continental dollars and to a lesser extent Continental dollars borrowed through issuing loan office certificates and as direct loans from the states. Almost half of all net new Continental dollars ever printed would be spent out of the Continental Treasury in 1779 (see table 1.1).

Continental dollars, however, were rapidly losing purchasing power. As more and more Continental dollars were emitted, the expected face-value redemption of those dollars was pushed further and further into the future, thus driving their present value (current purchasing power) down (see chap. 10). By the last quarter of 1778 the emission of new Continental dollars yielded only about ten cents of purchasing power (forecast present value) per face-value dollar emitted based on rational bond pricing (see table 10.1). In the marketplace, based on Philadelphia price indices, a similar result can be seen where only 10 to 15 cents of purchasing power was realized per face-value dollar spent (see fig. 11.1).

Congress was between a rock and a hard place with its Continental dollar financing system. Further emissions accelerated the gap between face value and present value (purchasing power), given rational bond pricing based on reasonable forecasts of when redemption at face value would occur. It was not just a widening gap between the Continental dollar's face value and its present value that was coming into view in 1778, but a clear, ever-accelerating, widening gap that was apparent in late 1778 and would be experienced through 1779. Financing congressional spending by emitting new Continental dollars was quickly becoming unsustainable (see appendix C, especially fig. C.1).

Congress had to do something to rectify this situation and stop from running off this fiscal cliff. Assuming Congress could not control the spending side of its budget short of surrender meant that Congress had to vastly improve the revenue side of its budget. Congress either had to find new revenue sources or to improve the current purchasing power of newly emitted and newly borrowed Continental dollars. Congress had no independent taxing power and would not achieve any such power under the Articles of Confederation. Borrowing from foreign powers was limited and declined from 1778 into 1779 (see table 6.5). That left trying to increase the purchasing power (present value) of the mass of newly printed as well as newly borrowed Continental dollars that Congress would spend in 1779.

Two avenues to increasing the present value of any new spending of Continental dollars by Congress in 1779 were (a) establishing a shorter redemption window and having it be closer to the present than what was being currently forecast, and (b) setting a hard limit on the total net new Continental dollars that could ever be emitted. The first element is obvious given the nature of time-discounting. The second element is necessary because of how legal-tender laws affected present value calculations—that is, any expected new emissions in the future would drive down the present value of all current dollars in circulation (see chap. 10).

Given this backdrop of Congress's financial situation in late 1778, I will now explain the redemption rule change Congress implemented in January 1779 for all Continental dollars and explain why Congress's new redemption rule deviated substantially from the pattern established with the first two emissions in 1775. First, I will explain what this rule change was. Second, I will explain the personnel changes in Congress that contributed to a loss of institutional memory and so shaped the rule change adopted in terms of disregarding the need for fiscal credibility. Third, I will explain the "ideal" outcome that this redemption rule change could have generated. Fourth, I will explain what Congress was up to with this rule change and what Congress hoped to gain by it. Finally, I will explain how this rule change failed to achieve its goal, contributed to undermining the Continental dollar system, and so caused depreciation of the Continental dollar to manifest itself for the first time.

The January 2, 1779, Redemption Rule Change

On January 2, 1779, twelve days prior to authorizing what would be the last emission of Continental dollars (emission no. 11), Congress changed redemption requirements for all Continental dollars. The Board of Treasury and Congress finally responded to their administrative failure to explicitly establish redemption windows for emissions nos. 3 through 10. This failure had been noted by the state commissioners' meeting in New Haven in their January 1778 letter to Congress (see chap. 5). The Board of Treasury's preamble to the January 2, 1779, resolution read:

> Whereas, these United States, unprovided with revenues, and not heretofore in a condition to raise them, have, in the course of the present war, repeatedly been under the necessity of emitting bills of credit [Continental dollars], for the redemption of which the faith of these United States has been solemnly pledged, and the credit of which their honor and safety, as well as justice, is highly concerned to support and establish; and whereas, to that end, it is essentially necessary to ascertain the periods of their redemption, and seasonally establish funds which, in due time, without distressing the people, shall make adequate provision for the same. (*JCC* 12:1266–67; 13:20)

All the structural procedures from 1775 were kept in place except the redemption installment amounts and the length of the contiguous-year redemption window. The face-value specie-redemption option for citizens at the Continental Treasury was not mentioned in the January 2, 1779, resolution. However, Congress indicated that it was still operative on June 14, 1779.[1] All past and future emissions were now to be fungible in redemption, explicitly codifying nationally what had only been an implicit outcome of legal-tender laws enacted piecemeal in 1777 by individual states (see chap. 10). The resolution also indicated that net new emissions would end in 1779. The states were now to redeem $15 million in 1779, by November 30, and an equal amount each year through 1797, the amount needed to exhaust the remainder (see table 1.1).

On September 1, 1779, Congress set a $200 million limit for total net new emissions. Congress made sure it reached that limit by November 29, 1779, the day before the first redemptions were scheduled to be received by the Continental Treasury. Thus, by the end of 1779 the states were required to remit 10,277,222 Continental dollars each year from 1780 through 1797 to the Continental Treasury to be burned. Eighteen years times 10,277,222 plus 15,000,000 for 1779 equals 199,989,995 net new Continental dollars actually emitted, versus the $200 million Congress thought it had emitted (see table 1.1 and appendix A). This number is the net of some undetermined amount of Continental dollars remitted by the states after 1779 that the resolution allowed to be respent, rather than destroyed, to pay off loan office certificate principal and interest on loans issued before 1780 (see chap. 8). Total state remittances of Continental dollars after 1779, therefore, had to be somewhat higher than 10,277,222 per year to achieve the permanent removal of these respent Continental dollars from circulation.

The Loss of Institutional Memory and Triumph of the Debt Hawks

By 1779 little institutional memory based on personal knowledge was left in Congress regarding the rationale for the initial structural design of the Continental dollar. The original designers, explainers, and advocates were gone. No core group of congressmen involved with, and voting on, all monetary and finance matters existed continuously from 1775 through 1780. The current Board of Treasury that brought the January 2, 1779, resolution before Congress consisted of Oliver Ellsworth, Elbridge Gerry, Richard Huston, Richard Henry Lee, Gouverneur Morris, Edward Telfair, and John Witherspoon. Only Lee had been in Congress in 1775 for the debate and passage of the resolutions establishing the structural design and redemption windows for the first two emissions of Continental dollars (see chap. 1).

Only Ellsworth, Gerry, and Witherspoon from the Board of Treasury, however, were present in Congress for the January 2, 1779, vote on the resolution (members of the Board were all congressmen). The resolution passed nine states to two, with only William Whipple of New Hampshire and John Henry of Maryland opposed. Only six of the twenty-three congressmen voting on this resolution were present in Congress in 1775 for the debates and passage of the resolutions establishing the structural design and redemption windows for the first two emissions. These six included three members of the New York delegation, John Jay, James Duane, and William Floyd; Eliphalet Dyer of Connecticut; Samuel Adams of Massachusetts; and Francis Lightfoot Lee of Virginia.[2]

Of these six individuals, Duane's proposal in 1775 to shorten the redemption window for emission no. 2 had been rejected by Congress, and Jay and Adams had sat on a committee that in early 1776 had its proposal to call in all Continental dollars and replace them with much larger-value interest-bearer bonds rejected by Congress. For these three individuals, educating the other congressmen in 1779 on the principles and rationale underlying Congress's 1775 structural design of the Continental dollar may not have been a priority or in their personal interest. It may also have even been outside their understanding. Whipple, who was not in Congress in 1775 but was there in early 1776 and sat on the coin rating committee, may have absorbed enough about the 1775 structural design to understand that the changes to that design made by the January 2, 1779, resolution were problematic, which would explain his vote against that resolution.

The change in congressional personnel by 1779 led to the triumph of the debt hawks in Congress. From the rhetoric at the time, numerous congressmen advocated a pay-as-you-go approach to Congress's budget. Not only should current war expenses be paid out of current state taxes or state revenues provided to Congress, but current congressional debts should be paid off quickly by states' raising taxes so Congress could extinguish its debts. In other words, debt financing was seen as a bad thing that should not be practiced, and all current debts should be eliminated as soon as possible. These congressmen did not worry about the fiscal credibility of states' raising their taxes, apparently thinking that those taxes could be raised infinitely without ramifications. James Duane's proposal in 1775 that subsequent emissions of Continental dollars all be redeemed in the same short redemption window, a proposal that was defeated in 1775 because it was seen by most congressmen then as not fiscally credible (see chap. 1), now gained ascendance. Whether Duane, who was still in Congress in 1779, personally rallied other new congressmen to his view is unknown, but such an effort would be consistent with the new redemption rule adopted in 1779.

The Ideal Expected Present Value Time Path
of Continental Dollar Values

Establishing the time path of the ideal expected present value of Continental dollars under the January 2, 1779, resolution comes with caveats. If these caveats are ignored, then that ideal at the inception of emission no. 11 would become 62 percent of face value, which was 48 and 52 percentage points higher than that projected by face-value redemption forecasts 1 and 2, respectively (see table 10.1). Figures 10.3 and C.1 show this revaluation in the ideal expected present value and how it would slowly appreciate to face value by 1797 (*JCC* 14:728). If this resolution was credible, a radical revaluation of the Continental dollar would have been achieved that would dramatically raise the Continental dollar's current purchasing power.

The January 2, 1779, resolution's radical reevaluation of the ideal expected present value of the Continental dollar, compared with forecasts 1 and 2, was caused by substantially shortening the redemption window from what prevailed in these forecasts. The resolution's redemption window ran for eighteen years, from 1779 to 1797, with more redeemed in the first year than in subsequent years. By contrast, the redemption windows for forecasts 1 and 2, at the inception of emission no. 11, ran for forty-three and seventy-three years, respectively. These windows were not frontloaded as the January 2, 1779, window was. Having more redeemed in the early years of a redemption window compared with the latter years raised the ideal expected present value over that of an evenly spaced redemption window.

What Congress did with the January 2, 1779, resolution was also consist with the advice sent to them by the state commissioners meeting in New Haven in January 1778 (see chap. 5). These commissioners recommended that Congress remedy the missing redemption instructions for emissions after no. 2 by establishing a "short period" for the redemption. They thought that such a short period would give the public "confidence in the money" and "establish its currency." Apparently Congress in early 1779 now agreed with that view (Hammond 1889a: 293; appendix C).

While the January 2, 1779, resolution filled in the missing redemption instructions for the eight preceding emissions, thus giving the system more certainty than before, it also altered the redemption pattern set in the first two emissions passed by Congress in 1775. As such, the expectations built into forecasts 1 and 2 were no longer valid. Given that those expectations were based on the likely fulfillment of ideal conditions, such as certainty of redemption at face value in specie as promised, the ideal expected present value calculated for the January 2, 1779, resolution, as shown in figures 10.4 and 12.3, may be outside the bounds of reality.

Emissions nos. 1 and 2, and consequently forecasts 1 and 2, were predicated on redemption taxes being within historically acceptable and fiscally feasible limits. This allowed the calculation of an ideal expected present value. Table 10.1 shows that with emission no. 11, under the January 2, 1779, redemption structure, per-year per-white-capita taxes would need to average nine times above these historically acceptable and fiscally feasible levels. They would have to be even 1.7 times above the tax levels achieved by the federal government from 1792 through 1795 after it had acquired direct taxing powers under the US Constitution. That tax level was just to cover Continental dollar redemption. When added to additional taxes needed to cover other government expenses and debts, it is doubtful that citizens had the resources to pay such high taxes.

These observations raise questions about the fiscal credibility of the January 2, 1779, redemption structure and thus about the presumed certainty of redemption as promised—an assumption needed to make an ideal present value calculation.[3] While the Board of Treasury, in its preamble to the resolution, intended to "establish funds"—that is, taxes—"without distressing the people," it is hard to see the level of implied taxation as anything short of "distressing." As such, the ideal expected present value calculation may not be valid for the January 2, 1779, redemption structure (see fig. 10.4).

What Was Congress Up To? The Goal of the January 2, 1779, Redemption Rule Change

What Congress's goals were in enacting the January 2, 1779, redemption rule change was not clearly articulated by anyone in or out of Congress. Thus, Congress's goals must be inferred. First, the January 2, 1779, redemption rule change is a clear indication that congressmen regarded the Continental dollar to be a zero-coupon bond currency and not a fiat money. Redemption mattered. Second, it is difficult to interpret the rule change as anything other than an attempt to raise the present value of the Continental dollars Congress intended to spend in 1779 and so raise those dollars' purchasing power in the marketplace over what prevailed at the end of 1778. Finally, Congress had a lot to gain by this rule change if it worked. Those potential gains are consistent with what underlay Congress's motives in passing the January 2, 1779, resolution.

Congress would emit 98,552,475 net new Continental dollars in 1779 (see table 1.1). If no redemption rule changes were made, using forecasts 1 and 2, that sum would yield only 10 to 15 percent, and using the Philadelphia price indices only about 5 percent, of its face value as purchasing power in 1779 (see table 10.1 and fig. 11.1). Thus, the $98,552,475 emitted would yield only between $4,927,624 and $14,782,871 in purchasing power for Congress in 1779. By contrast, if the January 2, 1779, redemption rule change was successful, then the 98,552,475 net new Continental dollars emitted by Congress in 1779 would yield $61,477,034 in purchasing power (present value) (see table 10.1 and figs. 10.4 and 12.3). This would markedly improve Congress's budget, helping to meet or even exceed the escalating spending demands of 1779–80 (see table 6.5).

For 1779, two other revenue sources denominated in Continental dollars were affected by the January 2, 1779, redemption rule change. First, Congress was seeking to borrow already-spent Continental dollars via loan office certificates to spend as a new revenue source (see chaps. 6 and 8). Improving the purchasing power of these borrowed Continental dollars by increasing their present value (via shortening the time to redemption) would be to Congress's financial advantage.

Over half of all the loan office certificates, 40 million Continental dollars (face value), to be borrowed and spent by Congress were authorized by Congress in February and June 1779, shortly after Congress made its January 1779 Continental dollar redemption rule change (see table 8.1). Under the present value calculation in forecast 1 for 1779 that $40 million in face value had only about $5.8 million in purchasing power (see table 10.1), and, using the Philadelphia price indices for 1779, it had only about $2 million in purchasing power (see fig. 11.1). If the January 2, 1779, redemption rule change was successful, then this $40 million in borrowed Continental dollars in 1779 would have about $24.5 million in purchasing power, a marked improvement in purchasing power for this congressional revenue source.

Second, Congress also asked the states to loan a sizable number of Continental dollars to Congress in 1779, so Congress could respend them. The states were asked to impose taxes on their citizens to raise this money and then directly loan that Continental dollar tax revenue to Congress. States were given individual loan quotas to fill (see table 6.1). The total amount of loans requested in 1779 was 60 million Continental dollars (face value): a 45 million Continental dollar loan requested on May 21, 1779, and a 15 million Continental dollar loan requested on October 6–7, 1779.[4]

If these amounts were actually loaned by the states to Congress, they would help cover the residual deficit estimated in table 6.5 for the years

1779 and 1780. However, neither the amounts the states remitted as loans nor when the loans were remitted is quite clear. Little compliance with these loan requests can be found. The states may have ignored them because the per-year per-white-capita taxes needed to comply with these loan requests in Continental dollars at their face value, around $33, were around eighty times higher than what had been historically feasible (see table 10.1). When added to the other taxes that would be required to remit state quotas of Continental dollars to the Continental Treasury to be burned, to pay off loan office certificates, and to cover other state-specific spending obligations, it is doubtful that citizens had the resources to pay such high taxes. The lack of state compliance with these loan requests is implied by the language used in the redemption rule-change resolution Congress made on March 18, 1780 (see chap. 14).[5]

Initially, if Congress expected the states to meet this request for a loan of 60 million Continental dollars in 1779, it had much to gain if it could successfully implement the January 2, 1779, redemption rule change. Under the present-value calculation in forecast 1 for 1779, that $60 million loan in face value had only about $8.7 million in purchasing power (see table 10.1), and, using the Philadelphia price indices for 1779, had only about $3 million in purchasing power (see fig. 11.1). If the January 2, 1779, redemption rule change was successful, then these 60 million borrowed Continental dollars in 1779 would have about $37.2 million in purchasing power, a marked improvement in the purchasing power for that congressional revenue source.

The total Continental dollars both newly emitted and potentially borrowed in 1779 by Congress that it could spend that year amounted to about $198.5 million in face value. If Congress did nothing, that $198.5 million would yield only around $10 million to $30 million in purchasing power. However, if the January 2, 1779, redemption rule change was successful, that purchasing power would rise to about $123 million—an amount that would more than solve Congress's looming post-1778 budget crisis. As such, the January 2, 1779, redemption rule change can be interpreted as a desperate, and ultimately misguided, attempt by Congress to fix its looming financial deficits for 1779 and 1780 (see table 6.5).

Failure, the Lack of Fiscal Credibility, and the Emergence of True Depreciation

The January 2, 1779, redemption rule change did not improve the purchasing power of the Continental dollar. At the start of 1779 with the adoption of the new redemption rule, using the Philadelphia price indices, the market exchange value of the Continental dollar did not increase but remained at about 6 percent of its face value. By the end of 1779 it declined further to about 1.5 percent of its face value (see figs. 11.1 and 12.2).

By mid-June 1779 Congress must have been aware of the January 2, 1779, resolution's failure to raise the Continental dollar's present value and must have given up on its having any chance of future success. This can be deduced from the June 29, 1779, resolution for the last authorization of loan office certificates—the last one slated to be in the "borrow and spend" category. In that resolution, Congress added the precursor to its 1780 depreciation table, namely an indexing of interest payments to the growth in the amount of Continental dollars outstanding (see chaps. 8 and 11; *JCC* 14:783–85). If the January 2, 1779, resolution had been successful, there would have been no reason for Congress to enact this indexation scheme in mid-1779 or adopt the subsequent depreciation table in 1780.[6]

Congress's recognition of the failure of the January 2, 1779, resolution to raise the present value of the Continental dollar can also be deduced from Congress's resolving at the end of 1779 (finally) to compensate military personnel for the falling real value of their nominal pay—military salaries had been fixed in nominal Continental dollars in 1775. On December 1, 1779, Congress agreed to compensate officers for the declining value of the Continental dollars in which their salaries were paid, and on April 10, 1780, it agreed to do the same for soldiers of the line (*JCC* 15:1336; 16:344–45). Where Congress would get the money to do this back-pay compensation was unclear. They had little in terms of purchasing power at the time they passed these resolutions.

The percentages of face value that the Continental dollar was trading for in the marketplace, the 6 percent at the start of 1779 falling to 1.5 percent by the end of 1779 mentioned above, correspond to MEV in the model of money in chap. 9, where $MEV \equiv (APV - RD) + TP$. That model will now be used to explain the rise in real depreciation after 1778. From 1777 to the end of 1778, $MEV \approx APV$, and so $RD = 0$ and $TP = 0$ (see chap. 12). In other words, in the two years prior to 1779, the Continental dollar suffered no depreciation ($RD = 0$) but also had no extra "moneyness" value ($TP = 0$). Its market value was determined almost exclusively by rational bond pricing under the expectation of successful face-value redemption based on the fiscally credible patterns set in the first two emissions and embodied in forecasts 1 and 2. Those expectations were upended by the January 2, 1779, redemption rule change.

The APV of the Continental dollar under the new January 2, 1779, redemption architecture, if credibly executed, would be 62 percent of face value at the start of 1779, rising to 63 percent by the end of 1779 (see table 10.1 and fig. 10.4). These numbers imply that the RD attached to the Continental dollar had jumped to 56 percent of face value at the inception of the new January 2, 1779, redemption architecture and then increased to 61.5 percent of face value by the end of 1779 (with $TP = 0$ in both cases). Thus, at the start of 1779, $MEV = APV - RD$ or $6 = 62 - 56$, and at the end of 1779, $MEV = APV - RD$ or $1.5 = 63 - 61.5$. These large RD (depreciation) values indicate that citizens did not believe that face-value redemption under the January 2, 1779, rules would actually occur. From the vantage point of the "ideal" present value that the new January 2, 1779, redemption rule was to create, almost all of the Continental dollar's market value was now the result of depreciation, namely an expected loss of principal.

The January 2, 1779, redemption rule change still occasioned a rise in depreciation even if citizens held to their old redemption forecasts (e.g., see forecast 1 in figs. 10.4 and 12.2). Under forecast 1, APV was about 15 percent of face value at the start of 1779 and about 16 percent of face value at the end of 1779. Even if citizens clung to forecast 1 as their expectation of face-value redemption, the RD attached to the Continental dollar jumped to 9 percent of face value at the inception of the new January 2, 1779, redemption architecture and then increased to 14.5 percent of face value by the end of 1779 (with $TP = 0$ in both cases). In other words, at the start of 1779, $MEV = APV - RD$ or $6 = 15 - 9$, and at the end of 1779, $MEV = APV - RD$ or $1.5 = 16 - 14.5$. Even using redemption forecast 1, the majority of the Continental dollar's market value in 1779 was now made up of depreciation (RD). Under any scenario, the January 2, 1779, redemption rule change was a turning point. Real depreciation of the Continental dollar—an expected loss of principal—became clearly manifest for the first time in 1779.

What lay behind this rising depreciation after Congress passed the January 2, 1779, redemption rule change was the lack of fiscal credibility embedded in that resolution. With the January 2, 1779, redemption rule change, the implied face-value redemption tax per year per white capita was driven from averaging $0.33 for emissions pre-1779 to averaging $3.66 for the January 2, 1779, redemption schedule (see table 10.1). The January 2, 1779, resolution had face-value redemption taxes per year per white capita ranging between $6.95 and $2.59. Raising annual per-white-capita taxation amounts by a factor of eleven on average, and in some years by a factor of twenty-one, was simply not fiscally credible—people did not have the resources to pay those tax amounts at the face-value specie equivalent printed on the Continental dollar.[7] These redemption taxes also did not include the taxes needed to run the government's day-to-day operations or to pay off other domestic and foreign debts. Citizens simply could not pay these taxes, so not only was the scheduled redemption of Continental dollars in doubt, but citizens must have realized that it simply could not happen.[8]

As far as can be determined, these high levels of taxes were never paid, and they appear not even to have been implemented (since it was known that they could not be paid; see chap. 15). Table D.2 shows that across all the states. none of the redemption quota set by the January 2, 1779, resolution for 1779 had been filled, and through 1780 only 5 percent of the combined 1779 and 1780 redemption quota had been filled. This outcome imparted for the first time an *RD* to the Continental dollar. Default to some degree on redemption as promised (or rationally forecast) was now clearly expected. Real depreciation—in other words, an expected loss of principal—was the result.

By mid-1779 it was clear that the January 2, 1779, redemption rule change had failed to increase the purchasing power of the Continental dollars that Congress was spending in 1779. In fact, as argued here, that resolution made things worse for Congress in terms of the Continental dollar's purchasing power. The value of those dollars was rapidly approaching zero—nearing one cent on the dollar by 1780 (see figs. 11.1 and 12.2). Congress still had spending obligations in 1780 that had to be funded. What Congress turned to next in 1780 to meet its projected budget shortfall would completely collapse and destroy the Continental dollar funding system and lead to the abandonment of the Continental dollar as a functioning medium of exchange. That story is taken up next.

CHAPTER FOURTEEN

1780–1781

The Road to Abandonment

[The authors of the Articles of Confederation could not have foreseen] the havoc of paper money.[1] —Edmund Randolph, delegate from Virginia, at the Constitutional Convention in Philadelphia on May 29, 1787 (Farrand 1966, 1:18)

By the end of 1779 Congress faced a growing budget crisis. Driven by expansive spending by the Quartermaster and Commissary Departments, congressional spending was running far ahead of congressional revenues. The budget deficit in early 1780 was huge (see table 6.5). Congress faced a fiscal chasm. On June 27, 1780, the Board of Treasury reported to Congress that "the Treasury of the United States . . . [is] totally exhausted." They reported that the "Continental Loan offices in the respective States, have received but very little money" and indicated that tax revenues requested from the states for 1778, 1779, and the first two months of 1780 were in arrears. The Board reported that the balances due from the states on these requests came to $45,523,461 (*JCC* 17:563–64; Smith 1976–94, 17:363).[2] Finally, Congress's effort to raise the present value (purchasing power) of the massive amount of Continental dollars that it spent, both newly emitted and borrowed, in 1779 had failed (see chap. 13).

Assuming that Congress could not rein in spending short of surrender, it had to find new revenue sources outside the traditional one. Its traditional and primary spendable revenue source from 1775 through 1779 had been emitting new, and to a lesser extent borrowing already spent, Continental dollars (see chap. 6). By 1780 that traditional revenue source was gone. Congress also requested no borrowings of Continental dollars via loan office certificates as a spendable revenue source after mid-1779, and so that revenue source was gone as well (see table 8.1). In any event, the Continental dollar had almost no purchasing power in the marketplace by 1780, so Continental dollars were largely useless as a spendable revenue source in 1780 (see fig. 11.1).

Congress had no independent taxing power and would not be granted any such power under the Articles of Confederation. Borrowing from foreign powers was paltry and had been declining from 1778 into 1780 (see table 6.5). That left only finding some way to get the states to share their tax revenues with Congress or somehow getting the states to cough up resources and provide them to Congress, as the states had done in providing troops for the army (see table 6.1). Straight-out confiscation of resources from citizens on a limited basis had become the default option and was now becoming a growing and ever-present threat.

Congress had nothing more to gain from the Continental dollar financing system other than garnering a reputation for not defaulting on its obligations and so protecting its future creditworthiness. At this junction, Congress could have done nothing regarding the Continental dollar, or, restated simply, as established in emissions nos. 1 and 2, the states were required to redeem 750,000 Continental dollars a year at face value every year until all had been redeemed.[3] The redeemed dollars would be sent to the Continental Treasury to be counted and burned. That redemption pattern generated the expected present value time path of forecast 2 in figure 10.4, the least burdensome, in terms of taxes, of the redemption patterns established by emissions nos. 1 and 2. It was also fiscally credible in terms of the level of taxes required. Congress could point to its broadside, published in 1775, establishing yearly quotas for each state (see fig. 4.1) and indicate that those requirements were still operative. Each state could institute some random drawing to determine which Continental dollars presented by its citizens would be redeemed (accepted to cover a citizen's state tax obligations) at face value each year to meet the state's portion of the overall $750,000 yearly redemption quota.

But this did not happen. Instead, Congress used the remnants of the Continental dollar financing system to leverage an extraction of spendable resources from the states through a convoluted new scheme. This new scheme netted Congress only a tiny amount of spendable resources for 1780–81. The price of that scheme was that it collapsed the Continental dollar funding system, led to the abandonment of the Continental dollar as a functioning medium of exchange, and set the stage for the propagation of the myth that the Continental dollar was just a fiat currency whose value had always been at the mercy of the winds.

Given this backdrop of Congress's financial situation in early 1780, I will now explain Congress's March 18, 1780, resolution and its convoluted redemption rule changes regarding the Continental dollar (*JCC* 16:262–67). This resolution was Congress's last resolution regarding the Continental dollar before the Funding Act of August 4, 1790. First, I will explain what this resolution was—its requirements and options. Second, I will explain the personnel changes in Congress that allowed a major change in direction regarding the Continental dollar financing system. Third, I will explain what Congress was up to with this resolution—what Congress hoped to gain from it. Fourth, I will explain the outcome of the Continental-state paper dollar experiment embedded in the resolution. Fifth, I will explain how this resolution and its rule changes failed to achieve its goal and contributed to destroying the Continental dollar system. In addition, I will use this analysis to make interpretive sense out of Franklin's 1779 statement describing how the Continental dollar system functioned (see the introduction). Sixth, I will recap and summarize the fiscal credibility problem Congress created with its January 2, 1779, and March 18, 1780, redemption rule-change resolutions, and how that problem collapsed and destroyed the Continental dollar system. Finally, I will address the abandonment of the Continental dollar as a functioning medium of exchange.

The March 18, 1780, Resolution and Redemption Rule Changes

On March 18, 1780, Congress replaced the redemption structure legislated January 2, 1779, with a new redemption structure (*JCC* 16:262–67). States were now to redeem 15 million Continental dollars each month over the next thirteen months. Thirteen months times $15 million equaled $195 million, or 97.5 percent of the Continental dollars ever emitted. The remaining $5 million was due in the future from Georgia, which, having been invaded, was temporarily exempt from sending remittances. This redemption structure was an explicit acceptance that the January 2, 1779, redemption rule-change resolution (see chap. 13) had been a failure. It recognized that none of the 15 million Continental dollars had been redeemed in 1779 as required by the January 2, 1779, resolution, and so the present value of the Continental dollar had not been improved.

In addition, the states were now allowed to substitute one Spanish silver dollar in lieu of forty Continental dollars when filling their redemption quotas. Congress continued to credit state Continental dollar remittances at the 40-to-1 paper-to-silver dollar rate into 1790.[4] The March 18, 1780, resolution did not remove the option citizens had to redeem their Continental dollars directly at the Continental Treasury for their face value in specie, as stated in the July 26 and December 26, 1775, resolutions and in congressional discussions on June 14, 1779.[5] Doing so, however, would be impossible under the March 18, 1780, resolution requirements, and citizens likely would have deduced that—in effect recognizing that Congress's action would result in a de facto default on the Continental dollar.

In addition, seemingly in conjunction with the March 18, 1780, resolution, Congress recommended two days after passing that resolution, on March 20, 1780, that the states "revise their laws . . . making the continental bills of credit a tender in discharge of debts and contracts, and to amend the same in such manner as they shall judge most conducive to justice, in the present state of the paper currency." From late 1780 through mid-1781 states complied by revoking their laws making the Continental dollar a legal tender in their respective states. For example, Delaware passed its law revoking the legal-tender status of the Continental dollar on November 8, 1780; New Jersey on January 5, 1781; Virginia did so on May 5, 1781; and Pennsylvania made its temporary suspension of legal-tender status permanent on June 21, 1781.[6]

The removal of legal-tender laws in conjunction with the new redemption rules legislated on March 18, 1780, freed the states to redeem Continental dollars from their citizens at whatever current value they wished to legislate or at whatever rate they could impose on the market. It also allowed a state to flatly refuse to redeem any more Continental dollars once that state had reached its prescribed redemption quota (see chap. 15). As such, it effectively broke the link between redemption per se and redemption at face value in specie equivalents. The Continental dollar lost its value anchor—it had become untethered from any real value. In other words, the Continental dollar could now be treated more like a fiat currency in terms of value compared with how a bond-type currency was treated in terms of value.

Finally, the March 18, 1780, resolution allowed, but did not require, states to issue one Continental-state paper dollar on their own account for every twenty Continental dollars remitted to the Continental Treasury to be burned. Each state that emitted Continental-state dollars was required to give four-tenths of the amount authorized in their respective

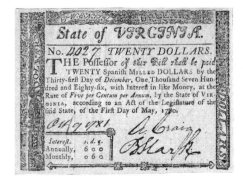

FIGURE 14.1. A Continental-state twenty-dollar bill issued by Virginia, May 1, 1780, front and back

Source: Newman (2008: 452). Reprinted by permission of the Eric P. Newman Numismatic Education Society.

Note: For examples of Continental-state dollars issued by other states, see Newman (2008: 177, 215, 245, 263, 291, 358, 400).

emission statutes to Congress for Congress to spend as it pleased. Each state, however, was still obligated to redeem the four-tenths that it had given to Congress.[7]

Continental-state dollars were different from Continental dollars both in how they looked and in how they were structured to perform. Citizens could easily distinguish between Continental-state dollars and Continental dollars. Figure 14.1 depicts the Continental-state dollar issued by Virginia. Compare it with the pictures of Continental dollars in figures I.1, I.2, I.3, and I.4. Continental-state dollars were state-specific paper monies and not financial obligations of Congress or the Continental Treasury. In 1795 Oliver Wolcott Jr., then the Secretary of the Treasury, stated in direct reference to the Continental-state currency, "This species of paper has never been considered as forming any part of the debt of the United States." A similar conclusion was reached in 1802 by Albert Gallatin, at that time the Secretary of the Treasury (*American state papers, class IX* 1834, 1:174, 215, 250). Each state that issued its own Continental-state dollars was responsible for eventually redeeming all of its own Continental-state dollars that it had emitted.

The March 18, 1780, resolution required the following language to be printed on all Continental-state dollars (see fig. 14.1):

> The possessor of this bill shall be paid [blank space where the denominated value of the bill would be printed] Spanish milled dollars, by the 31 day of December, 1786, with interest, in like money, at the rate of five per cent, per annum, by the State of [blank space were the respective state issuing the bill would be named], according to an act of the legislature of the said State, of the [blank space naming the day] day of [blank space naming the month], 1780.
>
> The United States ensure the payment of the within bill, and will draw bills of exchange for the interest annually, if demanded, according to a resolution of Congress of the 18 day of March, 1780. (*JCC* 16:264; 19:411)

Each state's Continental-state dollar followed this pattern, and so they looked somewhat similar across states. Just the state's name, state-law authorization date, denomination, and some engravings along the margin differed from state to state. The March 18, 1780, resolution stated that the last clause in the language stated above was only operative during war. Once the Revolution ended, the United States' payment-guarantee lapsed, and it would be purely each state's responsibility both to redeem the bills at face value in specie in 1786 and to pay the annual interest in specie. Between April 29 and July 2, 1780, eight states — Virginia, Maryland, Pennsylvania, New Jersey, New York, Rhode Island, Massachusetts, and New Hampshire — emitted Continental-state dollars. Five states did not emit Continental-state dollars: Georgia, South Carolina, North Carolina, Delaware, and Connecticut (*JCC* 16:264; 19:411; Newman 2008: 177, 215, 245, 263, 291, 358, 400, 452).

The Turnover of Congressional Personnel and the Vote on the March 18, 1780, Resolution

Only six of the twenty-eight congressmen — 21 percent — who voted on the March 18, 1780, resolution had voted on the January 2, 1779, resolution. While all six had voted for the January 2, 1779, resolution, two voted against the March 18, 1780, resolution, Thomas Burke of North Carolina and Cyrus Griffin of Virginia. Only one member of the Board of Treasury crafting the January 2, 1779, resolution, Oliver Ellsworth of Connecticut, was present and voted on the March 18, 1780, resolution, voting in favor.

Only four of the twenty-eight congressmen voting on the March 18, 1780, resolution—Roger Sherman of Connecticut, Robert R. Livingston and William Floyd of New York, and Thomas McKean of Delaware—or 14 percent, were congressmen in 1775 and present for at least some of the debate and passage of the initial structural design of the Continental dollar embedded in the first two emissions. Of these, only McKean voted against the March 18, 1780, resolution. Finally, only Floyd voted on both the March 18, 1780, and January 2, 1779, resolutions and was also present for part of the 1775 debate and passage of the initial structural design of the Continental dollar.[8]

The March 18, 1780, resolution passed six states in favor to five states opposed, with one state divided. This resolution was a more controversial change in redemption structure than that passed on January 2, 1779. Interestingly, the vote split sharply on a north-south divide. Not only did all the states south of Pennsylvania—Delaware, Maryland, Virginia, North Carolina, and South Carolina—vote against the resolution, but every single delegate from these states voted against it (no vote from Georgia was recorded). By contrast, not only did every single state north of Delaware vote in favor of the resolution (New Hampshire was divided), but every single delegate from these states, with the exception of Nathaniel Peabody of New Hampshire and John Fell of New Jersey, voted in favor of it.[9]

This north-south vote split may be due to how the resolution affected redemption relative to where Continental dollars were in the economy. From 1775 through 1779 most Continental dollars had been spent in the middle states and New England, and few in the states south of Pennsylvania (see chap. 6 and table 6.2). With the removal of legal-tender laws, the states north of Maryland could acquire Continental dollars cheaply at their current low market value (see fig. 11.1), and there were a lot of Continental dollars in their economies for them to acquire.

States south of Pennsylvania likely had relatively few Continental dollars in their local economies and so would find it harder to meet their remittance quotas. Remember the remittance quotas spanned only thirteen months in which to be completed—supposedly by the end of April 1781. Thus, if states are assumed to obey the March 18, 1780, resolution, then states south of Pennsylvania would likely have to fill some of their quotas with specie dollars rather than paper dollars at the 1-to-40 rate set by the resolution. This would drain the southern states of what little specie money they had in their economies. This expected outcome may explain why the southern states opposed the March 18, 1780, resolution.

What Was Congress Up To? The Goal of the March 18, 1780, Resolution

What Congress's motives and goals were in enacting the March 18, 1780, resolution and its redemption rule changes were not clearly articulated by anyone in or outside of Congress. As such, Congress's goals and motivates must be inferred from what it expected to gain from the resolution. The March 18, 1780, resolution had several moving parts, but when wedded together into a coherent whole the following interpretation is the result. After I give that interpretation, I will dissect several key individual components of the resolution and show that individually they cannot provide, on their own, a compelling story of Congress's motives and goals superior to that which now follows from treating its several components as a coherent whole.

Congress was in desperate need of spendable revenue in 1780–81 (see table 6.5). The only spendable revenue generated by the March 18, 1780, resolution was the provision to Congress of four-tenths of all Continental-state dollars issued by the individual states. For Congress to maximize its spendable revenue from this source for the year 1780–81, all Continental dollars ever emitted and currently outstanding (just under $200 million) had to be redeemed in this period. This explains the thirteen-month redemption window (April 1780–April 1781) set by the March 18, 1780, resolution for redeeming Continental dollars. The maximum spendable revenue Congress could get for 1780–81 from this scheme would then be 4 million Continental-state dollars (face value), namely 200 million Continental dollars redeemed reduced by the 1-to-20 emission rate for Continental-state dollars relative to Continental dollars redeemed, and then reduced to Congress's four-tenths share of the amount of Continental-state dollars emitted, that is, $200,000,000 * 0.05 * 0.4 = $4,000,000.

The states could not redeem 200 million Continental dollars over the designated thirteen-month period at face value. Face-value redemption over that period was impossible in terms of taxes. It would not be a fiscally credible demand (see the discussion below and table 10.1). Congress needed all the Continental dollars redeemed over this thirteen-month period to maximize its intake of spendable Continental-state dollars. As such, Congress had to make it possible for states to do a massive quick redemption without raising taxes to impossible heights. This condition explains the congressional request on March 20, 1780, that states remove their legal-tender laws with respect to the Continental dollar. This would allow states to acquire Continental dollars at their current market rates, about 1.0 to 1.5 percent of face value in mid-1780 (see fig. 11.1), rather than at face value.

Finally, the March 18, 1780, resolution allowed the states to substitute one dollar in specie for every forty Continental dollars they were supposed to redeem and send to the Continental Treasury. The 40-to-1 rate is the same as pricing the Continental dollar at 2.5 percent of its face value. This rate set by Congress was purely an accounting device for crediting state redemptions of Continental dollars.[10] The taxes needed to redeem Continental dollars even at this 40-to-1 rate were still impossibly high and so could not be met (see the discussion below and table 10.1). As such, Congress did not actually expect states to send them specie dollars in lieu of Continental dollars. At 2.5 percent of face value, the rate set by Congress was above the rate at which Continental dollars could be acquired in the marketplace, and so states had no incentive to substitute specie dollars for Continental dollars to meet their redemption quotas. In fact they had the opposite incentive, namely only to remit Continental dollars to meet their redemption quotas under the March 18, 1780, resolution.[11]

As far as I can determine, no specie dollars were sent to Congress by the states as part of the March 18, 1780, redemption scheme. When states could not meet their quota of Continental dollars that they were to redeem, they simply defaulted on their quota and sent no remittances at all to the Continental Treasury (see chap. 15). Lastly, it is unclear that any specie dollars sent to Congress under this scheme could be used as spendable revenue by Congress (see the discussion below). Congress was in a sounder position in terms of what it could legally spend if it got Continental-state dollars rather than specie dollars under the redemption scheme as laid out in the March 18, 1780, resolution.

Now I will assess the key individual components of the March 18, 1780, resolution, namely the shortened redemption window and the 40-to-1 Continental dollar–to–specie dollar remittance rate, and show that on their own they cannot provide a coherent interpretation of Congress's motives and goals superior to what was just articulated above. First, I will assess the resolution's new redemption window. The resolution shortened the redemption window to the next thirteen months. If all Continental dollars were redeemed at face value, then this short redemption window would have raised the present value of Continental dollars immediately to almost face value. Raising the present value of Continental dollars, however, could not have been the goal of Congress. Congress had nothing to gain by raising the present value or purchasing power of current Continental dollars. All Continental dollars delivered to the Continental Treasury had to be destroyed and could not be respent, and no new Continental dollars could be emitted.

In addition, redemption at face value over the next thirteen-month period was fiscally impossible, and Congress had to know that. The amount of taxes per year per white capita needed to achieve this redemption at face value would have to be 212 times above what had been historically acceptable and feasible and even 62 times above the tax level achieved by the federal government after it acquired taxing power under the US Constitution in 1792–95 (see table 10.1 and fig. 14.2). These tax levels were also way above the tax levels implied by the January 2, 1779, redemption resolution, which also could not be met. Congress had to have observed, based on the failure of the January 2, 1779, resolution, that such high tax levels were impossible for citizens to pay and so simply would not be paid. Thus, the March 18, 1780, resolution was not about raising the present value of the Continental dollar.

Second, the March 18, 1780, resolution's forty-to-one Continental dollar–to–specie dollar rate for crediting states with redemptions was just an accounting device for crediting state remittances and was set at a rate to induce states to remit Continental dollars rather than specie dollars to the Continental Treasury. Had states completely met their redemption quotas and then filled them only with specie dollars, the Continental Treasury would have received $5 million in specie money, that is, $200 million * 0.025 = $5 million. Having fulfilled their redemption quotas with specie dollars, each state had a mass of paper Continental dollars that would now be worthless, as far as the states were concerned. The face-value redemption of Continental dollars by individual citizens at the Continental Treasury, however, had never been rescinded. It was not discussed in the March 18, 1780, resolution, but was still considered operative in congressional discussions as late as June 14, 1779 (see chap. 13).

It is unclear whether Congress could legally spend this (hypothetical) $5 million in specie dollar remittances. And $5 million in specie was not enough in the Treasury to redeem all the outstanding Continental dollars ($200 million worth) at face value, as still required in law. If Congress did get this (hypothetical) $5 million in specie dollar remittances and then turned around and spent them, it would mean that most of the money in

Continental dollars (200 million) still out there in the hands of citizens was now worthless. All government obligations to them had now been satisfied; nothing more was legally required to be offered. Such an outcome would amount to transforming the Continental dollar from a bond-type currency into a pure fiat money.

Lastly, even at the forty-to-one redemption equivalence, the tax levels needed to extract Continental or specie dollars per year per white capita were impossibly high. That tax level would be over five times higher than what had been historically feasible and acceptable, and even over one and a half times higher than the tax level achieved by the federal government, after it acquired taxing power (see table 10.1 and fig. 14.2). Thus, Congress likely did not expect the March 18, 1780, resolution's 40-to-1 Continental dollar–to–specie dollar redemption rate to be operative other than as an accounting device. If it had been operative, it would have by itself completely destroyed the Continental dollar financing system and transformed Continental dollars into worthless pieces of paper.

Therefore, the March 18, 1780, resolution's two key components, the shortened redemption window and the 40-to-1 Continental dollar–to–specie dollar remittance equivalence, only make sense when combined with the request to remove legal-tender laws regarding the Continental dollar and with the Continental-state dollar emission scheme. You cannot interpret the resolution's components individually or separately. It was a single Rube Goldberg machine. Lastly, given what the March 18, 1780, resolution did, there was no meaningful "ideal" present value forecast or calculation that could be made under its auspices. This resolution, therefore, allowed later Federalist rhetoric, uncritically accepted by scholars up to the present day, to regard the Continental dollar as having *always* been just an unbacked fiat currency.

The Continental-State Dollar Experiment

Acquiring spendable Continental-state dollars was Congress's goal with the March 18, 1780, resolution. Continental-state dollars were state paper monies and so will not be analyzed at length here. Each state emitted its own inside paper monies during the Revolution, of which Continental-state dollars were a part. A full explication of each state's paper-money regime during the Revolution is still needed (Newman 2008; Ratchford 1941: 34); a complete understanding of Revolutionary War financing cannot be gained without it. A forensic accounting exercise to determine state paper-money accounts, emissions, and redemption structures for each state, and an analysis of the value and performance of each state's paper money during the Revolution, are tasks for future scholars.[12] I will focus here only on how the Continental-state dollar experiment affected Continental dollar redemptions and congressional finances.

The total amount of Continental-state dollars issued across all states in 1780 and 1781 were reported to Congress in 1790 by Nourse, to be 2,070,485. Alexander Hamilton, Secretary of the Treasury, reported a different total to Congress on May 11, 1790: 1,592,222 for the same period.[13] If these numbers are correct, then during 1780 and 1781 a total of either 41,409,700 or 31,844,440 in Continental dollars was called out of circulation via this mechanism—given the 20-to-1 rate allowed in Congress's requisition act of March 18, 1780.[14] These numbers are consistent with the estimate made in a report by a congressional committee that was assigned to assess the state of congressional finances and delivered to Congress on April 18, 1781. The committee's report used the Board of Treasury's report of February 16, 1781, which stated that the Board "supposed" that 160 million in Continental dollars was still unredeemed (*JCC* 19:405). Given that Congress thought that they had emitted 200 million Continental dollars with all outstanding by the start of 1780, the Board's "supposed" number implies that 40 million Continental dollars had been redeemed from early 1780 through early 1781.[15]

Because Congress was to be given four-tenths of the Continental-state dollars emitted by the states, the numbers above imply that Congress's revenue that it could spend in 1780–81, based on being given Continental-state dollars, was between $828,194 (Nourse) and $636,888 (Hamilton) in face value. Congress had designed the Continental-state dollar to maintain its face value if properly executed. It paid 5 percent annual interest in specie. Thus, the present value of the bill would be maintained close to its face value because the annual interest payment counterbalanced time-discounting. The redemption of the principal was set at the end of 1786, six years after emission, and in specie. Citizens could watch and assess how well states were doing in terms of finance in accumulating the funds needed to execute this redemption.

Thus, Congress likely thought that the Continental-state dollars it acquired would be worth close to their face value in purchasing power. What the actual purchasing power of these Continental-state dollars was in 1780–81 has yet to be determined accurately. But even at face value, these sums were a paltry amount of revenue and did not come close to solving Congress's budget deficit in 1780 (see table 6.5). The Board of Treasury's report to Congress on April 17, 1781, recognized this, namely that the states had only partially complied with the March 18, 1780, resolution and so the Continental-state dollars received by the Treasury were insufficient to meet spending needs (*JCC* 19:399–400).

The Price Paid for the Partial Success of the March 18, 1780, Resolution

Congress acquired between $636,888 and $828,194 Continental-state dollars (face value) to spend as revenue in 1780–81, magically, it seemed, out of whole cloth—revenue desperately needed to stave off collapse for which there seemed to be no other sources. It was a rather paltry amount of revenue and would not come close to covering expected spending in 1780–81, but it was better than nothing. The price of doing this was the destruction of the Continental dollar financing system, which in turn damaged Congress's reputation for honoring its financial obligations and so could have hurt its future creditworthiness.

The rather meager amount of Continental-state dollars attained by Congress was the consequence of the state's inability to raise taxes high enough to redeem all the 200 million Continental dollars outstanding over the thirteen-month redemption window set by the March 18, 1780, resolution. At best the states remitted only about 16 to 20 percent of the Continental dollars outstanding over that thirteen-month window. Even at a 40-to-1 rate of Continental dollars to specie dollars, taxes to redeem all Continental dollars would be impossibly high and so could not be paid (see fig. 14.2). The states also lacked any financial incentive to issue Continental-state paper money compared with just continuing to issue their own paper monies.

The Continental-state dollar scheme was short-lived, ending in 1781 (*JCC* 19:398–400, 411; 20:438, 577). Some states issued none of the new currency—for example, Connecticut, Delaware, North Carolina, South Carolina, and Georgia. Some that did issue the new currency apparently had a difficult time distinguishing between the old Continental dollars that still circulated and the new Continental-state dollars they emitted, in terms of how the public used them and how tax collectors regarded them.[16] The Board of Treasury's report to Congress on April 17 and 18, 1781, indicated as much (*JCC* 19:400, 416–17). The Board said that Continental-state dollars circulated below face value and at different values in different states, and the Board stated that some linkages in state laws between the old Continental dollar and the new Continental-state dollar created confusion and reduced the value of Continental-state dollars.

The specie interest payments may have been difficult for states to execute. The accumulation of specie by the states to meet face-value redemption (principal repayment) as scheduled by the end of 1786 may have been observationally deficient. If so, the present value of the Continental-state dollar would fall well below face value, and differentially so depending on the different financial conditions in each state issuing them (*JCC* 19:400). It is likely that state taxes needed to execute the Continental-state dollar scheme as designed, for the states that emitted Continental-state dollars, were simply too high to be credible, and so were unlikely to be paid— especially when added to all the other taxes required for running state government and servicing state debts. Being a state paper money, the Continental-state dollar and its performance will not be further analyzed here. How state paper monies performed during the Revolution is again a task for future scholars.

In any event, if states set the specie value of new taxes impossibly high, then, barring tax revolts, citizens would have to sell off goods, land, and paper monies to acquire the specie needed to pay these new taxes, thereby driving down the prices of all these assets. In addition, many citizens simply could not, and so did not, pay the taxes instituted. Thus, redemption of Continental dollars, even at relatively low rates like the 40-to-1 rate set by Congress, was in doubt. Even more Continental dollars would be required to trade for one dollar of specie than at Congress's 40-to-1 rate. In the mid-1780s, the United States experienced deflation in the specie value of goods and land, as well as tax revolts related to this deflation (Holton 2007).

State efforts to partially comply with March 18, 1780, resolutions forced massive depreciation onto the Continental dollar, which in turn led to its abandonment as a medium of exchange. After mid-1781 there are no dense market data to indicate what Continental dollars traded for relative to specie dollars. The presumption is that their market value was zero or so near zero, say 1 percent of face value, that it was effectively zero. Anecdotal evidence indicates that some citizens acquired and would continue to hold Continental dollars as a speculative investment in the hope that Congress might reverse itself and honor its obligations. But there was not enough trade action to generate a reliable value series. Throughout the rest of the 1780s, Congress frequently indicated that Continental dollars would be redeemed, and at face value, sometime in the future. But no definitive plan was ever made or actions taken.[17]

Using the model of money in chapter 9, from mid-1781 to 1790, $0 \approx MEV = APV - RD$. As such, whatever a citizen's expected APV was, based on guesses of possible future redemption at face value, it approximately equaled its RD on average, namely $APV \approx RD$ for this period. The Continental dollar's market value on average was all determined by its expected depreciation (expected loss of principal), which equaled the expected present value.

It is still unclear why Congress created the Continental-state dollar scheme within the March 18, 1780, resolution as its vehicle for extracting spendable resources from the states. In essence, Congress was simple asking the states to print some state-specific paper money and hand it over to Congress. All states had been printing and spending their own state-specific paper monies during the Revolution (Newman 2008; Ratchford 1941: 34). Why Congress did not simply ask each state to provide Congress with a quota of each state's paper-money emissions for Congress to use and spend as it wished is unclear. Such a request would have been structurally the same as the extraction of Continental-state dollars from the states, as in both cases the issuing state was obligated to redeem its own emissions using its own state taxes, thereby supporting the money's present value. Such a request would have been simpler than the rather convoluted design of the March 18, 1780, resolution and would not have necessitated the destruction of the Continental dollar financing system that the March 18, 1780, resolution perpetrated.

The best I can guess is that Congress realized that state paper monies were largely state specific and tended not to cross state boundaries. This was because only that state was responsible for its own paper money's redemption via taxes paid in that state by its citizens. This would create a spending problem for Congress if it used a plethora of various state paper monies in that Congress did not know where it would need to spend these monies. There was no guarantee that spending would be in the state that the paper money was from. Congress needed a paper money that it could use anywhere across the states without dealing with exchange rates across state paper monies.

That Congress needed a currency that was usable nationwide explains why Congress set the design of the Continental-state dollar to be uniform across the states. If properly executed, that design guaranteed that Continental-state dollars would all trade at an equal value regardless of which state issued them and which state's name was on them. The exchange rate would be one to one across different states' Continental-state dollar emissions. This was an outcome not realized by prior state paper monies. However, once doubts about a state's ability to pay interest in specie and the full principal in specie at the end of 1786 were realized, and if those doubts varied across states, that 1-to-1 exchange rate or equal value would be lost. This likely happened rather quickly. The Board of Treasury noted that this was the case in their report to Congress on April 17, 1781 (*JCC* 19:400). Its apparent failure to achieve this uniformity of value across states may partially explain why the Continental-state dollar experiment as outlined in the March 18, 1780, resolution was not continued past that resolution's redemption termination date of April 1781 (see chap. 15).

It is also unclear why the issuance of Continental-state dollars had to be linked to the removal of Continental dollars. The system could have been created without that linkage. As explained at the start of this chapter, Congress could have just left the Continental dollar financing system alone and reinstated a redemption plan following the least costly forecast 2. Then Congress could have implemented the Continental-state dollar requirement on its own as a stand-alone requisition from the states.

My best guess as to why Congress felt it had to link the emission of Continental-state dollars to the removal of Continental dollars is twofold. First, Congress's prior "naked" requisition requests of the states went largely unfilled (see chap. 13). Some incentive had to be given to the states to buy into this scheme. That incentive was that supposedly everyone knew there would be an accounting and reapportionment or rebalancing of war costs among the states once the Revolution was won. Giving the states an incentive to remit Continental dollars to the Continental Treasury on easy terms would appeal to states seeking to earn credits in this accounting process.

Second, many congressmen thought in crude quantity-theoretic terms. Reducing 200 million Continental dollars to 10 million Continental-state dollars, if the scheme was fully executed, was viewed as the way to support and maintain the new currency's value in terms of reducing the total quantity of paper money in circulation. A three-person congressional committee to assess the state of congressional finances, of which James Duane was a member, stated as much in its report to Congress on April 18, 1781 (*JCC* 19:411, 416–17).

Finally, all of this does not explain why states would participate in the Continental-state dollar scheme, and several did not. As far as I can tell, states had nothing to gain by issuing Continental-state dollars compared with issuing a comparable amount of their own prior state paper monies. States would come out ahead by just continuing to issue their own paper monies redeemed by their own taxes without having to give any to Congress.[18] The best I can say is that some states participated because for them patriotism counterbalanced free-riding (see chap. 6). This observation may also explain why the Continental-state dollar experiment was both short-lived and poorly attended by the states. On April 17, 18, and 25, and May 10 and 20, 1781, Congress complained bitterly about this lack of interest in the Continental-state dollar scheme by the states as well as about the general lack of state compliance with congressional funding requests (*JCC* 19:399–400, 402–20; 20:438–39, 472–73, 495, 577–78).

Assessing Benjamin Franklin's 1779 Description of the Continental Dollar Financing System

Franklin's 1779 "inflation-tax" statement describing Congress's Continental dollar financing scheme, quoted in the introduction, can now be put into its proper context. Franklin was advocating shifting to something like the outcome caused by the March 18, 1780, resolution. He supported raising taxes but allowing the public to pay taxes in Continental dollars not at their face value but only at their current market value (their current present value). Immediately before the passage quoted in the introduction—the passage often quoted in the traditional history of the Continental dollar—Franklin explained how he thought the Continental dollar financing system might be saved:

> The *only Remedy* now seems to be a Diminution of the Quantity by a vigorous Taxation, of great *nominal* Sums, which the People are more able to pay in Proportion to the Quantity & diminished Value; and the *only Consolation* under the Evil is that the Publick Debt is proportionably diminish'd; with the Depreciation; ... For it should always be remembered that the original Intention was to sink the Bills by Taxes, which as effectually extinguish the Debt as an actual Redemption. (Oberg 1992–98, 29:354–56)[19]

Franklin was advocating a policy in 1779 that would become Congress's 1780 policy.

Franklin's description, however, is a short offhand remark in a private letter to a friend. He did not go into detail about how what he was suggesting would need to be structured to work. I will fill in that understanding by taking the totality of Franklin's understanding of how bills of credit such as the Continental dollar functioned as zero-coupon bonds. In his speech to the Pennsylvania Assembly in 1764, Franklin clearly articulated that paper money structured as zero-coupon bonds was valued in the marketplace at its present value, not its face value, due to time-discounting. That present value required a face-value redemption anchor at some future date (Grubb 2016a: 171–73; Labaree 1966–70, 11:13–15).

Thus, to maintain a positive present value there had to be some credible commitment to redeem some amount at face value; otherwise the money's value would plummet toward zero. To maintain the system, the states could take additional Continental dollars in payment of taxes at their current present value rather than at their face value only if the states also continued to take some subset of Continental dollars concurrently at their face value. For example, using present-value forecast 2 in figure 10.4, where 750,000 Continental dollars a year were to be redeemed at face value, the states could say that they would continue to do that each year, maybe using a random draw to determine whose Continental dollars would be so redeemed that year at face value, and then also agree to accept additional Continental dollars as payment for other current taxes at the Continental dollar's current present value. If all Continental dollars so received would be destroyed after being redeemed by taxes, such a scheme would reduce the total mass of outstanding Continental dollars fasters than just the 750,000 redeemed each year — reducing it by the extra dollars redeemed at their current present value each year. This process would in turn shorten the length of the redemption window needed to eventually redeem all Continental dollars at face value from that using just the $750,000 amount redeemed at face value each year. This result would raise the present value of all current Continental dollars. Forecast 2 in figure 10.4 would ratchet up over time.

The March 18, 1780, resolution, however, did not maintain any subquota of Continental dollars to be redeemed at face value. The value anchor was lost, and thus the Continental dollar became untethered and plummeted toward zero value the way any fiat paper money would that had no guaranteed value or use. This result aided the transformation in how the Continental dollar was perceived: it was now seen as a money without a value anchored to its specie face value for government tax obligations when due, and thus more fiat than bond-like in nature.

Sinking the Ship: The Failure to Address Fiscal Credibility after 1778

Figure 14.2 presents the tax implications of Congress's changes in redemption policy after 1778. It sets the feasible, or historically acceptable, tax level of $0.33 per year per white capita at zero (see table 10.1). It then calculates the multiple factor increase in that tax level needed to accommodate the new legislation of January 2, 1779, March 18, 1780, and August 4, 1790, if Continental dollars were redeemed at face value and if Continental dollars were redeemed at their current expected average present value as estimated using forecasts 1 and 2, or were redeemed at the 40-to-1 paper-to-specie dollar rate set by Congress after March 1780. We are not talking about raising taxes by 20 percent or 50 percent or even 100 percent, but by multiple factors or by hundreds if not thousands of percent.

Figure 14.2 shows that the new redemption resolutions of 1779 and 1780 exploded the tax level for redemption at face value, peaking at nearly twenty-two times normal in 1779 for the January 2, 1779, resolution and at 263 times normal in 1781 for the March 18, 1780, resolution. If the March 18, 1780, resolution is ignored and states are assumed to have followed the redemption structure in the January 2, 1779, resolution, which in fact as a group the states did (see chap. 15), then redemption at face value between 1780 and 1790 would still entail tax levels between ten and fourteen times normal.

Figure 14.2 also shows that even if Congress intended in its new legislation of January 2, 1779, and then March 18, 1780, to redeem Continental dollars at their expected present value (forecasts 1 and 2), the tax levels needed to accomplish this were still multiple factors above normal. Using forecasts 1 and 2 to measure the expected present value of Continental dollars, figure 14.2 shows that redemption at those values under the March 18, 1780, resolution would require tax levels eleven to fifteen times above normal, and under the January 2, 1779, resolution would require tax levels three to four times above normal. Even if the redemption rate is taken as the 40-to-1 rate (paper-to-specie dollars) set in the March 18, 1780, resolution and thereafter maintained by Congress to 1790 for crediting state remittances, the tax level needed to redeem or buy up all Continental dollars still outstanding in 1790 at that rate would be almost two times normal.[20] These are tax levels separate from additional taxes im-

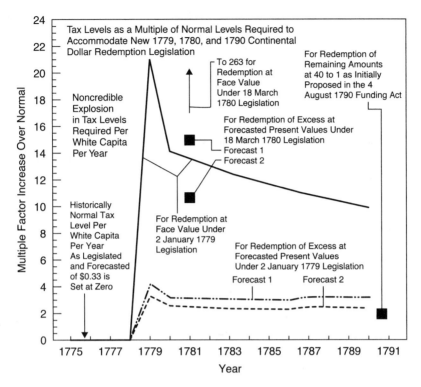

FIGURE 14.2. Tax levels needed to accommodate new Continental dollar redemption legislation, 1779, 1780, and 1790, as a multiple of normal levels

Sources: Tables 1.1 and 10.1; figs. 12.2 and 12.3.

Note: For construction, see the notes to tables 1.1 and 10.1; figs. 12.2 and 12.3; and the text.

posed to cover other government operating expenses and cover other
non-Continental dollar government debts.

When taxes are set beyond the real-resource capabilities of the public,
they simply cannot, and so will not, be paid. As such, the credibility behind the redemption of Continental dollars at any of the rates discussed
in figure 14.2 is lost. This loss of credibility means that citizens expected
an eventual loss of principal at any of the rates used to evaluate the Continental dollar, from face value down to a 40-to-1 (paper-to-specie dollar)
rating, namely redemption at 2.5 percent of face value. This expectation
created the massive depreciation the Continental dollar suffered after
1778, so much so that it could no longer function as a medium of exchange.

Abandonment of the Continental Dollar as a
Medium of Exchange and Unit of Account

Newspaper price currents, merchant account books, and George Washington's account book all stopped quoting prices in Continental dollars in May 1781 (Bezanson 1951: 12, 344; Breck 1843: 16; Ferguson 1961: 66; Webster 1969: 502). Interestingly, this date was also at the end of the thirteen-month redemption window set by the March 18, 1780, resolution. Thereafter, Continental dollars were abandoned as a circulating currency. Citizens also stopped using them as a unit of account (see fig. 11.5). Some authors claim this cessation was ordered by Congress and/or Congress formally repudiated the Continental dollar around this time. A definitive statement by Congress of such, however, cannot be found. Several proposals were put forth that might be interpreted as repudiation, but all were rejected or sent to committee, never to reappear.[21]

The traditional literature indicates that after 1780 Continental dollars were largely disposed of as trash, often in humorous demonstrations. However, the accounting in chapters 15 and 16 indicates that few Continental dollars were actually trashed in the 1780s.[22] While still in the economy, Continental dollars no longer served as a source of revenue to cover Congress's spending obligations.

One thing is clear, and that is that by 1781 the Revolution was on the brink of financial collapse, at least on the national level. In the absence of French involvement, and despite the heroic, though perhaps self-serving, efforts of Robert Morris as Superintendent of Finance from 1781 to 1784, the British would have soon outlasted the Americans in terms of war financing and thus likely defeated the revolutionaries (Carp 1984; Ferguson et al. 1973–99; Fowler 2011; Grubb 2007b; Ver Steeg 1976).

This observation puts renewed emphasis on the role of the French, and to a lesser extent the Spanish and Dutch, after 1778 in ultimately securing American independence from Britain. It was not just French naval and troop support that mattered, especially for the stunning victory at Yorktown in October of 1781, but French spending of hard currency (specie money) in North America and French loans of hard currency to the Americans that helps sustain the Revolution after 1780. For example, a congressional motion on April 17, 1781, anticipated receiving considerable sums of specie from France, and the motion's drafters laid out how they thought the sums received should be spent (*JCC* 19:398–99).

Perhaps more important, French entry into the war against the British in 1778, followed by Spanish entry in 1779, and finally Dutch entry in 1780 changed Britain's financial position. Britain was now in another global war against French, Spanish, and Dutch powers. The last global war against the French, the Seven Years' War, had been extremely costly, and the British were still paying on financial obligations incurred during that war. The financial pressure placed on the British by a new global war against French, Spanish, and Dutch powers had to change Britain's willingness to end the war in America and accept American independence sooner rather than later.

The Continental dollar does not factor into congressional finances or the budgetary process, either as debts or spendable revenues, after 1781 until it reappears in the August 4, 1790 Funding Act as a debt to be liquidated. As such, congressional finances from 1781 to 1790 will not be addressed here. That is the subject for another book. What happened to the Continental dollar after its abandonment as a money in 1781 is explored next in part III. Chapter 15 tracks state redemption of Continental dollars from 1779 through 1790, as states positioned themselves for credits in the reapportionment of war costs across the states. Chapter 16 addresses the 1790 Funding Act and the final irrevocable default on the Continental dollar. And lastly, chapter 17 identifies the transformation of monetary powers in the US Constitution and addresses why paper monies like the Continental dollar were constitutionally banned from ever being issued again.

PART III

Epilogue

CHAPTER FIFTEEN

State Redemption of Continental Dollars

Congress financed the War for Independence from 1775 through 1779 by issuing paper money—the Continental dollar. In these years net new emissions totaled almost $200 million (face value) and accounted for 77 percent of congressional spending. No new emissions occurred after November 1779 (see chaps. 1 and 6). Congress requested that beginning in 1779 the states start remitting prescribed quotas of Continental dollars to the national treasury to be burned. These quotas would run for enough years into the future that all Continental dollars would be eventually redeemed and removed from circulation. The credibility of Congress's war-financing strategy depended on the states' honoring this request.[1]

Congress's final Continental dollar remittance requirements were passed in 1779 and 1780 (see chaps. 13 and 14). They were never rescinded but were finally superseded by the Funding Act of August 4, 1790. From 1779 to 1790 the states were expected to redeem and remit Continental dollars, or their specie-rated equivalents as determined by Congress, to the Continental Treasury to be burned.[2] Did the states comply, and if so, which remittance resolution did they follow? In 1866 Henry Phillips concluded that "the history of the notes and the reasons why they were not fully liquidated, have been but imperfectly known." Only meager improvements in our knowledge have been achieved since.[3] Sorting out this history by compiling the quantitative evidence on state compliance with congressional resolutions regarding the redemption of Continental dollars will

help identify where the problems with the Continental dollar resided, assess the veracity of Federalist anti-paper-money rhetoric, and explain the
role played by the Continental dollar in the constitutional restructuring of
monetary powers in the early republic.

Reconstructing State Redemptions of Continental Dollars

Three documents spanning the period 1779–89 report remittances of Continental dollars from each state to the Continental Treasury by year. These
documents report final redemption remittances, as the Continental dollars received were burned rather than respent. Cross-corroboration of
the three documents is required to establish a comprehensive listing and
consistent interpretation of the remittances recorded. Close attention to
whether gross or net emissions are being counted is also required to make
sense of this evidence.

On January 14, 1786, Joseph Nourse, the Registrar of the Treasury from
1781 to 1829, reported to Congress the amount of Continental dollars—
face value—paid into the Continental Treasury from May 1779 through
1785 by month, year, and source (*JCC* 30:22–25). In May 1782 the Continental treasurer, Michael Hillegas, reported to state governors a portion of
the report given by Nourse to Congress in 1786—the portion covering from
November 25, 1780, through February 23, 1782 (Ferguson et al. 1973–99,
5:139). Hillegas's report is identical to Nourse's for the period that the two
overlap, except that Hillegas identifies which of the remittances were just
currency swaps, that is, those affecting gross but not net emissions.[4] Finally,
on May 11, 1790, Alexander Hamilton reported to Congress the amount
of Continental dollars—face value—paid into the Continental Treasury
from November 1780 through March 1789 by day, month, year, and state.[5]
With the exception of a few minor omissions and discrepancies, noted below, the three reports are the same for the periods when they overlap. This
cross-corroboration gives us confidence in the numbers reported by each
series when they do not overlap.

These series, slightly rearranged (put into chronological order), are reproduced in table D.1. The numbers in the Hillegas report, being redundant, are not listed separately.[6] Combining the three series gives a continuous quantitative monthly series from May 1779 through March 1789 of
the amount of Continental dollars—face value—remitted by each state to
the Continental Treasury. Eliminating the overlap or duplication between

the series yields a total of 153.5 million Continental dollars—face value—remitted to the Continental Treasury and burned by 1790. Interpreting this number, however, requires additional scrutiny.

The Hillegas report identifies the purpose of each remittance, something not done in the Nourse and Hamilton reports. In particular, Hillegas identifies which remittances from the May 20, 1777, and April 11, 1778, emissions were being swapped dollar for dollar for the emission of January 14, 1779.[7] Comparing the entries in the Hillegas report with those in the Nourse and Hamilton reports for the period when the three reports overlap reveals that the Nourse report includes the remittance of Continental dollars that were part of this currency swap, whereas the Hamilton report deliberately excludes these remittances. The Nourse and Hillegas reports thus count remittances in reference to gross emissions or total printings of Continental dollars (241,500,000), whereas the Hamilton report counts remittances in reference to net new emissions (199,989,995).[8] By inference, the numbers in the Nourse report for the period before Hamilton's report commences must represent only remittances that were part of the currency swap and so are not a reduction in net new emissions.

This interpretation of how to count remittances is consistent with the timing of congressional legislation. The period over which bills from the May 20, 1777, and April 11, 1778, emissions could be exchanged for bills of the January 14, 1779, emission ran from the spring of 1779 through January 1, 1781. While most of the currency swap took place before that deadline, some of the exchanged bills continued to trickle into the Continental Treasury through 1781. The total sum that was eligible for exchange was $41.5 million. Nourse's remittances through January 1, 1781, totaled $34.4 million and through April 1781 totaled $39.9 million. That total rises to $41 million when the amounts that Hillegas explicitly identifies as being exchanges of the May 20, 1777, and April 11, 1778, emissions that took place after April 1781 are added. The closeness of this total to $41.5 million, given that Nourse admits that his numbers are neither comprehensive nor complete, is further indication that Nourse's numbers, at least into late 1780, include mostly the return of old Continental bills that were being swapped for new Continental bills and not a reduction in the net amount of Continental dollars outstanding.[9]

The requisition act of March 18, 1780, with its Continental-state dollar scheme (see chap. 14), induced the first serious effort by the states to remit Continental dollars—a net removal of Continental dollars from circulation rather than just the currency swaps discussed above. Under this scheme, states removed between 31.8 and 41.4 million Continental dollars from the public and remitted them to the Continental Treasury between late 1780 and late 1781. The estimated range comes from conflicting statements over how many Continental-state dollars were issued by the various states under this scheme. For every twenty Continental dollars a state remitted to the Continental Treasury to be burned, that state was allowed to emit on its own account one Continental-state dollar. The Continental-state dollar experiment collapsed in mid-1781 and was never revived (see chap. 14).

The first remittances of Continental dollars under the Continental-state dollar scheme would not reach the Continental Treasury until late in 1780, which is consistent with the commencement date (November 1780) of the Hamilton report. The last remittances under this scheme, given its mid-1781 collapse, would be in mid-to-late 1781. Hamilton's total, starting in November 1780, reaches these amounts (31.8 and 41.4 million Continental dollars) by August and November 1781, respectively.

From July 1780 through 1781, Continental dollars were remitted to the Continental Treasury both as part of the Continental-state currency scheme and as part of the currency swap of the emissions of May 20, 1777, and April 11, 1778, for the emission of January 14, 1779. The evidence does not always distinguish the reason for each specific remittance. The Hamilton report is thought to exclude the currency swaps, whereas the Nourse report, with a starting date of May 1779, is thought to include them. By November 1781 total remittances across the entirety of both the Nourse and the Hamilton reports, minus overlap and duplication, were enough to fully account both for the $41.5 million currency swap and the upper estimate of $41.1 million remitted under the Continental-state currency scheme.

The sums remitted after 1781 were part of the normal quotas being filled by the states. Interestingly, both Nourse and Hamilton indicate that no Continental dollars were remitted to the Continental Treasury between late 1783 and mid-1786. With the surrender of the British army under General Cornwallis at Yorktown on October 17, 1781, the cessation of hostilities on land soon thereafter, and finally the Treaty of Paris recognizing US independence and sovereignty at the end of 1783, states lost interest and saw little need to continue remitting Continental dollars. From $41.1 million remitted from November 1780 through November 1781, remittances fell to $24.5 million for all of 1782 to under $1 million for all of 1783 and finally to zero for all of 1784 and 1785 (see table D.1). Only when it became clear that there would be a reckoning of accounts among the states did remittances of Continental dollars to the Continental Treasury pick up—presumably as states positioned themselves for credits with the national government in the reapportionment of the Revolution's war costs among the states (Ferguson 1961: 205–19, 224; *JCC* 22:83–86).

For example, Thomas Jefferson, writing to James Madison from Annapolis on April 25, 1784, reasoned, "Would it not be well for Virginia to empower persons privately to buy up her quota of old Continental money. I would certainly advise this were I not afraid that possession of her quota on such easy terms would tempt her to refuse justice to the other states on this matter. . . . If she would . . . do what is right, I should much wish to see her adopt secret measures for the purchase. I think some states will do this, and I fear with unjust views" (Boyd 1953–55, 7:120). With the removal of the Continental dollar's legal-tender status in state law, states could acquire Continental dollars at values well below their face value, even as low as 1 percent of face value (see fig. 11.1). Once it became clear that Congress would credit the states at the rate of forty Continental dollars to one silver dollar, as established by the March 18, 1780, resolution, states had an incentive to acquire Continental dollars at the lowest value possible.[10] States that acquired more of their Continental dollar quota at a rate higher than the 40-to-1 rate would come out ahead in the settlement of accounts vis-à-vis other states.

By 1790 the total amount of Continental dollars (face value) still unremitted was 80.5 million (200 million of net new emission minus 119.5 million remitted through 1789, as reported by Hamilton) or 88 million (241.5 million of gross emissions minus 153.5 million of gross remittances, as the result of combining the Hamilton and Nourse reports) (see table D.1). Because Nourse admitted that his numbers were not complete, the $80.5 million will be taken as the better estimate. Thus by 1790, eleven years after the issuance of Continental dollars had ceased and seven years after the end of the Revolution, the states had managed to remove from the public roughly 60 percent of the net new Continental dollars ever emitted (119.5 million / 200 million). This was quite an accomplishment—a success seldom noted in the literature—especially considering that 1784–87 were depression years for the US economy and Congress's January 2, 1779, resolution did not require states to complete their remittance of Continental dollars until 1797 (Holton 2007).

The 80.5 million Continental dollars, estimated above, that were still unremitted in 1790 is corroborated by other evidence. It is close to the

guess made by the Twenty-eighth Congress that $78 to $80 million remained unredeemed and unfunded as of 1791, and it is close to Hamilton's implied estimate for 1789. Hamilton placed the national debt at
$77,124,465 for 1789/1790. In this number Hamilton included 2 million
Continental dollars which he calculated at its specie value of forty Continental dollars to one silver dollar as set by Congress on March 18, 1780,
for crediting state remittances: 80,527,631 Continental dollars outstanding
in 1790 in face value converts to $2,013,191 in specie value at that rate.[11]

The Time Path of State Redemption of Continental Dollars

The quantitative time path of emissions and remittances of Continental
dollars from 1775 to 1790 is presented in figure 15.1 as the cumulative
net total still outstanding by year (face value). Emissions began in June
1775 and ended in November 1779. They totaled $199,989,995 net new
emissions, and all were still outstanding as of 1780. Congress printed an
additional $41,510,000 to be swapped one for one with already emitted
Continental dollars, replacing existing Continental dollars that were either too torn or ragged to continue in circulation or were under threat
of being counterfeited. Most of these currency swaps took place between
1779 and 1781. Adding the $41,510,000 issued for currency exchange to the
$199,989,995 net new emissions yields $241,499,995 in gross emissions or
total printings of Continental dollars (see appendix A). Separating gross
from net emissions is necessary to evaluate the evidence on remittances.

Remittances to reduce net new emissions were to begin in 1779. Yet no
remittances for that purpose were made in 1779, and only $1,302,387 for
that purpose was made in 1780. In 1779 remittances for currency swaps
only were made, and most of the remittances made in 1780 were for currency swaps as well. Before 1779 the states were expected to remit, in
total, only 750,000 Continental dollars in 1779, and the same amount again
in 1780, toward the reduction of net new emissions (see chaps. 1 and 10).
By the end of 1780 the states as a whole were close to being on target
with that pre-1779 remittance expectation: $1.5 million expected versus
$1,302,387 actually made. This remittance rate is what comprises forecast 2
in table 10.1 and figures 10.3 and 10.4.

The change in remittance requirements made by Congress on January 2, 1779, to a total of $15 million for 1779 and $10,277,778 for 1780,
may have caught the states unprepared for such an unexpectedly large in-

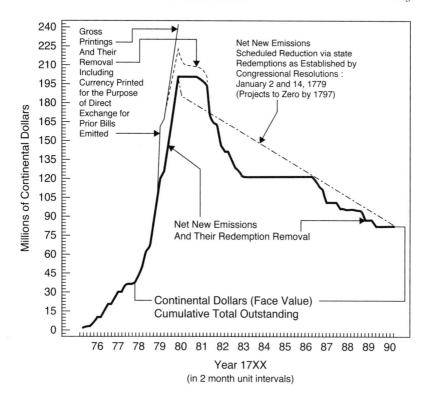

FIGURE 15.1. The Continental dollar, 1775–90: cumulative outstanding totals emitted and removed—face value

Sources: Grubb (2008); appendix A; tables D.1 and D.2.

Note: See the text for construction. The two-month unit intervals combine January with February, March with April, and so on.

crease in remittances. It was also unachievable through taxes at face value. The war was not over, and taxable commerce had not returned to normal levels. The tax rate needed to raise such a sum was well outside feasible and historically acceptable limits (see chaps. 10 and 13 and table 10.1). Yet, between 1781 and 1782, total remittances for the purpose of reducing net new emissions accelerated, surpassing the level needed to adhere to the January 2, 1779, resolution schedule of yearly redemptions. While remittances stayed ahead of this schedule from 1781 through 1790, after 1785 they tracked it closely (see fig. 15.1).

After 1780 the states as a whole appear to have adhered to the January 2, 1779, remittance schedule and largely ignored the new remittance schedule set by Congress on March 18, 1780 (see chap. 14). The 1780 schedule changed remittances to $15 million per month through April 1781, for a total of $195 million remitted by that date. In fact, just $7.3 million was remitted by that date, and only another $47.7 million was remitted through the rest of 1781.

How the states were able to meet the remittance schedule that they actually did is unclear and a topic for future research. The methods for redeeming Continental dollars were left to the individual states. They likely varied considerably from state to state. One thing is clear: to meet the remittance schedule that the states actually met, either tax amounts per year per white capita, especially in 1781 and 1782, had to be well above what had been historically acceptable, and/or states had to acquire Continental dollars from their citizens at significant discounts off their face value. For example, 1781 and 1782 were the two years with the most remittances, 53,690,923 and 24,506,561 Continental dollars, in face value, respectively. The per-year per-white-capita tax amounts needed to raise these two sums at face value were 57.6 and 26.3 times higher than the average per-year per-white-capita tax amounts of $0.41 in the colonies for all taxes levied between 1770 and 1774 (see table 10.1). Alternatively, to hold the average per-year per-white-capita tax amounts at $0.41 solely for the purpose of acquiring the Continental dollars that were redeemed and remitted would entail acquiring Continental dollars at rates considerably below face value, namely 57.6 Continental dollars equal to $1 in specie for 1781, and 26.3 Continental dollars equal to $1 in specie for 1782. Some combination of higher tax rates and below-face-value acquisitions were likely, with considerable variation across the states.

Adhering to the remittance schedules passed by Congress after 1778, and the actual remittances observed after 1780, forced three outcomes: (1) the removal of the Continental dollar's legal-tender status, (2) steep discounts given when paying taxes in anything other than Continental dollars, and (3) excessively high tax levels by historical standards.

State Adherence to Congressional Redemption Instructions

Broadly interpreted, after 1780 the states as a whole appear to have adhered to the remittance schedule set by Congress on January 2, 1779 (see fig. 15.1). This was an adherence in nominal amounts redeemed, but not to redemption at face value. Some states ran well ahead of that schedule,

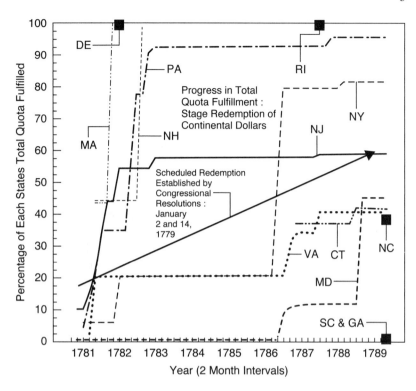

FIGURE 15.2. Progress in total quota fulfillment by states in remitting Continental dollars, 1780–89

Sources: Tables D.1 and D.2.

Note: See the text for construction. Square markers indicate that only a single payment was observed for that state. Lines start at the first payment remitted for each state, respectively, and chart the cumulative progress in fulfilling that state's total assigned quota. The two-month unit interval counts January with February, March with April, and so on.

while others lagged far behind. Only on average was that schedule of re-mittances the one to which the states appear to have adhered. Table D.2 and figure 15.2 illustrate the variation in remittance compliance among the states. Table D.2 tracks the remittance requirements (quotas) per year for each state as established by Congress on January 2, 1779. It calculates the percentage of these yearly quotas each state had filled as well as the percentage each state had filled of its accumulated yearly quotas to that date. The last columns in table D.2 provide a yearly summary of the re-mittance information in table D.1. Figure 15.2 combines the information in table D.2 with Hamilton's evidence in table D.1 to chart the progress each state had made toward filling its entire assigned quota of Continental dollar remittances for the purpose of final removal from circulation and destruction at the Continental Treasury.

Delaware was the first to fill its entire quota, doing so with a single payment on January 7, 1782. Massachusetts and New Hampshire also quickly filled their quotas, completing their payments by late September 1782. As states filled their quotas, or came close to filling their quotas, they discouraged the use of, and even refused to accept any more, Continental dollars. For example, on February 8, 1783, Delaware enacted the following law:

> Whereas it appears, that considerable balances of taxes directed by law to be raised within this state in Continental bills of credit, in the years One Thousand Seven Hundred and Seventy-eight, One Thousand Seven Hundred and Seventy-nine, and One Thousand Seven Hundred and Eighty, are yet due and uncollected: *And whereas* the said bills of credit have been called out of circulation, and this state hath paid Congress their computed quota of all the said bills, for the purpose of sinking and destroying the same; whereby it is become inexpedient and useless to levy said balances in such bills;
>
> *Be it therefore enacted by the General Assembly of Delaware*, That from and after the passing of this act, no Collector of the said taxes shall receive any of the bills aforesaid in payment of the taxes. . . .[12]

Such actions by states that had filled their redemption quotas must have further reduced the value of the now superfluous Continental dollars still in possession of the citizens in those states. It would also likely have driven those now superfluous bills into other states, the states that had not yet filled their redemption quotas, which in turn would drive the value of the Continental dollars in these other states down even further.

After 1782 only Rhode Island, with a single payment on August 13, 1787, completely filled its entire quota. Pennsylvania reached 90 percent of its entire quota by 1783, and New York reached 80 percent in 1786. New Jersey reached just over 50 percent by 1783 but made little progress thereafter. The other states, with the exception of South Carolina and Georgia, which recorded no remittances in the 1780s, made slow and intermittent progress but never reached over 50 percent of their total assigned quotas.

The behavior of New York, Virginia, Rhode Island, and Maryland after 1785 is consistent with Jefferson's rationale, quoted above, for how states reacted to positioning themselves for credits with the national government, given the pending reckoning of accounts between the states and the national government over apportioning war debts. These states were most likely able to acquire Continental dollars in the late 1780s at lower rates than that paid by Massachusetts, Delaware, New Hampshire, and Pennsylvania in the early 1780s. Given that the national government credited state remittances of Continental dollars at the same rate (40 to 1 in specie) throughout the 1780s, the former states came out ahead in the reckoning of accounts with the national government compared with the latter states. Finally, no state was recorded as having remitted more than its total assigned quota of Continental dollars.

In the early 1780s New Hampshire, Massachusetts, New Jersey, Pennsylvania, and Delaware were far ahead; New York and Virginia were somewhat behind; and the rest of the states were far behind the remittance schedule set by Congress on January 2, 1779. If we consider remittances just through the end of 1782, it appears that some states were more closely adhering to the remittance schedule set by Congress on March 18, 1780. This schedule asked each state to remit its entire quota (last row in table D.2) by mid-1781. By the end of 1782 New Hampshire, Massachusetts, and Delaware had completely filled their quotas, and Pennsylvania had filled 91 percent, and New Jersey 54 percent of their quotas. By contrast, through 1782 Virginia and New York appear to have been trying to adhere to the January 2, 1779, remittance schedule. The rest of the states were ignoring remittance requirements.

The extreme variation in remittances across the states implies that the per-year per-white-capita tax amounts, and/or the acquisition of Continental dollars at below-face-value rates, that was necessary to achieve the remittance amounts observed were in some states accentuated well above, and in other states depressed well below, the average calculated above for all states as a whole. To what extent this extreme state-level variation caused confusion and conflict among the states regarding the remittances of Continental dollars is unclear and a topic for future research (Grubb 2011b; Holton 2007).

CHAPTER SIXTEEN

The 1790 Funding Act and Final Default on the Continental Dollar

All Debts contracted and Engagements entered into before the Adoption of the Constitution, shall be as valid against the United States under this Constitution, as under the Confederation.
—US Constitution, Article VI

Congress adopted the US Constitution in 1789. This new Constitution gave Congress, for the first time, the power to levy taxes and thus an independent revenue source that it controlled directly. With this new revenue source Congress proceeded to restructure its finances with the Funding Act of August 4, 1790 (Peters 1845: First Congress, Second Session, chap. 34). The nation had incurred substantial debts waging the War for Independence. Most were in default, with payments of both principal and interest suspended and with arrears of interest accumulating between the end of the Revolution and 1790 (Taylor 1950: 2).[1]

First, I will show what Congress's annual tax revenues were from 1789 through 1800 and note their sources and limitations. Second, I will catalogue the debts—amount, type, and source—owed by Congress at the start of 1790. Third, I will report how the August 4, 1790 Funding Act identified these various debts and the resources reserved for funding them. Fourth, I will document how the August 4, 1790 Funding Act designed the actual servicing of these debts and explain the reasons that the debt servicing in the Act took the particular form it did, including how Congress fit the Continental dollar into the 1790 Funding Act. Fifth, I will measure the amount of default imposed on various debts by the 1790 Funding Act, including on the Continental dollar. Finally, I will explore whether Congress could have fully funded the remaining Continental dollars outstanding in 1790, as well as all its other debts, in some way that would have been in keeping with the US Constitution, as quoted above. How Congress could get away with defaulting on the Continental dollar while mostly funding its other debts without hurting its creditworthiness will be taken up in the final chapter.

Congress's Annual Tax Revenue, 1789–1800

Table 16.1 reports the annual revenue Congress received from 1789 through 1800 expressed in Spanish silver dollar units of account.[2] Over 90 percent of this revenue was from customs duties on imports and fees on shipping tonnage. Customs duties remained the principal source of federal revenue well into the nineteenth century (Edling 2014; Sylla 2011: 73). The US Constitution gave Congress the power to tax imports but not exports. It also prohibited the states from taxing imports or exports. From $1.6 million in 1790, this revenue grew to $6.1 million by 1795 and then to $10.8 million by 1800. This increase in annual revenue was primarily due to the growth in foreign trade, which increased the amount of customs duties and tonnage fees paid, with improvements in the efficiency of customs duties operations and increases in dutiable items and duties charged contributing some to the increased revenue stream over time.[3]

This revenue stream was likely the best that could be achieved at this time. The ability to raise taxes was severely constrained by public resistance. In late 1789 James Madison, congressman from Virginia, wrote to Alexander Hamilton, the newly installed Secretary of the Treasury in the first Washington administration: "In my opinion, in considering plans for the increase of our revenue, the difficulty lies, not so much in the want of objects as in the prejudices which may be feared with regard to almost every object. The Question is very much What further taxes will be *least* unpopular?" (Syrett and Cooke 1962–72, 5:439, italics in the original). The public was willing to engage in large-scale violent tax revolts, as witnessed by Shays' Rebellion (1786–87), the Whiskey Rebellion (1794), and Fries's Rebellion (1798). All three rebellions were tax revolts that forced the administration to call out the regular army to confront its own citizens. The Whiskey Rebellion was the only time a sitting US president as commander-in-chief has taken the field at the head of the army.[4]

TABLE 16.1 **Federal government revenue, 1789–1800**

Year	Annual revenue	Federal government annual operating expenses (est.)		Projected funds remaining for debt servicing
1789	$162,000	?	=	$162,000
1790	$1,640,000	− $829,000	=	$811,000
1791	$2,648,000	− $829,000	=	$1,819,000
1792	$3,675,000	− $829,000	=	$2,846,000
1793	$4,653,000	− $829,000	=	$3,824,000
1794	$5,423,000	− $829,000	=	$4,603,000
1795	$6,115,000	− $829,000	=	$5,286,000
1796	$8,378,000	− $829,000	=	$7,549,000
1797	$8,689,000	− $829,000	=	$7,860,000
1798	$7,900,000	− $829,000	=	$7,071,000
1799	$7,547,000	− $829,000	=	$6,718,000
1800	$10,849,000	− $829,000	=	$10,020,000
1789–1800 Totals	$67,688,000			$58,569,000

Source: Sylla (2011: 67, 73). See also Grubb (2007a: 281); *Historical statistics of the United States* (1975, 2:1104).
Notes: Revenue is the actual revenue received each year. In 1790, the first full year of operation, domestic operating expenditures were $829,000 (Sylla 2011: 67). See also the "support of government" borrowing authorized for 1793, which was $800,000 (*Laws of the United States . . .* 1896, pt. 1:18). The $829,000 number is used as the expectation of the minimum annual operating expenses from the viewpoint of 1790 for the near future.

Hamilton expected revenue shortfalls in the 1790s. In late 1789 he suggested quietly approaching the French to see "if the installments of the Principal of the debt [the United States owed France] could be suspended for a few years, [as] it would be a valuable accommodation to the U.S." (Syrett and Cooke 1962–72, 5:426, 429). Hamilton's suggestions for new taxes in addition to the tariff, such as the Whiskey Tax, in his December 13, 1790 "First Report on the Further Provision Necessary for Establishing Public Credit" helped spark the 1794 Whiskey Rebellion (Syrett and Cooke 1962–72, 7:225–36; Tindall 1988: 301, 320). Given these limitations on increasing taxes, I will assume that the actual revenue stream as shown in table 16.1 is the maximum reasonably attainable during the 1790s.

Congress's annual tax revenue had to pay for the annual operating costs of the federal government, such as salaries of government officials and employees, military outlays, and so on. In the first full year of operation, 1790, this spending amounted to $829,000. The amount of yearly revenue left after subtracting these operating costs is the revenue that could be applied, and by law as stated in the August 4, 1790 Funding Act was required to be and could only be applied, to servicing the debt (Peters 1845: First Congress, Second Session, chap. 34). I will assume that $829,000 was the least that was needed annually to cover operating expenses looking forward from 1790 for the rest of the 1790s, and so the rest of the revenue in table 16.1 was available for debt servicing. This assumption yields the most revenue available for debt servicing and is therefore a biased-high or optimistic view of Congress's ability to service its debts over the 1790s. Obviously, congressmen would want to add pet projects to the annual operating mechanisms of government over time and claim more and more of the revenue stream for operating expenses.

The Federal Government's Debts in 1790

Table 16.2 lists the federal government's debts as of 1790—their amounts by type and source. I separated the debts into interest-bearing debts and non-interest-bearing debts. The only non-interest-bearing debts were Continental dollars, estimated to be $80.5 million face value outstanding as of 1790 (see chap. 15). The interest-bearing debts consisted of foreign debts undertaken by Congress, domestic debts issued by Congress, and the assumption of some debts issued by state governments to fund war expenses. Interest arrears are included in these debt totals. The face value of the Continental dollar debt outstanding in 1790 was slightly larger than the face value of all the interest-bearing debts outstanding in 1790. The assumption of some state war debts by Congress was expected or even considered as a requirement, given that the new US Constitution had

TABLE 16.2 **Federal government debts, 1790 (face value in Spanish silver dollars)**

Type	Name	Source	Face-value amount outstanding as of 1790
Non-interest-bearing debt	Continental dollars	Direct spending by Congress	$80.5 million
Interest-bearing-debt	(a) Domestic bonds	Direct borrowings by Congress	$42.4 million
	(b) Foreign bonds	Direct borrowings by Congress	$11.7 million
	(c) Domestic bonds	State borrowings assumed by Congress	$25.0 million
Interest-bearing total			$79.1 million
Grand total (face value)			$159.6 million

Sources: See chap. 8, n. 2; chap. 15; Grubb (2007a: 280–81); Sylla (2011: 66–67).
Notes: The totals for the interest-bearing debts include interest arrears. Most of the domestic bonds were loan office certificates (see chaps. 6 and 8).

removed the power to tax imports and exports from the states and shifted it to Congress (for imports only). Taxing imports and exports had been an important revenue source for many states and was what some states had counted on to fund their war debts. States having lost the power to do so to Congress, the expectation was that the repayment of some state debts would also have to pass to Congress.

The amounts listed in table 16.2 for the interest-bearing debt are slightly different from the preliminary debt amounts listed in the August 4, 1790 Funding Act. For example, the Funding Act listed the foreign debt at $12 million and the state debts to be assumed at $21.5 million. The amounts as listed in table 16.2 rely on the work of Richard Sylla (2011) and are taken as being closest to the actual debts Congress had to fund. After 1790 Congress frequently extended the date for submitting debts that were required to be funded under the 1790 Funding Act.[5]

Comparing Congress's annual revenue stream for the 1790s (table 16.1) with the debts it owed in 1790 (table 16.2) shows that Congress did not have enough revenue to retire all its debts in 1790, or to retire them all using the revenue from the entire decade of the 1790s (1789–99). Even if the Continental dollar debt was discarded and left totally unfunded, there was not enough revenue to retire just the interest-bearing debts over the decade of the 1790s. Finally, even if the state debts were not assumed by Congress, Congress did not have enough revenue over the entire decade of the 1790s to retire the remaining interest-bearing debt. Simply retiring the debt was not feasible without picking and choosing which to pay off and which to not pay off, and then Congress could only at best pay off a small percentage (in the single digits) of that debt each year, resulting in the continued accumulation of interest arrears on the debts not yet paid off. Some other funding strategy for serving the debt other than retirement was sought.

If the debt traded in the marketplace at its face value, then debt holders could always get a face-value payoff for their debts from other citizen buyers of debt in the marketplace even if the government was incapable of retiring the debt at face value. If the government could cause the debt to trade in the marketplace at face value, then it could be said to be fully serviced. The minimum annual amount of current government revenue needed to pay on the debt that would cause it to reinflate to face value in the marketplace would be to pay annual market interest but no principal on the debt in perpetuity.

This method was well-known, for the British had adopted it in 1751 to fund its war debts. British Consol bonds (short for consolidated annuities) were callable perpetuities. The idea comes from simple finance present-value calculations for a perpetuity that pays a constant coupon each year. Let FV = face value of the debt instrument; PV = the present value of the debt instrument; i = the market interest rate; and C = the annual coupon of interest paid on the debt instrument. Then, if the government pays $C = FV*i$ each year on the debt instrument, and given that $PV = C/i$ for a perpetuity, it follows that $PV = (FV*i)/i$, and so $PV = FV$. The present value of the debt instrument will equal its face value. C represents the minimum amount the government has to pay each year on the debt to cause it to reinflate to face value in the marketplace so the debt could be considered fully funded.

Given a market interest rate of 6 percent (see chap. 9), could Congress reinflate all its debts listed in table 16.2 to face value by turning them into callable perpetuities and paying only annual interest each year on this debt out of its current revenue stream? The answer is no, unless Congress eliminated some of its debts from the books. Comparing the revenue stream in table 16.1 with the debts in table 16.2 indicates that at 6 percent, the yearly C would have to be over $9 million on a total of $160 million in debt. Congress's yearly revenue was well under $9 million throughout the 1790s (1789–99).

Even if the Continental dollar debt was discarded and left totally unfunded, there would not be enough yearly revenue to pay C on just the interest-bearing portion of the debt until after 1794. Finally, even if state debts were not assumed by Congress, Congress did not have enough yearly revenue before 1793 to pay annual C on just the remaining interest-bearing debt.

Turning the debts into callable perpetuities was a good strategy for funding the debt (reinflating it to face value), as it minimized the amount of yearly revenue that had to be dedicated to paying on the debt; but doing so would still require defaulting on some debts, especially over the first half of the decade of the 1790s. The "callable" part is largely irrelevant to this assessment (setting aside issues of interest-rate arbitrage if market interest rates changed). The government could always just step into the market and buy some of the debt at face value when it wanted to and retire it. Being "callable" just meant that the government had first purchase rights at face value in the marketplace.

The August 4, 1790 Funding Act: How Congress Addressed Its Debts and What Revenues to Use

The first paragraph of the Act makes a distinction between foreign and domestic debts: "provisions should be made for fulfilling the engagements of the United States in respect to their foreign debts." The phrase "fulfilling the engagements" indicates that foreign debts will be funded in full at face value. The Act goes on to say, "and for funding their domestic debt upon equitable and satisfactory terms," a phrase indicating that domestic debts may not be fully funded at face value.

Immediately following this first paragraph, sections 1 and 2 of the Act state that all revenue arising from the customs duties and tonnage fees after paying for the necessary expenses for operating the government (what is called "support of government") must be used first to pay interest on foreign loans, and then any remaining amounts could be used to pay interest on domestic loans. It also authorizes more borrowing to meet payments on foreign loans if necessary. Again, foreign debts are distinguished from domestic debts in sections 1 and 2.

Section 3 of the Act lists the domestic debts incurred by Congress to be funded. It includes seven categories of domestic debt that will be combined into a new debt issue. The Continental dollar is one of the seven categories listed. This indicates that Congress regarded the Continental dollar as a debt that had to be repaid or funded, not a fiat currency. If the Continental dollar was a fiat currency, Congress would have done nothing—it would not even have mentioned the Continental dollar in the Funding Act. Congress could have just walk away from it. Instead, the Continental dollar was listed as one of the seven debt categories incurred by Congress that were to be funded. The other six debt categories were notes issued by the Continental Treasury; loan office certificates; quartermaster, commissary, hospital, clothing, and marine department notes; notes issued by commissioners for adjusting accounts between the states; army paymaster-general notes; and vouchers issued to cover interest arrears, known as "indents" (see table 6.5; chap. 8).

The Act treated the assumption of state debts differently than other debts and did not address them until section 13. Finally, the last section of the Act, section 22, explicitly stated that any proceeds arising from the sale of western lands had to be used to pay off debts, being included in the "callable" part of the debt-funding act. Substantial land sales, however, would not occur until well after the 1790s (Grubb 2011a: 265).

The August 4, 1790 Funding Act:
How Congress Actually Serviced Its Debts

Congress converted all debts into new callable perpetuities. For foreign debts, any conversion to new bonds would be at face value. In addition,

Congress intended to pay the full market interest (6 percent) on foreign debts, thus making the present value of the foreign debts in 1790 equal their face value (reinflating that debt to face value).

For the domestic debts incurred by Congress, the Continental dollar would be converted at a rate of 100 Continental dollars per 1 dollar face value in the new bonds when turned in. The other domestic debts incurred by Congress, including their arrears of interest, would be converted into new bonds at their face value. Likewise, the state debts, including interest arrears, assumed under the Funding Act were converted to new bonds at their face value. A clear distinction was being made between funding interest-bearing debts and non-interest-bearing debts, namely between the Continental dollar debt and all other debts. The Continental dollar was a zero-coupon bond that was being converted into an interest-bearing bond by the Funding Act. As such, it had to have its face value (principal) reduced by some amount to yield its proper present value as a zero-coupon bond in 1790. Whether a 100-to-1 reduction in face value was an equitable adjustment is addressed below.

While the domestic debts incurred by Congress would be converted into new perpetuity bonds at their face value—except that for the Continental dollar, which was converted to face value at 100 to 1, the interest rate or annual coupon C to be paid on that face value was not always the market rate, and so the new debt package would not be raised to face value in the marketplace. When turning in old domestic debts for all six categories of interest-bearing debt, except for indents, the debt holder was given a package of new perpetuities where two-thirds paid 6 percent annual interest starting from when they were issued and one-third would pay 6 percent annual interest but starting only in 1800. For indents (vouchers representing interest arrears), new perpetuities would be issued that paid 3 percent annual interest starting when issued.

State debts that were assumed under the Funding Act would be converted to perpetuities at face value. But again, the annual interest rate paid, or annual coupon C paid, was not the market rate, and so these perpetuities would not reinflate this debt to its face value in the marketplace. For state debts, the holder was given a package of perpetuities where 44 percent of the package paid 6 percent annual interest starting from when issued, 33 percent of the package paid 3 percent annual interest starting from when issued, and 22 percent of the package paid 6 percent interest but only starting in 1800.

The rather convoluted payment packages of perpetuities used to convert old debts to new ones appears to have served two goals. The first was

TABLE 16.3 **Expected annual interest costs of the 1790 Funding Act for the 1790s**

Debt category	Face value	Adjustments	Interest rate	Annual interest due
Foreign debt	$11,700,000		* 0.06=	$702,000
Domestic debts				
Interest-bearing—congressional[a]	$42,400,000	* 0.66 = $27,984,000	* 0.06=	$1,679,040
Interest-bearing—state	$25,000,000	* 0.44 = $11,000,000	* 0.06=	$660,000
		* 0.33 = $8,250,000	* 0.03=	$247,500
Non-interest-bearing—Continental dollars	$80,500,000 / 100 = $805,000	* 0.66 = $531,300	* 0.06=	$31,878
[Actual	$6,000,000 / 100 = $60,000	* 0.66 = $39,600	* 0.06=	$2,376]
Total				$3,320,418
[Actual				$3,290,916]

Sources: Peters (1845: First Congress, Second Session, chap. 34); tables 16.1 and 16.2.

Notes: Only $6 million in Continental dollars were turned in for new bonds.

[a] Indents that paid only 3 percent annual interest were not separated out of this total, so this estimate is biased high.

to reduce the amount of annual payments needed to service the debt into the range of the government's anticipated annual revenues. The second was to provide what was considered some equitable distribution of losses across domestic debt holders. Foreign debts had to be fully funded to maintain the government's credit position in foreign markets in case the government had to borrow in those markets in the future. For domestic debt holders, everyone got a package with some bonds that would trade at face value and some that would trade at some discount off their face value, namely a permanent discount for indents and a portion of state debts converted to the new bonds, and a discount that slowly disappeared by 1800 for new bonds that had their interest payment deferred until that date. The Continental dollar was the exception. Holders of that debt received almost nothing relative to their face value. I will assess the default structures imposed by the Funding Act—the fact that the $PV < FV$ for the new bond packages of perpetuities, after assessing whether this payment structure met the first goal of bringing annual debt service payments within reach of annual government revenues.

Table 16.3 takes the Funding Act's payment structure and combines it with the debts listed in table 16.2 to estimate the government's annual interest payments. Comparing these estimates with the government's annual revenues in table 16.1 shows whether the government could meet the debt servicing as set up in the Funding Act. Congress would be able to meet the annual interest payments as established in the Funding Act out of annual revenues only after 1792. Before 1793, annual revenues were insufficient to meet even the reduced structure of debt payments imposed by the Funding Act. To meet annual interest payments before 1793, an even greater portion of the domestic debt's interest payments would have had to be deferred to 1800 than was actually deferred in the 1790 Funding Act. This also explains both the efforts by Congress in the early 1790s to impose new taxes on its citizens, such as the Whiskey Tax, and to borrow additional sums to meet its new debt obligations under the Funding Act (Peters 1845: First Congress, First Session, chap. 47; Second Session, chap. 34; Third Session, chap. 25).[6]

After the 1790 Funding Act, the federal government's interest-bearing debt held fairly constant at about $80 million from 1792 through 1800. No net progress in overall debt retirement occurred regarding interest-bearing debt in the decade of the 1790s (Grubb 2007a: 281). The non-interest-bearing debt—the Continental dollar—was a different story: it was almost completely wiped off the books via default in 1790. Only $6 million of the $80.5 million Continental dollars still outstanding in 1790 were turned in at the 100-to-1 rate for the new perpetuity bonds between 1791 and 1797, when the exchange program was ended.[7] This puts the annual interest expense of the funded Continental dollars at only $2,376, basically almost nothing (table 16.3).

Continental dollars not swapped for the new perpetuity bonds by 1797 became worthless. Thus, by 1797, $125.5 million of the $200 million net new Continental dollars ever emitted (63 percent) can be accounted for as remittances to the national treasury. What happened to the rest of the Continental dollars? Some were likely lost or destroyed.[8] Judging by the numerous petitions sent to Congress and to the Secretaries of the Treasury after 1790, most were held by citizens hoping for a better redemption rate than the 100-to-1 rate set by the 1790 Funding Act. They were ultimately disappointed. Redemption ceased at the end of 1797, and Congress would give nothing for Continental dollars thereafter. Future Secretaries of the Treasury would point to the 1790 Funding Act as the last word on the government's obligation regarding the Continental dollar. In 1843 the Twenty-eighth Congress, when investigating what happened to the Continental dollar, concluded that $72 to $74 million (face value) had been a total loss to the public, never funded or redeemed.[9]

Evaluating the Default on Debts Imposed by the 1790 Funding Act

Article VI of the US Constitution, quoted at the start of this chapter, indicates that the federal government was responsible for all debts incurred by Congress under the Confederation. The spirit, if not the letter, of this responsibility was that after 1789 the federal government had to fully service, fund, or otherwise pay off all debts that Congress undertook prior to 1789. The 1790 Funding Act seemed to reaffirm this view, for that act states "that nothing herein contained, shall be construed to annul or alter any appropriation by law made prior to the passing of this act" (Peters 1845: First Congress, Second Session, chap. 34). The Funding Act also stated that citizens bringing in their old debts to be converted to new loans as laid out in the Act would not be a requirement, but would be "done by a *voluntary* loan on their part" (italics added). Yet, as far as can be determined, anyone who did not convert their old debts into new loans as laid out in the Funding Act, including its subsequent deadline extensions, received nothing.

I will consider default as being when the actual present value of what a citizen is given is less than the face value (properly time-discounted when required) owed that citizen, the size of the default being the gap between the debt's present value (PV) and the debt's face value (FV). The Funding Act, while funding old foreign debts in full, did not service or fund all the old domestic debts in full. It partially defaulted on domestic debts, a default whose lost value would never be made up. On some domestic debts the default was small, but on others it was large. As such, it appears that the federal government violated the Constitution with the 1790 Funding Act.[10]

How big a default was built into the Funding Act? On foreign debts there was no default. Their present value was raised to their face value in the 1790 marketplace by paying the market interest rate annually, starting in 1790, on that debt in perpetuity. On domestic interest-bearing debts incurred by Congress, the Funding Act gave the debt holder in 1790 only 85 percent of the old debt's face value. The present value of that debt in 1790 when funded was less than its face value in 1790, namely $[(0.67 * e^{-0.06*0}) + (0.33 * e^{-0.06*10})] = PV$ in 1790 = 0.85 of FV in 1790. That present value would slowly rise from 1790 to face value by 1800 when the deferred interest finally kicked in on one-third of the bond package given citizens.[11]

On interest-bearing domestic state debts assumed under the Funding Act, the Funding Act gave the debt holder in 1790 only 74 percent of the old debt's face value. The present value of that debt in 1790 when funded was less than its face value in 1790, namely $[(0.45 * e^{-0.06*0}) + (0.22 * e^{-0.06*10}) + (0.33 * e^{-0.06*0} * 0.03/0.06)] = PV$ in 1790 = 0.74 of FV in 1790. That present value would slowly rise from 1790 to 84 percent of face value by 1800 when the deferred interest finally kicked in on 22 percent of the bond package given citizens.

Regarding the Funding Act's default on the Continental dollar, Hamilton initially proposed reducing the Continental dollar's face value at a rate of forty paper dollars to one specie dollar in the anticipated 1790 Funding Act. This rate followed from the March 18, 1780, congressional resolution that allowed states to substitute one specie dollar for forty Continental dollars in their required remittances to Congress (see chap. 14). Congress changed Hamilton's proposed 40-to-1 reduction to 100 to 1 in the 1790 Funding Act. As such, the Funding Act gave the Continental dollar debt holder in 1790 only 0.85 percent of the Continental dollar's face value. The present value of that debt in 1790 when funded was less than its face value in 1790, namely $[\{(0.67 * e^{-0.06*0}) + (0.33 * e^{-0.06*10})\} / 100] = PV$ in 1790 = 0.0085 of FV in 1790. That present value would slowly rise from 1790 to 1 percent of face value by 1800, when the deferred interest finally kicked in on a third of the bond package.[12] At Hamilton's proposed 40-to-1 reduction, paper to specie, the above calculation would have been a present value of 2.1 percent of face value in 1790.

Was this a large default on the Continental dollar debt? The Continental dollar was a zero-coupon bond that was being converted into an interest-bearing bond by the Funding Act. As such, it had to have its face value (principal) reduced by some amount to yield its proper present value as a zero-coupon bond in 1790. The 100-to-1 reduction in face value in 1790 was excessive compared with what the expected (forecast) present value of the Continental dollar in 1790 was, based on the fiscally credible pattern of promised future face-value redemptions as established by Congress in the first two emissions in 1775–76 (see chaps. 1 and 10). These forecast present values in 1790 stood at 24 and 15 percent of face value for forecasts 1 and 2, respectively (see fig. 10.3). In 1790 the Funding Act offered citizens 0.85 percent of face value on their Continental dollars, whereas congressionally established patterns of redemption yielded an expected 15–24 percent of face value payoff in 1790. This was a substantial loss in expected present value terms. Given the 80.5 million Continental dollars outstanding in 1790, this loss amounted to between 11.4 and 18.6 million dollars in 1790 in present value terms.

To fund the Continental dollar at its 1790 forecast present value, based on the face-value redemption patterns established by Congress in 1775 and 1776, would entail reducing Continental dollars to specie dollars at a rate between 4 to 1 (25 percent of face value) and 6 to 1 (17 percent of face value), paper to specie, rather than the 100 to 1 (1 percent of face value) set by the Funding Act. Such a reduction would be in keeping with the US Constitution's Article VI requirement, quoted above, that all debts incurred by Congress prior to 1789 be honored, as well as with the 1790 Funding Act's statement on the Act not annulling prior obligations.

Doing so was possible and would not change the ability to meet annual interest payments out of federal government annual revenues by more than half a year. Substituting a 4-to-1 or 6-to-1 paper-to-specie reduction in the face value of the Continental dollar in place of the 100-to-1 reduction in table 16.3 changes the total expected annual interest payments during the 1790s from $3,320,418 to $4,085,490 or $3,819,840, respectively. This annual interest payment could be met out of the federal government's annual revenue stream by 1793 and certainly by 1794, and then easily thereafter. By comparison, the federal government was not able to meet total annual interest payments before 1793 anyway when using the 100-to-1 reduction rate (see table 16.1). Default on the Continental dollar in terms of lowering its present value well below that expected in 1790 (fig. 10.3) was not necessary because it was within the federal government's funding ability, given how it funded and partially defaulted on its other debts.

Was Default on Any Debts Necessary in the 1790s?

I believe the answer to the question of whether debt default was necessary is no. There may be many different funding schemes that could generate a no-default outcome over the 1790s. I will present one that is relatively easy to lay out. Again, default is taken as being when $PV < FV$ for any old interest-bearing bonds funded in the 1790s, and actual $PV <$ forecast PV for old zero-coupon bonds (Continental dollars) funded in the 1790s. A no-default outcome would be to fund or service old interest-bearing debt in such a way that they would trade in the marketplace at their $PV = FV$ throughout the 1790s, and fund old zero-coupon bond debts in such a way that they would trade in the marketplace at their pre-1779 forecast PV for

TABLE 16.4 **A full-funding plan for the federal debt in 1790**

Year	Interest-bearing debt (start of year)		Plus new interest arrears	Minus revenue available to payoff interest-bearing debt net of Continental dollars retired (end of year)	Equals end-of-year interest-bearing debt
1790	$79,100,000ᵃ	+		− ($973,000ᵇ − $750,000)	= $78,877,000
1791	78,877,000	+	$4,732,620 = $83,609,620	− (1,819,000 − 750,000)	= 82,540,620
1792	82,540,620	+	4,952,437 = 87,493,057	− (2,846,000 − 750,000)	= 85,397,057
1793	85,397,057	+	5,123,823 = 90,520,800	− (3,824,000 − 750,000)	= 87,446,880
1794	87,397,057	+	5,246,813 = 92,693,693	− (4,603,000 − 750,000)	= 88,840,693
1795	88,840,693	+	5,330,442 = 94,171,135	− (5,286,000 − 750,000)	= 90,181,135
1796	90,181,135	+	5,410,868 = 95,592,003	− (7,549,000 − 750,000)	= 88,793,003
1797	88,793,003	+	5,327,580 = 94,120,583	− (7,860,000 − 750,000)	= 87,101,583
1798	87,010,583	+	5,220,635 = 92,231,218	− (7,071,000 − 750,000)	= 85,910,218
1799	85,910,218	+	5,154,613 = 91,064,831	− (6,718,000 − 750,000)	= 85,096,831
1800	85,096,831	+	5,105,810 = 90,202,641	− (10,020,000 − 750,000)	= 80,932,641
1801	80,932,641				

Sources: Derived from tables 16.1 and 16.2.

Notes: The figure of 6 percent is used to compute new interest arrears added for each year, so for 1791 the starting value is $78,877,000 times 0.06 annual interest, which equals $4,732,620 new interest added to the interest-bearing debt for 1791.

ᵃ Near end-of-year value for 1790, so no new interest arrears are added for 1790.

ᵇ This combines revenue from 1789 and 1790 for paying off interest-bearing debt in 1790.

1790. This would be in keeping with the spirit, if not the letter, of what the US Constitution required in Article VI.

Table 16.4 presents a funding scheme that would generate a "no default" outcome and leave the US federal government in the same interest-bearing debt position, approximately $80 to $81 million still outstanding at face value, at the end of 1800 as where it actually ended up under the 1790 Funding Act (Grubb 2007a: 281). This funding scheme would require no additional foreign borrowings to be added to the debt, something that the 1790 Funding Act allowed and was then required to meet its funding obligations (Peters 1845: First Congress, First Session, chap. 47; Second Session, chap. 34; Third Session, chap. 25).[13]

This scheme takes the federal government annual revenue as shown

in table 16.1 as given. It takes all the non-interest-bearing debt in 1790—
80.5 million Continental dollars—and retires $750,000 of it each year at
face value out of current revenue. To determine which Continental dollars
get redeemed at face value each year, the government would institute a
random lottery to select the $750,000 to be redeemed that year. It would
repeat the lottery each year until all were redeemed. Government-run
lotteries to deal with finances were well-known and well tried in both colonial and revolutionary America (see table 8.1).

Redeeming the outstanding Continental dollars at face value starting
in 1790 at a rate of $750,000 a year would be in keeping with the redemp-
tion pattern set by Congress for the first two emissions of Continental
dollars and would serve as a forecast of the redemption structure for future emissions (see chaps. 1 and 10). Such a redemption rate would yield
a present value in 1790 for Continental dollars still outstanding in 1790 of
16 percent of face value, which is the present value of forecast 2 in figure
10.3. This is the lowest expected present value consistent with the redemption pattern established by Congress in 1775–76, which was in turn based
on what was considered fiscally credible. As such, it is in keeping with the
requirements of the US Constitution Article VI on debt obligations.

The scheme takes the annual revenue net of government operating
costs from table 16.1, nets out the $750,000 used to redeem Continental
dollars each year, and then uses the remaining revenue to retire interest-
bearing debts at face value. To determine which interest-bearing debts get
retired at face value that year, the government would institute a lottery
to select those debts to be retired at face value. Those debts not selected
to be retired that year would continue to generate interest arrears, which
would be added to their debt amounts. Because interest arrears would
continue to accumulate on debts not selected to be retired that year, the
present value of that debt in the marketplace would continue to equal its
face value, and so be fully funded (a no-default outcome).

The interest arrears would cause the interest-bearing debt to continue
to grow (the interest arrears each year being greater than the revenue
used to retire debt) through 1795, when it would decline (the interest arrears each year being less than the revenue used to retire debt after 1795).
By the end of 1800 the interest-bearing debt would stand at $81 million,
or almost exactly where it stood under the 1790 Funding Act. The difference here is that over the 1790s there would be (1) no additional foreign
borrowings required and (2) no default on any debt in terms of lost or
reduced present value from what it should have been.

Conclusion

The default on the Continental dollar as executed by the 1790 Funding Act was not financially necessary. In fact, the default on any of Congress's debts in 1790 was not financially necessary. The federal government had the annual revenue stream to fund the Continental dollar at its forecast no-default present value of at least 16 percent of face value rather than at under 1 percent of face value, as was done in the 1790 Funding Act. The amount this funding of the Continental dollar would have added to annual interest costs would not have altered the timing of when the government was funding deficient versus funding sufficient in covering its annual interest cost by more than half a year. In addition, no default on any of its debts could have been achieved with feasible alternative funding schemes.

So what else might have been a motive to default on the Continental dollar in 1790 and effectively wipe it off the books? What else might be gained by such a default and removal of that debt from the government's ledger? Elsewhere I have shown that if you think in terms of net worth, that is, if you consider the difference between the federal government's total assets at face value and its total debts at face value, then a case can be made for eliminating the Continental dollar debt from the books via default. Total debts in table 16.2 were well in excess of the federal government's total assets. The US national government was in a negative net worth position. Given that the ability to borrow in foreign markets, and some measure of creditworthiness, was predicated on a positive net worth position, the federal government had to shed the face value of some of its debts off its books. I show that if the Continental dollar was eliminated from the ledger in 1790, then the federal government's net worth position instantly changed from a negative $40 million to a positive $40 million (Grubb 2007a: 282; 2011a). It is this positive net worth that likely helped the United States garner an excellent credit rating in European markets by the mid-1790s.

This still prompts the question of how the United States could default on the Continental dollar in 1790 and still garner an excellent credit rating by the mid-1790s—how could this default not affect its creditworthiness? Gaining a positive net worth position is only part of the answer. The other part has to do with how the United States constitutionally barred itself from ever issuing debt like the Continental dollar in the future. That constitutional bar is taken up in the final chapter.

CHAPTER SEVENTEEN

The Constitutional Transformation of the US Monetary System

A depreciating Currency, We must not have. It will ruin Us. The Medium of Trade ought to be as unchangeable as Truth: as immutable as Morality. The least Variation in its Value, does Injustice to Multitudes, and in proportion it injures the Morals of the People, a Point of the last Importance in a Republican Government. — John Adams to James Warren, February 12, 1777 (Smith 1976–94, 6:262)

The Monied interest will oppose the plan of Government, if paper emissions be not prohibited. — Gouverneur Morris at the Constitutional Convention, August 16, 1787 (Farrand 1966, 2:309)

In 1787, just three years after the Treaty of Paris recognized US independence, the founding fathers met from May 25 through September 17 in Philadelphia to craft a new national constitution to replace the Articles of Confederation. This new US Constitution, ratified by the states and then adopted by Congress in 1789, profoundly altered the nation's monetary structure. It was nothing short of revolutionary regarding monetary practice. Before the Constitution, the primary "inside" paper money in circulation was bills of credit issued directly by government legislatures and backed by future taxes and land mortgages, and not by specie coins (the "outside" money of the times). Few banks existed—none before 1782 and only three by 1787. After the Constitution was adopted, both state and national governments were prohibited from issuing bills of credit as paper money. Instead, government-chartered but privately run and largely unregulated banks proliferated, numbering seventy-six by 1805. They filled the paper-money void by issuing banknotes backed by fractional reserves in specie coins. By constitutionally banning the chief alternative paper-money competitor to banknotes, the Constitution established the legal framework for the ascendance in the United States of the modern bank-based financial system.[1]

The constitutional monetary powers of interest are defined here as (1) the power to emit bills of credit—zero-coupon bonds used as a paper-money medium of exchange, (2) the power to declare what money is a legal tender, and (3) the power to charter banks. The Constitution did not directly or legally impose a common monetary unit of account or medium of exchange onto the nation. After the ratification of the Constitution, a plethora of different private banknotes and specie coins in different foreign monetary standards circulated as currency (Criswell 1965; Muhleman 1895). The Constitution at best limited the medium of exchange to specie and specie-linked paper instruments. A common monetary unit of account—the US dollar—would emerge as a by-product of the market's optimal transaction-cost adjustment to the restructured means of payment brought about by the Constitution.[2]

At the 1787 Constitutional Convention the founding fathers explicitly voted to remove the power to emit bills of credit from and explicitly voted not to add the power to charter corporations—including chartering banks—to the list of enumerated powers to be granted Congress in the new Constitution (Article 1, Section 8).[3] Article 1, Section 10 of the new Constitution absolutely prohibits individual states from emitting bills of credit and making anything other than gold and silver coin a legal tender. States, however, retained the right to charter corporations, including chartering banks. These radical changes in the constitutionally determined monetary structure of the United States did not emerge until late in the Convention's deliberations and were not anticipated by prior deliberations. They were not only revolutionary in impact, but unexpected.

This transformation of governmental monetary powers was not a reason the Constitutional Convention was called. It was not an issue at the 1785 Mount Vernon conference or the 1786 Annapolis convention (precursors that lead to the call for the 1787 Constitutional Convention), nor was it an issue in the numerous amendments to the Articles of Confederation from 1781 through 1786. The 1787 Constitutional Convention was convened mainly to solve trade-tariff and navigation disputes between the states and to secure an independent source of tax revenue for the national government.[4] By giving the national government independent power to tax and to regulate trade between the states, the structural allocation of power among the states within the national legislature became a paramount concern and occupied most of the Convention's time. However, the issue of monetary powers, like the issues of slavery and curbing the excesses of democracy, became a prominent subtext of the Convention's deliberations, but also a subtext that was only loosely related to the main purposes of the Convention. Regarding the constitutional transformation of monetary powers, Convention delegates were driven by other motives—motives often connected to personal gain (Grubb 2003, 2006, 2007b).

After 1779 the national government did not issue new bills of credit—Continental dollars (see table 1.1). New issues of bills of credit by individual states were also less common after the Revolution compared with before 1784. Within three years of the Treaty of Paris, seven of the thirteen states—Pennsylvania, North Carolina, and South Carolina in 1785; Rhode Island, New York, New Jersey, and Georgia in 1786—issued new state-specific bills of credit that could be used to pay state taxes and fund land mortgages. State legislatures in Virginia, Maryland, New Hampshire, and Massachusetts were debating whether to issue their own new bills of credit, considerations undertaken because of the substantial post-Revolution trade depression that devastated their economies between 1782 and 1788. The problem facing the United States and the founding fathers in the half decade leading up to the Constitutional Convention was not inflation, but deflation and a scarcity of money caused by a temporary but substantial trade deficit that drained foreign reserves (specie) out the economy (see figs. 11.4 and 11.5; Grubb 2003; Holton 2007; Nettels 1962: 45–64, 105).

The Constitutional Prohibition on States Emitting Their Own Bills of Credit

The debate over how to control state monetary powers had a legitimate purpose in terms of designing how a new government would function, and this debate in some form was present from the beginning of the Convention. The slippery and often vacuous rhetoric used in the debate to justify the outcome, namely an absolute constitutional ban on states emitting bills of credit, set the stage for the debate at the end of the Convention that led to prohibiting Congress from emitting bills of credit like the Continental dollar in the future.

The new Constitution would give the federal government the power to tax the public directly. In what monies these federal taxes would be paid was thus a legitimate concern of the founding fathers in crafting the Constitution. If state legislatures could emit their own state-specific bills of credit as paper money and make those bills legal tender within their respective states, then federal taxes could be paid in each state with these state-specific bills of credit. This would create a payment-pricing problem for federal taxes, because bills of credit are worth less than their face value owing to time-discounting. Given that the redemption structure and thus the extent of time-discounting could vary from state to state, the present value of state bills of credit could differ substantially across states even if all states used the same face-value unit of account on their respective bills.[5]

When bills of credit are made a legal tender within a given jurisdiction, then market pricing gravitates to being in that legal tender as the only way to correctly account for the fact that a bill's present value is less than its face value (see chap. 7; Grubb 2016a: 189–97). Under these conditions, to be paid the correct amount of taxes that Congress intended in its legislation, the federal government would have to price its taxes separately by state and in the bills of credit in each state, and would also have to price federal taxes to account for each state bill's current present value as well as how that value would change over time. Doing so would be not just cumbersome but fraught with errors and perceived injustices, and likely almost impossible to achieve accurately. In addition, given that colonial (state) bills of credit seldom circulated outside the colony (state) of issue, federal taxes paid in state bills of credit would be a difficult revenue for the federal government to spend; the government would have to convert state bills of credit into other monies when spent outside the state in which they were received.[6]

The solution to this looming problem would be to give Congress the power to override state legal-tender laws with regard to the payment of federal taxes. Some early suggestions at the Constitutional Convention amounted to just that, namely, giving Congress the power to determine in what money federal taxes could be paid (Grubb 2006: 50–53). A slightly broader solution would be to prohibit the states from making anything but gold and silver coin a tender in payment of debts, which was adopted into Article 1, Section 10 of the Constitution late in the Convention's deliberations. This solved the federal tax-pricing problem by allowing the federal government either to flat-out refuse to accept state bills of credit in payment of federal taxes or to post a two-price payment schedule — one price in specie and a different price in local bills of credit for paying the same tax (see chap. 7; Grubb 2016a: 189–97).

The problem was state legal-tender laws and not the emission of state bills of credit per se. Colonial bills of credit (which were identical to state bills of credit in design and structure) had functioned as an inside paper money just fine while not being allowed to be a legal tender, with little performance difference to when they were a legal tender. The British Parliament had banned making bills of credit a legal tender after 1764, yet little value and performance difference can be seen pre- versus post-1764 (Celia and Grubb 2016; Cutsail and Grubb 2021: 481; Grubb 2016a: 179; 2016b: 1223; 2018a).

Eliminating state power to make their state bills of credit a legal tender within their respective state's jurisdiction would also remove all the problems nascent bankers had complained about regarding accepting deposits and payments in state bills of credit (Grubb 2003, 2006, 2007b). A banknote's present value was its face value, or close to its face value depending on the distance from the bank (liquidity crises excepted). Banknotes would be paid off or redeemed at face value in specie on demand at the issuing bank. Thus, banknotes and bills of credit had differing present values relative to their stated face value. To do correct valuation accounting bankers needed to impose a two-price system, one in banknotes at their face-value specie equivalence and one in bills of credit at the bill's proper time discount off its face value. While a somewhat cumbersome exercise, it was doable, but only if states were prohibited from making bills of credit a legal tender.

In the absence of legal tender laws, pricing in the marketplace and the preferred medium of exchange would have gravitated to banknotes. A banknote's present value was always at or very near its face value (liquidity crises excepted), which made it a superior or less cumbersome medium of exchange compared with bills of credit (see chaps. 1, 10, 11, and 12; Cutsail and Grubb 2021; Grubb 2016a, 2016b, 2018b, 2019b). Once citizens had had time to become familiar with banknotes and how banks worked, banknotes would have triumphed in the marketplace, outcompeted bills of credit for use as the primary medium of exchange, and driven bills of credit into being held as just tax-payment coupons.

This prospective outcome, however, was not enough for the nascent banking interests, and the 1787 Constitutional Convention was stacked with delegates connected to banking. The whole Pennsylvania delegation, the largest at the Convention and with members who spoke the most on monetary matters at the Convention, were all connected to the Bank of North America. They had just finished a lengthy legal battle with the Pennsylvania legislature regarding the state's emission of new bills of credit, which had threatened the bank's profitability and even its very existence (Grubb 2003, 2006, 2007b). These delegates sought to eliminate any competition with banknotes for what would be the primary paper medium of exchange by eliminating legislature-issued bills of credit.

To be fair to nascent bankers, the public in the 1780s was unfamiliar with banks and banknotes. They were unknown and untried before 1782, and how fractional reserve banking actually worked was also something of a mystery. Could private-corporation bankers be trusted? Would they always pay off on their banknotes in specie at face value on demand? Citizens were reluctant to use and accept banknotes as a medium of exchange compared with the more familiar state bills of credit. If bankers could eliminate the competition, they could issue more banknotes, make more loans; banknotes would circulate as a medium of exchange longer in the economy, and bankers would make more profits. In the absence of legal-tender laws, this outcome would eventually happen on its own without banning legislature-issued bills of credit, but in the mid-1780s it had not happened yet, and how long that transformation would take in the marketplace was unclear. The banking interests had a profit motive to speed up this transformation.

At the Convention, as well as in some speeches beforehand, delegates in the anti–bills of credit, nascent banking-interest "party" employed three rhetorical devices to achieve their end of eliminating altogether legislature-issued bills of credit. First, they constantly conflated legal-tender laws with the emission of bills of credit in their speeches. Legal-tender laws were the problem, not the emission of bills of credit per se, but by conflating the two, the banking interests sought to eliminate both. Second, they constantly referred to bills of credit as evil and the power to emit them as bad. They never explained what made bills of credit evil; they were just evil. Third, they repeated the first two rhetorical devices often, even when dealing with constitutional issues that were only at best tangentially related to monetary matters (Grubb 2006). Vacuous rhetoric repeated ad nauseam is effective. These three rhetorical devices would be carried over into the effort to constitutionally eliminate Congress's power to emit bills of credit such as the Continental dollar.

James Wilson, delegate from Pennsylvania, slipped in the prohibition on states emitting bills of credit in the last draft of the constitution to emerge from the Committee of Detail on August 6. On August 28 that clause was taken up for discussion. It generated some debate but no strong opposition. The vote on this clause (in Article 1, Section 10) was divided into two votes. The first was on prohibiting states from emitting bills of credit, which passed eight to two. The second was on prohibiting states from making anything other than gold and silver a legal tender, which passed eleven to none (Farrand 1966, 2:435, 439; Grubb 2006: 57–59, 63).

This vote indicates that many delegates understood that the emission of bills of credit per se and legal-tender laws were separate powers causing different outcomes. In the debate that day, however, the anti–paper money delegates continued their conflation of the two powers. The sequence of the vote mattered. As shown above, the problem was legal-tender laws and not the emission of bills of credit per se. The vote was ordered to consider prohibiting the state emission of bills of credit first, and only after that vote to consider restricting state legal-tender powers. If delegates had any doubts about the outcome of the second vote, they might have been induced to vote for the absolute ban on state emission of bills of credit in the first vote. By contrast, if the delegates had voted on and approved the legal-tender clause first, they might have taken a less severe stance on the state emission of bills of credit (Farrand 1966, 2:435, 439; Grubb 2006: 63).

The Constitutional Prohibition on Congress Emitting Bills of Credit

From the initial Virginia Plan at the onset of the Convention through all the Convention's deliberations given to the Committee of Detail on July 26 to draft a working constitution, the national legislature was designed to have all the rights and powers it possessed under the Articles of Confederation, including the power to emit bills of credit. The Committee of Detail drafted a list of new and enlarged powers to be explicitly added to these prior powers. In the Committee of Detail's last draft, drafted by James Wilson, but not in earlier drafts by the Committee of Detail, that list included the explicit power to "emit bills of credit of the United States"' (Farrand 1966, 1:21; 2:131, 142–44, 158–59, 167–69, 181–83). Yet, under the Articles of Confederation, Congress already possessed, and had exercised, this power. Why the Committee of Detail took the unprecedented step of inserting an "old" power into the last draft of their specifically enumerated "new and enlarged" powers of Congress is unclear. One thing is clear: it made this "old" power easier to attack and expunge.

The Committee of Detail submitted its draft constitution to the Convention to debate on August 6. From this point on, as the Convention debated various issues to revise, the anti–paper money delegates, in particular Gouverneur Morris and James Wilson, delegates from Pennsylvania who were also officers of the Bank of North America, took every opportunity, no matter how tangential, to proclaim the evils of paper money (Grubb 2006: 59–60). Having set the stage, late on August 16 Morris moved to strike out the phrase "and emit bills of credit of the United States" from the enumerated powers granted to Congress. "If the United States had credit," he reasoned, "such bills would be unnecessary: If they had not unjust & useless." The debate that followed is worth quoting at length:

Mr Madison. Will it not be sufficient to prohibit the making them a *tender*? This will remove the temptation to emit them with unjust views. And promissory notes in that shape may in some emergencies be best.

Mr Gouverneur Morris. Striking out the words will leave room still for notes of a *responsible* minister which will do all the good without the mischief. The Monied interest will oppose the plan of Government, if paper emissions be not prohibited.

Mr Gorham was for striking out, without inserting any prohibition. If the words stand they may suggest and lead to the measure.

Col. Mason had doubts on the subject. Congress he thought would not have the power unless it were expressed. Though he had a mortal hatred to paper money, yet as he could not foresee all emergencies, he was unwilling to tie the hands of the Legislature. He observed that the late war could not have been carried on, had such a prohibition existed.

Mr Gorham. The power as far as it will be necessary or safe, is involved in that of borrowing.

Mr Mercer was a friend to paper money, though in the present state & temper of America, he should neither propose nor approve of such a measure. He was consequently opposed to a prohibition of it altogether. It will stamp suspicion on the Government to deny it a discretion on this point. It was impolitic also to excite the opposition of all those who were friends to paper money. The people of property would be sure to be on the side of the plan, and it was impolitic to purchase their further attachment with the loss of the opposite class of Citizens.

Mr Ellsworth thought this a favorable moment to shut and bar the door against paper money. The mischiefs of the various experiments which had been made, were now fresh in the public mind and had excited the disgust of all the respectable part of America. By withholding the power from the new

Government more friends of influence would be gained to it than by almost any thing else—Paper money can in no case be necessary—Give the Government credit, and other resources will offer—The power may do harm, never good.

Mr Randolph, notwithstanding his antipathy to paper money, could not agree to strike out the words, as he could not foresee all occasions that might arise.

Mr Wilson. It will have a most salutary influence on the credit of the United States to remove the possibility of paper. This expedient can never succeed whilst its mischiefs are remembered. And as long as it can be resorted to, it will be a bar to other resources.

Mr Butler remarked that paper was a legal tender in no Country in Europe. He was urgent for disarming the Government of such a power.

Mr Mason was still averse to trying the hands of the Legislature *altogether*. If there was no example in Europe as just remarked it might be observed on the other side, that there was none in which the Government was restrained on this head.

Mr Read thought the words, if not struck out, would be as alarming as the mark of the Beast in Revelations.

Mr Langdon had rather reject the whole plan than retain the three words "and emit bills."

[The motion to strike out "and emit bills" was passed nine to two.] (Farrand 1966, 2:308–10)

Five key points can be taken from this debate and the ensuing vote. First, the opposition in the debate quoted above to letting Congress retain the power to emit bills of credit among its enumerated powers in Article 1, Section 8 was fervent. Thus, the final vote to remove it from the list of enumerated powers must have been intended to absolutely prohibit Congress from exercising it. It was also a lopsided vote against allowing Congress to retain that power. The vote to remove that power trumps the implied powers clause.[7] The power to emit bills of credit could not be sneaked in later as an implied corollary of the enumerated powers in Article 1, Section 8. Mason's statement above, that "Congress he thought would not have the power unless it was expressed," supports that view.

Basic logic also supports this interpretation. If the delegates thought the power to emit bills of credit by Congress was already subsumed in the implied powers clause, then there would be no reason to vote to strike that clause from Article 1, Section 8. That clause was only half of a single line of text. No economy of expression was gained by striking it. Any possible doubt that Congress could exercise that power under the implied powers clause meant that the delegates should have left the clause in, especially given its brevity, if they intended Congress to have that power under the auspices of the implied powers clause.

In addition, if it was just parsimony that mattered, and the implied powers clause covered whatever was missing, then all the delegates had to do was say that Congress had the power to govern and protect the country. No other enumerated powers would be needed, as they would all be subsumed under the implied powers clause. The basic logic is that explicitly enumerating particular congressional powers in Article 1, Section 8 had some circumscribing role to play, else their listing served no purpose. To assume the founding fathers engaged in writing down superfluous or irrelevant clauses in the Constitution challenges the legitimacy of the Constitution as ratified.

Again, the basic logic is that an explicit vote to remove a power from the list of enumerated powers granted Congress must trump the implied powers clause. The explicit vote to remove a power was an absolute prohibition. If it were not, then delegates were engaged in intentionally deceiving the public—pretending to strike that power while sneaking it back in under the implied powers clause. Under this scenario, the Constitution was ratified under fraudulent auspices, as part of an intentional deception of the public, and so the ratification lacked legitimacy.

This same logic applies to powers proposed to be added to the list of enumerated powers to be granted Congress in Article 1, Section 8 but were explicitly voted not to be so added, such as the vote near of the end of the Convention to give Congress the power of chartering corporations. That power was explicitly voted not to be added to the list of enumerated powers granted Congress, and so Congress does not have the power to charter corporations, including a national bank. The implied powers clause cannot overcome that logic and allow that power back in, even though Alexander Hamilton and George Washington did exactly that by not vetoing Congress's chartering of the First Bank of the United States in 1791.[8]

Second, the above debate illustrates how vacuous Federalist anti–government paper money rhetoric was. The argument against Congress emitting bills of credit was that it would cause "mischiefs" or be "mischievous." This term was used by three different delegates opposing Congress emitting bills of credit in the above-quoted debate. It also shows up in Hamilton's writings in 1790 (see the introduction, n. 7). Going even more hyperbolic, George Read, delegate from Delaware, in the above debate labeled Congress's power to emit bills "the mark of the Beast in Revelations," that is, the devil. These terms do not mean anything, but their use frightens people. No explanatory, evidence-based, or structural-performance arguments are given for why Congress should not have the power to emit bills of credit.

In addition, in the above-quoted debate, for only the second (and last) time at the Convention a delegate—in this case James Madison, delegate from Virginia—explicitly distinguished between legal-tender powers and the emission of bills of credit. Moreover, he identified legal-tender laws, as opposed to the emission of bills of credit per se, as the culprit causing the other delegates concern. As explained above, if Congress's bills of credit were made a legal tender, then pricing in the marketplace would gravitate to being in that legal tender. Pricing in only bills of credit would be needed to correctly value goods in the marketplace, given that bills of credit traded below their face value owing to time-discounting. Banknotes, however, traded at or near their face value. A two-price system could not be posted, one price in banknotes and one in bills of credit, because legal-tender laws would force people to pay the bill-of-credit posted price (which would be higher than the value-equivalent banknote posted price), even if they were paying in banknotes or specie (see chap. 7; Grubb 2016a: 189–97). Thus, banknotes would not circulate as readily or as long as a medium of exchange, which in turn would depress bankers' ability to make loans and generate profits.

If bills of credit could not be made a legal tender, then pricing could be posted in two parts, one price in banknotes and one price in bills of credit. Eventually banknotes would outcompete bills in the marketplace as the primary medium of exchange, because banknotes always traded at or near their face value whereas bills of credit traded at varying amounts off their face value over time owing to variations in the time-discounting needed to assess their present value. Eliminating Congress's power to make bills of credit a legal tender solved the problem facing the Convention delegates connected to the banking interest (Grubb 2006, 2007b).

This restriction, however, was not enough for the delegates with banking interests. They wanted to eliminate any competition with banknotes as to what would be used as the primary paper medium of exchange in the marketplace. These delegates wanted an absolute elimination of Congress's power to emit bills of credit. Morris's blunt and absolute rejection of Madison's suggestion to curb just Congress's power to make bills a legal tender in the above debate, and the continued conflation of legal-tender laws with the emission of bills of credit per se in the rest of the above debate, illustrates why the delegates with banking interests engaged in such vacuous and grandstanding rhetoric against government-issued bills of credit. They could not honestly admit their true banker-interest motives. To conclude otherwise would be to claim that these delegates, some of the most prominent writers on financial and money matters among the founding fathers (see chap. 5), were stupid. I do not think they were that stupid. Self-interested and devious, yes; but stupid, no.

Third, the debate quoted above shows that Congress's power to emit bills of credit was a zero-sum breaking point for many delegates. The whole plan of government would be rejected unless Congress's power to emit bills of credit was removed. Morris basically said as much when he stated, "The Monied interest will oppose the plan of Government, if paper emission be not prohibited." John Langdon, delegate from New Hampshire, would "rather reject the whole plan of government than retain the three words 'and emit bill.'" These comments are powerful grandstanding in that they place Congress's power to emit bills of credit on the same plane as issues dealing with slavery and with the division of power in the national legislature among the states, in terms of what would have ended the whole Convention with no new constitution if particular delegates did not get their way.

Fourth, Morris's cryptic response in the above debate to Madison's legal-tender question was that the power to emit paper money be left to "a *responsible* minister which will do all the good without the mischief." This "*responsible* minister" could not be an agent of a newly constituted federal government, as Morris had just said that "the Monied interest will oppose the plan of government, if paper emissions be not prohibited." So whom did he mean? It is likely he was referring to his own Bank of North America, which since 1782 had been trying to get its banknotes to circulate as a national paper currency.[9]

Why did Morris not say "bank" or "Bank of North America" in his remark? Why was his remark so cryptic as to who he thought should emit paper money? It was because banks were even more controversial than paper money. The mere mention of them, even indirectly, threatened the ratification of the Constitution. The only time banks were mentioned in the Convention's debates was on September 14, near the end of the Convention. It was brought up in the debate over whether Congress should be given the power to charter corporations. Rufus King, delegate from Massachusetts, noted that the issue of incorporation would include that of establishing a bank, and that banks were a subject of contention and that it would cause prejudice and divide the states into parties (Farrand 1966, 2:615–16; Grubb 2006: 64–69).

Fifth, in the above debate several delegates indicated that what the federal government really needed was credit and the ability to borrow, as opposed to emitting paper money. They act as though bills of credit were not a debt-credit instrument and were not a borrowing against future taxes. Their rhetoric marks the beginning of a transition to reinterpreting the Continental dollar as being a fiat currency as opposed to what it actually was—a zero-coupon bond.

Even worse, several delegates indicated that the power to emit bills of credit made Congress less creditworthy and reduced its ability to borrow. Morris started the debate by saying, "If the United States had credit such bills would be unnecessary: If they had not unjust & useless." Nathaniel Gorham, delegate from Massachusetts, stated, "The power as far as it will be necessary or safe, is involved in that of borrowing." As though bills of credit were not a borrowing! Oliver Ellsworth, delegate from Connecticut, proclaimed, "Give the government credit, and other resources will offer—The power [to emit bills of credit] may do harm, never good." Wilson stated, "It will have a most salutary influence on the credit of the United States to remove the possibility of paper [bills of credit] ... as long as it can be resorted to, it will be a bar to other resources."

These delegates certainly believed that removing Congress's power to emit bills of credit would improve the government's creditworthiness and thus its ability to borrow funds. They do not say directly that removing Congress's power to emit bills of credit meant that the government could thereafter default on the Continental dollars still outstanding with impunity, but the logical connection is there. The federal government could not achieve a position of positive net worth without erasing some its debts off its books. If the debts to be erased were not really debts because—by a rhetorical sleight of hand—they were now seen as a fiat currency, and given that the government could now never constitutionally emit such currency again, then a creditworthy position with a positive net worth might be achieved (Grubb 2007a, 2011a).

Conclusion—Endgame

Future emissions of Continental dollars were constitutionally eliminated at the 1787 Constitutional Convention, and this was confirmed with the ratification and then adoption of that Constitution in 1789 by Congress. The final and irrevocable default on outstanding Continental dollars was achieved with the August 4, 1790 Funding Act (chap. 16). Thus ended this portion of the monetary history of America. A fundamental transformation in the monetary powers that elected legislatures were allowed to exercise had been achieved.

Acknowledgments

I thank John Bockrath, Nayla Dahan, Stephen Douglas, Kimberley Fersch, Jiaxing Jiang, Eric O'Connor, Kelly Lynn Perkins, Nathan Richwine, and Zachary Rose, who, as students long ago, provided research assistance at the beginning of this project. Preliminary versions of material in some of the chapters were presented at various conferences and university seminars over the years, sometimes in unrecognizable form. These conferences and university seminars include the Economic History Association annual meetings of 2005 and 2011; the National Bureau of Economic Research meetings of 2006, 2007, and 2011; University of Delaware seminars of 2006, 2008, and 2011; the World Economic History Congress of 2006 and 2009; the Southern Economic Association annual meeting of 2006; SUNY-Binghamton seminar of 2007; the American Economic Association annual meeting of 2008; the American Institute of Economic Research, Great Barrington, Massachusetts, seminar of 2008; Universidad de Las Palmas, de Gran Canaria, Spain, seminar, 2009; the National Maritime Museum, Greenwich, United Kingdom, seminar, 2009; Newnham College, University of Cambridge seminar, 2010; Queens University, Kingston, Canada, seminar, 2010; University of Georgia seminar, 2013; the World Congress of Cliometrics, 2013; Columbia University Law School seminar, 2013; Harvard University Law School seminar, 2013; the Treasury Historical Association meetings, Washington DC, of 2014 and 2021; University of Applied Sciences seminar, Warburg, Germany, 2015; and the Pennsylvania Historical Association annual meeting, 2019.

I wish to thank the many participants at these conferences and presentations as well as numerous other scholars who over the years gave me kind words of encouragement. While no one gave me substantive research-altering advice or insights that I remember, I should mention four people who, probably unbeknownst to themselves, made brief yet helpful offhand remarks some years ago that substantially affected my thinking, approach, and investigative efforts. They are Charlie Calomiris, Edwin Perkins, Peter Rousseau, and Eugene White. I also want to thank a small handful of scholars who over the years actively worked to discourage me and prevent me from pursuing this topic for the stimulation their efforts gave me.

I would be remiss if I did not thank my professors at the University of Chicago and the University of Washington: Gary S. Becker, Robert W. Fogel, Robert E. Lucas Jr., Douglass C. North, and George J. Stigler. While they are not directly connected to this particular research project, they gave me the opportunity to acquire a deep understanding of economics and thus in a foundational way contributed to this book. I have likely missed thanking others that I should thank. But an aging memory and increasing forgetfulness over a multidecade project has overtaken me. I apologize for such lapses.

Getting the Numbers Right

Reconciling the Disparate Statements in the Secondary Literature Regarding Continental Dollar Emissions

The secondary literature presents a confusingly wide range of total net new Continental dollars emitted (see figs. A.1 and A.2).[1] Current scholars, unaware of this confusion, often report an emission total taken from just one secondary source, not knowing that the total reported is contingent on which source they happened by chance to have run across. In the old "authoritative" literature the total ranges from $191.5 to $387.5 million in face value. In the modern literature, it ranges from $204 to $250 million in face value. If a current consensus exists, prior to this study, it would be $241 million in face value.[2] Little has been done to reconcile these conflicting estimates. This appendix corrects this oversight, reconciles all estimates to one definitive number, and provides the underlying support for the numbers reported in tables 1.1, and elsewhere in the book.

Table A.1 presents the corrected estimate of net new emissions of Continental dollars—also shown as the *JCC* lines in figures A.1 and A.2. The first emission was authorized on June 22, 1775, and the last on November 29, 1779. The cumulative total was $199,989,995 in face value. All were still outstanding as of 1780. For example, the US Treasury Office issued a table on December 3, 1779, indicating that they projected $200,000,000 in face value to still be in circulation by the end of February 1780, and on June 28, 1781, the Secretary of Congress, Charles Thomson, reported that $195 million was still outstanding.[3] With one exception, the estimate presented in table A.1 is the lowest total in the literature—20 percent lower than the prior consensus. Table A.1 relies on original evidence found in the *JCC* and *PCC—Report of the Board of Treasury on the State of Emissions and Loans, September 17, 1779*. These two original sources, however, do not fully cohere. As such, they require reconciliation as well.

The September 17, 1779, Board of Treasury report sent to Congress recorded emissions through September 2, 1779, with the cumulative total to that date being stated as $159,948,880—the only time Congress recorded such a total in the *JCC* prior to permanently ending emissions.[4] While scholars have used this total, they have not often noted the details of its construction. These details make several corrections to the evidence in

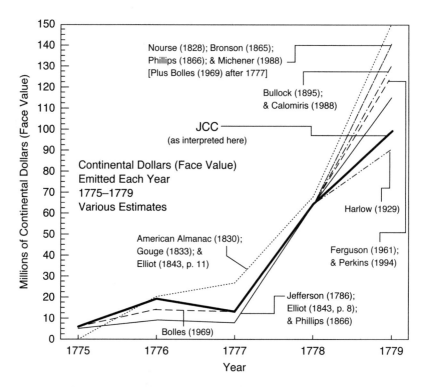

FIGURE A.1. Net new Continental dollars emitted each year from 1775 through 1779 (face value)—various estimates

Sources: American almanac (1830: 183); Bolles (1969, 1:31, 38–50, 70, 74, 88); Boyd (1953–55, 10:42–43); Bronson (1865: 1:88–89, 112–15); Bullock (1895: 135–36); Calomiris (1988: 57–58); Elliot (1843: 8, 11); Ferguson (1961: 29–30); Gouge (1833, pt. 2:25); Harlow (1929: 50–51); Michener (1988: 690); Nourse (1828: 7); Perkins (1994: 97); Phillips (1866: 198–99). See table A.1 for the *JCC* estimate.

Note: Robinson (1969: 108, 293, 323–26) cannot be placed in this pantheon because he fails to commit to an interpretation of several of his numbers, that is, whether they should be counted or not as net new emissions. His total emission count could range anywhere between $200 and $241.5 million in face value.

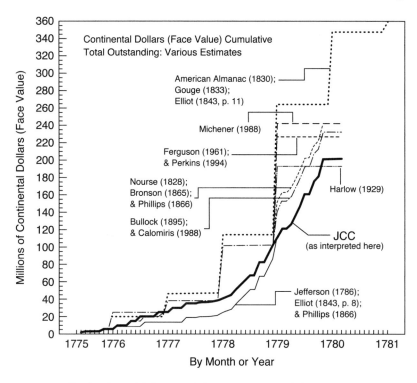

FIGURE A.2. The Continental dollar: cumulative total net new emissions outstanding to date (face value), 1775–81 — various estimates

Sources: See fig. A.1 and table A.1.

Note: See the note to fig. A.1.

the *JCC*, but also include errors — information in the *JCC* that was not assimilated by the *PCC* Board of Treasury report.

The Board's report corrected the *JCC* by revealing that only \$3,937,220 of the \$4 million authorized on February 17, 1776, was printed, and that the \$500,000 mentioned on November 2, 1776, was never printed. The report also showed how the emissions of May 20, 1777, and April 11, 1778, were counted. The Board's report, however, failed to assimilate pertinent information recorded by Congress in the *JCC*. It erroneously counted \$10,000 from January 5, 1776, as a new emission when in fact it was not — an error that Congress did not catch in the Board's report. Those ten thousand dollars were exclusively marked to be swapped one for one for worn bills that could not continue in circulation (*JCC* 4:42; 5:697). Being a swap for existing bills, this sum was not a new emission. The Board of Treasury

TABLE A.1 **Continental dollars emitted by Congress, 1775–79: Corrected estimates of total net new emissions (face value)**

Year	Month/Day	$ in face value
1775	June 22	2,000,000
	July 25	1,000,000[a]
	Nov. 29	3,000,000
1776	Feb. 17	3,937,220
	May 9	5,000,000
	July 22	5,000,000
	Nov. 2	5,000,000
1777	Feb. 26	5,000,000
	May 20	5,000,000
	Aug. 1	1,000,000
	Nov. 7	1,000,000
	Dec. 3	1,000,000
1778	Jan. 8	1,000,000
	Jan. 22	2,000,000
	Feb. 16	2,000,000
	Mar. 5	2,000,000
	Apr. 4	1,000,000
	Apr. 11	5,000,000
	Apr. 18	500,000
	May 22	5,000,000
	June 20	5,000,000
	July 30	5,000,000
	Sept. 5	5,000,000
	Sept. 26	10,000,100
	Nov. 4	10,000,100
	Dec. 14	10,000,100
1779	Jan. 14	8,500,395[b]
	Feb. 3	5,000,160
	Feb. 19	5,000,160
	Apr. 1	5,000,160
	May 5	10,000,100
	June 4	10,000,100
	July 17	15,000,280
	Sept. 17	15,000,260
	Oct. 14	5,000,180
	Nov. 17	10,050,540
	Nov. 29	10,000,140
	End of emissions	
Total cumulative net new emissions outstanding		199,989,995[a]

Sources: Tables A.2 and 1.1; *JCC* (2:103, 105, 207; 3:390; 4:32, 157, 339; 5:599, 651, 697; 6:912, 918; 7:161, 373; 8:377–80, 597, 646; 9:873, 993; 10:28, 82–83, 174–75, 223, 309, 337–38, 365; 11:524, 627, 731; 12:884, 962, 1100, 1218; 13:64, 139, 209, 408; 14:548, 557–58, 687–88, 848–49; 15:1019, 1053, 1076–77, 1171–72, 1285, 1324–25, 1436); *PCC* (microfilm 247, reel 146, item 136:647).

Notes: The date is the day Congress first authorized the amount listed. See table 1.1 for how these authorized amounts are grouped by emission banks.

TABLE A.1 (*continued*)

[a] On July 25, 1775, Congress ordered $1,000,000 struck in $30 bills (*JCC* 2:207). This is not possible. Either $999,990 or $1,000,020 can be struck, but not $1,000,000. Which was done and whether other denominations of Emission no. 1 were adjusted to accommodate the $1,000,000 target in $30 bills is not known. Because no change in the $1,000,000 total authorized was ever noted by Congress or the Board of Treasury, it is assumed that the discrepancy was rectified by adjusting the printing of bills of other denominations from this emission, thus yielding the reported total here of $199,989,995. However, the total cumulative net new emissions could vary between $199,989,985 and $199,990,015, depending on how Congress resolved its order to emit $1,000,000 in $30 bills on July 25, 1775 — an outcome that is currently unknown.

[b] The original authorization of $50,000,400 was subsequently reduced by $5. On May 7, 1779, Congress altered a portion of the denominational structure of the January 14, 1779, authorization by ordering that "instead of 116,280 bills of the denominations of 20, 8, 7, 5, 4, 3, 2, 1, respectively, there shall be emitted 31,427 bills, each of the denominations of 80, 70, 20, 5, 4, 3, 2, 1, which will reduce the sum ordered to be struck by the resolution aforesaid five dollars." See *JCC* (13:64; 14:557–58). This reduction was missed previously in Grubb (2008: 286).

erroneously included it as new in its September 17, 1779, report, thus overstating the true total amount — an error not noticed until now.

In addition, the Board's report failed to make the $5 reduction in the emission of January 14, 1779, that was enacted on May 7, 1779 — an error that Congress did not catch in the Board's report and one missed by most scholars. On May 7, 1779, Congress altered the denominational structure of the portion of emission no. 11 authorized on January 14, 1779. This alteration reduced that emission total by $5 in face value, which was so noted by Congress (*JCC* 13:64; 14:557–58). Emission no. 11 had multiple issuance dates (see table 1.1). Because all bills of emission no. 11 were from the same cut and so identical, regardless of authorized issuance date, it is possible that this $5 reduction in the January 14, 1779, issuance was made up by printing extra bills in one of the other authorizations of emission no. 11. While this is a possibility, no evidence has been found so far in either the *JCC* or the *PCC* that this was done. Therefore, the failure to note the $5 reduction is assumed to be an accounting error in the report issued by the Board of Treasury.

Why are the estimates in table A.1 preferred? The answer is that entropy has overtaken the literature on the Continental dollar. Errors in early estimates were uncritically copied by subsequent scholars who in turn added their own errors until now a plethora of different estimates coexist. When these errors are identified and corrected, all collapse to that in table A.1. This reconciliation exercise is given in table A.2. Prior estimates suffer from errors of omission, of addition, of transcription, and of definition. For example, Thomas Jefferson erroneously omitted $16 million from his 1786 account. This error was repeated in the report given to Congress by Jonathan Elliot in 1843. Elliot, in turn, is one of the primary sources used by James Ferguson. Henry Bronson erroneously included $500,000 from November 2, 1776. Albert Bolles erroneously omitted $5 million from May 1776. Henry Phillips made several transcription errors, and Charles Bullock made an addition error of $9.95 million when summing his entries—errors often uncorrected by subsequent scholars.[5]

The highest estimate—$357 million—comes from an error in definition. It counts all disbursements measured in Continental dollar units of account rather than the emission of Continental dollars per se. While the current literature follows Ferguson in discarding this estimate, a credible case for doing so, or even for establishing the estimate's origin, has never been made.[6] It turns out this estimate comes from tables complied by Knox that were included in a report assembled by Nourse on August 30, 1790, for a congressional committee. Therein, on page 35, Nourse states that Knox's tables (so converted and listed there in specie value) included "Loan Office Debt." This affirms that the $357 million estimate is measuring more than just the emission of Continental dollars.[7]

Correcting these errors leaves only one remaining point of discrepancy: how to count the emission authorized on January 14, 1779. Because of extensive counterfeiting, Congress on January 2, 1779, called in "the whole emissions of May 20, 1777, and April 11, 1778." These old bills were to be exchanged for new bills—with the old bills being "examined and burned." On January 14, 1779, Congress authorized a total of $50,000,400 in bills of a new design "to be emitted for exchanging others, agreeable to the resolutions of the 2nd instant, *or for supporting the war the ensuing year*" (*JCC* 13:22, 64–65; italics added). On May 7, 1779, Congress altered the denominational structure of the January 14 authorization, thereby reducing the total emitted to $50,000,395 (*JCC* 12:1224; 13:64; 14:557–58). How much of this amount was new spending and how much was bill swapping was not recorded. Guesses in the literature vary widely. At one extreme, Joseph Nourse and Ron Michener counted the entire amount initially authorized as new. At the other, Ralph Harlow assumed that none of the initial authorized amount was new.[8]

One obvious question is, how many old bills were eligible to be swapped for new? The authorizing legislation of January 2 and 14, 1779, explicitly

TABLE A.2 **Continental dollars emitted by Congress, 1775–81: Reconciliation of estimates of total net new emissions (face value)**

Listed by **Year** *Month* [Day][a]	20th Congress 1828 Nourse (1828), Bronson (1865), and Phillips (1866)	Thomas Jefferson's 1786 table Boyd (1953–55) and 28th Congress Elliot (1843: 8) and Phillips (1866)	Bullock (1895) and Calomiris (1988)	[*American Almanac* (1830) [*AA*] Gouge (1833) Elliot (1843: 11)] Harlow (1929) Ferguson (1961) Perkins (1994) Robinson (1969) Michener (1988) Bolles (1969)	Newman (1997) (2008)	*JCC* and [*PCC*, Sept. 14, 1779]
1775				$6,000,000		
				AA, Elliot, and Gouge = 0 Bolles, Ferguson, Harlow, and Michener = $6,000,000		
June [22]						
[23]	$2,000,000				$2,000,000	$2,000,000 [2,000,000]
July [25]	1,000,000	$2,000,000			1,000,000	1,000,000[u] [1,000,000]
Nov. [29]	3,000,000	?			3,000,000	3,000,000 [3,000,000]
1776		3,000,000		AA & Elliot = 20,064,667 Gouge = 20,064,465[k] Ferguson and Harlow = 19,000,000 Michener = 18,947,220 Bolles = 14,000,000		
Jan. [5]						(10,000)[q] [10,000][q]
Feb.			4,000,000			

continues

TABLE A.2 *(continued)*

Listed by **Year** *Month* [Day][a]	20th Congress 1828 Nourse (1828), Bronson (1865), and Phillips (1866)	Thomas Jefferson's 1786 table Boyd (1953–55) and 28th Congress Elliot (1843: 8) and Phillips (1866)	Bullock (1895) and Calomiris (1988)	[*American Almanac* (1830) [AA] Gouge (1833) Elliot (1843: 11)] Harlow (1929) Ferguson (1961) Perkins (1994) Robinson (1969) Michener (1988) Bolles (1969)	Newman (1997) (2008)	*JCC* and [*PCC,* Sept. 14, 1779]
[17]	4,000,000	4,000,000[b]			4,000,000	4,000,000 [3,937,220][r]
May [9 and 22]			5,000,000		5,000,000	5,000,000 [5,000,000]
or 27] *July* [22]	5,000,000	?				5,000,000 [5,000,000]
and *Aug.* [13]	5,000,000	5,000,000	5,000,000		5,000,000	5,000,000 [5,000,000]
Nov. [2]	500,000[c] [Bronson only]					(500,000)[c] [(500,000)][c]
Nov. [2] and *Dec.* [28]	5,000,000	?	5,000,000		5,000,000	5,000,000
1777						
Feb.			5,000,000	AA, Elliot, and Gouge = 26,426,333 Bolles, Ferguson, Harlow, and Michener = 13,000,000		[5,000,000]

Date				
[26]	5,000,000	5,000,000		5,000,000 [5,000,000]
May [20]	5,000,000	5,000,000	5,000,000*	5,000,000 [5,000,000]⁻
[May 20, 1777– Apr. 18, 1778]	?		5,000,000ᵈ	16,500,000#
Aug. [1]	1,000,000	1,000,000	1,000,000	1,000,000 [1,000,000]⁻
[15]	1,000,000	1,000,000	1,000,000	1,000,000 [1,000,000]⁻
Nov. [7]	1,000,000	1,000,000	1,000,000	1,000,000 [1,000,000]⁻
Dec. [3]	1,000,000	1,000,000	1,000,000	1,000,000 [1,000,000]⁻
1778				
Jan. [8]	1,000,000	1,000,000	3,000,000	1,000,000 [1,000,000]⁻
[22]	2,000,000	2,000,000		2,000,000 [2,000,000]⁻
Feb. [16]	2,000,000	2,000,000	2,000,000	2,000,000 [2,000,000]⁻
Mar. [5]	2,000,000	2,000,000	2,000,000	2,000,000 [2,000,000]⁻
Apr.			6,500,000	2,000,000 [2,000,000]⁻

Ferguson = 63,400,000
AA, Elliot, and Gouge = 66,965,269
Harlow and Michener = 63,500,300
Bolles = 63,500,000

continues

TABLE A.2 *(continued)*

Listed by **Year** *Month* [Day][a]	20th Congress 1828 Nourse (1828), Bronson (1865), and Phillips (1866)	Thomas Jefferson's 1786 table Boyd (1953–55) and 28th Congress Elliot (1843: 8) and Phillips (1866)	Bullock (1895) and Calomiris (1988)	[American Almanac (1830) [AA] Gouge (1833) Elliot (1843: 11)] Harlow (1929) Ferguson (1961) Perkins (1994) Robinson (1969) Michener (1988) Bolles (1969)	Newman (1997) (2008)	*JCC* and [*PCC*, Sept. 14, 1779]
[4]	1,000,000	1,000,000				1,000,000 [1,000,000]⁻
[11]	5,000,000	5,000,000*			5,000,000[#]	5,000,000 [5,000,000]⁻
[18]	500,000	500,000				500,000 [500,000]⁻
May [22]	5,000,000	5,000,000	5,000,000			5,000,000 [5,000,000]ʳ
June [20]	5,000,000	5,000,000	5,000,000		5,000,000[#]	5,000,000 [5,000,000]ʳ
July [30] [31]	5,000,000	5,000,000	5,000,000		5,000,000[#]	5,000,000 [5,000,000]ʳ
Sept. [5]	5,000,000	5,000,000	15,000,000		5,000,000[#]	5,000,000 [5,000,000]ʳ
[26]	10,000,100[e]	10,000,100				10,000,100 [10,000,100]
[Sept. 26, 1778–July 17, 1779]					75,001,080	

Date							
Nov. [4]	10,000,000			10,000,100	10,000,100	10,000,100	[10,000,100]
Dec. [14]	10,000,000			10,000,100^e	10,000,100	10,000,100	[10,000,100]
1779				*(see block below)*	95,051,695		
Issued	50,000,400^e	50,000,400	50,000,000	50,000,400	50,000,400	50,000,395	[50,000,400]
Exchanged	−0^f	−25,552,780^++	−10,000,000^*	−15,300,000^**	−41,500,000^#	−41,500,000^+	[−41,500,00]^+
Equals net new	50,000,400	24,447,620	40,000,000	34,700,400^**	8,500,400	8,500,395	[8,500,400]
Feb [3]	5,000,160	5,000,163	10,000,000			5,000,160	[5,000,160]
[12]	5,000,160	5,000,160				5,000,160	[5,000,160]

Block for **1779**:
Bolles = 140,052,480
AA, Elliot, and Gouge = 149,703,857
Harlow = 90,052,080
Michener = 140,052,480
Ferguson = 90,099,600

Block for Equals net new:
Harlow = 0
Michener = 50,000,000
Bolles = 50,000,400
AA, Elliot, & Gouge = ?

Adjustment made for January 14, 1779

On January 14, 1779, Congress voted $50,000,400, reduced to $50,000,395 on May 7, 1779, to be exchanged for the May 20, 1777, and April 11, 1778, emissions that were being counterfeited (*JCC* 13:64–65; 14:557–58; *PCC*, microfilm 247, reel 146, item 136:647, September 14, 1779). Estimates about how much of this amount represented a net new emission vary. ++ = the exchanged sum chosen by Jefferson and Elliot such that "**C. Discrepancy [A − B]**" equals zero, sans correcting for the $10,005 Board of Treasury errors (see below). * = emissions exchanged as interpreted by Bullock. ** = emissions exchanged as implied in Ferguson. # = emissions exchanged as interpreted by Newman + = the total of all emissions interpreted by Newman + = the total of all emissions in the style, tenor, and design of the May 20, 1777, and April 11, 1778, emissions designated for exchange as described in the *JCC* and as explicitly identified as such in the *PCC*, with ^ designating emissions that were part of the May 20, 1777, emission and ^ designating those that were part of the April 11, 1778, emission.

continues

TABLE A.2 *(continued)*

Listed by **Year** *Month* [Day][a]	20th Congress 1828 Nourse (1828), Bronson (1865), and Phillips (1866)	Thomas Jefferson's 1786 table Boyd (1953–55) and 28th Congress Elliot (1843: 8) and Phillips (1866)	Bullock (1895) and Calomiris (1988)	[American Almanac (1830) [AA] Gouge (1833) Elliot (1843: 11)] Harlow (1929) Ferguson (1961) Perkins (1994) Robinson (1969) Michener (1988) Bolles (1969)	Newman (1997) (2008)	*JCC* and [*PCC*, Sept. 14, 1779]
[19]	5,000,160					5,000,160 [5,000,160]
Apr. [1st]	5,000,160		5,000,000			5,000,160 [5,000,160]
[2]		5,000,160				
May [5]	10,000,100	10,000,100	10,000,000			10,000,100 [10,000,100]
June [4]	10,000,100	10,000,100	10,000,000			10,000,100 [10,000,100]
July [17]	15,000,280	15,000,280[d]	15,000,000			15,000,280 [15,000,280]

Comparison interlude

A. Totals so far—to Sept. 2, 1779

	20th Congress 1828	Thomas Jefferson's 1786 table	Bullock (1895) and Calomiris (1988)	American Almanac etc.	Newman (1997) (2008)	JCC and [PCC]
	201,501,660	159,948,883[++]	191,500,000	Ferguson = 186,148,880[g] Michener = 201,448,480[g] Harlow = 151,501,260[g]	155,001,480[g]	160,001,055 [159,948,880]
	202,001,660[c] [Bronson]					

B. Total Congress declared in circulation on Sept. 2, 1779 (*JCC* 15:1019, 1052–53; *PCC*, microfilm 247, reel 146, item 136:647, Sept. 14, 1779)

	159,948,880	159,948,880	159,948,880	159,948,880	159,948,880[g] [159,948,880][s]
Correction of Board of Treasury errors	−10,005	−10,005	−10,005	−10,005	−10,005 [−10,005]
Equals	159,938,875	159,938,875	159,938,875	159,938,875	159,938,875 [159,938,875]
C. Discrepancy [A − B] =	+41,562,785	+10,008[h]	+31,561,125	−4,937,395	+62,780[t] [+10,005][s]
	+42,062,785[c] [Bronson]			Ferguson = +26,210,005 Michener = +41,509,605 Harlow = −8,437,615	
Sept. [17]	15,000,260[e]	15,000,260[e]	15,000,000		15,000,260[u]
Oct. [14]	5,000,180	5,000,180	5,000,000		5,000,180
Nov. [17]	10,050,540	10,050,540	20,050,000		10,050,540
[29]	10,000,140	10,000,140			10,000,140
None thereafter except				1780 *AA*, Elliot, and Gouge = 82,908,320[p] 1781 *AA*, Elliot, and Gouge = 11,408,095[p]	
Total implied, summed, or reported 1775–81	241,552,780	200,000,003[h]	241,500,000	195,052,605[j] Harlow = 191,552,380 Michener = 241,500,000 Ferguson = 226,200,000 Bolles = 236,552,480 *AA*, Elliot, & Gouge = 357,476,541[k,p]	200,052,780[p] or 200,000,000[i]

continues

TABLE A.2 (*continued*)

Listed by **Year** *Month* [Day][a]	20th Congress 1828 Nourse (1828), Bronson (1865), and Phillips (1866)	Thomas Jefferson's 1786 table Boyd (1953–55) and 28th Congress Elliot (1843:8) and Phillips (1866)	Bullock (1895) and Calomiris (1988)	[*American Almanac* (1830) [AA] Gouge (1833) Elliot (1843: 11)] Harlow (1929) Ferguson (1961) Perkins (1994) Robinson (1966) Michener (1988) Bolles (1969)	Newman (1997) (2008)	*JCC* and [*PCC*, Sept. 14, 1779]
	242,052,780[c] [Bronson]					
Corrected for addition, omission, and transcription errors	0 −500,000[c] [Bronson]	+15,999,997[h]	−9,950,000[l]	0 +5,000,000 [Bolles]	+5,000,180	0
Then recorrected using [C. Discrepancy [A − B]}, such that net new emissions for Jan. 14, 1779, are uniform at 8,500,395 and the Jan. 5, 1776, Board of Treasury error of 10,000 is corrected[m]	−41,562,785	−16,010,005[h]	−31,561,125	Harlow = +8,437,615 Michener = −41,509,605 Ferguson = −26,210,005 Bolles = −41,562,485 AA, Elliot, & Gouge = ?	−62,780	−62,780[n] or −10,005[j]
Final corrected total amount (face value) outstanding at the beginning of 1780 (end of 1781)[m]	199,989,995	199,989,995	199,988,875[o]	Harlow = 199,989,995 Bolles = 199,989,995 Ferguson = 199,989,995 Michener = 199,990,395[o] (AA, Elliot, & Gouge = 357,476,541[p])	199,989,995	199,989,995[u]

Sources: American Almanac (1830: 183); Bolles (1969, 1:31, 38–54, 70, 74, 88); Boyd (1953–55, 10:42–43); Bronson (1865: 88–89, 112–15); Bullock (1895: 135–36); Calomiris (1988: 57–58); Elliot (1843: 8, 11); Ferguson (1961: 29–30); Gouge (1833, part 2:25); Harlow (1929: 50–51); *JCC* (2:103, 105, 207; 3:390; 4:32, 157, 339; 5:599, 651, 697; 6:912, 918; 7:161, 373; 8:377–80, 597, 646; 9:873, 993; 10:28, 82–83, 174–75, 223, 309, 337–38, 365; 11:524, 627, 731; 12:884, 962, 1100, 1218; 13:64, 139, 209, 408; 14:548, 687–88, 848–49; 15:1019, 1053, 1076–77, 1171–72, 1285, 1324–25, 1436); Michener (1988: 690); Newman (1997: 58–69; 2008: 62–73); Nourse (1828: 7); Phillips (1866: 198–99); *PCC* (microfilm 247, reel 146, item 136:647—*Report of the Board of Treasury on the State of Emissions and Loans, September 14, 1779*); Perkins (1994) simply repeats Ferguson (1961) and so is not listed separately in the table.

Notes: Numbers in parentheses are amounts mentioned in the record but do not actually add to net new emissions because they either were not printed or were designated for currency swaps. These amounts are not counted in that column's total. Numbers in brackets represent those reported in the *PCC* (microfilm 247, reel 146, item 136:647—*Report of the Board of Treasury on the State of Emissions and Loans, September 14, 1779*). Robinson (1969: 108, 293, 323–26) cannot be placed in this pantheon because he fails to commit to an interpretation of several of his numbers, i.e., whether they should be counted or not as net new emissions. His total emission count could range anywhere between $200 and $241.5 million in face value.

a "The difference in the [day] reported by different scholars for what are the same emissions represents the difference between the [day] that Congress first authorized the emission versus a later [day] when Congress commented on some aspect of the implementation of its initial authorization. The first date is used for the column derived directly from the *JCC*.

b Jefferson's original entry was for $1,000,000, as listed in Boyd (1953–55, 10:42–43). This clearly is a typo as this entry was also listed as being worth $4,000,000 silver dollars with no depreciation. Elliot's (1843: 8) transcription of this table reported it as $4,000,000.

c Bronson (1865: 113–14) erroneously included this $500,000 in his list of net new emissions. He is the only scholar to do so. Other scholars have excluded it based on the fact that searches over the years have failed to uncover any vestiges of its existence; see, e.g., Bolles (1969, 1:49–50); Bullock (1895: 134); Phillips (1866: 57). This should not be surprising; largely unnoticed by prior scholars, the *PCC* (microfilm 247, reel 146, item 136:647) explicitly indicates that this $500,000 sum, separate from the $5 million authorized on November 2, was never printed. The *PCC* also does not count it therein when tallying up total emissions. The *JCC* (6:918) indicates that this $500,000 sum, while mentioned on November 2, was part of the $5 million authorized on that date, namely that part which was to be hastily emitted. The *JCC* also indicates that this hasty emission was not followed through on. As such, this $500,000 sum is not regarded as part of, or counted toward, the amount of net new emissions derived from the *JCC* separate from (or in addition to) the $5 million authorized on November 2.

d Phillips (1866: 199) erroneously transcribed the entry for May 20, 1777, as $5,000,090 and erroneously transcribed the entry for July 17, 1779, as June 17, 1779.

e Phillips (1866: 198) erroneously transcribed the entry for September 26, 1778, as $10,000,000; the entry for December 14, 1778, as $10,000,000; the entry for January 14, 1779, as $50,000,100; and the combined entry for September 17, 1779, as $15,000,360.

f Bronson (1865: 113) claimed to have omitted from his list of total emissions "the $10,000,000 less five dollars, authorized January fourteenth and May seventh, 1779, which were designed to take the place of the counterfeited emissions of May twentieth, 1777, and April eleventh, 1778." In fact, he did not subtract that sum from the list of emissions he reported.

g Because Jefferson's and Elliot's (1843: 8) numbers for 1779 and for September 26, 1778–November 29, 1779, sum to the same total as those for Newman, Harlow, and Michener (and close to those for Ferguson once adjusted for rounding), the values reported by Jefferson and Elliot (1843: 8) were used to apportion Newman's, Ferguson's, Harlow's, and Michener's numbers for 1779 into before versus after September 2, 1779, subtotals. Not enough information is given in Bolles, Elliot (1843: 11), or Gouge to do this kind of comparison.

h Jefferson omitted $16,000,000 between 1775 and early 1777, designated as "?" in the table here [also omitted in Elliot's (1843: 8) transcription], and his individual entries sum to $200,000,003, not the total in his table ($200,000,000) as reported in Boyd (1953–55, 10:42–43). The extra three dollars in the February 3, 1779, entry is most likely a transcription error. Elliot (1843: 8) transcribed Jefferson's table without the extra three dollars. Both Jefferson and Elliot (1843: 8) set the amount of net new emissions from the January 14, 1779, authorization to be the residual needed to add up to the cumulative total net new emission stated by Congress of $159,948,883 through September 2, 1779. Because this stated sum included an erroneous $10,005 that had gone unnoticed by Congress, Jefferson's and Elliot's residual calculation is off by an additional $10,005 here—to which the missing $16 million mentioned above will be added later.

continues

TABLE A.2 (*continued*)

i Newman's list of emissions can be aggregated in two ways. Both start with the subtotal of $71,500,000 emitted through September 5, 1778. To this number add the $75,001,080 Newman reported for the period September 26, 1778–July 17, 1779 (the total for this period derived from the *JCC* is $80,001,260). Then add in the emissions after July 17, 1779 ($40,051,120) as reported in Nourse (1828), Boyd (1953–55), and Elliot (1843: 8). Finally, add in the estimated amount of the January 14, 1779, emission that was new ($8,500,395). This yields a grand total of $195,052,605 emitted, which is the method used and the total reported here. Alternatively, to the $71,500,000 emitted through September 5, 1778, add the amount emitted through the rest of 1778 ($30,000,300) as reported in Nourse (1828), Boyd (1953–55), and Elliot (1843: 8), and then add in the total Newman reports for 1779 ($95,051,695) (the total for this period derived from the *JCC*, sans the January 14, 1779, emission, is $90,052,080). This yields a grand total of $196,551,995. Whether Newman included in his 1779 total the estimated amount of the January 14, 1779, emission that was new ($8,500,395) is unclear. If he did not, then adding that amount in would yield a grand total of $205,052,390. Newman does not give enough detail in his accounting of separate emissions after September 26, 1778, to identify where the problem lies and resolve the discrepancies in these different grand-total estimates for him.

j The figure of $200 million was explicitly stated by Congress to be its final cumulative total net new emissions (*JCC* 15:1019, 1036, 1053, 1055, 1171). This number was based on the Board of Treasury report (PCC, microfilm 247, reel 146, item 136#47, September 14, 1779), which claimed that $159,948,880 had been emitted through September 2, 1779. When this Board of Treasury number is added to that emitted from September 17–November 29, 1779, after which emissions were permanently discontinued, the total is to $200 million. The Board of Treasury report, however, erroneously included $10,000 from January 5, 1776, as a net new emission in its $159,948,880 total emitted through September 2, 1779, when in fact this $10,000 was not a new emission and missed the $5 reduction in the January 14, 1779, authorization enacted May 7, 1779. As such, Congress thought it had emitted $10,005 more than it actually had. See also notes n, q, s, and t below.

k Gouge (1833, part 2:25) reported the same total for his table of emissions as the *American Almanac* (1830: 183) and Elliot (1843: 11), even though Gouge's yearly numbers sum to $357,476,339. The $202 difference between Gouge's and AA-Elliot's summed totals comes from what they reported for 1776. Gouge's number for 1776 may just be a typo, and it should really be the same as the AA-Elliot number for 1776.

l Bullock's individual entries sum to $231,550,000 and not to the $241,500,000 he reported as the total—an addition error that was left uncorrected in table 2 of Calomiris (1988: 58). This addition error does not occur in or affect the analysis in fig. 1 of Calomiris (1988: 56).

m The January 14, 1779, adjustment is made uniform across estimates, i.e. [$50,000,395 − $41,500,000 (exchanged)] = $8,500,395 of net new emissions. This adjustment also uniformly accounts for the $10,005 oversight errors in the Board of Treasury report where applicable. The remaining differences are due to rounding or minor transcription errors. This correction, when made to Bullock's estimate, solves the anomaly that Bullock himself puzzled over (Bullock 1895: 136). This estimate also accords closely with Ferguson (1961: 45), who claims that $41,500,000 was exchanged out of the $50,000,400 authorized for exchange on January 14, 1779, which would then potentially leave $8,500,400 as a net new emission from that date—even though Ferguson did not use this observation when constructing his estimate of net new emissions. Finally, this estimate also accords with the limit set by Congress on September 3, 1779, of a maximum of $200,000,000 Continental dollars that could be emitted before emissions were permanently discontinued (Ferguson 1961: 46; *JCC* 15:1019, 1036, 1053, 1055, 1171; and Jefferson's assessment in Boyd 1953–55, 10:25, 42), which, when the $10,005 Board of Treasury errors are subtracted (see notes n and q below), yields the true final cumulative total outstanding.

[n] This total represents the sum of the authorized net new emissions mentioned in the *JCC*: $160,001,655 to September 2, 1779, plus $40,051,120 emitted September 17–November 29, 1779, as opposed to the final total stated by Congress (see note j above). The $52,780 in excess of the $200 million Congress stated as emitted represents the fact that the authorized net new emissions mentioned in the *JCC* failed to note that $62,780 of the $4 million authorized on February 17, 1776, was not printed (see note r below) and that the amount declared by Congress as emitted through September 2, 1779 ($159,948,880) was erroneously overstated by $10,005 due to Board of Treasury errors on the January 5, 1776, emission and the May 7, 1779, adjustment to the January 14, 1779, emission (see notes j above and q below). In other words, Congress set a $200 million limit on emissions but did not realize that its true emission numbers, when summed up, were $62,780 long on one account (the February 17, 1776, emission) and $10,005 short on another account (the amount it could emit after September 2, 1779, before it reached $200 million).

[o] The difference between the number listed and $199,989,995 is due to rounding.

[p] This total represents an error of definition and so cannot be reconciled with the other estimates. It should, therefore, be discarded. See the text for further analysis.

[q] On January 5, 1776, Congress resolved "that the sum of ten thousand dollars, be struck, for the purpose of exchanging ragged and torn bills of the continental currency; That the bills, making this sum . . . be lodged in the treasury, to be applied to the sole purpose aforementioned" (*JCC* 4:32; 5:697). Being a swap for existing bills outstanding, this $10,000 does not represent a net new emission, nor does it add to the cumulative total of bills outstanding. That these kinds of swaps actually took place is corroborated by a statement recorded in Congress on February 9, 1779, that a "quantity of torn bills, was laid before Congress, soliciting that the same be exchanged" (*JCC* 13:158) Therefore, this $10,000 is not counted here as a net new emission when summing the entries in the *JCC* column. No subsequent scholar has counted this $10,000 as a net new emission (see also Bronson 1865: 113). However, the Board of Treasury, in its report to Congress, where it stated that $159,948,880 had been emitted through September 2, 1779—a sum accepted by Congress—had included (erroneously) this $10,000 as a net new emission in constructing its $159,948,880 estimate (PCC, microfilm 247, reel 146, item 136:647, Sept. 14, 1779). Thus, the Board of Treasury overstated the true amount of net new emission by $10,000—an overstatement that Congress, as well as all subsequent scholars, did not catch (see also notes j above and t below).

[r] The report by the Board of Treasury to Congress on emissions through September 2, 1779, listed the $4 million Congress had authorized on this date but indicated that only $3,937,220 were printed out of this authorization (PCC, microfilm 247, reel 146, item 136:647, Sept. 14, 1779). This $62,780 shortfall has not been previously noted in the literature. See notes n above and t below.

[s] See notes j and q above.

[t] The *JCC* entry for February 17, 1776 (item A of the comparison) overstates emissions by $62,780 compared with the *PCC* entry for that date (item B of the comparison). In addition, the *JCC* cumulative total through September 2, 1779 (item A of the comparison) does not include the overstatement errors of $10,005 from January 5, 1776, and May 7, 1779, that are in the *PCC* cumulative total reported to Congress (item B of the comparison), and so the *JCC* entry for item A of the comparison does not need to be corrected for that $10,005 error. See also note r above.

[u] The *PCC* evidence on emissions does not continue past September 14, 1779 (PCC, microfilm 247, reel 146, item 136:647); thus, only the *JCC* estimate can be carried through to the end of emissions, and only the *JCC* evidence can generate a final corrected total amount emitted. This total of cumulative net new emissions assumes that Congress made up for the discrepancy produced on July 25, 1775. On that date Congress ordered $1,000,000 to be struck in $30 bills (*JCC* 2:207). This is not possible: either $999,990 or $1,000,020 can be struck, but not $1,000,000. Which was done and whether other denominations of emission no. 1 were adjusted to accommodate the $1,000,000 target in $30 bills is not known. Because no change in the $1,000,000 total authorized was ever noted by Congress or the Board of Treasury, it is assumed that the discrepancy was made up by adjusting the printing of bills of other denominations from this emission, thus yielding the total reported here of $199,989,995. However, the total cumulative net new emissions could vary between $199,989,985 and $199,990,015, depending how Congress resolved its order to emit $1,000,000 in $30 bills on July 25, 1775—an outcome that is currently unknown. No prior secondary source notes this discrepancy or adjusts for it, accepting the $1,000,000 number from July 25, 1775, as the realized amount issued.

listed the entire emissions of May 20, 1777, and April 11, 1778—and no others—as eligible. Thereafter, only these two dates were mentioned, and mentioned often, in reference to exchanging bills.[9] Scholars differ over how to count these emissions. Bullock assumes that each authorization date represents a unique emission. Because only $5 million was authorized on May 20, 1777, and another $5 million on April 11, 1778, he assumes that only $10 million was eligible for exchange—the residual $40,000,400, as he counted it, would then be a net new emission (Bronson 1865: 113; Bullock 1895: 135–36). Congress, however, had never authorized more than $10 million in new emissions on a single date before.

By contrast, Eric Newman assumes that authorization dates do not represent unique emissions. A given emission represented all authorized amounts—even if authorized on different dates—that were printed from the same cut. (This interpretation is adopted here and used throughout the book; see, e.g., see table 1.1.) Thus, the emission of May 20, 1777, included not only the amount authorized on May 20, 1777, but also that authorized on August 15, November 7, and December 3, 1777, and on January 8, January 22, February 16, March 5, April 4, and April 18, 1778. The bills from these separate authorization dates were all indistinguishable from one another but were distinguishable from all other emissions (Newman 1997: 64–69; 2008: 68–69).[10]

Newman considers the emission of April 11, 1778, to include not only the amount authorized on April 11, 1778, but also that authorized on May 22, June 20, July 30, and September 5, 1778. The bills from these separate authorizations were all indistinguishable from one another but were distinguishable from all other emissions. In total, then, the emissions of May 20, 1777, and April 11, 1778, amounted to $41.5 million (Newman 1997: 64–69; 2008: 68–69). If all $41.5 million of these two emissions was exchanged, it would leave $8,500,395 out of that authorized on January 14, 1779, as amended on May 7, 1779, as a net new emission—an amount clearly within the $5 to $10 million typical of new emissions authorized on a single date.

The authorizing language supports this interpretation. The nine authorizations Newman identified after May 20, 1777, carried the same instructional language "that the bills shall . . . be of the same tenor and date as the emission now executing." The language authorizing the April 11, 1778, emission explicitly stated that for these bills "new cuts be used for striking off and printing: That the form of the bills be as follows: . . . according to a resolution passed by Congress, at York, 11 April, 1778." The next four authorizations Newman listed as belonging to the April 11, 1778, emission carried the same instructional language: "That the bills shall . . . be of the same tenor and date as the emission directed on the eleventh day of April last."[11]

The *PCC* provides definitive corroboration for this interpretation. Therein the Board of Treasury explicitly identifies the emissions of May 20, 1777, and April 11, 1778, as comprising the additional authorization dates listed above with the cumulative total listed as $41.5 million emitted (*PCC* microfilm 247, reel 146, item 136:647). William Whipple, congressman from New Hampshire, in a letter to Josiah Barlett dated February 28, 1779, stated the same: that $16,500,000 of the May 1777 and $25,000,000 of the April 1778 emissions were to be called in. In 1780, Pelatiah Webster came close to this amount when he claimed that $25 million from the April 11, 1778, and $8 million from the May 20, 1777, emission were to be exchanged— apparently overlooking an additional $8.5 million from the May 20, 1777, emission (Smith 1976–94, 12:122; Webster 1969: 92). The Board subtracted this sum, the $41.5 million, from the $50,000,400 authorized on January 14, 1779, missing the $5 reduction in this authorization enacted on May 7, 1779, when tallying up the cumulative net new emissions outstanding as of September 2, 1779—which was then stated to be $159,948,880.

Congress accepted this total. However, the sum of new emissions authorized as of September 2, 1779, as listed in the *JCC*—counting the January 14, 1779, emission as $8,500,395—totaled $160,001,655. The difference between the *JCC* and *PCC* totals to that date equals $52,775. This discrepancy is fully accounted for by the fact that the *PCC*, but not the *JCC*, adjusted the February 17, 1776, authorization down by $62,780 to account for bills not printed, and by the fact that the *PCC*, but not the *JCC*, mistakenly counted $10,000 from January 5, 1776, as new and failed to adjust the January 14, 1779, authorization down by $5 owing to denominational restructuring on May 7, 1779. Thus, the true *JCC* total ($160,001,655 − $62,780) = the true *PCC* total ($159,948,880 − $10,000 − $5) for cumulative net new emissions as of September 2, 1779 (*JCC* 15:1019, 1052–53).

In 1786 Thomas Jefferson used the discrepancy between *JCC* and *PCC* totals as of September 2, 1779, to determine how much of the January 14, 1779, authorization should be counted as new (Boyd 1953–55, 10:42–43; Elliot 1843: 10–12). Because Jefferson erroneously omitted $16 million of pre-1779 emissions, and because he did not know about the required reduction of $62,780 and overage errors of $10,005 in the *PCC* numbers relative to the *JCC* numbers, his residual estimate is off by exactly

$15,947,225 ($16,000,000 − $62,780 + $10,005). This adjustment perfectly realigns Jefferson's estimate with that reported in table A.1.

Were all $41.5 million Continental dollars eligible for exchange actually exchanged? Ferguson assumes that little of the eligible amounts was swapped, leaving more as a net new emission. He erroneously assumed that none were so exchanged after August 1779 and that because only $15.3 million was sent out to be exchanged between late June and early August 1779, the rest ($34.7 million) must have been new (Ferguson 1961: 29 n. 13, 45; *JCC* 15:1436). The Treasury Office Report of April 21, 1779, contradicts Ferguson's assumption, concluding:

> It is no longer probable that the expedient of calling in the emissions of May 20th, 1777, and April 11th, 1778, will afford any other extensive advantage than that of defeating frauds by counterfeits. . . . that little comparatively of those emissions will be drawn into the Loan offices: a vast proportion of the amount must consequently be exchanged after the first of August, and pass again into circulation. (*JCC* 14:519, 731)

Congress and the Board of Treasury had hoped that citizens would turn in their Continental dollars dated May 20, 1777, and April 11, 1778, for loan office certificates, rather than just swapping them for new Continental dollars dated January 14, 1779. The Loan Office and Treasury would then swap these bills received on loan for the new bills, destroy the old bills, and spend the new bills as loaned sums. Their thinking, somewhat erroneous, was that spending loaned sums removed the loaned amounts from the stock of currency outstanding (as though the velocity of circulation did not matter). By contrast, if citizens simply swapped old bills for new bills, the swapped amount stayed in circulation, with no net reduction in the amount of currency outstanding. Lastly, they saw that most bills from the May 20, 1777, and April 11, 1778, emissions would be exchanged after August 1779, making Ferguson's conclusions erroneous.

Direct evidence from the Continental Treasury can be used to estimate the quantity of old bills actually swapped for new. On January 14, 1786, Nourse reported to Congress the amount of Continental dollars paid into the Continental Treasury through 1785. These amounts included bills sent in as part of the exchange of the emissions of May 20, 1777, and April 11, 1778, for the emission authorized on January 14, 1779. The *JCC* recorded the total of new bills sent out to be exchanged during late June through early August 1779: $15.3 million. The *Pennsylvania Packet* stated that $19.8 million in old bills had been exchanged for new bills by January 1780. These numbers are close to the total Nourse reported ($19.1 million) as being sent in to the Treasury in 1779 to be destroyed.[12]

Francis Hopkinson, Treasurer of Loans, reported the cumulative total amount of the emissions of May 20, 1777, and April 11, 1778, that had been received and destroyed, namely those that had been swapped for new bills, as being $3,852,766 by July 19, 1779; $19,847,268 by January 1, 1780; and $32,304,372 by March 22, 1780.[13] Hopkinson's totals fully account for Nourse's remittance totals to those dates as reported to Congress in 1786. Nourse's totals to the end of March 1780 are $710,441 less than Hopkinson's totals as of March 22, 1780, for the amount of bills swapped.

Although the exchange of old bills for new ended on January 1, 1781, the Treasury was still destroying old bills that had been exchanged for new as late as January 1782. Cross-referencing Nourse's and Hillegas's Treasury reports indicates that the remittances in the Nourse report through April 1781 were mostly exchanges of the May 20, 1777, and April 11, 1778, emissions (see chap. 15).[14]

The total sum eligible for exchange was $41.5 million. Nourse's report of remittances from May 1779 through January 1, 1781, totaled $34.4 million and through April 1781 totaled $39.9 million. This total rises to $41 million when the amounts that Hillegas explicitly identifies as being exchanges of the May 20, 1777, and April 11, 1778, emissions that took place after April 1781 are added. The closeness of these estimates ($41.5 million eligible versus $41 million swapped), given that Nourse admits that his remittance numbers are not complete, is further corroboration that of the $50,000,395 Continental dollars authorized on January 14, 1779, and amended on May 7, 1779, only $8,500,395 should be counted as a net new emission.

When the addition, omission, transcription, and definition errors in the past literature are corrected, the discrepancy between the *JCC* and *PCC* evidence is taken into account, and the method for calculating the net new emission from the January 14, 1779, authorization described above is used, the discrepancies across the literature, sans rounding, are eliminated — revealing a single estimate of $199,989,995 net new Continental dollars emitted from 1775 through 1779 and still outstanding as of 1780 (see table A.2). All the different time paths of emissions across the literature also collapse onto the one reported in table A.1 and shown as the *JCC* lines in figures A.1 and A.2.

On September 3, 1779, Congress set a limit of $200 million for the cumulative total net new emissions of Continental dollars, after which new emissions would be discontinued.[15] Except for missing the $10,005 of overage accounting errors, they were right on the mark with their last issuance authorized on November 29, 1779. Several contemporary and subsequent scholars—among them the 1779 US Treasury Office, Thomas Jefferson, Benjamin Franklin, Charles Thomson, Pelatiah Webster, Samuel Breck, and B. U. Ratchford—merely accepted Congress's $200 million emission limit as their estimate of total net new emissions.[16] As such, these scholars ended up being closer to the true cumulative total amount of net new emissions of Continental dollars—$199,989,995—than all other scholars until the present.

The Denominational Structure of American Paper Monies, 1755–1781

The denominational spacing of various American paper monies in terms of the percentage emitted per unit and per value, and how those denominational values align with Spanish silver dollars and pounds sterling, and in 2012 US dollars, is presented in the following tables and discussed in chapter 3. Table B.1 presents these data for the Continental dollar by emission from 1775 through 1779, as well as aggregated totals for all emissions. Table B.2 presents these data for the paper monies emitted by colonial Virginia, Pennsylvania, New Jersey, and New York during the Seven Years' War, 1755–64. Table B.3 presents these data for the paper monies emitted by the states of Virginia, Pennsylvania, New Jersey, and New York for the early years of the Revolution, 1775–77, before the states were asked by Congress to curtail emission except for smaller denominations. Tables B.4 and B.5 present the denominational structure of loan office certificates (see chap. 8).

TABLE B.I Denominational structure of the Continental dollar in face value per emission, 1775–79

In $ (Spanish silver dollars)	In 2012 US dollars[a]	May 10, 1775 No. 1: $3,000,000		Nov. 29, 1775 No. 2: $3,00,000[c]		Feb. 17, 1776 No. 3: 4,000,000[d]		May 9, 1776 No. 4: $5,000,000		July 22, 1776 No. 5: $5,000,000		Nov. 2, 1776 No. 6: $5,000,000		Feb. 26, 1777 No. 7: $5,000,000	
		Units %	Value %	Units %	Value %	Units %	Value %	Units %	Value %	Units %	Value %	Units %	Value %	Units %	Value %
0.17	5.2	—	—	—	—	18.85	2.50	—	—	—	—	—	—	—	—
0.33	10.3	—	—	—	—	18.85	5.00	—	—	—	—	—	—	—	—
0.50	15.5	—	—	—	—	18.85	7.50	—	—	—	—	—	—	—	—
0.67	20.7	—	—	—	—	18.85	10.00	—	—	—	—	—	—	—	—
1.00	31.0	11.21	1.63	12.50	2.78	4.10	3.26	12.50	2.78	—	—	—	—	—	—
2.00	62.0	11.21	3.27	12.50	5.56	4.10	6.52	12.50	5.56	12.50	3.08	12.50	3.08	12.50	3.08
3.00	93.0	11.21	4.90	12.50	8.33	4.10	9.78	12.50	8.33	12.50	4.62	12.50	4.62	12.50	4.62
4.00	124.0	11.21	6.53	12.50	11.11	4.10	13.04	12.50	11.11	12.50	6.15	12.50	6.15	12.50	6.15
5.00	155.0	11.21	8.17	12.50	13.89	2.05	8.15	12.50	13.89	12.50	7.69	12.50	7.69	12.50	7.69
6.00	186.0	11.21	9.80	12.50	16.67	2.05	9.78	12.50	16.67	12.50	9.23	12.50	9.23	12.50	9.23
7.00	217.0	11.21	11.43	12.50	19.44	2.05	11.41	12.50	19.44	12.50	10.77	12.50	10.77	12.50	10.77
8.00	248.0	11.21	13.07	12.50	22.22	2.05	13.04	12.50	22.22	12.50	12.31	12.50	12.31	12.50	12.31
20.00	620.0	2.70	7.87	—	—	—	—	—	—	—	—	—	—	—	—
30.00	930.0	7.63[b]	33.33	—	—	—	—	—	—	12.50	46.15	12.50	46.15	12.50	46.15
35.00	1,085.0	—	—	—	—	—	—	—	—	—	—	—	—	—	—
40.00	1,240.0	—	—	—	—	—	—	—	—	—	—	—	—	—	—
45.00	1,395.0	—	—	—	—	—	—	—	—	—	—	—	—	—	—
50.00	1,550.0	—	—	—	—	—	—	—	—	—	—	—	—	—	—
55.00	1,705.0	—	—	—	—	—	—	—	—	—	—	—	—	—	—
60.00	1,860.0	—	—	—	—	—	—	—	—	—	—	—	—	—	—
65.00	2,015.0	—	—	—	—	—	—	—	—	—	—	—	—	—	—
70.00	2,170.0	—	—	—	—	—	—	—	—	—	—	—	—	—	—
80.00	2,480.0	—	—	—	—	—	—	—	—	—	—	—	—	—	—
		100.00	100.00	100.00	100.00	100.00	100.00	100.00	100.00	100.00	100.00	100.00	100.00	100.00	100.00

TABLE B.1 *(continued)*

May 20, 1777 No. 8: 16,500,000		Apr. 11, 1778 No. 9: $25,000,000		Sept. 26, 1778 No. 10: $75,001,080		Jan. 14, 1779 No. 11: $95,051,695[e]		1775–79 Total[f]		In $ (Spanish silver dollars)	In 2012 US dollars[a]
Units %	Value %	Units %	Value %	Units %	Value %	Units %	Value %	Units %	Value %		
—	—	—	—	—	—	—	—	3.69	0.04	0.17	5.2
—	—	—	—	—	—	—	—	3.69	0.08	0.33	10.3
—	—	—	—	—	—	—	—	3.69	0.12	0.50	15.5
—	—	—	—	—	—	—	—	3.69	0.17	0.67	20.7
12.50	3.08	12.50	3.33	—	—	5.43	0.15	3.33	0.22	1.00	31.0
12.50	4.62	12.50	4.17	—	—	5.43	0.29	6.32	0.85	2.00	62.0
12.50	6.15	12.50	5.00	—	—	5.43	0.44	6.32	1.27	3.00	93.0
12.50	7.69	12.50	5.83	—	—	5.43	0.59	7.60	2.04	4.00	124.0
12.50	9.23	12.50	6.67	12.50	2.27	5.43	0.74	9.30	3.13	5.00	155.0
12.50	10.77	12.50	16.67	—	—	—	—	6.34	2.56	6.00	186.0
12.50	12.31	12.50	25.00	12.50	3.18	—	—	8.44	3.97	7.00	217.0
—	—	—	—	12.50	3.64	—	—	8.44	4.54	8.00	248.0
12.50	46.15	12.50	33.33	12.50	9.09	7.07	2.94	4.31	5.80	20.00	620.0
—	—	—	—	12.50	13.64	7.07	5.75	7.69	15.52	30.00	930.0
—	—	—	—	—	—	7.07	6.70	1.12	2.64	35.00	1,085.0
—	—	—	—	12.50	18.18	7.07	7.66	4.50	12.11	40.00	1,240.0
—	—	—	—	—	—	7.07	8.62	1.12	3.39	45.00	1,395.0
—	—	—	—	12.50	22.73	7.07	9.58	3.22	10.83	50.00	1,550.0
—	—	—	—	—	—	7.07	10.54	1.12	4.15	55.00	1,705.0
—	—	—	—	12.50	27.27	7.07	11.49	3.22	12.99	60.00	1,860.0
—	—	—	—	—	—	7.07	12.45	1.12	4.90	65.00	2,015.0
—	—	—	—	—	—	5.43	10.30	0.86	4.05	70.00	2,170.0
—	—	—	—	—	—	5.43	11.77	0.86	4.63	80.00	2,480.0
100.0	100.0	100.0	100.0	100.0	100.0	100.0	100.0	100.0	100.0		

continues

TABLE B.1 (*continued*)

Sources: JCC (2:105, 207; 3:398; 4:164, 281; 5:651; 6:918, 1047; 7:161; 8:377, 646; 9:873, 993; 10:28, 83, 175, 223, 309, 337, 365; 11:524, 627, 732; 12:884, 962, 1100, 1218; 13:64, 139, 209, 409; 14:548, 557–58, 688, 848–49; 15:1076, 1172, 1285, 1325); Newman (2008: 62–73).

Notes: $ = Spanish silver dollars, in which the Continental dollar was denominated at face value.

[a] From http://eh.net, "measuring worth—relative value of U.S. Dollars" using the 1775-to-2012 *CPI* conversion algorithm.

[b] See table A.2, note u. The number $999,990 is used here for percentage calculation purposes.

[c] Newman (2008: 64) presents erroneous denominational counts for the November 29, 1775, emission. See instead *JCC* 3:398.

[d] Only $3,937,220 were printed. Which denominations were shorted is not known. The $4,000,000 number is used for percentage calculation purposes.

[e] This is a gross emission number (total bills printed). Out of this gross emission, $41,500,000 were swapped for the emissions of May 20, 1777, and April 11, 1777 (emissions no. 8 and no. 9), yielding a net new emission of $53,551,695. Which bills by denomination were swapped is not known, so the denomination structure is reported on the gross rather than on the net new emission total.

[f] This is out of total scheduled printings ($241,552,775) and not net new emissions ($199,989,995). Not all bills were printed, and some printed bills were simply swapped for other bills that had already been emitted, which explains the difference in these two sums. Which denomination totals were affected by nonprinting and currency swaps is unknown. See notes b, d, and e.

TABLE B.2 Face-value denominational structure of colonial paper monies during the Seven Years' War, 1755–64

| | | | Virginia | | | | Pennsylvania | | New Jersey | | New York | | | | |
| | | | 1757–62 | 560,107 | 370,588 | | 1,307,931 | 550,000 £PA | 374,998 | 347,603 £NJ | 1755–64 72,600 | 340,000 £NY | | | |
Face value in £s	$ (face value in Spanish silver dollars)	Value in 2012 US dollars	Denominations £VA	Units %	Value %	Denominations £PA, £NJ, & £NY	Units %	Value %	Units %	Value %	Units %	Value %	Face value in £s	$ (Face value in Spanish Silver dollars)	value in 2012 US dollars
0.0400	0.1739	5.39	0.0500	15.6	1.2	0.0125	8.1	0.2	—	—	—	—	0.0125	0.0094	1.26
0.0500	0.2174	6.74	0.0625	15.6	1.5	0.0167	6.3	0.3	—	—	—	—	0.0167	0.0125	1.69
0.1000	0.4348	13.48	0.1250	16.8	3.2	0.0250	6.2	0.4	—	—	—	—	0.0250	0.0188	2.53
0.2000	0.8686	26.96	0.2500	16.8	6.3	0.0375	6.2	0.6	—	—	—	—	0.0375	0.0282	3.80
0.4000	1.7391	53.91	0.5000	12.9	9.7	0.0500	6.2	0.7	15.1	0.8	—	—	0.0500	0.0376	5.07
0.8000	3.4783	107.83	1.0000	12.9	19.4	0.0750	5.8	1.0	11.7	1.0	—	—	0.0750	0.0564	7.60
1.6000	6.9565	215.65	2.0000	2.8	8.5	0.1000	5.7	1.4	—	—	—	—	0.1000	0.0752	10.13
2.4000	10.4348	323.48	3.0000	2.8	12.8	0.1250	5.7	1.7	—	—	—	—	0.1250	0.0940	12.67
4.0000	17.3913	539.13	5.0000	2.8	21.3	0.1500	—	—	9.3	1.5	—	—	0.1500	0.1128	15.20
8.0000	34.7876	1,078.42	10.0000	1.1	16.2	0.2500	13.8	8.2	10.8	3.5	4.4	0.2	0.2500	0.1880	25.34
				100	100	0.3000	—	—	—	—	—	—	0.3000	0.2256	30.40
						0.5000	12.0	14.2	—	—	4.1	0.4	0.5000	0.3759	50.67
						0.6000	—	—	10.8	7.0	—	—	0.6000	0.4511	60.80
						0.7500	9.9	17.7	15.0	12.1	5.7	1.2	0.7500	0.5639	76.01
						1.0000	11.2	26.5	—	—	—	—	1.0000	0.7519	101.34
						1.5000	—	—	15.3	24.8	—	—	1.5000	1.1278	152.01
						2.0000	—	—	—	—	31.1	13.3	2.0000	1.5038	202.68
						2.5000	1.5	9.1	—	—	—	—	2.5000	1.8797	253.35
						3.0000	—	—	8.6	27.8	3.6	2.3	3.0000	2.2556	304.02

continues

TABLE B.2 (continued)

	Virginia		Pennsylvania		New Jersey		New York				
	1757–62		1755–64		1755–64		1755–64			$ (Face value in Spanish Silver dollars)	value in 2012 US dollars
Denominations	$£_{VA}$		$£_{PA}$		$£_{NJ}$		$£_{NY}$		Face value in $£_S$		
$£_{PA}, £_{NJ}, \& £_{NY}$	560,107	370,588	1,307,931	550,000	374,998	347,503	72,600	340,000			
	Units %	Value %	Units %	Value %	Units %	Value %	Units %	Value %			
4.0000	—	—	—	—	—	—	0.8	0.7	3.0075	13.0762	405.36
5.0000	—	—	1.5	18.1	—	—	24.1	25.7	3.7594	16.3452	506.70
6.0000	—	—	—	—	3.3	21.5	—	—	4.5113	19.6143	608.04
10.0000	—	—	—	—	—	—	26.3	56.2	7.5188	32.6905	1,013.41
	100	100	100	100	100	100	100	100			

Sources: Bush (1980: 314–15, 348–49, 373–74, 417, 466, 501, 517, 549, 572–73, 631–32, 673–74; 1982: 83–84, 135–36, 207–8, 299–300); Hening (1969, 7:82–83, 175, 259–60, 350, 360–61, 498); McCusker (1978: 10); Newman (2008: 259–61, 281–83, 336–43).

Notes: Shillings and pence are converted to decimalized pounds. $ = Spanish silver dollars. $£_S$ = pound sterling. $£_{xx}$ = pounds in the respective colonial paper monies with VA = Virginia, PA = Pennsylvania, NJ = New Jersey, and NY = New York. At face value, $1.25£_{VA} = 1£_S$ and $1.33(£_{PA}, £_{NJ}, £_{NY}) = 1£_S$. Pre-1772, $1£_S = \$4.34783$.

TABLE B.3 **Face-value denominational structure of state paper monies during the American Revolution, 1775–77**

Value in 2012 US dollars ($)	Denominations ($)	New York 1775–77 $ (757,868) Units %	(750,000) Value %	Denominations (£PA & £NJ)	Pennsylvania 1775–77 £PA (1,307,931) Units %	(550,000) Value %	New Jersey 1776 £NJ (346,882) Units %	(175,000) Value %	Face value in £s	$ (Face value in Spanish silver dollars)	Value in 2012 US dollars	Denominations (£VA)	Virginia 1775–76 £VA (460,796) Units %	(447,404) Value %	Value in 2012 US dollars
2.02	0.0650	14.0	0.9	0.0125	14.0	0.6	—	—	0.0094	0.0427	1.32	0.0500	5.33	0.27	5.64
3.88	0.1250	17.9	2.3	0.0167	14.0	0.8	—	—	0.0125	0.0568	1.76	0.0625	18.39	1.18	7.05
5.17	0.1667	4.0	0.7	0.0250	14.0	1.2	—	—	0.0188	0.0855	2.65	0.1000	5.33	0.55	11.27
7.75	0.2500	17.9	4.5	0.0375	14.0	1.8	23.4	2.3	0.0282	0.1282	3.97	0.1250	18.38	2.37	14.09
10.33	0.3333	4.0	1.3	0.0500	4.7	0.8	18.0	2.7	0.0376	0.1709	5.29	0.2500	6.31	1.63	28.18
15.50	0.5000	18.6	9.4	0.0750	4.7	1.2	—	—	0.0564	0.2564	7.95	0.3750	3.90	1.51	42.27
20.67	0.6667	4.0	2.7	0.1000	4.7	1.6	—	—	0.0752	0.3418	10.60	0.5000	3.95	2.03	56.36
31.00	1.000	5.3	5.3	0.1250	2.8	1.2	14.4	4.3	0.0940	0.4273	13.25	0.6250	3.90	2.51	70.45
62.00	2.000	3.6	7.3	0.1500	1.9	1.0	—	—	0.1128	0.5127	15.89	1.000	10.15	10.45	112.73
93.00	3.000	3.6	10.9	0.2000	2.1	1.5	—	—	0.1504	0.6836	21.19	1.2000	5.33	6.59	135.27
155.00	5.000	3.6	18.2	0.2500	0.4	0.3	12.3	7.3	0.1880	0.8545	26.49	1.5000	5.33	8.23	169.09
310.00	10.0000	3.6	36.5	0.3000	2.1	2.2	—	—	0.2256	1.0255	31.79	2.0000	5.00	10.30	225.45
		—	—	0.4000	1.9	2.7	—	—	0.3008	1.3673	42.39	3.0000	3.52	10.88	338.18
		100	100	0.5000	2.7	4.8	10.8	12.9	0.3759	1.7086	52.97	4.0000	0.43	1.79	450.91
				0.6000	1.9	4.0	—	—	0.4511	2.0505	63.57	5.0000	1.78	9.18	563.64
				0.7000	0.2	0.5	9.1	13.6	0.5263	2.3923	74.16	8.0000	1.31	10.80	901.82
				0.7500	0.4	1.0	—	—	0.5639	2.5632	79.46	10.0000	0.30	3.11	1,127.27
				0.8000	2.1	5.8	—	—	0.6015	2.7341	84.76	12.0000	1.35	16.62	1,352.73
				1.0000	4.6	16.1	—	—	0.7519	3.4177	105.95		—	—	
				1.5000	2.4	12.3	6.5	19.3	1.1278	5.1264	158.92		100	100	

continues

TABLE B.3 (*continued*)

	New York		Pennsylvania £PA		New Jersey			Virginia £VA	
	1775–77 $		1775–77		1776 £NJ			1775–76	
	757,868	750,000	1,307,931	550,000	346,882	175,000		460,796	447,404

Denominations $	Units %	Value %	Denominations £PA & £NJ	Face value in £s	$ (Face value in Spanish silver dollars)	Value in 2012 US dollars	PA Units %	PA Value %	NJ Units %	NJ Value %	Denominations £VA	VA Units %	VA Value %
			2.0000	1.5038	6.8354	211.90	3.2	21.9	—	—			
			2.5000	1.8797	8.5441	264.87	0.2	1.8	—	—			
			3.0000	2.2556	10.2527	317.83	—	—	4.5	27.0			
			4.0000	3.0075	13.6704	423.78	0.8	11.2	—	—			
			5.0000	3.7594	17.0882	529.73	0.2	3.7	—	—			
			6.0000	4.5113	20.5059	635.68	—	—	0.9	10.7			
							100	100	100	100			

Sources: See the source note to table B.2; Newman (2008: 259–61, 286–90, 350–57, 444–46).

Notes: See the notes to table B.2. Post-1772, 1£$_s$ = \$4.54545. For Virginia, to get the value in 2012 US dollars, take the denomination value × 0.8 × 4.54545 × 31; for Pennsylvania and New Jersey, take the denomination value × 0.75188 × 4.54545 × 31. New York state money was denominated in Spanish silver dollars; thus, to get the value in 2012 US dollars, just take the denomination value × 31.

TABLE B.4 **Denominational structure of loan office certificates per authorization**

Face value of loan office certificates in Continental dollars	Equivalence of this face value in 2012 US dollars[a]	Authorization no. 1 Oct. 3, 1776 $5,000,000		Authorization no. 2 Jan. 1, 1777 $2,000,000		Authorization no. 3 Feb. 22, 1777 $13,000,000		Authorization no. 4 Jan. 17, 1778 $10,000,000		Authorization no. 5 May 2, 1778 $250,000	
		In units %	In value %	In units %	In value %	In units %	In value %	In units %	In value %	In units %	In value %
$200	$6,200	33.33	22.05			8.32	3.85	16.57	6.67		
$300	$9,300	26.67	23.52			30.55	21.20	16.57	10.00		
$400	$12,400	20.00	22.05			24.45	22.62	16.57	13.33		
$500	$15,500	13.33	17.64	100.00	100.00	18.34	21.20	16.57	16.67	88.89	80.00
$600	$18,600	6.68	14.74			12.22	16.96	16.57	20.00		
$1,000	$31,000					6.13	14.18	16.57	33.34	11.11	20.00
$2,000	$62,000										
$3,000	$93,000										
$4,000	$124,000										
$5,000	$155,000										
$10,000	$310,000										
$15,000	$465,000										
$20,000	$620,000										
$30,000	$930,000										
Totals		100.01	100.00	100.00	100.00	100.01	100.01	100.02	100.01	100.00	100.00

continues

TABLE B.4 (continued)

Authorization no. 6[b]		Authorization no. 7		Authorization no. 8[c]		Authorization no. 9		Authorization no. 10		Maximum total[d]			
Feb. 3, 1779		Apr. 27, 1779		June 29, 1779		Oct. 30, 1779		Jan. 2, 1781		1776–81			
$20,000,000		$4,000,000		$20,000,000		$600,000		$850,000		$75,700,000			
In units	In value	In units	In value	In units	In value	In units	In value	In units	In value	Units	Value	Units	Value
%	%	%	%	%	%	%	%	%	%	No.	$	%	%
10.82	2.50									18,333	3,666,600	16.26	4.84
10.82	3.75									18,693	5,607,900	16.58	7.41
21.63	10.00									18,623	7,449,200	16.52	9.84
17.30	10.00			47.88	14.25	87.42	68.33	82.24	58.82	22,971	11,485,500	20.38	15.17
17.30	12.00									12,478	7,486,800	11.07	9.89
10.16	11.75			19.73	11.75	10.66	16.67	16.45	23.53	14,962	14,962,000	13.27	19.76
4.33	10.00	100.00	100.00	8.40	10.00					2,000	4,000,000	1.77	5.28
2.89	10.01			8.96	16.01					1,734	5,202,000	1.54	6.87
2.16	10.00			7.14	17.00					1,350	5,400,000	1.20	7.13
1.73	10.00			5.38	16.00	1.92	15.00	0.82	5.88	1,068	5,340,000	0.95	7.05
0.87	10.00			2.52	15.00			0.16	2.35	502	5,020,000	0.45	6.63
								0.16	3.53	2	30,000	0.00	0.04
								0.08	2.35	1	20,000	0.00	0.03
								0.08	3.53	1	30,000	0.00	0.04
100.01	100.00	100.00	100.00	100.01	100.01	100.00	100.00	99.99	99.99	112,718	75,700,000	99.99	99.98

Sources: JCC (6:955; 7:36, 143; 10:59; 11:416; 13:112, 141; 14:717–20, 783–85; 15:1225–26; 16:392; 19:7); table 8.1.

a From http://eh.net, "measuring worth—relative value of U.S. Dollars" using the 1775-to-2012 CPI conversion algorithm.

b On January 23, 1779, the Committee on the Treasury proposed a denominational structure for $40 million in loan office certificates. On February 2, 1779, Congress reduced the $40 million request to $20 million and left the denominational structure up to the Board of Treasury. What the Board actually implemented as the denominational structure is currently unknown. It is assumed here that the Board simply reduced the denominational structure proposed for the $40 million request proportionately to meet the $20 million Congress authorized. See JCC (13:112, 141).

c On June 11 and 29, 1779, Congress authorized $20 million in loan office certificates, specifying only that none be issued for under $500. Congress apparently left the rest of the denominational structure to the discretion of the Board of Treasury. On April 27, 1780, Congress ordered that the $4,800,000 in $600 denominations intended by the Board to be prepared in loan office certificates to meet the June 11 and 29, 1779, authorization be replaced with certificates of denominations $3,000, $4,000, $5,000, and $10,000, and specified how many of each. This change indicates that the Board was likely using the same denominational pattern as that for the $20 million authorized on February 3, 1779 (no. 6), with the exception that the amounts in the $200–$400 denominational range were spread over the $500 and $600 denominations. Using this presumption in combination with the explicit denominational changes ordered on April 27, 1780, yields the structure reported here. See JCC (14:717–20, 783–85; 16:392).

d See table 8.1, notes e and h.

TABLE B.5 **Denominational structure of loan office certificates as of November 10, 1780**

Face value of certificate denominations in Continental dollar values	Face value in 2012 values[a]	Number lent by Dec. 31, 1779[b] (face value)	Additional number lent to Nov. 10, 1780[c] (face value)	Number still on hand and unlent as of Nov. 10, 1780 (face value)	Total accounted for as of Nov. 10, 1780[d] (face value)	Maximum total authorized through Nov. 10, 1780 (face value)
$200	$6,200	7,748 ($1,549,600)	1,389 ($277,800)	3,109 ($621,800)	12,246 ($2,449,200)	18,333 ($3,666,600)
$300	$9,300	11,162 ($3,348,600)	1,638 ($491,400)	2,024 ($607,200)	14,824 ($4,447,200)	18,693 ($5,607,900)
$400	$12,400	10,466 ($4,186,400)	1,454 ($581,600)	3,217 ($1,286,800)	15,137 ($6,054,800)	18,623 ($7,449,200)
$500	$15,500	9,082 ($4,541,000)	4,010 ($2,005,000)	2,143 ($1,071,500)	15,235 ($7,617,500)	21,971 ($10,985,500)
$600	$18,600	6,456 ($3,873,600)	1,095 ($657,000)	1,439 ($863,400)	8,990 ($5,394,000)	12,478 ($7,486,800)
$1,000	$31,000	7,872 ($7,872,000)	3,825 ($3,825,000)	1,084 ($1,084,000)	12,781 ($12,781,000)	14,762 ($14,762,000)
$2,000	$62,000	756 ($1,512,000)	304 ($608,000)	39 ($78,000)	1,099 ($2,198,000)	2,000 ($4,000,000)
$3,000	$93,000	472 ($1,416,000)	387 ($1,161,000)	378 ($1,134,000)	1,237 ($3,711,000)	1,734 ($5,202,000)
$4,000	$124,000	440 ($1,760,000)	201 ($804,000)	198 ($792,000)	839 ($3,356,000)	1,350 ($5,400,000)
$5,000	$155,000	381 ($1,905,000)	226 ($1,130,000)	62 ($310,000)	669 ($3,345,000)	1,058 ($5,290,000)
$10,000	$310,000	196 ($1,960,000)	143 ($1,430,000)	2 ($20,000)	341 ($3,410,000)	502 ($5,020,000)

Sources: PCC (microfilm 247, reel 41, item 34, "Reports of a Committee Appointed to State the Public Debt and Estimates of Expenses, with Related Papers 1779–1781," no. 143 and no. 145); table 8.2.

[a] From http://eh.net, "measuring worth—relative value of U.S. Dollars" using the 1775-to-2012 *CPI* conversion algorithm.

[b] Denomination compositions are missing for this period from New York, New Jersey, Virginia, South Carolina, and Georgia. Denomination compositions are also missing for North Carolina after September 10, 1779.

[c] Denomination compositions are missing for this period from New York, New Jersey, North Carolina, South Carolina, and Georgia. The time span for this period is December 31, 1779–September 30, 1780, but with end dates ranging between July 31, 1780, and October 31, 1780, for some states. The start date for New York is November 2, 1779. See the notes to table 8.2.

[d] Actual end dates by state are listed in table 8.2. Denomination compositions in this category are missing for New Jersey, South Carolina, and Georgia.

The Cumulative Value of Continental Dollars Emitted, 1775–1780

Face Value versus Present Value

Table C.1 presents the cumulative value of Continental dollars emitted and currently outstanding over the period of active emissions from August 1775 through November 1779. The time path of the cumulative face value, as well as the cumulative present value using forecasts 1 and 2 under perfect foresight, are presented. For 1779, the cumulative present values, both for the counterfactual applications of forecasts 1 and 2 and for the new January 2, 1779, redemption structure, are reported (see table 10.1).

When an amount was authorized, it was not instantly put into circulation; there was a certain lag between authorization and the spending of the bills by Congress. That lag is currently unknown. From the comments in the *JCC*, the longest lag was with the first emission. Substantial portions of that emission did not go into circulation until the fall of 1775. Thereafter, from the statements by Congress that the Continental Treasury was empty prior to authorizing the next issuance of bills, and from a rough tracking of the spending resolutions in the *JCC*, it appears that each new authorized amount was spent between its initial authorization and the next authorization of a new issuance of bills.[1] Thus, the cumulative flows reported in table C.1 are reasonably accurate from authorization date to authorization date.

While the flow of spending between authorized amounts is currently unknown, the range of that flow is depicted in figure C.1. Given that the public expected that a given authorized amount would be spent before

TABLE C.1 **Cumulative values of Continental dollars emitted and currently outstanding, 1775–80**

Procedural authorization dates	Date printed on the bill (emission no.)	Face value of new emission	Face value of cumulative emissions to date	Expected present value discounted at 6% of cumulative emissions to date using	
				Forecast 1	Forecast 2
				(Discount factor)	
July 29, 1775	May 10, 1775 (Emission no. 1)	$3,000,000[a]	$3,000,000	$2,091,900 (0.6973)	$2,091,900 (0.6973)
Dec. 26, 1775	Nov. 29, 1775 (Emission no. 2)	$3,000,000	$6,000,000	$3,862,200 (0.6437)	$3,862,200 (0.6437)
Feb. 21, 1776	Feb. 17, 1776 (Emission no. 3)	$3,937,220	$9,937,220	$5,685,084 (0.5721)	$5,680,115 (0.5716)
May 22, 1776	May 9, 1776 (Emission no. 4)	$5,000,000	$14,937,220	$7,540,309 (0.5048)	$7,525,371 (0.5038)
Aug. 13, 1776	July 22, 1776 (Emission no. 5)	$5,000,000	$19,937,220	$9,101,341 (0.4565)	$9,041,529 (0.4535)
Nov. 2, 1776	Nov. 2, 1776 (Emission no. 6)	$5,000,000	$24,937,220	$10,398,821 (0.4170)	$10,338,971 (0.4146)
Feb. 26, 1777	Feb. 26, 1777 (Emission no. 7)	$5,000,000	$29,937,220	$11,531,817 (0.3852)	$11,504,874 (0.3843)
May 22, 1777	May 20, 1777 (Emission no. 8)	$5,000,000	$34,937,220	$4,685,081 (0.1341)	$3,357,467 (0.0961)
Aug. 15, 1777	"	$1,000,000	$35,937,220	$4,891,056 (0.1361)	$3,503,879 (0.0975)

Nov. 7, 1777	"	$1,000,000	$36,937,220	$5,101,030 (0.1381)	$3,653,091 (0.0989)
Dec. 3, 1777	"	$1,000,000	$37,937,220	$5,265,686 (0.1388)	$3,770,960 (0.0994)
Jan. 8, 1778	"	$1,000,000	$38,937,220	$5,431,742 (0.1395)	$3,889,828 (0.0999)
Jan. 22, 1778	"	$2,000,000	$40,937,220	$5,710,742 (0.1395)	$4,089,628 (0.0999)
Feb. 16, 1778	"	$2,000,000	$42,937,220	$6,019,798 (0.1402)	$4,315,191 (0.1005)
Mar. 5, 1778	"	$2,000,000	$44,937,220	$6,336,148 (0.1410)	$4,538,659 (0.1010)
Apr. 4, 1778	"	$1,000,000	$45,937,220	$6,509,304 (0.1417)	$4,662,628 (0.1015)
Apr. 11, 1778 (Emission no. 9)		$5,000,000	$50,937,220	$7,217,801 (0.1417)	$5,170,128 (0.1015)
May 20, 1777 (Emission no. 8)		$500,000	$51,437,220	$7,288,651 (0.1417)	$5,220,878 (0.1015)
Apr. 11, 1778 (Emission no. 9)		$5,000,000	$56,437,220	$8,036,660 (0.1424)	$5,756,596 (0.1020)
June 20, 1778	"	$5,000,000	$61,437,220	$8,791,666 (0.1431)	$6,297,315 (0.1025)
July 30, 1778	"	$5,000,000	$66,437,220	$9,553,672 (0.1438)	$6,843,034 (0.1030)
Sept. 5, 1778	"	$5,000,000	$71,437,220	$10,379,828 (0.1453)	$7,436,615 (0.1041)

continues

TABLE C.1 (*continued*)

Procedural authorization dates	Date printed on the bill (emission no.)	Face value of new emission	Face value of cumulative emissions to date	Expected present value discounted at 6% of cumulative emissions to date using		
				Forecast 1	Forecast 2	Jan. 2, 1779, redemption resolution[b]
				(Discount factor)		
Sept. 26, 1778	Sept. 26, 1778 (Emission no. 10)	$10,000,100	$81,437,320	$11,832,843 (0.1453)	$8,477,625 (0.1041)	
Nov. 4, 1778	"	$10,000,100	$91,437,420	$13,413,870 (0.1467)	$9,610,073 (0.1051)	
Dec. 14, 1778	"	$10,000,100	$101,437,520	$14,941,747 (0.1473)	$10,711,802 (0.1056)	
				Counterfactual as if the Jan. 2, 1779, redemption rules were nonoperative $		Jan. 2, 1779, redemption resolution[b] $
Jan. 2, 1779	Jan. 14, 1779 (Emission no. 11)	$8,500,395	$109,937,915	16,270,811 (0.1480)	11,664,413 (0.1061)	68,579,270 (0.6238)
Feb. 3, 1779	Sept. 26, 1778 (Emission no. 10)	$5,000,160	$114,938,075	17,079,798 (0.1486)	12,263,893 (0.1067)	71,698,372 (0.6238)
Feb. 19, 1779	"	$5,000,160	$119,938,235	17,822,822 (0.1486)	12,797,410 (0.1067)	74,817,471 (0.6328)
Apr. 1, 1779	"	$5,000,160	$124,938,395	18,728,265 (0.1499)	13,468,359 (0.1078)	77,936,571 (0.6238)

May 5, 1779	"	$10,000,100	$134,938,495	20,321,737 (0.1506)	14,613,839 (0.1083)	84,174,633 (0.6238)
June 4, 1779	"	$10,000,100	$144,938,595	21,914,716 (0.1512)	15,783,813 (0.1089)	90,412,696 (0.6238)
July 17, 1779	Jan. 14, 1779 (Emission no. 11)	$5,000,180	$149,938,775	22,760,706 (0.1518)	16,403,302 (0.1094)	93,546,802 (0.6239)
July 17, 1779	Sept. 26, 1778 (Emission no. 10)	$10,000,100	$159,938,875	24,278,721 (0.1518)	17,497,313 (0.1094)	99,785,864 (0.6239)
Sept. 17, 1779	Jan. 14, 1779 (Emission no. 11)	$15,000,260	$174,939,135	26,783,182 (0.1531)	19,330,774 (0.1105)	109,144,526 (0.6239)
Oct. 14, 1779	"	$5,000,180	$179,939,315	27,674,667 (0.1538)	19,991,258 (0.1111)	112,264,139 (0.6239)
Nov. 17, 1779	"	$10,050,540	$189,989,855	29,334,434 (0.1544)	21,202,868 (0.1116)	118,553,670 (0.6240)
Nov. 29, 1779	"	$10,000,140	$199,980,995[b]	30,878,455 (0.1544)	22,318,883 (0.1116)	124,793,757 (0.6240)

Sources: Derived from tables 1.1 and 10.1; and appendix A.

Notes: After emission no. 7 the perfect-foresight assumption is used for forecasts 1 and 2; see table 10.1.

[a] See note d of table 1.1.

[b] These values assume that redemption could and would be executed as legislated. Given that this plan was not fiscally credible, these values are presented for comparative purposes only. See the text for further discussion.

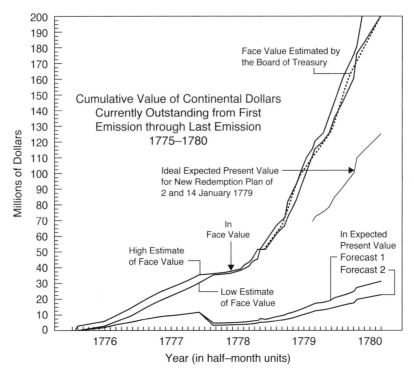

FIGURE C.1. Cumulative value of Continental dollars emitted and currently outstanding from first emission to last, 1775–80

Sources: See table C.1; see also *Early American imprints* (1983, microfiche S 269, nos. 16634, 16635).

the next new amount was authorized, once Congress told the public the amount being currently authorized, the public would know the amount that would be soon spent. Therefore, because all bills from an authorization were put into circulation by the next amount authorized, a low estimate of the amount currently in circulation is the cumulative amount of past authorizations on the date Congress authorized the next new amount to be issued. A high estimate is the cumulative amount of past authorizations on the date Congress authorized the next new amount to be issued, inclusive of that new amount. Figure C.1 presents these high and low estimates for the cumulative face value in circulation over time. Up to mid-1777 the gap between the high and low estimate is about $3 million to $5 million. Between mid-1777 and mid-1778 the gap is $1 million to $3 million. After mid-1778 the gap grows to between $10 million and $20 million.

On December 3, 1779, the Board of Treasury reported the cumulative face value amount in circulation each day from June 1, 1778, through February 28, 1779, and each day from June 1, 1779, through February 28, 1780. While the Board claimed these were the actual amounts in circulation, they must have been estimates, because the incremental increase from day to day is too consistently the same number to capture the actual day-to-day flow of spending that put Continental dollars into circulation. The Board's report assumes that Continental dollar emissions would total $200 million in face value, with that entire sum still in circulation by the end of February 1780 (see appendix A).

Figure C.1 shows the Board's estimate. Except for a brief period in late 1779, the Board's estimate tracks the low estimate shown in figure C.1 for the cumulative face value in circulation. This indicates that a good estimate of the cumulative face value amount in circulation on any date would be to take the cumulative amount authorized so far in table C.1 and place that amount on the date listed for the next authorized sum. The Board's estimate also indicates that they expected that the last sums authorized, those in late November 1779 amounting to $20 million in face value, would take three months to put into circulation.

The trajectory of the cumulative face-value sums in circulation was approximately linear from August 1775 through mid-1777, with $1,455,718 added on average each month. In August–December 1777 this trajectory briefly flattened out, with only $600,000 added on average each month. This flattening of the trajectory coincided with the adoption of legal-tender laws. Thereafter, the trajectory changed to a steeper linear path, with $6,232,799 added on average each month from January 1778 through February 1780.

Figure C.1 also shows the cumulative amount in circulation in present value. The time path of these cumulative flows uses the low-estimate method, placing each sum presented in table C.1 at the next authorization date and the last sum on February 28, 1780. From August 1775 through March 1777, the cumulative present value in circulation, while rising at a slower pace than the cumulative face value, was roughly half that of the cumulative face value. The trajectories of the cumulative face value and the cumulative present value parted ways around March 1777. This coincided with the adoption of legal-tender laws and illustrates the dramatic effect those laws had on the cumulative present value of Continental dollars compared with their cumulative face value. From March to June 1777, cumulative present values collapsed 30 to 40 percent, while cumulative face values continued to grow. Cumulative present values did not recover to their March 1777 level until between October 1778 and January 1779.

The temporary gain in the purchasing power of new emissions gained by Congress with the adoption of legal-tender laws (see fig. 10.2) coincided with the deceleration in the growth of the cumulative face value in circulation from March 1777 to January 1778. This gain came at the cost not only of the collapse in the present value of the cumulative sums in the hands of the public, but of accelerating the eventual collapse of the Continental dollar financing system. Figure C.1 shows that beginning in 1778 the growth in cumulative face value accelerated relative to the growth in cumulative present values. The relatively constant widening gap between their trajectories before March 1777 became an accelerating widening gap. It took an ever-increasing amount of face-value emissions to generate a given increase in cumulative present values. This widening gap meant that after January 1778 the Continental dollar financial system would be unsustainable in the long run—a long run that was likely not that far off.

Table C.1 and figure C.1 also illustrate the idealized effort by Congress on January 2, 1779, to reflate present values through the adoption of a new redemption structure. If that structure had been credible, it would have pushed the cumulative present value to approximately 62 percent of the cumulative face value. In addition, the trajectory of this cumulative present value through 1779 would have been only slightly less than that for the cumulative face value—roughly $5 million versus $8 million added on average per month, respectively. Had this redemption plan worked, it would have made the Continental dollar financial system sustainable for much longer. Figure C.1 helps make sense of what Congress was attempting to do in 1779 compared with the continue-as-before alternative. Their failure to understand that this change was not fiscally credible doomed their effort (see table 10.1).

The Redemption of Continental Dollars by Individual States over Time

TABLE D.1 **Continental dollars paid by each state from 1779 through 1790 to the federal government as part of their tax revenues and currency swaps owed to Congress that were examined, counted, and then burned by the US Treasury (face value in nominal dollars)**

Year Month Day	Reported by Joseph Nourse, Registrar of the US Treasury, Jan. 14, 1786		Reported by Alexander Hamilton, Secretary of the US Treasury, May 11, 1790	
	Received From	Amount	Received From	Amount
1779				
May	Delaware state treasurer	224,524		
	Paymaster-general's dept.	233,098		
	Pennsylvania state treasurer	166,000		
June	New York—loan office	1,841,856		
	New Jersey—loan office	768,466		
	Pennsylvania—loan office	73,600		
	Delaware state treasurer	150,003		
	Delaware—loan office	157,894		
	Paymaster-general's dept.	24,851		
	Board of War	83,233		
July	Rhode Island—loan office	746,372		
	Rhode Island state treasurer	195,018		
	New Jersey—loan office	483,444		
	Pennsylvania—loan office	537,401		
Sept.	Massachusetts—loan office	6,635,550		
	Paymaster-general's dept.	15,335		
Oct.	New Jersey—loan office	554,505		
Nov.	New York—loan office	5,130		
Dec.	Pennsylvania—loan office	1,397,002		
	Virginia—loan office	4,848,100		

continues

Year Month Day	Reported by Joseph Nourse, Registrar of the US Treasury, Jan. 14, 1786		Reported by Alexander Hamilton, Secretary of the US Treasury, May 11, 1790	
	Received From	Amount	Received From	Amount
1780				
Jan.	Connecticut—loan office	1,592,159		
	Connecticut state treasurer	1,367,537		
Feb.	Pennsylvania—loan office	6,220,313		
Mar.	Rhode Island state treasurer	8,238		
	Pennsylvania—loan office	1,445,914		
	Delaware—loan office	3,899		
	South Carolina—loan office	1,814,471		
June	New Hampshire state treasurer	200,000		
	New Hampshire—loan office	501,522		
	Paymaster-general's Dept	8,893		
	Managers of the US lottery	184,513		
Nov.	New Jersey—loan office	949,430		
	Maryland—loan office	115,117		
25			New Jersey	949,430
25			Maryland	115,117
Dec.	New Jersey—loan office	237,840		
23			New Jersey	237,840
1781				
Jan.	New York—loan office	599,396		
1			New York	599,396
Feb.	Pennsylvania—loan office	1,400,527		
13			Pennsylvania	1,400,527
Mar.	New Jersey—loan office	631,523		
23			New Jersey	631,523
Apr.	Pennsylvania—Loan office	2,599,987		
	Virginia—Loan office	105,433*		
	Virginia—Loan office	802,717		
3			Pennsylvania	2,599,987
17			Virginia	802,717
May	Pennsylvania—Loan office	1,999,995		
	Virginia—loan office	5,785,555		
	New Jersey—loan office	712,824		
15			Pennsylvania	1,999,995
29			Virginia	5,785,555
30			New Jersey	712,824
June	New Hampshire—loan office	2,299,769		
	Massachusetts—loan office	12,984,687[a]		
11			New Hampshire	2,299,769
11			Massachusetts	12,984,001[a]
July	Massachusetts—loan office	46,959*		
	Massachusetts state treasurer	821,152*		
Aug.	New Jersey—loan office	1,456,417		
	Pennsylvania—loan office	28,323*		
	Pennsylvania—loan office	4,402,413		
2			New Jersey	1,456,417
4			Pennsylvania	4,402,413
Oct.	New Jersey—loan office	1,139,180		
6			New Jersey	1,139,181

Year Month Day	Reported by Joseph Nourse, Registrar of the US Treasury, Jan. 14, 1786		Reported by Alexander Hamilton, Secretary of the US Treasury, May 11, 1790	
	Received From	Amount	Received From	Amount
Nov.	Massachusetts—loan office	16,876,618		
6			Massachusetts	16,876,618
1782				
Jan.	Delaware—loan office	2,246,683		
	New York—loan office	1,373,811		
	New York—loan office	3,817*		
	South Carolina—loan office	221,387*		
7			Delaware	2,210,000
30			New York	1,373,811
Feb.	New Jersey—loan office	1,207,111		
23			New Jersey	1,207,111
May	Pennsylvania—loan office	3,367,670		
	Delaware—loan office	243,127		
30			Pennsylvania	3,367,670
June	Pennsylvania—loan office	2,805,318		
3			Pennsylvania	2,805,318
July	Pennsylvania—loan office	5,009,343		
30			Pennsylvania	5,009,343
Aug.	Pennsylvania—loan office	1,599,758		
	Massachusetts—loan office	38,725[b]		
7			Pennsylvania	1,599,758
31			Massachusetts	387[b]
Sept.				
18			New Hampshire	2,900,231[c]
Nov.	Pennsylvania—loan office	2,954,918		
22			Pennsylvania	2,954,918
Dec.	Pennsylvania—loan office	1,000,391		
	Pennsylvania—loan office	77,623		
6			Pennsylvania	1,000,391
19			Pennsylvania	77,623
1783				
Jan.	Pennsylvania—loan office	47,535		
	Pennsylvania—loan office	331,369		
20			Pennsylvania	47,535
29			Pennsylvania	331,369
Feb.	New Jersey—loan office	392,833		
21			New Jersey	392,833
July	New Hampshire State Commissioner	29,231[c]		
1784	None		None	
1785	None		None	
1786				
June				
9			New York	2,758,217
July				
2			New York	848,776
25			Maryland	827,490
Aug.				
2			New York	2,151,478

continues

Year Month Day	Reported by Joseph Nourse, Registrar of the US Treasury, Jan. 14, 1786		Reported by Alexander Hamilton, Secretary of the US Treasury, May 11, 1790	
	Received From	Amount	Received From	Amount
22			Maryland	430,969
22			Maryland	473,779
Sept.				
5			Maryland	151,417
12			Maryland	26,650
16			Maryland	132,929
16			Virginia	2,880,720
Nov.				
1			Virginia	1,523,224
9			Maryland	62,481
Dec.				
7			Connecticut	8,102,425
13			Maryland	40,072
29			Maryland	21,750
1787				
Jan.				
22			Maryland	89,905
July				
5			Virginia	2,048,160
Aug.				
13			Rhode Island	2,593,353
17			New Jersey	99,516
Nov.				
13			Pennsylvania	857,827
1788				
Mar.				
28			New York	172,6277
Aug.				
25			Connecticut	1,049,060
Sept.				
5			Maryland	6,780,026
1789				
Mar.				
18			North Carolina	5,066,861
Separate subtotals		$111,435,353[d]		$119,462,369
Combined total (minus overlap)			$153,526,347	

Continental dollars still outstanding and unredeemed as of 1790:
If currency emitted for currency swaps and the destruction of said swapped currency are included in the totals: (241,500,000 − 153,526,347) = $87,973,653[e]
If only net new emissions (minus currency swaps) and their removal are considered: (199,989,995 − 119,462,369) = $80,527,626

Sources: Derived from Joseph Nourse, Registrar's Office, Board of Treasury, January 14, 1786, report as recorded in the *JCC* (30:22–25); and Alexander Hamilton's May 11, 1790, report to Congress, "Schedule E. *Statement of the sums, in the old continental emissions, paid by the following States into the treasury of the United States, on account of their several quotas of the requisitions of Congress, of March 18, 1780*" (*American state papers* 1832, Class III, Finance, 1:58–59; Elliot 1843: 73–76; US Congress 1834, 2:1544, 1566). Both sources record no payments made by Georgia and South Carolina, and no payments by any states made for the years 1784 and 1785.

Notes:

* Identified by Michael Hillegas, Continental Treasurer, in May of 1782 as being bills of the May 20, 1777, and April 11, 1778, emissions remitted as part of the authorized currency exchange for new bills that occurred between November 25, 1780, and February 23, 1782 (Ferguson et al. 1973–99, 5:139).

[a] These appear to be the same entry. Which is correct and which is a typo is unclear.

[b] These appear to be the same entry. Which is correct and which is a typo is unclear.

[c] These might be the same entry, though that is not entirely clear. If they are, which is correct and which is a typo is not clear. For the purpose of calculating the "Grand combined total (minus overlap)" they were counted as independent and separate entries.

[d] Nourse indicated that his numbers were neither comprehensive nor complete. As such, they represent a lower boundary of what was actually removed and destroyed in this period.

[e] Because the number in note d above is a lower boundary, this value is biased high.

TABLE D.2 **1779 quotas and compliance fulfillment for remitting Continental dollars by state by year**

| Year | Jan. 2, 1779, quota totals | New Hampshire | | | Massachusetts | | |
| | | 2.60% of quota total [2.67%][a] | % of quota filled | | 14.95% of quota total [15.33%] | % of quota filled | |
			Yearly	Cumulative to date		Yearly	Cumulative to date
1779	$15,000,000	$390,000	0.00%	0.00%	$2,242,500	0.00%	0.00%
1780	10,277,778	267,222	0.00	0.00	1,536,528	0.00	0.00
1781	10,277,778	267,222	860.62	248.77	1,536,528	1,943.38	561.76
1782	10,277,778	267,222	1,085.33	436.36	1,536,528	0.03	435.79
1783	10,277,778	267,222	0.00	356.44	1,536,528	0.00	355.97
1784	10,277,778	267,222	0.00	301.26	1,536,528	0.00	300.86
1785	10,277,778	267,222	0.00	260.87	1,536,528	0.00	260.53
1786	10,277,778	267,222	0.00	230.03	1,536,528	0.00	229.73
1787	10,277,778	267,222	0.00	205.71	1,536,528	0.00	205.45
1788	10,277,778	267,222	0.00	186.05	1,536,528	0.00	185.80
1789	10,277,778	267,222	0.00	169.81	1,536,528	0.00	169.59
1790	10,277,778	267,222	0.00	156.18	1,536,528	0.00	155.98
1791	10,277,778	267,222	0.00	144.58	1,536,528	0.00	144.39
1792	10,277,778	267,222	0.00	134.58	1,536,528	0.00	134.40
1793	10,277,778	267,222	0.00	125.87	1,536,528	0.00	125.71
1794	10,277,778	267,222	0.00	118.23	1,536,528	0.00	118.07
1795	10,277,778	267,222	0.00	111.46	1,536,528	0.00	111.31
1796	10,277,778	267,222	0.00	105.42	1,536,528	0.00	105.28
1797	10,277,778	267,222	0.00	100.00	1,536,528	0.00	99.87
Total[b]	$200,000,000	$5,200,000	100.00%	100.00%	$29,900,000	99.87%	99.87%

TABLE D.2 — (*continued*)

| | Rhode Island | | Connecticut | | | New York | | |
| | % of quota filled | | | % of quota filled | | | % of quota filled | |
1.30% of quota total [1.33%]	Yearly	Cumulative to date	11.05% of quota total [11.33%]	Yearly	Cumulative to date	4.88% of quota total [5.00%]	Yearly	Cumulative to date
$195,000	0.00%	0.00%	$1,657,500	0.00%	0.00%	$732,000	0.00%	0.00%
133,611	0.00	0.00	1,135,694	0.00	0.00	501,555	0.00	0.00
133,611	0.00	0.00	1,135,694	0.00	0.00	501,555	119.51	34.55
133,611	0.00	0.00	1,135,694	0.00	0.00	501,555	273.91	88.22
133,611	0.00	0.00	1,135,694	0.00	0.00	501,555	0.00	72.06
133,611	0.00	0.00	1,135,694	0.00	0.00	501,555	0.00	60.91
133,611	0.00	0.00	1,135,694	0.00	0.00	501,555	0.00	52.74
133,611	0.00	0.00	1,135,694	0.00	0.00	501,555	1,148.32	182.25
133,611	1,950.97	205.19	1,135,694	713.43	84.34	501,555	0.00	162.98
133,611	0.00	185.57	1,135,694	0.00	75.42	501,555	34.43	150.69
133,611	0.00	169.38	1,135,694	92.37	77.04	501,555	0.00	137.54
133,611	0.00	155.78	1,135,694	0.00	70.32	501,555	0.00	126.50
133,611	0.00	144.21	1,135,694	0.00	64.67	501,555	0.00	117.10
133,611	0.00	134.24	1,135,694	0.00	59.87	501,555	0.00	109.01
133,611	0.00	125.55	1,135,694	0.00	55.73	501,555	0.00	101.95
133,611	0.00	117.92	1,135,694	0.00	52.12	501,555	0.00	95.76
133,611	0.00	111.17	1,135,694	0.00	48.96	501,555	0.00	90.28
133,611	0.00	105.15	1,135,694	0.00	46.15	501,555	0.00	85.39
133,611	0.00	99.74	1,135,694	0.00	43.65	501,555	0.00	81.08
$2,600,000		99.74%	$22,100,000		41.41%	$9,750,000		81.08%

continues

TABLE D.2 — (*continued*)

5.85% of quota total [6.00%]	New Jersey % of quota filled		Pennsylvania 14.95% of quota total [15.33%]	Pennsylvania % of quota filled		Delaware 1.11% of quota total [1.13%]	Delaware % of quota filled	
	Yearly	Cumulative to date		Yearly	Cumulative to date		Yearly	Cumulative to date
$877,500	0.00%	0.00%	$2,242,500	0.00%	0.00%	$166,500	0.00%	0.00%
601,250	197.47	80.29	1,536,528	0.00	0.00	114,083	0.00	0.00
601,250	655.29	246.50	1,536,528	677.04	195.71	114,083	0.00	0.00
601,250	200.77	236.25	1,536,528	1,904.35	397.22	114,083	1,937.19	434.40
601,250	65.34	204.94	1,536,528	24.66	328.98	114,083	0.00	354.83
601,250	0.00	173.21	1,536,528	0.00	278.05	114,083	0.00	299.90
601,250	0.00	149.99	1,536,528	0.00	240.78	114,083	0.00	259.70
601,250	0.00	132.26	1,536,528	0.00	212.31	114,083	0.00	229.00
601,250	16.55	120.03	1,536,528	55.83	195.77	114,083	0.00	204.79
601,250	0.00	108.55	1,536,528	0.00	177.05	114,083	0.00	185.21
601,250	0.00	99.08	1,536,528	0.00	161.60	114,083	0.00	169.05
601,250	0.00	91.13	1,536,528	0.00	148.63	114,083	0.00	155.48
601,250	0.00	84.36	1,536,528	0.00	137.59	114,083	0.00	143.93
601,250	0.00	78.52	1,536,528	0.00	128.07	114,083	0.00	133.97
601,250	0.00	73.44	1,536,528	0.00	119.79	114,083	0.00	125.31
601,250	0.00	68.98	1,536,528	0.00	112.51	114,083	0.00	117.69
601,250	0.00	65.03	1,536,528	0.00	106.07	114,083	0.00	110.95
601,250	0.00	61.51	1,536,528	0.00	100.32	114,083	0.00	104.94
601,250	0.00	58.35	1,536,528	0.00	95.17	114,083	0.00	100.00
$11,700,000		58.35%	$29,900,000		95.17%	$2,210,000		100.00%

TABLE D.2 — (*continued*)

	Maryland			Virginia			North Carolina	
		% of quota filled			% of quota filled			% of quota filled
10.27% of quota total [10.53%]	Yearly	Cumulative to date	16.25% of quota total [16.67%]	Yearly	Cumulative to date	6.50% of quota total [6.67%]	Yearly	Cumulative to date
$1,540,500	0.00%	0.00%	$2,437,500	0.00%	0.00%	$975,000	0.00%	0.00%
1,055,528	10.91	4.43	1,670,139	0.00	0.00	668,056	0.00	0.00
1,055,528	0.00	3.15	1,670,139	395.47	114.03	668,056	0.00	0.00
1,055,528	0.00	2.45	1,670,139	0.00	88.46	668,056	0.00	0.00
1,055,528	0.00	2.00	1,670,139	0.00	72.26	668,056	0.00	0.00
1,055,528	0.00	1.69	1,670,139	0.00	61.07	668,066	0.00	0.00
1,055,528	0.00	1.46	1,670,139	0.00	52.88	668,056	0.00	0.00
1,055,528	205.35	25.56	1,670,139	263.29	77.80	668,056	0.00	0.00
1,055,528	8.52	23.76	1,670,139	122.63	82.54	668,056	0.00	0.00
1,055,528	642.34	82.90	1,670,139	0.00	74.65	668,056	0.00	0.00
1,055,528	0.00	75.67	1,670,139	0.00	68.14	668,056	758.45	66.19
1,055,528	0.00	69.59	1,670,139	0.00	62.67	668,056	0.00	60.87
1,055,528	0.00	64.42	1,670,139	0.00	58.01	668,056	0.00	56.35
1,055,528	0.00	59.97	1,670,139	0.00	54.00	668,056	0.00	52.45
1,055,528	0.00	56.09	1,670,139	0.00	50.51	668,056	0.00	49.06
1,055,528	0.00	52.68	1,670,139	0.00	47.44	668,056	0.00	46.08
1,055,528	0.00	49.66	1,670,139	0.00	44.72	668,056	0.00	43.44
1,055,528	0.00	46.97	1,670,139	0.00	42.30	668,056	0.00	41.09
1,055,528	0.00	44.45	1,670,139	0.00	40.12	668,056	0.00	38.98
$20,540,000		44.56%	$32,500,000		40.12%	$13,000,000		38.98%

continues

TABLE D.2 — (*continued*)

	South Carolina			Georgia				Row (yearly) totals	
		% of quota filled			% of quota filled			% of quota filled	
7.80% of quota total [8.00%]	2.50% of quota total [0.00%]	Yearly	Cumulative to date		Yearly	Cumulative to date	Total remittances	Yearly	Cumulative to date
$1,170,000	0.00%	0.00%	0.00%	$375,000	0.00%	0.00%	$0	0.00%	0.00%
801,667	0.00	0.00	256,944	0.00	0.00	1,302,387	12.67	5.15
801,667	0.00	0.00	256,944	0.00	0.00	53,609,923	521.61	154.44
801,667	0.00	0.00	256,944	0.00	0.00	24,506,561	238.44	173.28
801,667	0.00	0.00	256,944	0.00.	0.00	771,737	7.51	142.91
801,667	0.00	0.00	256,944	0.00.	0.00	0	0.00	120.79
801,667	0.00	0.00	256,944	0.00	0.00	0	0.00	104.60
801,667	0.00	0.00	256,944	0.00	0.00	20,433,377	198.81	115.73
801,667	0.00	0.00	256,944	0.00	0.00	5,688,761	55.35	109.35
801,667	0.00	0.00	256,944	0.00	0.00	8,001,763	77.85	106.34
801,667	0.00	0.00	256,944	0.00	0.00	5,066,860	49.30	101.43
801,667	0.00	0.00	256,944	0.00	0.00	0	0.00	93.29
801,667	0.00	0.00	256,944	0.00.	0.00	0	0.00	86.36
801,667	0.00	0.00	256,944	0.00.	0.00	0	0.00	80.39
801,667	0.00	0.00	256,944	0.00	0.00	0	0.00	75.19
801,667	0.00	0.00	256,944	0.00	0.00	0	0.00	70.62
801,667	0.00	0.00	256,944	0.00	0.00	0	0.00	66.67
801,667	0.00	0.00	256,944	0.00	0.00	0	0.00	62.97
801,667	0.00	0.00	256,944	0.00	0.00	0	0.00	59.73
$15,600,000	0.00%	0.00%	$5,000,000	0.00%	0.00%	$119,462,369	59.73%	59.73%

Sources: JCC (13:20–22, 64–65); table 1.1.

Notes: The congressional resolution of January 2, 1779, established remittance amounts through 1797. The August 4, 1790 Funding Act, however, removed state remittance obligations.

[a] The percentage in brackets by each state is the quota assigned on October 7, 1779, when Georgia was exempt because it had been invaded. Georgia, however, was required to eventually raise "its proportion"; see *JCC* (15:1150). The percentage used in the calculation, the unbracketed percentage by each state, assumes that Georgia was eventually assigned $5 million out of the total of $200 emitted as its share to remit. The percentage distribution was then recalculated among the states. The $5 million for Georgia comes from the residual between the amount emitted ($200 million) and the amount assigned to be remitted to all the other states except Georgia ($195 million) in 1781. See the accounting as stated by Charles Thomson, Secretary of Congress, on June 28, 1781, in Ferguson et al. (1973–99, 1:194).

[b] Congress thought it had issued a total of $200 million in net new emissions when in fact it had only issued $199,989,995. See table 1.1: appendix A. No adjustment is made here for this discrepancy.

Notes

Introduction

1. *Journals of the Continental Congress* (hereafter *JCC*) 1:13–124; 2:11–78.

2. Newman (2008); and Ratchford (1941: 34). All state and congressional currencies during the Revolution were comprised of paper monies only. Foreign (specie) coins, which were typically considered scarce, were the only coins in use in North America in this period. A small number of brass, pewter, and silver coins appear to have been minted, maybe in 1776, with the term "Continental Currency" on them. They were not authorized or issued by Congress or the Continental treasury. To date, there have been no clues discovered as to the origin, value, or usage of these coins, or who minted them (Mossman 1993: 150–52). They were few in number compared with the amounts of paper money issued. I thank Steve Hatfield for information on this issue.

3. For examples, see Atack and Passell (1994: 71–72); Baack (2001, 2008); Bezanson (1951); Bolles (1969); Breck (1843); Bronson (1865); Bullock (1895: 117–40; 1900: 60–78); Calomiris (1988); Ferguson (1961: 25–35); Edling (2014: 24–25); Gouge (1833, pt. 2:25–31); Hall and Sargent (2014: 151–56); Harlow (1929); Henretta, Brownlee, Brody, and Ware (1987: 190–92); Hepburn (1967: 13–19); Hughes and Cain (2011: 73); Myers (1970: 24–28); Newman (2008: 62–73, 481); Perkins (1994: 95–105); Phillips (1866); Ratchford (1941: 33–39); Studenski and Krooss (1963: 25–29); Sumner (1968, 1:35–103); Walton and Rockoff (2014: 114); Webster (1969); and https://en.wikipedia.org/wiki/Early_American_currency, accessed April 18, 2019. By contrast, I can find no intentional policy of inflation-tax finance by Congress during the Revolution. In fact, in the original sources, at least through 1779, I find an ongoing promise, expectation, effort, and commitment to redeem the Continental dollar as promised in the future at face value in specie.

4. I have not been able to locate the origin or first use of this phrase. I have not run across it in any documents or correspondence between 1775 and 1800. I suspect that the phrase is a product of later generations and not a sentiment of the times. The Online Etymology Dictionary indicates that the phrase's first use might date from as

late as 1851 (https://www.etymonline.com/search?q=not+worth+a+continental, accessed November 21, 2020). I thank Robert S. Wick for pointing me to this reference. If anyone knows the origin or first use of this phrase, I would appreciate their informing me.

5. On the quantity theory of money, see Bordo (1987); Fisher (1912); Grubb (2004, 2012b, 2019a); and chap. 3.

6. Oberg (1992–98, 29:354–56). From Franklin, letter to Samuel Cooper, April 22, 1779, France.

7. A fuller assessment of Federalist anti–government paper money rhetoric, along with its underlying motivation and why it was so vacuous, is provided in chap. 17. Note that Hamilton uses a favorite word found in Federalist anti–paper money rhetoric—"mischievous." This word does not mean anything, but its use frightens people.

8. See the recent work in macroeconomics on the fiscal structure of money and credit, briefly and ably summarized in Sargent (2012: 1–10).

Chapter One

1. See *JCC* (2:22; 3:342–43) and Newman (1997: 58–69; 2008: 62–73). Congressmen's private letters at the time reveal little (Bolles 1969, 1:27; and Smith 1976–94, 1–2).

2. Figures whose numbering begins with a roman numeral are in the introduction. Figures and tables whose numbering begins with an arabic numeral are in the chapter of that numeral, and those whose numbering begins with a letter are in the appendix of that letter (e.g., fig. 3.1 is in chap. 3, and table B.1 is in appendix B).

3. For examples, see the paper money issued by Massachusetts between 1690 and 1738; by Connecticut between 1709 and 1734, and in 1740 and 1746; New Hampshire between 1709 and 1741; by Rhode Island between 1710 and 1739; by New York between 1709 and 1724; New Jersey between 1709 and 1725, and from 1754 through 1763; by Pennsylvania in 1723, by Maryland after 1732, and by Virginia from 1755 through 1775 (Bush 1977: 63–66, 68–70, 109–13, 209–13; 1980: 220; Celia and Grubb 2016; Grubb 2015, 2016a, 2016c, 2017, 2018a, 2019b; and Newman 2008: 90–97, 102, 184–97, 224–31, 248–49, 270–76, 332, 372–81).

4. Smith (1976–94, 1:567). The same inference can be gleaned from the final redemption date attached to the paper money emitted by the state of Virginia in July 1775 and May 1776 to support that state's war spending. These notes were to be redeemed by January 1, 1784. Virginia appears to have been less sanguine about how short the war might be and when normal commerce would recommence. See Hening (1969, 9:69, 147) and Newman (2008: 444–46).

5. On congressional trade embargos, see *JCC* (1:41, 43, 51–53, 57, 62, 75–81, 113; 2:54, 67, 70–72, 78, 125, 184–85, 200–202, 235, 238–39, 247, 251–52; 3:268–69, 280, 292–94, 306, 308, 314–15, 317, 362–64, 389–90, 395–96, 408–9, 420–22, 429–30, 437–39, 455, 457, 460–61, 464–65, 476–85, 493–504; 4:62, 96, 172, 183, 257–59; 6:1071–72; 12:1165).

See also Buel (1998) and O'Shaughnessy (2000). For examples of comparable assessments expressed by leading American revolutionaries, such as Charles Carroll, Samuel Chase, Silas Deane, James Duane, Benjamin Franklin, John Jay, Thomas Jefferson, Henry Laurens, Richard Henry Lee, Francis Lewis, Robert R. Livingston, Jr., James Madison, Gouverneur Morris, John Rutledge, Joseph Warren, Oliver Wolcott, George Wythe, John Joachim Zubly, and the Board of Treasury, see Boyd (1953–55, 10:25); Hutchinson and Rachal (1962–65, 1:305); *JCC* (2:25; 3:477, 479–80, 498, 499, 501, 503; 6:1071–72; 12:1048–50; 13:20; 14:649; 15:1052, 1055–57; 16:262; 19:406–8); Oberg (1992–98, 34:229); Smith (1976–94, 7:462–63, 13:351–52); and Sparks (1832, 1:38).

6. Derived from Carter, Gartner, Haines, Olmstead, Sutch, and Wright (2006, 1:25; 5:652–53); McCusker (1978: 10); and Rabushka (2008: 796, 825, 862–63).

7. A similar outcome can be gleaned from the state of Virginia's emission of its own paper money to pay for its own war expenditures. Virginia set explicit redemption dates for each emission of its paper money. It pushed the redemption of each new emission forward in time, thus spreading the tax costs of redemption over time to keep per-year taxes from being too burdensome. The final redemption dates for each emission issued in 1775, 1776, 1777, and 1778 were rolled forward so they spanned from 1784 to 1790. See Hening (1969, 9:69, 147, 224, 288, 367, 457) and Newman (2008: 444–50). Of all the states, Virginia emitted the most state-issued paper money during the Revolution (Ratchford 1941: 33–34).

8. Smith (1976–94, 3:83). This November 23, 1775, committee was comprised of John Jay, Benjamin Franklin, Samuel Adams, Thomas Johnson, George Wythe, Edward Rutledge, and Thomas Jefferson (*JCC* 3:367–68).

Chapter Two

1. Derived from Bush (1980: 15–39, 65–74, 81–82, 104, 124–27, 168–72, 195–213, 219–51, 269–88, 303–4, 307–19, 323–24, 327–55, 373–409, 413–36, 451–88, 495–502, 517–31, 539–55, 559–78, 581–97, 621–56, 663–79; 1982: 5–13, 24–28, 73–89, 97–103, 107–11, 125–40, 153–54, 159–66, 191–98, 207–21, 273–76, 289–316, 385–88, 394, 427–31, 453–56, 505–8, 523–64; 1986: 25–29, 53–59, 64–68, 115–21, 171–77, 212–35, 250–51, 301–6, 327–32, 379–93, 419–22, 437–56); Fisher (1911: 289); Grubb (2015, 2016b, 2016c); Kemmerer (1940: 279; 1956: 136); Lester (1939: 122–34); Newman (2008: 247–59); Sherwood (1851: 147); and Wicker (1985: 874). Per capita amounts rely on population estimates in Carter, Gartner, Haines, Olmstead, Sutch, and Wright (2006, 5:652) with interpolated values between the reported decadal estimates. Currency conversions are taken from McCusker (1978: 8–10). In face value, 1 £$_{NJ}$ (New Jersey pound) = 2.9163 ounces of silver = 0.7533 £$_S$ (pounds sterling). This means that 1.3275 £$_{NJ}$ = 1£$_S$ = $4.5457 (Spanish silver dollars). Therefore, 1 £$_{NJ}$ = $3.4243. See the notes to fig. 2.1.

2. Recent analysis has shown that the paper monies of several colonies were also structured as zero-coupon, bond-type currencies and performed as such, possessing

only minor procedural differences from how colonial New Jersey pounds and Continental dollars were structurally designed and then performed. Thus, most Americans would have been familiar with the structural design of the Continental dollar, what that design was intended to accomplish, and how that paper money was expected to perform. See Celia and Grubb (2016); Cutsail and Grubb (2019, 2021); and Grubb (2015, 2016a, 2016b, 2016c, 2017, 2018a, 2019a, 2019b, 2020).

Chapter Three

1. *PCC* (microfilm 247, reel 179, item 161:339–41), "Samuel H. Parsons to John Jay (Camp in the Highland), 6 August 1779." I have reordered the clauses slightly to improve clarity. See also Puls (2008: 187) and Smith (1976–94, 13:388).

2. Derived from Fortescue (1910–30, 4, pt. 2:935); Grubb (2018b); *JCC* (2:89–90, 93–94, 209–10, 220–23; 3:322–23, 384, 417, 427; 11:539–43); *Pennsylvania Gazette* (August 14, 1776); Smith (1976–94, 3:588–89); Williamson (1796: 27); and http://foot guards.tripod.com/01ABOUT/01_payscale.htm, accessed January 30, 2013. Currency conversions are from McCusker (1978: 10).

3. By "outside money" I mean money that is used to clear international (trans-government-jurisdictional) debts arising from trans-jurisdictional transactions for both private and public trades. See also Ferguson (1983: 404–5). In the eighteenth century the outside money was specie in the form of gold and silver coins, bullion, and plate.

4. The simple quantity theory of money dominated American thinking in this era; see Bullock (1900: 65); Davis (1964, 1–4); *JCC* (9:954); and Sumner (1968, 1:43–44).

5. By "inside money" I mean money that does not readily cross government-jurisdictional borders because it is only that particular governmental jurisdiction (location) that is providing the legal and functional support for enforcing the recognition of that item as a money and its potential conversion to an equivalence in outside money.

6. Grubb (2016a: 147–224) and Hammond (1991: 3–67). Running a bank where the bank's reserves were an inside paper money rather than an outside money, such as specie coins, was unknown and untried in this era. Backing an inside paper money, such as banknotes, with another inside paper money as its reserves, such as federal government bonds, would not be tried in the United States before the National Banking Act of 1864.

Chapter Four

1. For congressional discussions about publishing their proceedings, see *JCC* (2:208; 3:263–64, 393, 427, 431) and Smith (1976–94, 1:503, 525–26, 695; 6:404; 13:383; 15:484).

2. See *JCC* (3:367–68, 424, 455; 4:49–50); *Pennsylvania Gazette* (January 17; April 17 and 24; June 19, 1776); and Smith (1976–94, 2:464).

3. See Cutsail and Grubb (2021); Grubb (2016a, 2016b, 2018a, 2020); and Smith (1976–94, 4:295, 424, 678).

Chapter Five

1. For examples, see Davis (1964, 1:384–85; 2:314, 318; 3:158–59, 182, 191, 196–98, 247, 430–31, 433, 440, 445, 454, 462, 471; 4:49, 179–80, 185, 223, 386, 398, 401 2); Grubb (2012b); Labaree (1966–70, 11:13–15, 14:35–36); Ricord (1892, 17:159); Smith (1937: 310–12).

2. See *JCC* (4:293–94, 381–83; 5:608, 724–28). The actual quotation is from *JCC* (4:382). This committee went beyond its mandate and proposed other resolutions that were incoherent and internally inconsistent.

3. Hammond (1889a: 293). The commissioners offer other observations not wholly consistent with this last observation.

4. Brookhiser (2003: 31–93); Grubb (2003: 1787–90; 2006: 54–64; 2007b: 41–50;); *JCC* (11:731, 779–87; 12:929–33); Smith (1976–94, 7:xviii; 8:xx; 9:xx; 10:xx; 11:xxi; 12:xx; 13:xx; 14:xxi); and Sparks (1832).

5. Barlow (2012: 73, 75). Gouverneur Morris's analysis of money involves alternatives that are inconsistent with the passage quoted here. Morris's statement here maps into the model of monetary value presented in chap. 9. For Morris, the money's value (MEV) depends on its "want," which is the transaction premium (TP); the "distance ... of payment," which is its asset present value (APV); and its "certainty ... of ... payment," which is its risk discount (RD). In other words, $MEV \equiv (APV - RD) + TP$ (see chap. 9).

6. Morris was referring to Congress's most recent resolutions of January 2 and 14, 1779, which set redemption of the Continental dollar to run to 1797 (see table 1.1).

7. Madison is referencing Congress's January 2 and 14, 1779, resolutions on the redemption of the Continental dollar (see table 1.1).

8. Hutchinson and Rachal (1962–65, 1:304–5, 308, 310). Madison's treatise on money was published in the *National Gazette*, December 19 and 22, 1791. I thank Alan Gibson for bringing Madison's treatise to my attention.

Chapter Six

1. A variant of this report is reproduced in, but not analyzed by, Carp (1984: 69) and Ferguson (1961: 28–29). The numbers reported are clearly the same as those in Knox (1790). A noted exception is Dougherty, who in his study (2001) makes excellent use of the Knox report.

Chapter Seven

1. In chapter 9 I show that legal-tender laws may have contributed to increasing the *TP* component of the money object's value. This would be, at best, only a minor contribution to total value, as it would not affect the non-money real-value portion (that is, the *APV*) of the money object. This is because embedded in the definition of money as a transaction-premium value is a trader's faith that subsequent traders will continue to see the object as a more convenient transacting medium than the next-best alternative. It is that expected ongoing convenience in transacting compared with using the next-best alternative that generated a willingness to pay for the money object over and above the money object's non-money real value when that object was a government-issued bill of credit. Legal-tender laws, and the designation by the government of which media could be used to pay taxes, contribute to that faith in an ongoing transacting convenience. Legal-tender laws did not force people to use the legal tender as a medium of exchange. It only legally sanctioned the nonacceptance of its use when offered to mediate an exchange.

2. See *Acts of the council and general assembly of New-Jersey* (1784: 157); Grubb (2012b); Hening (1969, 13:412–13); *JCC* (16:269); *Laws of the state of Delaware* (1797, 2:718–19); Smith (1976–94, 15:295; 17:87); and *Statutes at large of Pennsylvania* (1903–4, 10:204–5, 228–29, 247–49, 337–44).

3. See also Grubb (2012b) and Smith (1976–94, 11:136, 306–7).

Chapter Eight

1. Congress raised revenue by running several lotteries. Lotteries for raising public revenue were well-known in the colonial period. The public would buy lottery tickets using Continental dollars with given odds of winning prizes in Continental dollars. The prizes were less than the total value of tickets sold, thus yielding a net revenue to the government. The prizes in the cases listed in table 8.1 were to be covered with newly authorized loan office certificates.

2. Starting at $27 million loan office certificates outstanding in 1782, if no principal or interest were paid on that sum through 1789, then the accumulation of interest arrears at 6 percent per year would yield a total debt of about $40,598,017 in 1789. This estimate closely matches the estimate of $40,414,086 reported for this debt by Alexander Hamilton for 1789 (Syrett and Cooke 1962–72, 6:86; and Taylor 1950: 1–2). Nonredemption of loan office certificates after 1782 is consistent with the states' removal of the Continental dollar's legal-tender status, with Congress's redemption rule change to paying off Continental dollars at 40 to 1 in specie (see chap. 14), and with the states' nonredemption of Continental dollars between mid-1783 and mid-1786 (see table D.1). Given Congress's 40-to-1 rule change, holders of loan office certificates may have been inclined to not redeem them but continue to hold them

and collect interest arrears in the hope that the rule would be changed back to face-value redemption in specie equivalents in the near future.

3. See table 6.1, the November 22, 1777, column. For any of these loan amounts actually made to Congress, states were to receive a credit for the principal loaned plus 6 percent interest per annum accruing on the amount loaned. The credit states received on the principal loaned were not remittances of Continental dollars for the purpose of their final redemption and removal from circulation (see chap. 1). The states were still required ultimately to redeem these respent Continental dollars and cause them to be permanently removed from circulation by remitting them under the procedures that led to their being burned at the Continental Treasury (see chaps. 13 and 15).

Chapter Nine

1. Celia and Grubb (2016); Grubb (2012b, 2019b); Newman (2008); and Ratchford (1941: 34).

2. Conventional monetary models in the quantity-theoretic tradition too often just assume money—or, more precisely, assume that the opportunity cost of using the thing they call money—to execute transactions is infinite. No transactions can occur without using this money. In other words, a money's transaction premium over the next-best alternative for executing transactions is assumed to be large enough to anchor its exchange value given its quantity relative to the amount of real transactions in the economy. This view of money presumes that only a single money exists. The traditional story and quantity-theory-of-money explanations of the Continental dollar rest on these assumptions. However, if there are numerous near-perfect alternative monies in use, then the opportunity cost of using one particular money to execute transactions is no longer infinite, but instead may be near zero. Under such conditions, simple quantity-theoretic monetary models are no longer applicable. The Continental dollar might possess no transaction premium—that is, it might have a zero opportunity cost for executing current transactions—because numerous alternative monies existed that were as good. As such, the perspective offered here turns the assumption embedded in the conventional monetary models that underlay the traditional story on its head. Instead of assuming that the opportunity cost of using Continental dollars to execute transactions is infinite, it notes that it could be zero, and its size needs to be estimated rather than assumed. If near zero, then the value and performance of the Continental dollar will depend mostly on its structural design and linkage to real assets or other monies in the economy rather than just on its quantity in circulation.

3. For some historical economies, just assuming what is and what is not money may be sufficient for successful economic macro/monetary-modeling applications. For example, in the nineteenth- and early twentieth-century US economy, money seems obvious and easy to define and measure in a way that captures most domestic

transactions: money consisted of coins, banknotes, and bank accounts. See Friedman and Schwartz (1963) and Rockoff (1971).

4. Barter, and so a barter good, involves the exchange of real (non-money) value for real (non-money) value, whether contemporaneously or over time. The benchmark model in price theory is the Arrow-Debreu formalization of the Walrasian general equilibrium model. There is no money in this model. Goods trade for goods until their relative prices adjust in terms of what one good will trade for in terms of other goods so that all markets clear, thereby yielding a Pareto optimal outcome for society (Banerjee and Maskin 1996: 955–61, and Starr 2012: viii–35). I use the term "barter" to refer to such trades. See also Grubb (2012b).

5. Some assumptions must always be made to translate theory into specific empirical applications. While a range of values for TP and RD that yield a particular $(TP - RD)$ is mathematically possible, what is logically possible restricts that range. For example, suppose $(MEV - APV)$ is measured as equal to 1 and therefore $(TP$ $RD) = 1$. That outcome could be mathematically produced, for example, either by $TP = 1$ and $RD = 0$ or by $TP = 101$ and $RD = 100$. The latter possibility, however, is not logically possible. Transactions always have some time-flow dimension. If $RD = 100$ then the money "thing," namely the carrier of value, has evaporated and disappeared by the end of the transaction and so there is nothing, no valued object, to carry the TP value and so, by definition, TP cannot have a positive value. Second, TP is measured in opportunity cost terms. Thus, for any given time-location transaction there can only be one money "thing" that has a $TP > 0$. You cannot have two different money "things" with $TP > 0$. Thus, in the above example you cannot have two different money "things" with each one having an $(TP - RD) = 1$ caused by $TP = 4$ and $RD = 3$ for one money "thing" and $TP = 1$ and $RD = 0$ for the other money "thing." This possibility is ruled out by the opportunity cost construction of TP. Taken to the limit, this logic yields the assumptions I use. Those assumptions also mean that positive measures of TP under my assumptions are the lowest TP possible, i.e., are biased low, in terms of the "moneyness" value attached to that money "thing" in question.

6. See Celia and Grubb (2016); Cutsail and Grubb (2021); and Grubb (2016a, 2016b, 2018a, 2019a, 2019b, 2020).

7. For 6 percent being the typical rate mentioned during the revolutionary period, see Barlow (2012: 110, 125, 128); Elliot (1843); Homer and Sylla (1991: 274–313); Hutchinson and Rachal (1962–65, 1:308); *JCC* (2:25–26; 6:1037; 7:102–3, 158, 168; 8:725–26; 9:955, 989; 10:59; 11:416; 12:929–30, 932, 1074, 1256; 13:112, 141, 146–47, 441, 497; 14:717, 720, 731–32, 783, 820, 901; 15:1147, 1197, 1210, 1225, 1245–46, 1288, 1319, 1405; 16:264–65, 288; 17:464, 568, 804; 18:1017; 19:6, 167; 21:903; 23:831; 24:39; 26:32; 27:395–96); Ferguson et al. (1973–99, 7:547); *Pennsylvania Gazette* (April 30; May 21 and 28; June 25; July 2, 16, and 23, 1777); Puls (2008: 181); and Smith (1976–94, 4:295; 6:117–18, 212–13, 228–29, 238–39, 245, 252, 259–62, 270, 277, 295, 346, 368, 372, 386, 400–401, 404; 7:524, 581, 617, 623, 635, 642–43; 8:25; 10:205; 11:94, 137–38, 361; 13:132, 604–5; 14:51, 463, 500; 15:377, 396; 16:307–8, 490, 531; 17:365; 19:139; 21:467). On 6 percent being the typical interest rate in mid-eighteenth-century America, see Brock (1975: 260,

328, 332, 435, 462); Davis (1964, 1:326; 2:38, 68, 83, 99–100, 315, 321; 3:168; 4); Grubb (2016a: 163–64); and Nettels (1934: 267). On the rate the US government borrowed at in the 1790s, see *Laws of the United States* (1896 1:15, 18, 20–22, 24, 33, 35–36, 40).

Chapter Ten

1. Derived from Fortescue (1910–30, 4, pt. 2:935); *JCC* (2:89–90, 93–94, 209–10, 220–23; 3:322–23, 384, 417, 427; 11:539–43); *Pennsylvania Gazette* (August 14, 1776); Smith (1976–94, 3:588–89); Williamson (1796: 27); and http://footguards.tripod.com /01ABOUT/01_payscale.htm, accessed January 30, 2013. Currency conversions are from McCusker (1978: 10). Relative to privates' pay, the pay of upper ranks increased less in the American than in the British army, so comparisons by any rank above private are less informative.

2. See chap. 6; *JCC* (15:1335; 16:344; 19:413); Puls (2008: 174–76, 181); and Smith (1976–94, 9:326, 691; 13:139, 296, 414; 15:24, 29, 31, 56).

3. *JCC* (4:293–94, 380–83; 5:608, 724–28; 7:35–36).

4. See Cushing (1981: 599–602); Hening (1969, 9:297–98); *JCC* (4:294, 381–83; 5: 608, 724–28; 7:35–37); Smith (1976–94, 6:261); and *Statutes at large of Pennsylvania* (1903–4, 9:34–40). When a state made the Continental dollar a legal tender within its jurisdiction, this meant that state-imposed fees and taxes could now be paid in Continental dollars at a legally set equivalence to that state's paper money. This may have been an effort to add some current positive transaction premium to the Continental dollar. Given that states did not remit Continental dollars to the Continental Treasury until November 1779, state taxes paid in Continental dollars under the auspices of their being a legal tender did not materially affect the redemption of Continental dollars ahead of that legislatively scheduled and prudently forecast; see appendix D and Grubb (2012a: 156–60, 170).

5. *JCC* (7:136–38). Congress did not adopt this part of the committee's recommendation. The committee's report was written by Roger Sherman. See also Smith (1976–94, 9:491–92, 632).

6. See also the *Pennsylvania Gazette* (February 10 and 17, and April 7 and 14, 1779).

7. See *JCC* (8:453; 14:719, 728, 730, 732, 783, 901, 1013–14; 15:1019, 1053, 1171, 1324); O'Shaughnessy (2013); and Smith (1976–94, 11:487–88; 12:500; 25:641).

8. The example is derived from tables 1.1 and 10.1. For the rest, see appendix C; *JCC* (14:1013; 15:1019, 1053, 1171, 1324); and Smith (1976–94, 11:487–90).

9. See Smith (1976–94, 6:602, 606; 7:21, 24, 172, 462; 8:35, 374; 9:3–4, 326).

Chapter Eleven

1. See the sources cited in n. 3 of the introduction.

2. The precursor to Congress's depreciation table was a statement by Congress

on June 29, 1779, that it would adjust the interest paid on loan office certificates not to observed market values but in proportion to the growth in the amount of Continental dollars outstanding (see chap. 8). See also the sources in fig. 11.1. See also *JCC* (5:845–46, 850; 6:949, 955–56; 7:36, 143, 225; 8:578; 9:955); Oberg (1992–98, 34: 231–32); and Smith (1976–94, 5:307–8, 349, 470, 623, 639; 15:49–50, 377, 384). Some writers thought that approximately $30 million was required to transact commerce (*JCC* 15:1054; Smith 1976–94, 13:495, 532; Webster 1969: 6). They assumed that no depreciation could occur until that sum was exceeded. Continental dollars did not exceed 30 million emitted into public circulation until May 1777 (see table 1.1). Jefferson's 1786 depreciation table (Boyd 1953–55, 10:42–44) shows depreciation only after May 1777, so he may have simply assumed that no depreciation was possible before that date.

3. Bezanson (1951: 65) also reports a value series charting the amount of Continental dollars needed to purchase specie and a value series charting the same commodities priced in both Continental dollars and specie. These two value series are line 5 and line 6, respectively, in fig. 11.5. These value series appear to be a small subset of the overall price data. The composition of goods in these two value series, and whether that composition was consist over time, are not provided. These two series also have missing values in some months and suffer from high error variance owing to small sample sizes. Referring to these two value series, Bezanson (1951: 60–62) concluded, "As might be expected, both specie and commodity transactions suffer from some erratic quotations, arising from a sparse number of entries, [and] from differences in individual practices.... The differences arising from uncertainties of the rate of exchange between currencies would be expected to average out only if the number of transactions were larger than is likely ever to be available." That "erratic" behavior can be seen in fig. 11.5 by comparing lines 5 and 6 with the import and export price indices, which were created using a larger data sample. Fig. 11.5 also shows that these two value series track the export-only price index more or less closely for the most part. For these reasons, the import and export price indices are consider superior to these two other value series for measuring the Continental dollar's market exchange value.

4. John Adams indicated on October 12, 1775, that Continental dollars were not yet in general circulation (*JCC* 3:491). The evidence in fig. 7.1 comes from the same market, but is different from that used to construct the Bezanson price index in fig. 11.1.

5. See *JCC* (3:367–68, 424, 455; 4:49–50); *Pennsylvania Gazette* (January 17, April 17 and 24, June 19, 1776); and Smith (1976–94, 2:464).

Chapter Thirteen

1. *JCC* (13:20–23, 64–65; 14:728). The preamble to a discussion on finances on June 14, 1779, read: "In consequence [to the discontinuance of emission of new

bills] . . . it may be expected that the currency will gradually appreciate until the time limited for its redemption, when possessors will be entitled to receive the amount expressed in each bill in gold and silver" (*JCC* 14:728). The January 2 and 14, 1779, congressional resolutions on paper money were reprinted on the front page of the *Pennsylvania Gazette* on January 27, 1779.

2. See *JCC* (11:731; 12:1130, 1134; 13:23) and Smith (1976–94, 1:xxvi–xxxii; 2: xvi–xxii). Lee was not present for the debate and passage of emission no. 1 resolutions, and Floyd may not have been present when that resolution passed.

3. That the public and Congress were concerned about the fiscal credibility of this change is revealed in the front-page editorial in the *Pennsylvania Gazette* on May 19, 1779, and in the address to the public by John Jay, President of Congress, on September 13, 1779 (*JCC* 15:1051–62; *Pennsylvania Gazette*, September 29, 1779). See also Hammond (1889a, 9:283, 285, 291; 1889b, 9:300); Smith (1976–94, 11:361–62, 370–71, 406; 12:236; 13:24, 85–86, 90–91, 388, 524–25, 529–33, 603–4; 14:41–42, 50, 241, 286, 288–90, 292, 298, 437, 452; 15:89–90, 140, 405, 490, 628; 16:127, 192, 286, 485–98, 506, 641; 17:34–35, 49, 128, 150, 192, 212–13, 363); and Sumner (1968, 2:76–77).

4. *JCC* (8:650, 731; 9:953–58; 14:626; 15:1147–50; 16:263). States were to receive a credit for the principal loaned plus 6 percent interest per annum accruing on the amount loaned. These were not remittances of Continental dollars for the purpose of their final redemption and removal from circulation. The states were still required ultimately to redeem these respent Continental dollars and cause them to be permanently removed from circulation by remitting them under the redemption procedures in the emission acts that led to their being burned at the Continental Treasury.

5. Congress had no way to enforce its requisitions on the states, which could ignore it with impunity. On the relatively small portions of Congress's requisitions actually filled by the states and on the fact that requisition fulfillments lagged far behind what was requested, see the reports by Joseph Nourse for 1781–84 in Ferguson et al. (1973–99, 1:196; 8:57, 749; 9:139, 908). A congressional committee report submitted to Congress on April 18, 1781, also noted the lack of state compliance with congressional funding requests (*JCC* 19:408–10). In Congress, efforts in April and May 1781 to create enforcement mechanisms were rebuffed by the majority, rejected or buried in committee (*JCC* 20:440, 445, 471, 495, 578).

6. See also this chapter, n. 3.

7. See also this chapter, n. 3, as well as fig. 14.1.

8. A different way of looking at the impossibility of Congress's successfully raising the present value and therefore the purchasing power of the Continental dollar in 1779 can be seen by looking at the situation in terms of the average per-white-capita money stock in the economy. By the last emission in November 1779, just under 200 million Continental dollars (face value) had been emitted. All were still outstanding as of the beginning of 1780, as state redemptions of Continental dollars were not required to begin before November 1779. This was a lot of paper money. By 1780 it averaged $91 per white capita in face value, or the equivalent of about twenty pounds in sterling equivalents (in face value). Using the January 2, 1779 "ideal"

expected present value, it averaged $57, and using the expected present value from forecast 1, it averaged about $13, or about 12.5 and 2.9 pounds in sterling equivalents, respectively. By contrast, the money stock of the colonies before the Revolution averaged around one pound sterling-equivalents per capita, and between 1795 and 1830 the US money stock averaged about 1.8 pounds sterling-equivalents per capita (Rousseau 2006). Trying to inject such a historically excessive money stock per white capita into the economy could not be sustained without some serious and detrimental macroeconomic adjustments.

Chapter Fourteen

1. The Articles of Confederation were laid before Congress in November 1777 (*JCC* 9:907–28).

2. These tax arrears amounted to $20.60 per year per white capita, or fifty times greater than the per-year per-white-capita tax level in the colonies for all taxes levied between 1770 and 1774 (see table 10.1). Adding these taxes to the taxes required for redeeming Continental dollars pushed per-year per-white-capita tax levels beyond comprehension. The fiscal impossibility of what Congress did in 1779 regarding redeeming Continental dollars was compounded by the fiscal impossibility of the tax revenues Congress requested from the states.

3. A three-person congressional committee to assess the state of congressional finances in its report to Congress on April 18, 1781, in summarizing the history of Continental dollar emissions, explicitly recounted the redemption instructions embedded in the first two emissions and laid out in table 1.1 (*JCC* 19:406–7). So it was not as if Congress did not remember, or did not now know, that information. See also table 16.4.

4. See *Archives of Maryland* (43:258–59); Bolles (1969, 1:97–98, 135–36); Boyd (1953–55, 7:221–23); Bullock (1895: 136–38; 1900: 72); Elliot (1843: 67, 77–82); Ferguson et al. (1973–99, 2:70–71); Grubb (2012a: 160–61); *JCC* (16:165, 217, 253, 262–67, 269; 23:560–61, 590); Phillips (1866: 160–66); Sumner (1968, 1:87–89); and Webster (1969: 111). See also Smith (1976–94, 8:366; 11:306–7, 382; 13:351–52, 388, 603–4; 14: 463–64, 500, 506, 514, 519–32).

5. Ferguson et al. (1973–99, 1:194) and *JCC* (14:728; 16:262–67). This act was printed in the *Pennsylvania Gazette* on March 29, 1780.

6. See *Acts of the council and general assembly of New-Jersey* (1784: 157); Grubb (2012b); Hening (1969, 13:412–13); *JCC* (16:269); *Laws of the state of Delaware* (1797, 2:718–19); Smith (1976–94, 13:129; 15:295; 17:87); and *Statutes at large of Pennsylvania* (1903–4, 10:204–5, 228–29, 247–49, 337–44).

7. See *American state papers, class IX* (1834, 1:172–81, 215, 250); Ferguson (1961, 51–52); *JCC* (16:263–65; 19:164, 411); Perkins (1994: 97); and Ratchford (1941: 37–38).

8. *JCC* (13:23; 16:267) and Smith (1976–94, 1:xxvi–xxxii; 2:xvi–xxii). Livingston and Floyd may not have been present when the 1775 resolutions on the structural design of the Continental dollar were passed.

9. *JCC* (16:267). For prior north-south vote splitting over finance issues, see *JCC* (12:1257–58, 1266). See Grubb (2011b) for an extended analysis of this north-south vote split.

10. See this chapter, n. 4.

11. Jefferson suggested to Madison that Virginia buy up Continental dollars on "easy terms" so as to fill Virginia's Continental dollar redemption quota. He implied that because all states would be credited at the 40-to-1 rate in the final apportionment of war costs by the national government, if Virginia could buy up Continental dollars at a cheaper rate than at 40-to-1 and cheaper than what other states could achieve, Virginia would come out ahead financially in that final reckoning and apportionment of war costs across the states. See chap. 15 and Boyd (1953–55, 7:120).

12. I hope future scholars can make use of the pioneering methods used to do such for the paper monies issued by individuals colonies as demonstrated in Celia and Grubb (2016); Cutsail and Grubb (2019, 2021); and Grubb (2015, 2016a, 2016b, 2016c, 2017, 2018a). State paper monies emitted during the Revolution resembled their colonial antecedents in terms of how they were structured to perform.

13. See *American state papers, class III* (1832, 1:58); *Archives of Maryland* (48:22); Elliot (1843: 11, 65–83); Nourse (1790, in Ferguson et al. 1973–99, 9:930–36); Syrett and Cooke (1962–72, 6:412–14); and United States Congress (1834, 2:1544, 1566). See also *American almanac* (1830: 183); Ferguson (1961: 30); Gouge (1833, pt. 2:25); Hepburn (1967: 16); and Perkins (1994: 97). Elliot (1843: 11) reported two different estimates by Senator Woodbury, former Secretary of the Treasury, namely $2,070,240 and $2,071,085 Continental-state dollars emitted.

14. The implied 31.8 to 41.5 million Continental dollars redeemed in 1780–81, based on Nourse's and Hamilton's reports on how many Continental-state dollars were emitted, is corroborated by the direct evidence on the redemption of Continental dollar in 1780 and 1781 (see chap. 15 and appendix D).

15. Several authors in the secondary literature have presented different numbers for the total number of Continental-state dollars emitted. I will note them here and explain why they are erroneous and thus why the numbers reported by Nourse and Hamilton are preferred. Ratchford (1941: 38) said that "$4,468,625 of these new bills [Continental-state dollars] were put into circulation," citing Harlow (1929: 62). However, Harlow (1929: 62) really said, "Less than half the authorized total—about $4,468,625—was put into circulation." Half of $4,468,625 is $2,234,313, which is almost the total given by Elliot (1843: 11); Gouge (1833, pt. 2:25); and Hepburn (1967: 16) and close to Nourse's number. Unfortunately, Harlow cited *JCC* (19:399–400, April 15, 1781) as his source. It turns out there is no entry in the *JCC* for April 15, 1781—it was a Sunday and Congress did not meet—and none of Harlow's numbers are mentioned on the pages he cited. For another possible source of this $4,468,625

number, see Bronson (1865: 125) and Bullock (1895: 138; 1900: 72). Bronson (1865: 126) estimated the total emission of Continental-state dollars to be 3,980,556. He arrived at this total by taking the number reported by Hamilton and assuming this was only the federal government's share, i.e., four-tenths of the total emitted. Scaling up from four-tenths yielded 3,980,556 for the total emission of Continental-state dollars. This also seems to be the source of Bullock's estimate of 4 million Continental-state dollars issued. Hamilton's statement is somewhat ambiguous as to whether the reported sum is the global total or just the federal government's four-tenths share. However, the 80 million Continental dollars that would have been called out of circulation by the states in 1780 and 1781, given the 20-to-1 rate set by Congress, to be consistent with the 4 million Continental-state dollars these authors say were emitted, cannot be sustained by the direct evidence on state redemption of Continental dollars (see appendix D and chap. 15) or made consistent with the other evidence these authors present.

The confusion can be straightened out by the report sent to Robert Morris by Charles Thomson, the Secretary of Congress, on June 29, 1781 (Ferguson et al. 1973–99, 1:193–94). Thomson reported 195 million Continental dollars outstanding, which, if all were cashed in for Continental-state dollars, would yield 9.75 million Continental-state dollars, of which Congress would get four-tenths, or 3.9 million Continental-state dollars. As such, 4 million is the *maximum amount possible* that Congress could acquire (200,000,000 * 0.05 * 0.4 = 4,000,000) of Continental-state dollars, and not what it *did* acquire. Bronson, Bullock, and Ratchford simply confused the maximum amount possible that Congress could have acquired for the actual amount of Continental-state dollars emitted by the states.

16. For example, on December 13, 1781, the state of Maryland reported that it had 73,082 "Maryland pounds" worth of Continental-state bills in circulation. Note in what money the amount of Continental-state dollars was evaluated. Regarding the confusion over how to treat these bills compared with other paper monies in Maryland, see *Archives of Maryland* (43:205, 258–59, 277, 279, 297–98, 460; 45:73–74, 279, 382, 397–98, 441, 453, 577; 47:37, 84, 107, 131, 142–43, 230–31, 437; 48:21–22, 101, 165). See also Bezanson (1951: 51–56); Bolles (1969, 1:101, 140–41); Bronson (1865: 126); and Phillips (1866: 171–72, 177, 182).

17. *JCC* (17:784–85; 19:266, 380–81, 413; 20:439, 471; 23:591; 24:357–58; 26:395–96; 27:540–45; 29:590–93). Statements by Franklin and Jefferson in personal letters and pamphlets also indicated as much; see Boyd (1953–55, 9:604–5; 10:17, 26, 127–28, 509, 584; 12:61) and Oberg (1992–98, 34:232).

18. See also *Archives of Maryland* (45:397–98; 48:22); Bezanson (1951: 51); Bronson (1865: 127); Bullock (1895: 137); Phillips (1866: 182); and Sumner (1968, 1:86).

19. From Franklin, letter to Samuel Cooper, April 22, 1779, France.

20. See also *Archives of Maryland* (43:258–59); Bolles (1969, 1:97–98, 135–36); Boyd (1953–55, 7:221–23); Bullock (1895: 136–38; 1900: 72); Elliot (1843: 77–82); Ferguson et al. (1973–99, 2:70–71); *JCC* (16:165, 217, 253, 262–67, 269; 23:560–61,

590); Phillips (1866: 160–66); Smith (1976–94, 8:366; 11:306–7, 382; 13:351–52, 388, 603–4; 14:463–64, 500, 506, 514, 519–32); Sumner (1968, 1:87–89); and Webster (1969: 111).

21. Bezanson (1951: 12, 344); Breck (1843: 16); Bullock (1895: 137, 240); Ferguson (1961: 51, 66); Harlow (1929: 61); Hughes and Cain (2011: 83, n. 10); Phillips (1866: 185, 190–91); Ratchford (1941: 38); Sumner (1968, 1:87); Tindall (1988: 265); and Webster (1969: 502). For examples of such proposals that were never enacted by Congress, see *JCC* (16:312; 19:165; 20:495).

22. See chap. 16, n. 8.

Chapter Fifteen

1. See table 1.1; appendix A; and *JCC* (2:103, 221–23; 3:390, 407, 457–59; 13:21–23, 64).

2. Elliot (1843: 12); *JCC* (16–34); Newman (1997: 69); Sumner (1968, 1:980); and United States Congress (1834, 2:2243–51).

3. Phillips (1866: v). Comprehensive documentation and discussion of state redemption of Continental dollars does not appear in Baack (2008); Bolles (1969); Breck (1843); Bronson (1865); Brown (1993); Bullock (1895, 1900); Calomiris (1988); Ferguson (1961); Gouge (1833); Harlow (1929); Hepburn (1967); Jensen (1981); Perkins (1994); Ratchford (1941); Sumner (1968); or any general-history or textbook treatment of the revolutionary period.

4. The January 2 and 14, 1779, congressional resolutions restructuring the remittance of the Continental dollar also entailed a currency swap. The entire emissions of May 20, 1777, and April 11, 1778, totaling 41,500,000 Continental dollars, were to be exchanged one-for-one for new bills, those with the date "January 14, 1779" on them. The emissions of May 20, 1777, and April 11, 1778, were under threat of being counterfeited. The currency swap was intended to remedy the counterfeiting problem. Remittances of Continental dollars by the states to the Continental Treasury for the purpose of this currency exchange need to be distinguished from remittances that were intended to remove Continental dollars permanently from circulation. See appendix A and *JCC* (13:20–22, 64–65).

5. *American state papers, class III* (1832, 1:58–59); Elliot (1843: 73–76); and United States Congress (1834, 2:1544, 1566).

6. The only major exception in the cross-corroboration is the May 1781 amount for Virginia ($5,785,555), which is missing from the Hillegas report. The numbers in the Hillegas report are not listed separately in table D.1 since they are both redundant and incomplete relative to the Nourse report.

7. See this chapter, n. 4, and appendix A.

8. See this chapter, n. 4, and appendix A This conclusion is consistent with what Nourse (1828) reported to the Twentieth Congress as total emissions. Therein he

included the full authorization of January 14, 1779 ($50 million) without netting out bills swapped for the bills of the May 20, 1777, and April 11, 1778, emissions.

9. See appendix A. Francis Hopkinson, Treasurer of Loans, reported the cumulative total amount of the emissions of May 20, 1777, and April 11, 1778, that had been received and destroyed—that is, swapped for new bills—as being $3,852,766 by July 19, 1779; $19,847,268 by January 1, 1780; and $32,304,372 by March 22, 1780 (*Pennsylvania Gazette*, July 28, 1779; January 12, 1780; and March 29, 1780; respectively). Hopkinson's totals fully account for Nourse's remittance totals to those dates, respectively. Nourse's totals to the end of March 1780 are $710,441 below Hopkinson's totals as of March 22, 1780.

10. See *Archives of Maryland* (43:258–59); Boyd (1953–55, 7:221–23); Bullock (1895: 136–38); Elliot (1843: 77–82); *JCC* (16:265; 23:560–61, 590).

11. Elliot (1843: 12), Sumner (1968, 1:98); Syrett and Cooke (1962–72, 6:85–87); and United States Congress (1834, 2:2243–51).

12. *Laws of the state of Delaware* (1797, 2:774–75) and *Statutes at large of Pennsylvania* (1903–4, 10:249–51).

Chapter Sixteen

1. As Madison wrote to Jefferson on October 24, 1787: "Such is the state & prospect of our fiscal department that any new loan however small, that should now be made, would probably subject us to the reproach of premediated deception. The balance of Mr. Adams' last loan will be wanted for the interest due in Holland, and with all the income here, will, it is feared, not save our credit in Europe from further wounds. It may well be doubted whether the present Govt. can be kept alive thro' the ensuing year, or until the new one may take its place" (Rutland and Hobson 1973–81, 10:218; Swanson 1963: 36).

2. The contents of US silver dollars, which were minted after the 1792 Mint Act, were based on a random sample of the content of Spanish silver dollars in circulation in the United States in the early 1790s. Foreign specie coins would remain legal tender in the United States until 1857 (Muhleman 1895: 39).

3. On tariff changes in this period, see Peters (1845: First Congress, First Session, chap. 47; Second Session, chap. 39; Third Session, chaps. 1, 26). Letters between Alexander Hamilton, who as Secretary of the Treasury was responsible for overseeing tariff-revenue tax collections, and his port agents and customs officials often alluded to the problem of smuggling, the difficulty of enforcing the tariff, and the difficulty of collecting actual tariff revenues. As one customs officer put it in late 1789, "The difficulties that have occurred in the Execution of the laws respecting the Customs have been infinite, and present themselves daily. The System itself is the most complicated and embarrassing of anything that has employed my attention . . . [and] the Owners pay with reluctance . . . others not at all without compulsion; and the law provides none" (Syrett and Cooke 1962–72, 5:422, 427, 459–64; 17:6–7). The yearly

value of imports fluctuated greatly in this period, which explains most of the variance in the revenue stream as well as its uncertainty (North 1966: 19–32, 228). Regarding problems with trade treaties in this period, see Rutland and Hobson (1973–81, 8:502–3); Syrett and Cooke (1962–72, 16:261–79); and Tindall (1988: 316–17, 330–31).

4. See Bouton (2007); Holton (2007); Richards (2002); Syrett and Cooke (1962–72, 17:2–6, 9–58, 61–72, 77–78); Szatmary (1980); and Tindall (1988: 320–21, 333–34). On tariff-revenue collection constraints, see this chapter, n. 3.

5. See Peters (1845: Second Congress, First Session, chap. 38, Second Session, chap. 26; Third Congress, First Session, chap. 36, Second Session, chap. 13; Fourth Congress, First Session, chap. 2, Second Session, chap. 25).

6. In the 1790s Congress had to authorize the president to borrow additional sums, up to a prescribed amount, to meet budget deficits, namely $523,000 on May 2, 1792; $800,000 on February 28, 1793; $1,000,000 on March 20, 1794; $1,000,000 on June 9, 1794; $2,000,000 on December 18, 1794; $1,000,000 per year on March 3, 1795; $324,539 on May 30, 1796; $5,000,000 on May 31, 1796; $650,000 on June 1, 1796; $800,000 on July 8, 1797; $5,000,000 on July 15, 1798; $3,500,000 on May 7, 1800 (*Laws of the United States* 1896, 1:15, 18, 20–22, 24, 33, 35–36, 40). Some of these borrowing were bridge loans between spending outflows and tariff-revenue inflows.

7. Elliot (1843: 12); Newman (1997: 69); Sumner (1968, 1:980); and United States Congress (1834–56, 2:2243–51). Ferguson (1961: 67) says in regard to the mass of Continental dollars issued and outstanding prior to the 1790 Funding Act, "Eventually the dead mass of currency was drawn in by the states. A good part of it was scattered or destroyed, and in 1790 only about $6,000,000 remained in the hands of individuals." Ferguson's source for his figure of $6 million is Elliot (1843: 12). However, Ferguson misinterpreted his source. The $6 million was the amount estimated to have been actually exchanged at the 100-to-1 rate for bonds after 1790, not the amount outstanding at this date in the hands of the public, which was estimated in the same source to be $78–$80 million. In addition, in reference to 1780 and the withdrawal of old Continental currency, Ferguson (1961: 181) says that the "states absorbed nearly $120,000,000." Ferguson's statement here also appears to be the source of the statement by Perkins (1994: 97) that "they [the states] collected monies [Continental currency] with a face value of $119 million ($3 million in specie) in the early 1780s, approximately half the total volume issued by Congress." These two statements are erroneous. No other sources show that much absorbed in 1780 or in the early 1780s. If by chance Ferguson and Perkins really meant that the total absorbed by the states between 1780 and 1790 was $120 million, then they would be close to that estimated here in table D1 and to the evidence in Ferguson's primary source (Elliot 1843: 12, item 3).

8. See the stories recounted in Breck (1843: 15–16); Ferguson (1961: 66); and Phillips (1866: 185).

9. *American state papers, class IX* (1834, 1:55, 172–81, 215, 250); Bullock (1895: 138); Elliot (1843: 12); Newman (1997: 69); Phillips (1866: 195); Sumner (1968, 1:98); Syrett and Cooke (1962–72, 6:85–87); and United States Congress (1834–56, 2:2243–51).

The report from the Twenty-eighth Congress summarized in Elliot (1843: 12, items 3 and 4) is often misinterpreted or ignored in the secondary literature.

10. Hamilton, as Secretary of the Treasury, and his Federalist allies in Congress seemed willing to violate the Constitution when it suited them, as they also did it with the congressional creation of the First Bank of the United States at about the same time; see Grubb (2006).

11. This is a biased-high estimate of the present value and so a biased-low estimate of the size of the default. This is because the package of bonds given citizens included a 3 percent perpetuity to cover "indent" debts, rather than a market rate of 6 percent used to pay on other debts. Not knowing how much of the bond package represented indent debts, for calculation purposes, I just assumed it was little or nothing and so the bond package would only consist of 6 percent perpetuities both current and deferred, and so the calculation yields a biased-high estimate of the bond package's present value to the extent that bonds to cover indent debts had their rate counted at 6 rather than 3 percent interest.

12. See this chapter, n. 11.

13. See this chapter, n. 6.

Chapter Seventeen

1. By "outside money" I mean money (specie—gold and silver) that is used to clear international (trans-government-jurisdictional) debts for both private and public trades. See also Ferguson (1983: 404–5).

2. Although the Constitution gave Congress a directly enumerated power to "coin money, regulate the value thereof, and of foreign coins" (Article 1, Section 8), Congress allowed any specie unit of account to be used in legal-tender transactions. The federal government accepted the gold coins of Great Britain, France, Spain, and Portugal, and the silver coins of France and Spain, as a legal tender until 1857 (Muhleman 1895: 39).

3. A common error repeated often in the secondary literature is the claim that the new Constitution was intentionally crafted to allow Congress the power to emit bills of credit because no explicit prohibition on issuing bills of credit by Congress was written into the Constitution. For example, see Baack (2001: 653); Ferguson (1969: 254, 258); Nettels (1962: 98–99); Rolnick, Smith, and Weber (1993: 3); and Schweitzer (1989: 311). The analysis here is a corrective in that it will show that under almost any logically consistent and coherent interpretation such a claim cannot be sustained. See also Grubb (2006).

4. On the reasons for calling the 1787 constitution convention, see Ferguson (1969, 1983); Grubb (2003); Jensen, Kaminski, and Saladino (1976, 1:140–229); and Rutland (1970, 2:814–22).

5. On how colonial bills of credit, which were the same as state bills of credit,

worked, and how time-discounting and thus their present value varied across the colonies, see Celia and Grubb (2016); Cutsail and Grubb (2021); and Grubb (2016a, 2016b, 2018a, 2019a, 2019b).

6. There was no discussion, not one word, raised at the Constitutional Convention regarding a monetary union among the states or the problem between states of states issuing their own individual bills of credit. Monetary unification among the states was never a topic of interest expressed by the Convention delegates; see Farrand (1966).

7. The implied powers clause is the last paragraph in Article 1, Section 8 of the Constitution, which enumerates the new powers to be granted Congress. It says, "To make all Laws which shall be necessary and proper for carrying into Execution the foregoing Powers, and all other Powers vested by this Constitution in the Government of the United States, or in any Department of Officer thereof." Since the Marshall court, the Supreme Court has engaged in interpreting whether a particular new law passed by Congress was implied by one of the enumerated powers listed in Article 1, Section 8 when judging whether that particular new law was indeed constitutional.

8. Over the years I have asked numerous law professors who specialize in constitutional law this question, namely, does an explicit vote at the convention to remove a specific power or an explicit vote not to add a specific power to the list of enumerated powers of Congress in Article 1, Section 8 trump the implied powers clause? Did such votes amount to absolute prohibitions on exercising those powers, and those powers could not be brought back in under the implied powers clause? I also asked the same question of Antonin Scalia when he was alive. Alas, to a person, not only was no opinion given, but no one seemed to comprehend the question or to have previously considered the logical problem it posed. See Grubb (2006: 64–69) for an extended discussion of the power to charter a national bank by Congress, the debate at the Convention and afterward regarding that power, and how banking interests overcame the logic above and got their way with the First Bank of the United States.

9. See Ferguson (1983: 402); Grubb (2003, 2006, 2007a); and Wilson (1942: 3–28).

Appendix A

1. While this appendix relies principally on Grubb (2008), some new information is added.

2. Examples from the older literature include *American almanac* (1830: 183); Bolles (1969, 1:31–88); Boyd (1953–55, 10:42–43); Breck (1843: 8, 15); Bronson (1865: 88–89, 112–15); Bullock (1895: 135, 174, 177); Elliot (1843: 8–9, 11); Gouge (1833, pt. 2:25); Harlow (1929: 50–51); Hepburn (1924: 16); Nourse (1828: 7); Phillips (1866: 198–99); and Ratchford (1941: 37). Examples from the modern literature include

Atack and Passell (1994: 71); Calomiris (1988: 58); Ferguson (1961: 28–30, 67); Hughes and Cain (2011: 79); Michener (1988: 690); Newman (1997: 58–59; 2008: 15–16, 37–41, 61–88); Perkins (1994: 97); Robinson (1969: 108, 293, 323–26); and Tindall (1988: 226).

3. *Early American imprints* (1983, microfiche S 269, nos. 16634, 16635; "U.S. Board of Treasury, 1779, A Table of First Year's Interest. Philadelphia, 1779" and "U.S. Board of Treasury, 1779. Table of the Sums Actually in Circulation. Philadelphia, 3 December 1779"); and Ferguson et al. (1973–99, 1:194).

4. *JCC* (14:1002–3; 15:1052–53; 19:410); *PCC* (microfilm 247, reel 146, item 136:647).

5. Bolles (1969, 1:42–54); Boyd (1953–55, 10:42–43); Bronson (1865: 113–14); Bullock (1895: 135–36); Elliot (1843); Ferguson (1961: 28–30); and Phillips (1866: 198–99).

6. See *American almanac* (1830: 183); Elliot (1843: 11); Ferguson (1961: 28–29, 64–65); Gouge (1833, pt. 2:25); and Hepburn (1924: 16).

7. Nourse is reprinted in Ferguson et al. (1973–99, 9:905–40). In May 1790 the United States Congress, *Debates and Proceedings* (2:1566), said that the Secretaries of War and the Treasury laid a report before Congress "of the sums of money, including indents and paper money of every kind." This report is the same as the Nourse report.

8. Harlow (1929: 50–51); *JCC* (13:53, 98–99, 140, 255, 259, 302, 392; 14:731, 774–75, 817, 820–21, 846, 881, 943; 15:1431, 1436); Michener (1988: 690); and Nourse (1828: 7).

9. See *JCC* (12:1224; 13:21–22, 53, 65, 74, 98, 129, 140, 255–56, 259, 302; 14:519, 557, 695, 731, 774–76, 795–96, 817, 820–21, 846, 881, 943; 15:1186, 1431, 1436, 1451–52; 16:312; 19:430).

10. The August 15, 1777, authorization was first mentioned on August 1, 1777 (see table A.1).

11. *JCC* (7:373; 8:646; 9:873, 993; 10:28, 83, 175, 223, 309, 365; 11:524, 627, 731; 12:884).

12. *JCC* (14:817, 821; 15:1436; 30:22–25) and Phillips (1866: 99).

13. *Pennsylvania Gazette*, July 28, 1779; January 12, 1780; and March 29, 1780, respectively.

14. See Ferguson (1973–99, 5:139); *JCC* (13:32; 14:695, 731, 774, 795–96; 16:312; 19:430); and appendix D.

15. *JCC* (14:1013; 15:1019, 1053, 1171, 1324; 19:405, 410).

16. See Boyd (1953–55, 10:25, 42); Breck (1843: 8, 15); Oberg (1992–98, 34:231); Ratchford (1941: 37); Webster (1969: 76); and n. 3 in appendix A.

Appendix C

1. See *JCC* (2–16, esp. 2:237, 245; 3:275, 342, 345, 387); Michener (1988: 686); and Smith (1976–94, 2:166, 355, 379–80; 5:521, 611; 6:79, 117–18, 146, 212–14, 270; 7:304; 9:479; 14:288–89, 547; 25:683).

References

Acts of the Council and General Assembly of New-Jersey. 1784. Trenton, NJ.

American almanac and repository of useful knowledge for the year 1830, vol. 1. 1830. Boston: Gray & Bowen.

American state papers, class III, finance, vol. 1 [*Documents, legislative and executive of the Congress of the United States, from the first session of the eighteenth Congress to the first session of the twentieth Congress: commencing April 19, 1824, and ending May 16, 1828. On Finance. vol. 5*]. 1832. Washington, DC: Gales & Seaton.

American state papers, class IX, claims, vol. 1 [*Documents, legislative and executive of the Congress of the United States, vol. {blank}*]. 1834. Washington, DC: Gales & Seaton.

Anderson, William G. 1983. *The price of liberty: The public debt of the American Revolution*. Charlottesville: University Press of Virginia.

Archives of Maryland, vols. 1–72. 1883–1972. Baltimore: Maryland Historical Society.

Atack, Jeremy, and Passell, Peter. 1994. *A new economic view of American history* (2nd ed). New York: W. W. Norton.

Baack, Ben. 2001. "Forging a nation state: The Continental Congress and the financing of the War of American Independence." *Economic History Review* 54: 639–56.

———. 2008. "America's first monetary policy: Inflation and seigniorage during the Revolutionary War." *Financial History Review* 15: 107–21.

Banerjee, A. V., and Maskin, E. S. 1996. "A Walrasian theory of money and barter." *Quarterly Journal of Economics* 111: 955–1005.

Barlow, J. Jackson, ed. 2012. *To secure the blessings of liberty: Selected writings of Gouverneur Morris*. Indianapolis: Liberty Fund.

Bezanson, Anne. 1951. *Prices and inflation during the American Revolution: Pennsylvania, 1770–1790*. Philadelphia: University of Pennsylvania Press.

Bolles, Albert S. 1969. *The financial history of the United States from 1774 to 1789, vols. 1–3*. New York: Augustus M. Kelly [originally published 1884].

Bordo, Michael D. 1987. "Equation of exchange." In John Eatwell, Murray Milgate, and Peter Newman, eds., *The new Palgrave: A dictionary of economics*. London: Macmillan, vol. 2: 175–77.

Bouton, Terry. 2007. *Taming democracy: The "people," the founders, and the struggle over the American Revolution*. New York: Oxford University Press.

Boyd, Julian P., ed. 1953–55. *The papers of Thomas Jefferson, vols. 7–12*. Princeton, NJ: Princeton University Press.

Breck, Samuel. 1843. *Historical sketch of Continental paper money*. Philadelphia: John C. Clark.

Brock, Leslie V. 1975. *The currency of the American colonies, 1700–1764: A study in colonial finance and imperial relations*. New York: Arno Press.

Bronson, Henry. 1865. "A historical account of Connecticut currency, Continental money, and the finances of the Revolution." *Papers of the New Haven Colony Historical Society* 1: 1–192 [New Haven, CT: Thomas J. Stafford, printer].

Brookhiser, Richard. 2003. *Gentleman revolutionary: Gouverneur Morris, the rake who wrote the Constitution*. New York: Free Press.

Brown, Roger H. 1993. *Redeeming the republic: Federalists, taxation, and the origins of the Constitution*. Baltimore: Johns Hopkins University Press.

Buel, Richard Jr. 1998. *In irons: Britain's naval supremacy and the American revolutionary economy*. New Haven, CT: Yale University Press.

Bullock, Charles J. 1895. *The finances of the United States from 1775 to 1789*. Madison: University of Wisconsin Press.

——. 1900. *Essays on the monetary history of the United States*. New York: Macmillan.

Bush, Bernard, ed. 1977. *Laws of the royal colony of New Jersey, 1703–1745*. Trenton: New Jersey State Library, Archives and History Bureau.

——. 1980. *Laws of the royal colony of New Jersey, 1746–1760*. Trenton: New Jersey State Library, Bureau of Archives and History.

——. 1982. *Laws of the royal colony of New Jersey, 1760–1769*. Trenton: New Jersey State Library, Bureau of Archives and History.

——. 1986. *Laws of the royal colony of New Jersey, 1770–1775*. Trenton: Division of Archives and Records Management, New Jersey Department of State.

Calomiris, Charles W. 1988. "Institutional failure, monetary scarcity, and the depreciation of the Continental." *Journal of Economic History* 48: 47–68.

Carp, E. W. 1984. *To starve the army at pleasure: Continental army administration and American political culture, 1775–1783*. Chapel Hill: University of North Carolina Press.

Carter, Susan B.; Gartner, Scott Sigmund; Haines, Michael R.; Olmstead, Alan L.; Sutch, Richard; and Wright, Gavin, eds. 2006. *Historical statistics of the United States: Earliest times to the present* (Millennium ed., vols. 1 and 5). New York: Cambridge University Press.

Celia, James, and Grubb, Farley. 2016. "Non-legal-tender paper money: The structure and performance of Maryland's bills of credit, 1767–1775." *Economic History Review* 69: 1132–56.

Cooke, Ebenezer. 1730. *Sotweed redivivus: Or, the planters looking-glass*. Annapolis, MD.

Criswell, Grover C., Jr. 1965. *North American currency*. Iola, WI: Krause.

Cushing, John D., ed. 1981. *The first laws of the state of Delaware, vol. 2, part 1*. Wilmington: Michael Glazier, State Printer of Delaware.

Cutsail, Cory, and Grubb, Farley. 2019. "The paper money of colonial North Carolina, 1712–74: Reconstructing the evidence." *Journal of the North Carolina Association of Historians* 27: 1–31.

———. 2021. "Colonial North Carolina's paper money regime, 1712–1774: Value decomposition and performance." *Journal of Post-Keynesian Economics* 44: 463–91.

Davis, Andrew McFarland. 1964. *Colonial currency reprints, 1682–1751, vols. 1–4*. New York: Augustus M. Kelley.

Dougherty, K. L. 2001. *Collective action under the Articles of Confederation*. New York: Cambridge University Press.

Early American imprints, 1639–1800: Based on the 13-volume Charles Evans bibliography, including supplements and corrections to Evans. 1983. New York: Readex Microprint Corporation.

Edling, Max M. 2014. *A Hercules in the cradle: War, money, and the American state, 1783–1867*. Chicago: University of Chicago Press.

Elliot, Jonathan. 1843. "Funding system of the United States and Great Britain." *House of Representatives Document No. 15* (Vol. II: Executive Documents), 28th Congress, First Session, read on December 16, 1843 [reprinted 1971, New York: Burt Franklin].

Ernst, Joseph E. 1973. *Money and politics in America, 1755–1775*. Chapel Hill: University of North Carolina Press.

Esposito, V. J., ed. 1995. *The West Point atlas of American wars, vol. 1: 1689–1900*. New York: Henry Holt.

Farrand, Max, ed. 1966. *The records of the Federal Convention of 1787, vols. 1–4*. New Haven, CT: Yale University Press.

Ferguson, E. James. 1953. "Currency finance: An interpretation of colonial monetary practices." *William and Mary Quarterly*, 3rd ser., 10: 153–80.

———. 1961. *The power of the purse: A history of American public finance, 1776–1790*. Chapel Hill: University of North Carolina Press.

———. 1969. "The nationalists of 1781–1783 and the economic interpretation of the Constitution." *Journal of American History* 56: 241–61.

———. 1983. "Political economy, public liberty, and the formation of the Constitution." *William and Mary Quarterly*, 3rd ser., 40: 389–412.

Ferguson et al., eds. 1973–99. *The papers of Robert Morris, 1781–1784, vols. 1–9*. Pittsburgh, PA: University of Pittsburgh Press.

Fisher, Edgar Jacob. 1911. *New Jersey as a royal province, 1738 to 1776*. New York: Columbia University, Longman, Green.

Fisher, Irving. 1912. *The purchasing power of money: Its determination and relation to international credit and crises*. New York: Macmillan.

Fortescue, John William. 1910–30. *A history of the British army*. London: Macmillan.

Fowler, William M., Jr. 2011. *American crisis: George Washington and the dangerous two years after Yorktown, 1781–1783*. New York: Walker.

Friedman, Milton, and Schwartz, Anne J. 1963. *A monetary history of the United States, 1867–1960*. Princeton, NJ: Princeton University Press.

Gouge, William M. 1833. *A short history of paper money and banking in the United States*. Philadelphia, PA: T. W. Ustick.

Grubb, Farley. 2003. "Creating the U.S.-dollar currency union, 1748–1811: A quest for monetary stability or a usurpation of state sovereignty for personal gain?" *American Economic Review* 93: 1778–98.

———. 2004. "The circulating medium of exchange in colonial Pennsylvania, 1729–1775: New estimates of monetary composition, performance, and economic growth." *Explorations in Economic History* 41: 329–60.

———. 2005. "State 'currencies' and the transition to the U.S. dollar: Reply—including a new view from Canada." *American Economic Review* 95: 1341–48.

———. 2006. "The U.S. Constitution and monetary powers: An analysis of the 1787 Constitutional Convention and the Constitutional transformation of the U.S. monetary system." *Financial History Review* 13: 43–71.

———. 2007a. "The net worth of the U.S. Federal government, 1784–1802." *American Economic Review—Papers and Proceedings* 97: 280–84.

———. 2007b. "The constitutional creation of a common currency in the U.S.: Monetary stabilization versus merchant rent seeking." In Lars Jonung and Jurgen Nautz, eds., *Conflict potentials in monetary unions*. Stuttgart: Franz Steiner Verlag: 19–50.

———. 2008. "The Continental dollar: How much was really issued?" *Journal of Economic History* 68: 283–91.

———. 2010. "Testing for the economic impact of the *U.S. Constitution*: Purchasing power parity across the colonies versus across the states, 1748–1811." *Journal of Economic History* 70: 118–45.

———. 2011a. "U.S. land policy: Founding choices and outcomes, 1781–1802." In Douglas A. Irwin and Richard Sylla, eds., *Founding choices: American economic policy in the 1790s*. National Bureau of Economic Research Conference Report. Chicago: University of Chicago Press: 259–89.

———. 2011b. "The distribution of Congressional spending during the American Revolution, 1775–1780: The problem of geographic balance." In Stephen Conway and Rafael Torres Sánchez, eds., *The spending of the states—Military expenditure during the long eighteenth century: Patterns, organisations, and consequences, 1650–1815*. Saarbrücken, Germany: VDM Verlag Dr. Müller GmbH: 257–84.

———. 2012a. "State redemption of the Continental dollar, 1779–90." *William and Mary Quarterly*, 3rd ser., 69: 147–80.

———. 2012b. "Chronic specie scarcity and efficient barter: The problem of maintaining an outside money supply in British colonial America." NBER working paper #18099, http://www.nber.org/papers/w18099.

——. 2015. "Colonial New Jersey's paper money regime, 1709–75: A forensic accounting reconstruction of the data." *Historical Methods* 48: 13–34.

——. 2016a. "Is paper money just paper money? Experimentation and variation in the paper monies issued by the American colonies from 1690 to 1775." *Research in Economic History* 32: 147–224.

——. 2016b. "Colonial New Jersey paper money, 1709–1775: Value decomposition and performance." *Journal of Economic History* 76: 1216–32.

——. 2016c. "Colonial New Jersey's provincial fiscal structure, 1709–1775: Spending obligations, revenue sources, and tax burdens during peace and war." *Financial History Review* 23: 133–63.

——. 2017. "Colonial Virginia's paper money regime, 1755–1774: A forensic accounting reconstruction of the data." *Historical Methods* 50: 96–112.

——. 2018a. "Colonial Virginia's paper money, 1755–1774: Value decomposition and performance." *Financial History Review* 25: 113–40.

——. 2018b. "Common currency versus currency union: The U.S. continental dollar and denominational structure, 1775–1779." In Nathalie Champroux, Georges Depeyrot, Aykiz Dogan, and Jurgen Nautz, eds., *Construction and deconstruction of monetary unions: Lessons from the past.* Wetteren, Belgium: MONETA: 15–34.

——. 2019a. "Colonial paper money and the quantity theory of money: An extension." *Social Science History* 43: 185–207.

——. 2019b. "Creating Maryland's paper money economy, 1720–1740: The confluence of political constituencies, economic forces, transatlantic markets, and law." *Journal of Early American History* 9: 34–58.

——. 2020. "Money and prices in colonial America." In Stefano Battilossi, Youssef Cassis, and Kazuhiko Yago, eds., *Handbook of the history of money and currency.* Singapore: Springer: 431–54.

Hall, George J., and Sargent, Thomas J. 2014. "Fiscal discrimination in three wars." *Journal of Monetary Economics* 61: 148–66.

Hammond, Bray. 1991. *Banks and politics in America: From the Revolution to the Civil War.* Princeton, NJ: Princeton University Press [originally published 1957].

Hammond, Isaac W., ed. 1889a. "Record of the commissioners' meeting at New Haven, 1778." *Collection of the New Hampshire Historical Society* 9: 272–95.

——. 1889b. "Record of a meeting of commissioners from the states of Massachusetts, New Hampshire and Connecticut, 1780." *Collection of the New Hampshire Historical Society* 9: 295–303.

Hanson, John R. II. 1979. "Money in the colonial American economy." *Economic Inquiry* 17: 281–86.

——. 1980a. "The economic development of the thirteen continental colonies, 1720 to 1775: A critique." *William and Mary Quarterly* 37: 165–75.

——. 1980b. "Small notes in the American colonies." *Explorations in Economic History* 17: 411–20.

Harlow, Ralph Volney. 1929. "Aspects of revolutionary finance, 1775–1783." *American Historical Review* 35: 46–68.

Hening, W. W., ed. 1969. *The statutes at large: Being a collection of all the laws of Virginia, vols. 7, 9, and 13.* Charlottesville: University Press of Virginia [originally published 1821, 1823].

Henretta, James A.; Brownlee, W. Elliot; Brody, David; and Ware, Susan. 1987. *America's history, vol. 1: To 1877.* Chicago: Dorsey Press.

Hepburn, A. Barton. 1967. *A history of currency in the United States.* New York: Augustus M. Kelly [rev. & enlarged ed. originally published 1924].

Historical statistics of the United States: Colonial times to 1970. 1975. Washington, DC: U.S. Department of Commerce.

Holton, Woody. 2007. *Unruly Americans and the origins of the Constitution.* New York: Hill & Wang.

Homer, Sidney, and Sylla, Richard. 1991. *A history of interest rates* (3rd ed.). New Brunswick, NJ: Rutgers University Press.

https://en.wikipedia.org/wiki/Early_American_currency. Accessed April 18, 2019.

http://footguards.tripod.com/01ABOUT/01_payscale.htm. Accessed January 30, 2013.

http://memory.loc.gov/service/rbc/bdsdcc/00301/0001.jpg. Accessed April 23, 2019.

https://www.etymonline.com/search?q=not+worth+a+continental. Accessed November 21, 2020.

Hughes, Jonathan, and Cain, Louis P. 2011. *American economic history* (8th ed.). New York: Pearson Education.

Hutchinson, William T., and Rachal, William M. E., eds. 1962–65. *The papers of James Madison, vols. 1–4.* Chicago: University of Chicago Press.

Jensen, Merrill, Kaminski, John P., and Saladino, Gaspare J., eds. 1976. *The documentary history of the ratification of the Constitution, vol. 1.* Madison: Wisconsin Historical Society Press.

Jensen, Merrill. 1981. *The new nation: A history of the United States during the Confederation, 1781–1789.* Boston: Northeastern University Press [originally published 1950].

Journals of the Continental Congress, 1774–1789, vols. 1–34 [hereafter *JCC*]. 1904–37. Washington, DC: Government Printing Office.

Kaminski, John P., and Saladino, Gaspare J., eds. 1981. *The documentary history of the ratification of the Constitution, vol. 13: Commentaries on the Constitution, public and private, vol. 1, 21 February to 7 November 1787.* Madison: State Historical Society of Wisconsin.

Kemmerer, Donald L. 1940. *Path to freedom: The struggle for self-Government in colonial New Jersey, 1703–1776.* Princeton, NJ: Princeton University Press.

———. 1956. "A history of paper money in colonial New Jersey, 1668–1775." *Proceedings of the New Jersey Historical Society* 74: 107–44.

Knox, Henry. 1790. "Report of the Secretary of War—*War-Office of the United States*, May 10, 1790." Listed as item E. in Joseph Nourse, "Statements of the receipts and expenditures of public monies, during the administration of the finances by Robert Morris." Submitted to the House of Representatives by the Treasury Department, Registrar's Office, August 30, 1790, and reprinted in Ferguson et al. 1973–99, 9:905–40.

Labaree, Leonard W., ed. 1966–70. *The papers of Benjamin Franklin, vols. 9–14*. New Haven, CT: Yale University Press.

Laws of the state of Delaware. 1797. Newcastle, DE.

Laws of the United States relating to loans, paper money, banking, and coinage, 1790 to 1895. 1896. Washington, DC: Government Printing Office (53rd Congress, Third Session, Senate Report 831), Part 1 — Loans: i–236.

Lester, Richard A. 1939. *Monetary experiments: Early American and recent Scandinavian*. Princeton, NJ: Princeton University Press.

McCusker, John J. 1978. *Money and exchange in Europe and America, 1600–1775: A handbook*. Chapel Hill: University of North Carolina Press.

Michener, Ron. 1988. "Backing theories and the currencies of eighteenth-century America: A comment." *Journal of Economic History* 48: 682–92.

Mossman, Philip L. 1993. *Money of the American colonies and confederation: A numismatic, economic and historical correlation*. New York: American Numismatic Society.

Muhleman, Maurice L. 1895. *Monetary systems of the world*. New York: Charles H. Nicoll.

Myers, Margaret G. 1970. *A financial history of the United States*. New York: Columbia University Press.

Neem, J. N. 2009. "Creating social capital in the early American republic: The view from Connecticut." *Journal of Interdisciplinary History* 39: 471–95.

Nettels, Curtis Putnam. 1934. *The money supply of the American colonies before 1720*. Madison: University of Wisconsin Press.

———. 1962. *The emergence of a national economy, 1775–1815*. New York: Holt, Rinehart, & Winston.

Newman, Eric P. 1997. *The early paper money of America* (4th ed.). Iola, WI: Krause.

———. 2008. *The early paper money of America* (5th ed.). Iola, WI: Krause.

North, Douglass C. 1966. *The economic growth of the United States, 1790–1860*. New York: W. W. Norton.

Nourse, Joseph. 1790. "Statements of the receipts and expenditures of the public monies, during the administration of the finances by Robert Morris." Submitted to the committee of the House of Representatives of the United States on the memorial of Robert Morris, August 30. Reprinted in Ferguson et al., 9:905–40.

———. 1828. "Amount of Continental money issued during the Revolutionary War and the depreciation of the same." *House document no. 107*, 20th Congress, First Session, January 30, 1828. Washington, DC: Gales & Seaton.

Oberg, Barbara B., ed. 1992–98. *The papers of Benjamin Franklin, vols. 29–34*. New Haven, CT: Yale University Press.

Olson, Mancur, Jr. 1965. *The logic of collective action: Public goods and the theory of groups*. Cambridge, MA: Harvard University Press.

O'Shaughnessy, Andrew Jackson. 2000. *An empire divided: The American Revolution and the British Caribbean*. Philadelphia: University of Pennsylvania Press.

———. 2013. *The men who lost America: British leadership, the American Revolution, and the British Empire*. New Haven, CT: Yale University Press.

Papers of the Continental Congress, 1774–1789 [hereafter *PCC*]. Washington, DC: National Archives Microfilm Publication, M247.

Perkins, Edwin J. 1994. *American public finance and financial services, 1700–1815*. Columbus: Ohio State University Press.

Peters, Richard, ed. 1845. *The public statutes at large of the United States of America, from the organization of the government in 1789, to March 1845*. Boston: Charles C. Little & James Brown.

Phillips, Henry, Jr. 1866. *Continental paper money: Historical sketches of American paper currency*, 2nd ser. Roxbury, MA: W. Elliot Woodward.

Puls, Mark. 2008. *Henry Knox: Visionary general of the American Revolution*. New York: Palgrave Macmillan.

Rabushka, Alvin. 2008. *Taxation in colonial America*. Princeton, NJ: Princeton University Press.

Randall, William Sterne. 1990. *Benedict Arnold: Patriot and traitor*. New York: Barnes & Noble Books.

Ratchford, U. B. 1941. *American state debts*. Durham, NC: Duke University Press.

Redish, Angela, and Weber, Warren E. 2008. "Coin sizes and payments in commodity money systems." Federal Reserve Bank of Minneapolis, Research Department Staff Report 416.

Richards, Leonard L. 2002. *Shay's Rebellion: The American Revolution's final battle*. Philadelphia: University of Pennsylvania Press.

Ricord, Frederick W., ed. 1892. *Documents relating to the colonial history of the state of New Jersey, vol. XVII*. Trenton, NJ: John L. Murphy [*Archives of the State of New Jersey*, 1st ser., vol. XVII].

Robinson, Edward Forbes. 1969. "Continental Treasury Administration, 1775–1781: A study in the financial history of the American Revolution." Ph.D. diss., University of Wisconsin.

Rockoff, Hugh. 1971. "Money, prices and banks in the Jacksonian era." In Robert W. Fogel and Stanley L. Engerman, eds., *The reinterpretation of American economic history*. New York: Harper & Row: 448–58.

Rolnick, Arthur J., Smith, Bruce D., and Weber, Warren E. 1993. "In order to form a more perfect monetary union." *Federal Reserve Bank of Minneapolis Quarterly Review* 17: 2–9.

Rousseau, Peter L. 2006. "A common currency: Early US monetary policy and the transition to the dollar." *Financial History Review* 13: 97–112.

Rutland, Robert A., ed. 1970. *The papers of George Mason, 1725–1792, vol. 2*. Chapel Hill: University of North Carolina Press.

Rutland, Robert A., and Hobson, Charles F., eds. 1973–81. *The papers of James Madison, vols. 8–13*. Charlottesville: University Press of Virginia.

Sargent, Thomas J. 2012. "United States then, Europe now." https://files.nyu.edu/ts43/public/research/Sargent_Sweden_final.pdf, accessed February 8, 2013; also: https://www.nobelprize.org/prizes/economic-sciences/2011/sargent/lecture/, Nobel Prize Lecture delivered December 8, 2011, Stockholm, Sweden.

Schweitzer, Mary M. 1989. "State-issued currency and the ratification of the U.S. Constitution." *Journal of Economic History* 49: 311–22.

Scott, Kenneth. 1957. *Counterfeiting in colonial America*. Philadelphia.

Sherwood, Joseph. 1851. "Letters of Joseph Sherwood [agent for New Jersey in Britain, 1761–1766]." *Proceedings of the New Jersey Historical Society*, 1st ser., 5: 147.

Smith, Adam. 1937. *The wealth of nations*. New York: Modern Library [originally published 1776].

———. 1976. *The theory of moral sentiments*. Indianapolis: Liberty Classics [originally published 1759].

Smith, Paul H., ed. 1976–1994. *Letters of delegates to Congress, 1774–1789, vols. 1–21*. Washington, DC: Library of Congress.

Smyth, Albert Henry. 1907. *The writings of Benjamin Franklin, vol. 9*. London: Macmillan.

Sparks, Jared. 1832. *The life of Gouverneur Morris, with selections from his correspondence and miscellaneous papers in three volumes*. Boston: Gray & Bowen.

Starr, R. M. 2012. *Why is there money? Walrasian general equilibrium foundations of monetary theory*. Northampton, MA: Edward Elgar.

Statutes at large of Pennsylvania, vols. 9–10. 1903–4. Harrisburg, PA: W. M. Stanley Ray, State Printer of Pennsylvania.

Studenski, Paul, and Krooss, Herman E. 1963. *Financial history of the United States* (2nd ed.). New York: McGraw-Hill.

Sumner, Scott B. 1990. "The transactions and hoarding demand for currency." *Quarterly Review of Economics and Business* 30: 75–85.

Sumner, William Graham. 1968. *The financier and the finances of the American Revolution, vols. 1–2*. New York: Augustus M. Kelly [originally published 1891].

Swanson, Donald F. 1963. *The origins of Hamilton's fiscal policy*. Gainesville: University of Florida Press.

Sylla, Richard. 2011. "Financial foundations: Public credit, the national bank, and securities markets." In Douglas A. Irwin and Richard Sylla, eds., *Founding choices: American economic policy in the 1790s*. National Bureau of Economic Research Conference Report. Chicago: University of Chicago Press: 59–88.

Syrett, Harold C., and Cooke, Jacob E., eds. 1962–72. *The papers of Alexander Hamilton*, vols. 5–17. New York: Columbia University Press.

Szatmary, David. 1980. *Shays' Rebellion: The making of an agrarian insurrection*. Amherst: University of Massachusetts Press.

Taylor, George Rogers, ed. 1950. *Hamilton and the national debt*. Boston: D. C. Heath.

Telser, Lester G. 1995. "Optimal denominations for coins and currency." *Economics Letters* 49: 425–27.

Tindall, George Brown. 1988. *America: A narrative history* (2nd ed.). New York: W. W. Norton.

Tschoegl, Adrian E. 1997. "The optimal denomination of currency." *Journal of Money, Credit and Banking* 29: 546–54.

United States Congress. 1834–56. *The debates and proceedings in Congress of the United States, vols. 1–18.* Washington, DC: Gales & Seaton.

United States Continental Congress. 1775. Philadelphia? http://memory.loc.gov/ser vice/rbc/bdsdcc/00301/0001.jpg, accessed January 30, 2013.

Van Hove, Leo. 2001. "Optimal denominations for coins and bank notes: In defense of the principle of least effort." *Journal of Money, Credit and Banking* 33: 1015–21.

Ver Steeg, Clarence L. 1976. *Robert Morris: Revolutionary financier.* New York: Octagon Books.

Wallace, Neil, and Zhou, Ruilin. 1997. "A model of a currency shortage." *Journal of Monetary Economics* 40: 555–72.

Walton, Gary M., and Rockoff, Hugh. 2014. *History of the American economy* (12th ed.). Mason, OH: South-Western.

Webster, Pelatiah. 1969. *Political essays on the nature and operation of money, public finances and other subjects.* New York: Burt Franklin [originally published 1791].

Wicker, Elmus. 1985. "Colonial monetary standards contrasted: Evidence from the Seven Years' War." *Journal of Economic History* 45: 869–84.

Williamson, John. 1796. *A treatise of military finance.* London: Oxford University.

Wilson, Janet. 1942. "The Bank of North America and Pennsylvania politics: 1781–1787." *Pennsylvania Magazine of History and Biography* 66: 3–28.

Wynne, Mark A. 1997. "More on optimal denominations for coins and currency." *Economic Letters* 55: 221–25.

Index

Page numbers in italics refer to figures and tables.